Capacity Development in Practice

Capacity Development in Practice

Edited by
Jan Ubels, Naa-Aku Acquaye-Baddoo
and Alan Fowler

publishing for a sustainable future

London · Washington, DC

First published in 2010 by Earthscan

Earthscan Ltd
Dunstan House
14a St Cross Street
London EC1N 8XA, UK

Earthscan LLC, 1616 P Street, NW, Washington, DC 20036, USA

Earthscan publishes in association with the International Institute for Environment and Development

For more information on Earthscan publications, see www.earthscan.co.uk or write to earthinfo@
earthscan.co.uk

ISBN: 978-1-84407-741-0 hardback
ISBN: 978-1-84407-742-7 paperback

Typeset by
Bookcraft Ltd, 18 Kendrick Street, Stroud, GL5 1AA

Cover design by Susanne Harris

A catalogue record for this book is available from the British Library

Library of Congress Cataloging-in-Publication Data

Capacity development in practice / edited by Jan Ubels, Naa-Aku Acquaye-Baddoo and
Alan Fowler.
    p. cm.
Includes bibliographical references and index.
    ISBN 978-1-84407-741-0 (hbk.) – ISBN 978-1-84407-742-7 (pbk.)
    1. Economic assistance–Developing countries. 2. Technical assistance–Developing countries.
3. Economic development–Developing countries. 4. Institution building–Developing countries.
I. Ubels, Jan, 1956- II. Acquaye-Baddoo, Naa-Aku. III. Fowler, Alan, 1947-
    HC60.C2925 2010
    338.9109172'4–dc22

                                                                        2009053544

Contents

Part I   Perspectives on Capacity

Part II   Establishing your Practice

Part III   Working with Connections

Part V   Looking Ahead

List of Figures, Tables and Boxes

Figures

Tables

Boxes

List of Contributors

Naa-Aku Acquaye-Baddoo is a Senior Strategy Adviser at SNV Netherlands Development Organisation. Before that, she was responsible for corporate Human Resource Development and Learning at the same organisation (www.snvworld. org). A practitioner herself, she has more than 20 years' experience of organizational, human resource and knowledge development in public and development organizations. She has also been extensively involved in strategy and practice development at SNV. Her current interests and work include how to stimulate and sustain practice based organizational learning, and development of methodologies for practitioner development.

Nils Boesen is a Danish development consultant specializing in organization, management and aid methodology issues (www.nilsboesen.dk). He has contributed extensively to methodology development related to capacity development, governance and sector-wide approaches, and led major multi-donor evaluations. Nils is currently lead adviser to the European Commission in its efforts to reform how it works with technical cooperation and capacity development, as well as assisting the OECD and bilateral donors in this field. He holds a BA in philosophy and a Master's in social science from Roskilde University in Denmark.

Marianne Mille Bojer is an experienced facilitator and designer of group dialogue and change processes. She is a partner at Reos Partners (www.reospartners.com), an international organization dedicated to supporting and building capacity for innovative collective action in complex social systems. After living and working for eight years in South Africa, she recently relocated to São Paulo, Brazil, where Reos is based. She is co-author of *Mapping Dialogue: Essential Tools for Social Change*, developed with Nelson Mandela Foundation, GTZ, and the Taos Institute.

Bruce Britton is a consultant with Framework, a consulting company based in the UK (www.framework.org.uk). Specializing in organizational development and organizational learning, he has worked with civil society organizations in Africa, Asia and Europe for almost two decades. Bruce has conducted organizational learning reviews and evaluations for INTRAC and SNV, and served as an adviser with the Aga Khan Foundation, Swedish Mission Council, RDRS Bangladesh and the Bernard van Leer Foundation, among others.

Catherine Collingwood is an Associate of the Community Development Resources Association (www.cdra.org.za) in South Africa. Specializing in organizational learning and practitioner formation she has worked with civil society organizations, mainly in Africa, for the past 12 years. Before that she was a social worker focusing on children and families. Catherine has conducted organizational evaluations and impact assessments for a number of international development organizations, as well as leadership development in networked, membership based organizations.

Brigitte Dia is a senior health adviser with SNV Netherlands Development Organisation, based in Benin since 2009. Also serving as coordinator of the SNV Leadership initiative in West Africa region, she has been active in capacity development of local actors such as civil servants, NGOs and mayors. She previously held the positions of Regional Millennium Development Goals adviser and regional strategy adviser for SNV West Africa. Prior to joining SNV, Brigitte worked on private sector promotion with, among others, UNDP and the government of Niger.

Jan Willem Eggink is an independent consultant with more than 20 years' experience as a coach and trainer in leadership development. Until 2003, he worked primarily for Dutch municipalities and multinational corporations. In 2003 he joined SNV West Africa, where he was involved in developing the 'Leadership for Change' programme. Since returning to the Netherlands in 2005 he has launched a consulting company focusing on leadership development in the healthcare sector. He combines this work with short-term consultancies in the development sector

Alan Fowler combines roles as an independent adviser on capacity-development theory and practice with academic appointments. Over some 30 years, this combination is found in professional assignments with non-governmental organizations; positions in foundations as well as in the World Bank; and in a wide range of (translated) publications on civil society and on development issues. He is a co-founder of the International NGO Training and Research Centre (INTRAC); and was an elected member of the boards of the International Society for Third Sector Research (ISTR) and Civicus, the World Alliance for Citizen Participation. He is currently affiliated as a professor at the Institute of Social Studies, Erasmus University in the Netherlands and at the University of KwaZulu Natal, South Africa.

Heinz Greijn has more than 20 years' experience as project manager and adviser on poverty reduction, capacity development and governance. He has worked in Kenya, Tanzania, Rwanda, Ethiopia and Yemen, among other countries. He is currently based at MUNDO, the international development unit at Maastricht University in the Netherlands, where he manages partnership projects with higher education institutions in developing countries. He is also editor of *Capacity.org*, a leading journal on capacity development and co-founder of 'Learning for Development' (L4D) consultancy.

Irene Guijt is an independent adviser, researcher, author and process facilitator. Her professional experience spans more than 20 years of involvement in learning processes and systems in rural development and natural resource management, particularly where this involves collective action. Among other publications, she is co-author of *Participatory Learning and Action: A Trainer's Guide,* and *Negotiating Learning: Collaborative Monitoring in Forest Resource Management.* Her recent work includes coordinating the monitoring and evaluation of a Latin America-wide programme linking research, policy influencing and capacity development, and the decentralization process of a leading Dutch NGO.

Rinus van Klinken is an experienced development practitioner who has worked for the past 30 years with SNV Netherlands Development Organisation in various capacities. Based primarily in East Africa (Kenya, Tanzania) and Ghana during this period, he has been involved in a number of corporate change and learning processes, amongst which was convening a series of Learning Platforms for bridging research and practice. Rinus has previously published on local governance processes.

Joseph McMahon is a consultant with Inter-Mediation International (www.inter-mediation.org). With a focus on organizational development aimed at improving collaboration and healthy approaches to conflict, he has worked with civil society organizations or government agencies in the USA, Africa, Asia, Latin America and Europe, including among others Water for People. Joe's specialization is in the design and conduct of environmental, water and public policy processes that connect government decisions with stakeholder interests and science.

Duncan Mwesige is a senior Economic Adviser with SNV Uganda in the area of value chain development and financing, business development services, organizational and institutional development, and facilitating multi-stakeholder engagement. He has worked intensively in the oilseed sub-sector in Uganda in recent years, helping to strengthen capabilities of individual actors involved as well as the value chain as a system. He holds degrees in Agriculture (BSc) and Business Administration in Finance (Master's).

Geoff Parcell is a business coach, mentor and speaker, and a master practitioner of knowledge management with Practical KM (www.practicalkm.com). He helps organizations in the private and public sectors identify and build on their capabilities. He was the senior advisor on Knowledge Management within BP and has applied his know-how to development topics following a secondment to UNAIDS. He is co-author of the business best-seller, *Learning to Fly: Practical Knowledge Management from Leading and Learning Organizations* (Capstone 2004) and the recently published book *No More Consultants: We Know More than We Think* (Wiley 2009).

Rakesh R. Rajani, a Tanzanian citizen, is the Head of Twaweza ('we can make it happen' in Swahili), a ten-year initiative to enhance access to information, citizen agency and public accountability in East Africa. Until the end of 2007 he served as the founding Executive Director of HakiElimu (www.hakielimu.org), an independent organization that promotes public engagement in Tanzania. Rakesh serves on several national and international boards and has been a fellow of Harvard University since 1998. He has written and/or edited over 300 papers and popular publications in English and Swahili.

Ingrid Richter is a consultant with Threshold Associates (www.thresholdas-sociates.ca), and an adjunct faculty at the University of Toronto. Specializing in complex systems change and leadership development, she has worked with government, profit and civil society organizations in Canada, Africa, Asia and Europe for 14 years. Prior to this she spent 16 years as a senior public servant in the government of Ontario (Canada). She has designed and facilitated leadership and organization development training for diverse international organizations as well as the Government of Canada. Ingrid is co-founder and co-Academic Director of the Canadian Organization Development Institute (CODI).

Rajesh Tandon is the founder President of the Society for Participatory Research in Asia (PRIA), based in New Delhi. He has led scores of programmes on organizational and institutional development, development management, governance and leadership, with a focus on the civil society sector. He also serves on the governing boards and advisory committees of numerous national and international agencies. Tandon holds a PhD in organizational science and has authored several books, articles and training manuals.

Jan Ubels is Senior Strategist with SNV Netherlands Development Organisation, prior to which he worked with several consultancy firms and in academia. His professional training was in irrigation engineering and sociology. Leading and facilitating change has become central to his work. Jan has worked for long periods in several countries in Asia and Africa and in the Netherlands. Through his different jobs and roles he developed extensive experience in the areas of strategy development, capacity development, knowledge development and learning and in change management, facilitation and coaching. He chairs the editorial committee of *Capacity.org*.

Hendrik Visser is an adviser in capacity development and complex change processes, with a special interest in the development of human consciousness and ethical action through systems-thinking approaches. He holds MSc degrees in Civil Engineering and Sustainable Development and has worked for over 15 years in rural infrastructure development, livelihood strengthening and empowerment processes. Hendrik currently lives in Bhutan where he also established and runs a charity for animal rescue, care and happiness.

David Watson is a development economist specializing in international development. He has served nearly 15 years in various developing countries, including stints as a volunteer economist for the governments of Fiji and Botswana earlier in his career, and team leader of multi-ethnic consultant teams in Indonesia and Ecuador. More recently he has focused on governance and capacity-development issues, and was a member of the ECDPM Capacity Study team, producing case studies in Ethiopia and Pakistan.

Jim Woodhill is Director of the Wageningen University Research Centre for Development Innovation in the Netherlands. He has over 20 years' experience supporting process of participatory learning, innovation and change in the agriculture, rural development and natural resources sectors in Africa, Asia and

Australia. Jim is an experienced facilitator, evaluator and trainer having worked for many different international organizations in a wide variety of contexts. He holds a PhD in political economics from the Australian National University.

Schirin Yachkaschi is an independent development practitioner and action researcher with extensive experience in community and organizational development, multi-stakeholder processes, training and dialogue facilitation in South Africa and recently also in Germany. She holds a Master's degree in environmental planning and a PhD in development studies. In a search for a suitable organizational development approach at a grassroots level, she has conducted action research with community-based organizations in South Africa, where she has lived since 2000.

Acknowledgements

A book like this does not come from the minds and hearts of just one or a few people. It grows, over many years. It is the result of concrete experiences, successes and errors; of professional debate and the gradual connection of, and interaction between, various strands of work. In shaping this book we, the three co-editors, have called on many people and experiences in our personal histories, which we wish to recognize and acknowledge.

Thanks go to the many actors and practitioners who live and grapple with the ambitions and dilemmas described in this volume. Their work forms the foundation and learning ground for all that is presented here. Within this group, special acknowledgement goes to the SNV colleagues and their clients and partners who have collaborated with us, in different innovative and personally taxing learning processes, over the last decade.

On a more personal level, it is impossible to list all those who over the years have directly challenged our assumptions, provided us with inspiring professional accompaniment and opportunities and asked difficult questions. Among those who have been part of our personal journeys are: Moussiliou Alidou, Niloy Banerjee, Worku Behonegne, Kees Biekart, Evan Bloom, Nils Boesen, Jessie Bokhoven, Greg Booth, Mariette Castellino, Sue Davidoff, Mohan Dhamotharan, Harm Duiker, Dirk Elsen, Paul Engel, Mike Edwards, Jan Willem Eggink, Martin de Graaf, Heinz Greijn, John Hailey, Volker Hauck, Hans Heijdra, Ad Hordijk, Lucas Horst, Annemiek Jenniskens, Mohamed Ali Jinnah, Yaouba Kaigama, Allan Kaplan, Connie Lenneberg, Hanne Lund Madsen, Chiku Malunga, Lucia Nass, Jan Willem Nibbering, Margriet Poel, Brian Pratt, Rakesh Rajani, Ingrid Richter, Bart Romijn, James Taylor, Thomas Theisohn, Tony Tujan, Laurent Umans, Fons van der Velden, Jaap Voigt, Quynh Anh Vu Thi, Hettie Walters, Andy Wehkamp, Jim Woodhill and Kees Zevenbergen. In addition, we thank all those people within the organisations that have provided the wide range of settings for our concrete experiences and comparative learning.

Moving to the creation of the book itself, firstly and most importantly a big 'thank you' goes to the authors who produced the chapters of this volume. You simply made this book! Your varied perspectives helped unravel the field of capacity development as it exists today and carved out essential logics, methods and concepts that stem from rich experiences. You endured rounds of feedback that were at times quite robust as we strove to achieve a particular rhythm and balance between the stories and the structure of the volume. We are very grateful for the richness that your combined contributions have created and exposed. Thank you!

At SNV, Kees Zevenbergen, Annemiek Jenniskens and Jessie Bokhoven continued to inspire and stimulate us in consolidating practitioner learnings. They did so not only to support SNV's own staff but also to reach out to the wider community of professionals. At the times when it was difficult financially or managerially, their support and belief in this initiative never wavered.

The staff and affiliates of Earthscan also played a vital and encouraging role. Particular appreciation goes to Camille Bramall, Rachel Butler, Claire Lamont, Julie Laws, Caroline Sheldrick, Kim McSweeney, Janet Reed and Rob West for their diverse roles in editing, layout, production, publishing and marketing of this volume. Earthscan's solid interest early in the process was a strong support and motivation.

And then there is the remarkable Wangu Mwangi. She facilitated the complex interactions with the large number of authors and coordinated the practical progress in developing the manuscript. More importantly, through a first round of critical reviews and editing of all chapters she contributed in no small measure to the overall quality of the volume. Wangu, we are very grateful for your patience with us, the professionalism of your work and stimulating presence as a team member.

Finally, thanks to everybody mentioned above. We are grateful for the fact that we have had the privilege to work on and complete this book.

It has been a personal and professional joy.

Jan Ubels, Naa Aku Acquaye Baddoo and Alan Fowler
Diepenveen, The Hague, Herbertsdale
25 June 2010

Preface

SNV is committed to supporting people's efforts to create their own futures in their own ways. In line with such an ambition, this book is about capacity and its development. Not in abstract concepts or policy prescriptions, but rooted in what people across the world do every day to improve living standards, to strengthen performance in sectors of work and to change their societies.

The creation of this book reflects a strategic choice. Some 10 years ago, SNV decided to pay increased attention to capacity development as a professional discipline. We saw that conventional project implementation methods were not doing enough to foster local capacities, ownership and sustainability. So we began to focus on providing advice, support and facilitation for changes led by local actors.

This proved to be an enriching journey. Meaningful lessons emerged from both good and difficult experiences. For example, we found ourselves focusing overly on demand, reacting to local 'needs' without sufficient understanding of wider problems and policy challenges in the sector concerned. We looked thoroughly into the internal workings and capabilities of clients, but at the cost of adequate concern for their external performance and collaboration. We struggled to combine change expertise with sector knowledge.

This accumulated practical experience has led to some provocative ideas. We would now assert, for example, that:

- Capacity is about concrete, real-life action. Abstract organizational abilities must be seen to be believed.
- Capacity develops as much through relationships between actors as its does within individual organizations. Capacity development therefore involves unleashing collaboration but also dealing with power and politics.
- Capacity is fuelled by local actors' ambitions and resources, which cannot be replaced by external inputs and finance.

To communicate these and many more insights in an accessible way, this book is in the style and form of a resource volume. It is intentionally full of practical examples and hands-on approaches. At the same time it doesn't shy away from more conceptual and complex questions on what capacity is and how it grows. It illustrates considerable advances in the 'theory' of capacity and its development. Progress is based on a rich compilation of insights and results from different people, disciplines and parts of the world. This resource is about real-life practice, about hands-on professionalism.

SNV's journey has not been alone. This book brings together experiences from a very broad set of practitioners and thought leaders, including people that have worked for the World Bank and the EU or activist NGOs, for national governments or the private sector, and for expertise centres such as ECDPM, CDRA, UNDP and Wageningen International. The breadth of their backgrounds and insights gives credibility and relevance to the publication. The content highlights a number of critical themes, including:

- The need to work with multiple actors within and across public, private and civil sectors
- How to combine a strong results-orientation with flexibility and learning
- Ways to build connections between local realities and macro policies or programmes
- Professional knowledge, attitudes and skills for doing effective capacity development
- The emerging market and service environment for capacity development support.

I believe that with the critical insights and down to earth knowledge shared in this book, capacity development is moving beyond the abstract towards a set of effective professional practices directly relevant to achieving concrete results.

Yet even with this major step forward in our understanding, much remains to be explored and achieved – for example, in deepening intervention and facilitation expertise and professionalization; or for financing to reverse how supply tends to dictate demand; and in expanding the availability and quality of local capacity development expertise.

Yes, the journey continues. And, as before, we will travel in close collaboration with others. I look forward to reporting on further progress towards supporting people to create their own futures in their own ways.

Dirk Elsen
Chief Executive
SNV Netherlands Development Organisation

List of Acronyms and Abbreviations

5Cs	Five Capabilities model or framework
AAA	Analysis and planning, Action and monitoring, Assessing results and Evaluation (Triple AAA model)
ADB	Asian Development Bank
AI	Appreciative Inquiry
AIDS	Acquired Immunodeficiency Syndrome
AusAID	Australian Agency for International Development
BMZ	German Federal Ministry for Economic Development Cooperation
CAS	Complex Adaptive Systems
CBO	Community-Based Organization
CD	Capacity Development
CDC	Civic-driven Change
CDGF	City District Government Faisalabad (Pakistan)
CDRA	Community Development Resource Association (South Africa)
CIDA	Canadian International Development Agency
CSCOM	Centres de Santé Communautaire (Mali)
CSO	Civil Society Organization
DANIDA	Danish International Development Agency
DANIDA-ASPS	Danish International Development Agency – Agriculture Sector Programme Support (Uganda)
DFID	UK Department for International Development
DGIS	Netherlands Directorate-General of Development Cooperation
DoR	Department of Roads (Bhutan)
ECDPM	European Centre for Development Policy Management
EFRC	Environmentally Friendly Roads Construction Programme (Bhutan)
ENA	National College for Administrators (Niger)
ENACT	Environmental Action Programme (Jamaica)
EU	European Union
GNH	Gross National Happiness index (Bhutan)
GTZ	Deutsche Gesellschaft für Technische Zusammenarbeit (Germany)
HIV	Human Immunodeficiency Virus
IDA	International Development Assistance
IDRC	International Development Research Centre
IDS	Institute of Development Studies, University of Sussex (UK)
IFAD	International Fund for Agricultural Development

INGO	International Non-Governmental Organization
ISS	Institute of Social Studies (Netherlands)
IUCN	International Union for the Conservation of Nature
KIT	Royal Tropical Institute (Netherlands)
LCD	Local Capacity Developer
LCDF	Local Capacity Development Facility
LFA	Logical Framework Approach
M&E	Monitoring and Evaluation
MDG	Millennium Development Goals
MSP	Multi-stakeholder Process(es)
NGO	Non-Governmental Organization
OA	Organizational Assessment
OD	Organizational Development
ODI	Overseas Development Institute (UK)
OECD	Organisation for Economic Co-operation and Development
OECD/DAC	Development Assistance Committee of the Organisation for Economic Co-operation and Development
PEAP	Poverty Eradication Action Plan (Uganda)
PEDP	Primary Education Development Plan (Tanzania)
PLC	Leadership Change Programme, West Africa
PRA	Participatory Rural Appraisal
PRIA	Society for Participatory Research in Asia (India)
PRSP	Poverty Reduction Strategy Paper
RBM	Results-Based Management
SARS	Severe Acute Respiratory Syndrome
SIDA	Swedish International Development Agency
SNV	SNV Netherlands Development Organisation
SWAps	Sector-wide Approaches (in donor-funded development programmes)
TA	Technical Assistance
TGN	Tanzania Governance Notice-board
UNADA	Uganda National Agro-input Dealers Association
UN	United Nations
UNDP	United Nations Development Programme
USAID	United States Agency for International Development
USAID-APEP	United States Agency for International Development – Agriculture Productivity Enhancement Project (Uganda)
VECO	Vredeseilanden (Belgian NGO) Country Office (Indonesia)
WB	World Bank
WBI	World Bank Institute
WUR	Wageningen University and Research (Netherlands)
ZOPP	Goal-oriented project planning (abbreviation in German)

A Resource Volume on Capacity Development

Jan Ubels, Alan Fowler and Naa-Aku Acquaye-Baddoo

Capacity development is one of the defining ideas within contemporary international development. This stems from the conviction and experience that addressing social, economic and environmental issues calls for greater capabilities everywhere in society: in individual human capital, in communities, groups, organizations, sectors and institutions.

'Capacity development' is supported and done by consultants, trainers and advisers, who function as 'external actors' to their clients. But it is also done, and even more widely, by managers, project team members, change agents, front-line workers and professionals within government, civil movements and private sector organizations. Across a wide variety of aid initiatives, capacity development enjoys substantial effort and investment. Through Technical Assistance (TA) alone, the aid system allocates annually over a quarter of its finance – US$25 billion or more – to capacity development. Using an eclectic set of methods and interventions, hundreds of thousands of people undertake this type of work (ActionAid, 2006). These efforts occur not only on the basis of external finance, but are also driven by endogenous change and development dynamics.

At the same time, uncertainty remains about what capacity is and what its development entails. Many people feel the term is vague and misused. There is also simple confusion. Some see capacity development as a central rationale, even a core function, of development work. Others see it as a means only. Some think of skills training, others of organizational development. The term capacity development is also sometimes used to refer to the funding of buildings or providing computers. Government officials will think of strengthening their policy development processes and public financial management procedures. For some non-governmental organizations (NGOs) capacity development is about increasing empowerment, voice and participation. All these different angles are created by development agencies themselves. No wonder there is doubt and misunderstanding; it is this that this book seeks to redress.

A practitioner's perspective

This volume is written by and for 'practitioners', that is, people whose work and concern is to try to stimulate the development of capacities in diverse ways. It is based on actual capacity-development activities that give substance to policies and conceptual frameworks. It is truly empirical. In looking through the eyes and talking with the voices of experienced practitioners, the contribution of this volume is new and distinctive. With their words and insights successes are explained. Yet difficulties, contradictions and struggles in this type of work are not glossed over. In fact, the opposite is the case. The problems encountered in capacity development are important sources of learning and are treated as such. The path from confusion to clarity is, therefore, not smooth and is far from fixed.

Yet, seen from the perspective of these practitioners, there has been significant progress in understanding what capacity is all about and what its development entails. This body of proven experience points towards a profile of methods, concepts, competencies and common challenges that are not limited to certain types of organizations or to specific technical sectors. We dare to propose, therefore, that a more and more coherent and consistent professional domain is emerging. In bringing together the contributions and experiences in this volume, it is intended to describe, explore and discuss the emerging professional field of capacity development. The progress the authors show in the practice and theory of capacity development will be of interest not only to the practitioners themselves, but also to government officials, donor staff, researchers and financiers that support and orient this field of work.

The writers form a mixed group. We are privileged to have contributions from practitioners and stories about experiences from places as varied as Albania, Australia, Bhutan, Cambodia, Cameroon, Canada, Colombia, Denmark, Ethiopia, Germany, Ghana, Brazil, India, Indonesia, Iran, Mali, Mozambique, Nepal, Niger, the Netherlands, Pakistan, Peru, South Africa, Sri Lanka, Tanzania, Thailand, Uganda, Vietnam , the United Kingdom and the United States. The experiences they discuss deal with development challenges in terrains as diverse as water supply, forestry, slum development, education, HIV-Aids, agricultural value chains, primary health care, land rights, road construction, local governance and much more. They have worked on capacity development with and for entities as varied as community-based organizations and NGOs, national and local governments, United Nations agencies and the private sector, and in arrangements that include public–private partnerships, networks and coalitions. Their assignments have been associated with social movements, public sector service delivery programmes, economic reform, public information and media, and much more. The breadth of these experiences and insights forms the basis of this volume and its main themes. From this diversity and richness, a set of professional orientations and patterns is emerging that has shaped the overall logic of the volume. It explores 'capacity-development support' as an intervention practice. By this we mean a repertoire of insights, knowledges, approaches, methods, skills, roles and attitudes used to deliberately stimulate and support growth of capacities. But why is this necessary?

It is almost a conventional wisdom of those involved in the international system that 'capacity matters' and that this certainty is here to stay. This policy position and imperative is reinforced by declarations from international conferences and agreements between official aid agencies and some NGOs seen, for example, in the Accra Agenda for Action (September 2008). Consequently, capacity and its development cannot be ignored in today's development debates about effectiveness and investment choices. And as indicated above, one can reasonably speculate that many hundreds of thousands of people have a significant capacity-development component in their work. However, explanations of the need for capacity development and its translation into what needs to be done or delivered have not been matched by professional knowledge to judge how it can actually be done well. And, in an area of debate and attention that is some 20 years old, this gap needs to be urgently filled – from below, so to speak – by those on the front line doing the work. This volume makes one step in this direction.

The issue of definitions

When a new topic appears on the aid landscape it is subjected to definitional scrutiny and endless prolonged debate. Participation, empowerment and ownership are well known examples. The case of capacity development is no different. The variety of definitions available (see box below for a small sample) are, amongst others, the result of significant interest and claim making by major aid organizations, such as the World Bank, the United Nations Development Programme (UNDP) and the International Development Research Centre (IDRC). Each definition reflects the politics and positioning of the institution concerned, as does ours. This diversity is actually valuable by illustrating the fact that – like the idea of organization – the images or frameworks employed for capacity development are up for discussion. And this helps mitigate against the dominance of a monolithic 'truth', thus inviting continual enquiry and testing.

Sample of capacity-development definitions

An organization with capacity has the ability to function as a resilient, strategic and autonomous entity (Kaplan, 1999, p20).

Capacity represents the potential for using resources effectively and maintaining gains in performance with gradually reduced levels of external support (LaFond and Brown, 2003, p7).

Capacity is [the] potential to perform (Horton et al, 2003, p18).

Capacity is the ability of people, organizations and society as a whole to manage their affairs successfully (OECD, 2006, p12).

Capacity is that emergent contribution of attributes that enables a human system to create development value (Morgan, 2006, p8).

In this volume different definitions of capacity development will also feature. But as a starting point we opt for the following definition because:

- we consider it reflects adequately what one sees and experiences;
- it is not overly prescriptive or excessively reductionist; and
- it reflects broader science and discussion on capacity and its development that exists outside the aid community.

Our working definition is, therefore:

Capacity is the ability of a human system to perform, sustain itself and self-renew.

This working definition makes clear that capacity is not a static state or quality. It is about creating some form of added value for the members and the outside world (perform), it is about staying alive and active (sustain), it is about adjusting and developing over time (self-renew) on the basis of external pressures and internal drivers.

Note that we use the term 'human system'. This implies that capacities exist in different scales or levels of human organization. Individuals can have capacities, teams have a capacity to do what they do, organizations have a capacity, networks of actors have a capacity to co-produce certain results and even socio-technical 'sectors' or nations have a capacity.

Capacity development is literally, therefore, changes in capacity over time. It is important to recognize that capacity development is in that sense an endogenous and continuous/spontaneous process. Because no context is static, the capacity of any entity will always evolve in interaction with its environment, for good or ill.

The term capacity development (or building) in practice is also used for something else: deliberate efforts to make capacities grow. We call this *capacity-development support*. And this is what this book is mainly about: the purposeful approaches and the professional repertoire used to deliberately stimulate, guide, strengthen, unleash, nurture and grow capacities beyond the existing condition. However, some humility is needed. Discussion of this repertoire cannot take place without reflecting on spontaneous processes of capacity growth and the nature of capacity itself. Authors in this volume frequently bring an appreciation of 'unaided' capacity development into their chapters.

Competencies and capabilities are two terms often used in relation to capacity. We adopt an interpretation of the relationship between the three – recently developed by Morgan (2006) – in seeing competencies and capabilities as components of capacity. In that logic, competencies are the specific abilities of individuals. Capabilities are specific abilities of the organizational (sub-)system concerned. Both underpin and contribute to the overall capacity of a system. In other words, they can be considered as smaller sub-components of capacity that interact in complex ways, also explained in Chapter 1. This interpretation is allied to some broader notions with regard to the nature of capacity.

A living view on capacity

When starting on this volume, we had rough ideas on what we would like it to contain. But over time, these ideas were re-shaped by engagement with and contributions from the various authors. This interactive process took more than two years from idea to manuscript. Over this time span, the field of capacity development expressed itself and became clearer to us.

After all the contributions we take stock, in Chapter 22, of what this 'field' looks like in more detail. But by way of orientation we would like to introduce key characteristics of capacity and its development that will emerge from these diverse contributions.

Three perspectives have oriented and informed the final shape of this volume. The first view is that capacity is about concrete results and impact. The second is that capacity is a 'living phenomenon'. And the third one is that it is relational and thus also political.

Firstly we see capacity development as directly *engaging with real-life issues and results*. It is not vague. One can and should always ask: capacity for what? If we define capacity as the ability to perform, sustain oneself and self-renew (as we did above), this means that the actual capacity that a system has simply expresses itself as the concrete level of performance, sustainability and renewal that it displays in its current reality and in its concrete area of activity. Whether we look to water management or minority rights, micro credit or education, if capacity exists and grows it makes a difference. It expresses itself in the ability of people concerned to (collectively) perform and deliver results in a chosen area, to sustain the activities required and adapt them over time. Capacity is the real thing, not an input, not a kind of theoretical ability or a secret ingredient that may be used or not. It is how vital a human system is, expressed in the degree to which it functions effectively.

Secondly, capacity is not just a technical or organizational capability or set of competencies. Based on the progress we observed and captured in this volume, it is clear that capacity can best be seen as a 'living phenomenon'. The definition that we have given above clearly goes beyond 'performance' in the sense of certain specific outputs alone. It is the broader ability of a system to live an active and meaningful life and demonstrate confidence and agency in determining its own future. It is the core of a system's 'vitality'. Chapter 1 of this volume uses two frameworks to take this view further and deeper. They show that, as in other living phenomena, capacity builds and draws upon various elements or sub-systems that interact with and depend upon each other. The sum of that interaction and interdependency is more than that of its constituent parts. This living, multi-faceted understanding of capacity will return as a recurring theme across the volume.

Thirdly, as capacity is a living phenomenon and about real-life effectiveness it is inherently *relational*. Every living system interacts with its environment, influencing and being influenced. This is also true for any form of human organization, whether we talk about individuals, teams, organizations, networks, sectors or even countries. They exist in relation. Capacity of any form of organization is also relational; it requires and works in connection with other elements in the 'eco-system' of human organization that it operates in. And this is also very obvious if one acknowledges that there are no development results that are produced by a single actor in isolation. And if capacity is relational, it is also *political*. It is also about power, politics and interests and about a system's ability to work with and through differences in view and power to achieve effective collaboration. It is about potential divergence and asymmetries between actors, and how these factors are dealt with.

These three perspectives are all strongly present in the volume: capacity as concrete effectiveness in real-life issues of human well-being; capacity as a multifaceted living phenomenon; and capacity as a relational outcome and thus, also, a political feature.

In this volume we try to look at the phenomenon of capacity and its development, not just from the perspective of 'aided development', the pursuit of specific objectives of certain development programmes, but in a wider context: that of the broader processes of the societies concerned towards increased abilities to steer and develop themselves. So we are especially interested in the underlying *endogenous dynamics,* that is, in self-propelled and self-guided processes of societies developing their own capacities. This does not mean that these processes are disconnected from external support. But their locus of control and dynamics are within the societies concerned and not primarily induced and pursued from the outside. This orientation informs several cases and methodological explorations in this volume and also informs some of the later chapters that try to look forward to the further development of this professional field.

The structure of the volume

As our work progressed, the substance of each chapter and relations between them became clearer. The end result is a resource volume in five parts. The contents of each are introduced by means of a practitioner-oriented question.

Part I *What is the substance of capacity?* The three chapters in this part discuss the multiple nature of capacity, the fact that capacity often exists between multiple actors and finally that capacity is embedded in different scales of human organization. By looking at these three types of multiples (multiple dimensions, multiple actors, multiple levels), the practitioner gains a landscape for clarifying their own views on capacity and their own place within it.

Part II *What establishes your practice?* The seven chapters in this part provide insights about critical features of practitioner work, that is, elements and topics that a practitioner needs to be knowledgeable about in order to do capacity-development work and further develop one's own experience, repertoire, style and choices. They range from roles and expertise to one's ability for dialogue and 'reading situations'.

Part III *How can one deliberately work with 'connections' that shape capacity and influence the client system?* Starting from the understanding that capacity is relational, the seven chapters in this part provide a range of insights, experiences and approaches on how to work with multi-actor and multi-tiered systems. Topics range, for example, from dealing with politics and accountability to working with value chains and knowledge networks.

Part IV *How can a practitioner combine a results orientation and learning?* This part explores the need to account for results and to learn 'on the go'. The four chapters illustrate the possibilities and challenges of combining these ambitions that are often seen as being in opposition, or difficult to reconcile.

Part V *From where we are, how can this professional field be advanced?* Here, the co-editors have brought together three chapters in which they take stock of the terrain as it has exposed itself in this volume, explore the 'market dynamics' and finally discuss the status of capacity development as a 'professional field in formation' and perspectives for its further development.

It is probably obvious that this volume has features of a compendium of topics, not a textbook. It is not necessary to read from cover to cover. There are also other ways in which we have tried to make this work accessible. We close, therefore, with a reader's guide.

Suggestions for the reader

Though often based on earlier work, a large majority of the texts are newly written for this volume. To quickly scan and judge what to read, we have developed a specific format. Each chapter has three elements:

- An introductory box that states why the topic is in the volume, as well as why the specific text for that chapter has been chosen and what it brings that is of interest to a reader.
- The main text of the chapter. The character of this varies strongly depending on the topic, the author and the writings available on the topic.
- A brief set of carefully selected Recommended Readings on the topic of the chapter.

By using this format we have created the space to use a fairly wide variation in style and scope of texts. Some are centred on case studies. Others provide an example of a successful method, or present a review of various experiences. And there are also explorations of dilemmas or challenges.

The reader may use the opening boxes to have a quick glance at what each chapter offers. The chapters are not necessarily read in a fixed sequence. One can pick up any topic that is relevant to one's own situation at that specific moment.

The recommended readings with each chapter have been carefully selected by the respective authors. They provide additional resources to those who want to further explore certain topics.

For readers wishing to use this volume as a handbook, it offers a structured view of the terrain. And the recommended reading lists cover some 20 sub-topics more or less systematically.

We envisage the volume to be a 'platform' on which new insights, learning, debate and additional content can be added and exchanged. We are therefore very interested to receive your comments, inputs and suggestions. The editors can be reached at: editors@CDinPractice.org

References

ActionAid (2006) *Real Aid 2: Making Technical Assistance Work*, ActionAid, London

Horton, D. et al (2003) *Evaluating Capacity Development: Experiences from Research and Development Organizations around the World*, ISNAR, CTA, IDRC, Ottawa

Kaplan, A. (1999) *The Developing of Capacity*, Community Development Resource Association, Cape Town

LaFond, A. and Brown, L. (2003) *A Guide to Monitoring and Evaluation of Capacity-Building: Interventions in the Health Sector in Developing Countries*, MEASURE Evaluation Manual Series, Carolina Population Center, UNC, Chapel Hill

Morgan, P. (2006) *The Concept of Capacity: Capacity, Change and Performance*, European Centre for Development Policy Management, Maastricht

OECD (2006) *The Challenge of Capacity Development – Working Towards Good Practice*, Organisation for Economic Co-operation and Development, Paris

Part I

Perspectives on Capacity

The three chapters in Part I set out a number of basic ideas, terms and concepts that help to shape our understanding of capacity. Together they give an initial answer to the question: 'what do we deal with when we do capacity development?'

Chapter 1 is the most conceptual, in setting out two powerful frameworks for understanding capacity that are derived from hands-on experience and dedicated study. The frameworks help define different elements or capabilities on which capacity is based and also discuss how capacity comes about. Chapter 2 looks at how capacity is located within and between stakeholders in capacity-development processes. These ideas are further illustrated in Chapter 3, by means of a case showing how such capacities are embedded in different levels of human organization; these range from the individual actor, through organizations, networks and a sector to the wider societal and (supra) national systems.

Taken together, these opening chapters provide a basic definition of capacity and its dimensions. They set a foundation for looking at the ways that capacity development is actually undertaken, described in the following four parts of the volume.

1

Multiple Dimensions

Working with capacity and its development requires recognition of the many dimensions involved. This text brings together two prominent perspectives on capacity from, respectively, a South African NGO and a European-based policy centre. Both show a non-mechanical view of capacity and its development that is applied throughout this volume.

These frameworks derive from extensive practical experience and propose different, but complementary, features of what capacity is all about. They bring similar observations on the nature of capacity and the implications that this has for practice. Familiarity with both will assist practitioners' awareness of their own understanding of capacity and what this means for their way of working. It will also enhance 'deeper' reading of other chapters.

The Multi-faceted Nature of Capacity: Two Leading Frameworks

Alan Fowler and Jan Ubels[1]

Introduction

Experienced practitioners know that capacity has many, often confusing, faces. Pinning it down is like trying to nail a multi-coloured jelly to the wall. For example, capacity can be experienced in the confidence of staff and the organization as a whole. Looking around an office to see if members of staff are sullen and withdrawn or full of energy and curiosity can speak a lot about its underlying condition. Capacity can show in the application of well-crafted expertise, procedures or skills. Spontaneous, external demands on an organization for advice can signal peer recognition of its competencies. Capacity can radiate in the quality of achievements and relations and reputations with clients and others. This chapter therefore gets to grips with the 'multi-dimensional' nature of capacity and what this means for its development. Doing so requires making choices between the array of ideas, concepts, stories, frameworks and practices on offer.

Our decision to describe the landscape of capacity and its development through two particular frameworks stems from a number of criteria. A first point for selection is that any 'framework' – a coherent set of features and a story which makes capacity understandable – must have its foundation in reflections on experience across many contexts and over time. Second, it needs to be supported by and contribute to the wider literature on the topic. Third, the framework is popular with and used by practitioners. Finally, it makes experiential sense to us and to the approach of authors agreeing to contribute to the volume. This filter focused our selection onto two frameworks, with different origins in terms of time period of 'discovery' and their international recognition (Kaplan, 1999; Baser and Morgan, 2008). The two draw on the governmental and non-governmental domains in society, operating at different scales within and across nation states. We are convinced that familiarity with both will benefit practitioners in their work as well as the professional development of the field as a whole.

The first perspective was developed in the early 1990s by Allan Kaplan and his colleagues at the Community Development Resource Association (CDRA), a South African non-governmental organization (NGO). With a special mix of experience in the anti-apartheid struggle and an anthroposophic philosophy, the CDRA team developed fundamental interpretations of what capacity is about. Developing capacity is explained through six inter-related elements. In doing so, an important distinction is made between elements that are tangible and those that are not. For more than ten years, this work has provided a valuable and enduring professional influence within, and increasingly beyond, the community of NGOs.

Alongside is an evolving framework for capacity and its development formulated recently by the Netherlands-based European Centre for Development Policy Management (ECDPM). This centre aims to build effective partnerships between the European Union and Africa, the Caribbean and the Pacific (ACP), particularly related to development cooperation. ECDPM is renowned for its exploratory contributions and constructive roles in the early days of the 'capacity development' discussion in the donor world. One example is initiating the magazine *Capacity. org*. The Centre has focused especially on multilateral and bilateral development aid. In 2007 it completed a study for members of the Development Assistance Committee of the Organisation for Economic Co-operation and Development (OECD-DAC) and other organizations. Building on earlier work based on original case studies and complementary papers, amongst advances on other themes and discussion topics – such as accountability and ownership – ECDPM developed the 'five capabilities' (5Cs) framework for both understanding and evaluating capacity.[2] The 5Cs framework is now being applied in many areas, for example in evaluation and learning from capacity development programmes.[3]

At first sight, the frameworks appear as alternatives. In some superficial ways they are. But they also share a deeper grounding. They are both developed on the basis of reflection on a considerable amount of practical experience and reveal the 'multi-faceted' nature of capacity. In both, capacity is a label for the uncertain results of interaction between what are referred to as elements in one and as capabilities in the other. In other words, capacity is not a specific substance but is an 'emergent' property based on the combination of a number of elements. In seeing capacity as 'living' and dynamic, they draw attention to the fact that understanding capacity means looking beyond measuring results only. They also illustrate the importance of clarity about the mental image that a practitioner brings to his or her work. These and other similarities are revisited in the conclusions. The immediate task is to introduce both frameworks in terms used by the authors.

CDRA: The development of capacity

Here is the view on capacity that Allan Kaplan of CDRA set out in a 1999 United Nations publication, 'Organisational Capacity: A different perspective'. Mainly retaining wording from the author, the indented text is extracted and edited from the original. The selection concentrates on the characteristics of capacity and does not include, for example, explanations of stages of organizational evolution also covered in his publication. It begins with an identification of organizational elements, moves on to the issue of 'invisibility' and then homes in on the significance of treating organizations as complex open systems, where the whole adds up to 'more than the sum of the parts'.

Elements of capacity

> *Context and Conceptual Framework:* The first requirement for an organization with capacity, the 'prerequisite' on which all other capacity is built, is the development of a conceptual framework which reflects the organization's understanding of its world. This is a coherent frame of reference, a set of concepts which allows the organization to make sense of the world around it, to locate itself within that world, and to make decisions in relation to it.
>
> Understanding context is accompanied by a particular organizational 'attitude' towards that context. An organization needs to build its confidence to act in and on the world in a way that it believes can be effective and have an impact. It has to believe in its own capacity to affect its circumstances, allied to an acceptance of responsibility for the social and physical conditions 'out there'.
>
> *Vision:* With clarity of understanding and a sense of confidence comes the possibility of developing organizational vision. There is a reality out there which must be responded to, and there is an inner inspiration that must be harnessed and focused. No two organizations will choose to respond to the same external situation in the same way. Every organization must get in touch with its own driving force. To be most effective, it must identify its own particular abilities and strengths in order to focus on the possibilities of its unique contribution. Interaction between understanding of particular context and appreciation of particular responsibility yields organizational vision.

Strategy: Organizational vision yields an understanding of *what* the organization intends to do; strategy is a translation into *how* the organization intends to realize its vision. Strategy entails the development of, as well as designing the organization around, particular methodologies of practice, with adaptation to particular circumstances. Strategic thinking involves prioritizing certain activities and approaches over others as well as marshalling and coordinating scarce resources in the service of chosen priorities.

Strategy is achieved through the constant interplay between doing, planning and evaluation. It has both to see what works and what does not work as well as to reflect in depth about what it means by its discernible impact, and what – perhaps unforeseen – consequences this impact releases. Given such evaluation, it has to rethink, re-plan, re-strategize; improve and adapt its methodology as well as its understanding of its context, its vision, and its relationships with others.

Culture: An important dimension of organizational attitude is that of culture. By culture we understand the norms and values which are practised in an organization; the way of life; the way things are done. Without changing culture, other changes are likely to be short-lived and ineffectual. Many of the cultural aspects of organizations exist and operate unconsciously: what people *say* they value and believe in and what is *practised* in the organization are often very different.

Over time every organization will develop particular ways of doing things – habits, norms, routines, mindsets. They become unconscious. The organization loses awareness of them and they begin to exert a tremendous power and force precisely because they become hidden. The organization that makes them conscious, however, which becomes aware of its own dynamics, and makes its values transparent and collective, is able to use that power as a source of liberation, creativity and energy.

Structure: Although these elements are not gained entirely sequentially, once organizational aims, strategy and culture are clear it becomes possible to structure the organization in such a way that roles and functions are clearly defined and differentiated, lines of communication and accountability untangled, and decision-making procedures transparent and functional. Put slightly differently, 'form follows function' – if one tries to do this the other way around the organization becomes incapacitated.

Too many attempts to intervene in organizational functioning take structure and procedure as their starting point, partly because this element is easily observable, partly because it can be more directly accessed and manipulated, and partly because it *seems* to be the cause of so much malfunctioning.

Skills: The next step in the march towards organizational capacity, in terms of priority and sequence, is the growth and extension of individual skills, abilities and competencies – the traditional terrain of training courses. Yet what emerges clearly from extensive experience is that there is a sequence, a hierarchy, an order. Unless organizational capacity has been developed sufficiently to harness training and the acquisition of new skills, training courses do not 'take', and skills do not adhere. The organization that does not know where it is going and why; which has a poorly developed sense of responsibility for itself; and which is inadequately structured, cannot make use of training courses and skills acquisition.

Material resources: Finally, an organization needs material resources: finances, equipment, office space, and so on. Without an appropriate level of these, the organization will always remain, in an important sense, incapacitated. Once again it is worthwhile to note the common misunderstanding displayed by incapacitated organizations – the thought that they would become capacitated if only they had access to sufficient material resources. Yet experience has shown that, by and large, those organizations that complain about their lack of material resources, and which attribute their failures to this organizational feature, lack the ability to counter these problems, while those organizations that accept their own incapacities and attempt to remedy them gain the ability to overcome or compensate for outer constraints.

Though written with an eye on the development of NGOs, readers will recognize this logic in relation to a variety of models that distinguish organizational 'sub-systems'. Examples are: Henry Mintzberg's Structure in Fives, the 'seven S-s' and other organizational and capacity frameworks that have been promoted and employed over the years.

The visible and invisible nature of capacity

A special quality of the CDRA work is its recognition of the 'integrity' of the organizational organism, and a certain degree of hierarchy in the sub-systems. But, just as important, is how it directs attention towards the '(in)visibility' of elements of capacity.

> If you look towards the bottom of the hierarchy you will see those things which are quantifiable, measurable, elements of organizational life, which can easily be grasped and worked with. Material and financial resources, skills, organizational structures and systems belong to the realm of the visible. If however, we turn our attention to the top of the hierarchy, we enter immediately an entirely different realm, the realm of the invisible. Sure, organizations may have written statements of vision, of strategy and of value, but these written statements do not in any sense indicate whether an organization actually has a working understanding of its world. They do not indicate the extent to which an organization is really striving to become a learning organization, to what extent it is manifesting a team spirit or endeavour. They do not indicate the extent to which an organization is reflective, non-defensive and self-critical. In short, the elements at the top of the hierarchy of elements of organizational life are ephemeral, transitory, not easily assessed or weighed. They are to a large degree observable only through the effects they have. And they are largely invisible to the organization itself as well as to those practitioners who would intervene to build organizational capacity.
>
> We are saying, then, that the most important elements in organizational life, those which largely determine the functioning of the organization,

are of a nature which make them more or less impervious to conventional approaches to capacity building. Capacitated organizations will manifest both stronger invisible elements as well as an ability to reflect on these elements – which is itself a feature of these stronger invisible elements situated at the top of the hierarchy. (Kaplan, 1999, p26)

Many, if not most, capacity development interventions tend to focus on the lower end of the hierarchy and because of that seem not to change the fundamental patterns in the organization. Also much support is in the form of advice-giving: 'trying to get organizations to make changes that we think will be good for them; rather than strengthening them through a form of facilitation which enables them to come to grips with their own business' and thus developing the top elements. Kaplan therefore calls for a paradigm shift or expansion to include the intangible with the tangible. Recognizing both and making sense of how they interact is a critical competency. In doing so, Kaplan identifies two important characteristics of organizational functioning and processes that bring about change that should lead to greater effectiveness. These characteristics are openness and complexity.

Openness and complexity in capacity and its development

Organizational change and development processes are too uncertain, ambiguous and contradictory for a standard intervention approach or sequence of actions producing a 'guaranteed' result. This experience leads Kaplan to call for a second paradigm shift: 'from static framework to developmental reading'. In terms of understanding and developing an organization's capacity this means seeing, appreciating and taking on board its inherent openness towards the environment as well as working with complexity in processes of human change.

If we look at these six elements of organizational life not as indicators, but in terms of the meaning they have for the whole, if we begin to apprehend them through their relationships to one another, and if we allow the organization as such to quite literally *emerge* from such an appreciation, then some quite new and perhaps radical insights arise concerning capacity and capacity building interventions.

The organization is a system in that it is greater than the sum of its parts. How it performs cannot be 'calculated' by 'adding up' all the work arrangements – like departments – with the resources and processes which connect it all together. In addition, parts themselves are only identifiable in relation to each other. A strategy department only makes sense once you know what other parts of the organization need and must apply a strategy. While there are various features of organizational life which may be separated out and shown, for example, in an organization chart, these component parts are continuously interacting. An organization arises, so to speak, from the ways in which the parts affect, and are affected by, each other. An organization is a form of greater complexity than any one of its parts. In attempting to understand the system, we must therefore look to the whole, rather than reduce our understanding to the components.

The organization is also open in the sense that, while it has boundaries, these boundaries are porous, with the result that contextual influences pervade and invade the system, ensuring continued growth and demanding adaptability. Each organization is an entity in itself, but not entirely. It interacts with its environment, it affects and is affected by that environment. It is one entity among many, and its specific identity is a combination of its own internal integrity and its relationship with others. The continued growth, and the continued life of the organization, depends largely on its interaction with its ever-changing context and environment. Without such interaction the organization – as with a biological organism – would soon become dormant and cease to function. (Kaplan, 1999, p20)

If an organization is an open system, on what basis or principles does it operate? For Kaplan, the answer lies in the fact that organizations are made up of individuals, who are themselves complex and their relationships equally so.

We have been describing the organization as an almost abstract system without taking account of the fact that it is composed of people. Organizing means dealing with individuals as systems in their own right, as well as in their relationships to achieve collective purposes. People bring many potentials, inspirations and struggles, each with their strengths and shadows which build the elements out of which organization arises. These elements take on the character of the strongest and weakest aspects of the people who build them. At the same time, organizational members are moulded by the organization itself and through their relationships to one another. Consequently, interventions towards organizational capacity have to recognise the significance of building individual capacity on the one hand and capacitated relationships on the other. Both are a requisite for capacity development. Put another way, capacity building has to respect the complexities generated by the interplay between individual and organization, and work as much with individuals and with small groupings as with the larger system.

The foundation laid by this view of capacity – albeit from a perspective of discrete organizations – is an important grounding. First, it establishes six, loosely hierarchical, categories to help 'unpack' organizations and see their roles in ways of organizing. In doing so, Kaplan points out that tangible and intangible elements create something more complex than before. This insight asks us to look beyond a combination of (in)visible elements in order to appreciate capacity as something qualitatively different that is expressed in performance. In addition, he highlights the role of both individuals and their interactions as 'sites' of capacity which interventions must take into account. These three features have significant influence on the effectiveness of capacity development efforts.

A more recent, complementary, way of explaining capacity and its development is provided by a multi-country study undertaken by ECDPM. Analysis of the evidence reaffirmed that capacity as understood and described by Kaplan is a valid and powerful perspective. Results of this study provide a new step forward in identifying what arises from the interaction between people's competencies, their collective capabilities and the capacity which arises from them. Set along-side Kaplan's explanation the ECPDM capacity framework makes a practitioner's terrain clearer, though not necessarily easier.

ECDPM: Five core capabilities

Based on 16 in-depth case studies, the ECDPM team 'unpacked' the concept of capacity in terms of five 'core capabilities' that seem to be present across all the situations where effective capacity is displayed. Despite having different 'labels', the substance of capacity has many similarities, refinements and illustrative applications, which reinforce the insights from Kaplan's earlier work. Retaining the original voice and formulations wherever possible, the following description is extracted and edited from the original material.[4]

Capacity is about the ability to do something. But such an aggregated meaning tells us little about what that ability might be. Based on our reading of the cases and the wider literature we conceptualize capacity as being built on five core capabilities which can be found, to a greater or lesser extent, in all organizations or systems: the capability to act, the capability to generate development results, the capability to relate, the capability to adapt and finally, the capability to integrate.

These five capabilities are separate but interdependent. All the actors in the cases tried in some way, with varying degrees of success, to balance all five as they did their work. All five were necessary. None were sufficient by themselves to ensure overall capacity.

The capability to act and self-organize
The first core capability may appear obvious. And yet its absence weakens efforts at building any kind of broader capacity. We are talking here about the capability to act deliberately and to self-organize. Organizations must be able to have volition, to choose, to exert influence and to move and develop with some sort of strategic intent. It is about the capability of a living system, to be conscious and aware of its place in the world, to configure itself, develop its own identity and then to act. And to do so over the resistance or non-cooperation of others. From this perspective, capability is about human, social, organizational and institutional energy. Can the organization develop a collective ability to make choices that its members will respect and work to implement? Can it overcome its contextual constraints and develop the commitment to go ahead with decisions that it has made? Does the system have a mastery and an energy that enable it to make progress? Does it have the collective drive and ambition to build its capabilities? Is it stuck or trapped or immobilized?

The reasons underlying an inability to act can be many and complex. Government agencies can be leaderless and directionless. They can struggle to deal with conflicting mandates and constituencies. They can decide it is not in their interest to make a serious effort to deliver a particular programme or service. They can be starved of resources and protection and/or can be captured or controlled by groups that have no interest in making them effective. Many civil society organizations in low-income states lack power to act. Government intrusions and control limit their policy and operating space. Many lack financial independence. Some are not able to build the international or even domestic linkages that could sustain their capability to act. Victimization and powerlessness takes over.

The capability to generate development results

This second capability is the most widely-used way of thinking about capacity issues. But our reading of the cases has broadened our view of what constitutes development results and how such a capability fits within the overall capacity of a system.

A first type of development results is improved capacity itself. Capacity building was a crucial developmental goal in its own right that entailed equipping a country, a region, an organization or an individual with attitudes, values, behaviours that they needed to make progress.

A second type of results is programmatic: for example, outputs and outcomes in the form of better maternal health, improved environmental protection policies, more comprehensive livestock protection services or declining levels of poverty. Capability from this perspective is about a group or organization or system executing or implementing projects and programmes to a certain standard. A key idea is capacity as an 'input' or as a means to achieve higher-order programme development results. In many cases, this capability is more or less equated with effective performance management in the form of better service delivery. Characteristic of this view is the constantly-repeated 'capacity for what' question.

Our case research, however, has highlighted the limitations of relying exclusively on a narrow, instrumental way of improving the capability for generating development results. To be effective, it needs to be integrated in some way and combined with the four other capabilities.

The 'results' perspective tends to emphasize the development of more functional, thematic or technical capabilities such as policy analysis, management information systems, research methodologies, financial management or service delivery. These represent a type of capability that is accorded particular importance by most stakeholders both in countries and in international development agencies. But less attention is given to other more generative, non-technical, less instrumental capabilities such as reflection and 'double-loop' learning, self-organization, bridging and linking. Without these latter capabilities, the technical core of the system cannot be sustained over the medium and longer term.

The capability to relate

This third type of capability appeared time and again in the cases. This is the capability to achieve a basic imperative of all human systems, i.e. to relate to other actors within the context in which it functions. From this perspective, capacity is not just about goal achievement and programme delivery. In the real world, systems need to gain support and protection. Protecting the technical core of the organization or system is key. They also need to leverage their resources by entering into informal alliances or formal partnerships. This capability is particularly relevant in many low-income countries that are still struggling to put in place an institutional and organizational infrastructure. Without this capability, the chances of achieving effectiveness are unlikely.

This has important implications for our understanding of capacity. First, organizations and systems worked to gain different kinds of legitimacy from other groups in society. Capacity was thus conferred from the outside as much as it was developed from the inside. Second, this type of capacity had political aspects. In the cases, institutions and organizations frequently had to compete for power, space, support and resources with a variety of other actors including individuals, informal groups and networks and other formal actors. This approach appears to operate as much through the informal and the intangible as it does through the formal and the tangible.

A good deal of donor behaviour can be explained from this perspective. In some of the cases, we can see the tension in the relationships between country participants and donors as both groups try to maintain their own legitimacy with different groups of stakeholders. In practice, much current emphasis on activities such as results-based management or monitoring and evaluation arise out of a need to maintain donor legitimacy and operating space. Actors need legitimacy, political support and alliances to function. But systems that become obsessed with their own survival and vested interests lose the capability to innovate and experiment.

The capability to adapt and self-renew
A fourth capability is adaptation and self-renewal. Capacity from this perspective is about the ability of an organization or system to master change and the adoption of new ideas. Many of the actors in the cases also had to confront dramatic shocks – the Asian tsunami, unforeseen government or funder decisions, changing needs of clients and beneficiaries, the loss of key staff, sudden economic changes, and so on. And many development agencies struggled to keep up with the demands of their constituents and clients as global pressures affected their behaviour.

Part of the capacity development challenge in all the cases was to balance the stability needed for developing key capabilities with the need to keep changing them as mandates and conditions altered.

In most cases, capacity development is likely to be a complex voyage of personal and collective discovery that evolves over time. This is a less instrumental, more process-oriented approach which stresses the emergence of inner human and organizational qualities such as resourcefulness, identity, resilience, confidence, innovation, collaboration, adaptiveness, courage, imagination, aspiration and even spirituality. Those on the outside will never have more than a limited understanding of, or leverage over, the process as it unfolds.

The capability to achieve coherence

All organizations, indeed all human systems, must deal with the tension between the need to specialize and differentiate versus the need to bring things together and achieve greater coherence. On the one hand, systems need different capabilities, separate country units, different kinds of skills and personalities, a range of services and products, a diversity of clients and funders and a variety of perspectives and ways of thinking. Yet at the same time, they must find ways to rein in fragmentation to prevent the system or organization from losing focus or breaking apart.

Centralization and control are increasingly not the answer to resolving this tension. Many organizations try this approach only to lose effectiveness as innovation and flexibility are lost. They enter into a period of oscillation in which the system swings back and forth from decentralization to centralization then back to decentralization. And they lose effectiveness as the cycle continues.

Actors also try multi-component strategies to achieve greater coherence including the upholding of certain values, the recruitment of particular types of people, the attention to communication and openness and the use of cross-functional, cross-country, cross-disciplinary teams and management groups. This differentiation–coherence dilemma is even more pervasive at the programme and sector level given the long-standing independence of many of the actors.

The achievement of a deeper, more resilient and coherent kind of capacity seems to depend critically on the effectiveness of this capability to bring things together. Systems that perform in the short term but cannot change or relate in the medium term lose effectiveness.

ECDPM suggests that, in essence, these five core capabilities are applicable to each level of human system, be it an individual, a team, an organization, a network of organizations, a sector or even a country. How these capabilities interact so that capacity emerges is not fixed. Their relative importance at different ages and stages of evolution at any scale of social organization and in different contexts is far from certain. How the development of each capability is best approached in reality and interacts with others is a critical issue for a practitioner to continuously consider and work with.

A practitioners' lens on capacity

The chapters in this volume illustrate that practitioners need and rely on images or mental 'pictures' with which they analyse the condition and situation of the entity they are dealing with (Morgan, 1986). The image adopted, and its specific components, forms a lens (or a set of lenses) with which one looks at and interprets the present, looks at history and anticipates possible interventions. It shapes ideas about the directions in which one would seek a more capacitated future. It is therefore important to realize what one's own framework and mix of capacity dimensions looks like. This self-understanding is also significant in order to appreciate that there will be different frameworks in play on which others rely. Such clarity makes for better communication. In short, multi-dimensionality is essential in any understanding of capacity. In our view, inter-connecting the two sets of dimensions described above is a powerful starting point for useful 'framing'. Differences in the two explanations, for example in relation to hierarchy, are mostly issues of emphasis. Their core similarities, summarized below, are more important.

- Capacity is a multi-faceted phenomenon. It is based on different competencies or capabilities that combine and interact to shape the overall capacity of a purposeful human system. Both frameworks identify key elements that contribute to overall capacity. Ways in which elements are present and combine can vary enormously within and between types of organization. It is therefore best to treat generalizations with great care, placing more trust in those that derive from experience with the type of entity or entities one is working with.
- Both frameworks see a single organization, a group of organizations, social institutions or a sector as a 'living and dynamic system'. They stress the need to understand not only concrete observable features of organizations, but also the more intangible dimensions and connections. In processes of capacity development, making 'the invisible' tangible is a vital professional skill.
- 'The whole is more than the sum of the parts'. It is the appropriate interrelation and interaction between different components that produce the energy, confidence, productivity and resilience typical for a 'capacitated organization'. The uncertain, 'emergent' nature of capacity also implies that its development is unlikely to be a linear, well-planned, predictable process. Consequently, active observation of unanticipated changes and professional responsiveness are important.
- A practitioner needs to be conscious about framework and specific dimensions that one uses and the assumptions one relies on. Such self-understanding positions the practitioner in relation to the frames used by others, which may be very different. Comparing perspectives is often a form of capacity development in its own right.
- The lens employed to see and read an organization in its history and context makes a big difference: in diagnosis, in negotiation and selection of remedies, in accountability for and commitment to change, and so on. From different angles one simply sees different things. To find an adequate intervention it is therefore important to develop a robust understanding of a situation by, for example, using different angles and/or dimensions from within a specific framework or a repertoire of options.
- Capacity is highly relational! Consequently, a sub-theme is that power matters. Practitioners need to be aware of what types of power are in play, where they are located and how they are applied.

The varied perspectives and dimensions of capacity and its development described in this chapter are to be seen in many of the practical cases described in the texts which follow. In some instances, direct reference is made to a framework included here. In others, for example when dealing with intangible and tangible features of capacity and its development, the reference is less explicit but present none-the-less. Whatever the case, an appreciation of both will be an advantage when reading this resource volume.

Notes

1   By prior agreement with Allan Kaplan (formerly of CDRA, South Africa) and the Director of ECDPM Paul Engel and his colleagues, this chapter draws both liberally and literally on their publications shown in the references. For reasons of style, quotation marks are not included. Responsibility for inclusion and explanation of their original texts rests with the authors of this chapter.
2   Two relevant ECDPM publications are: www.ecdpm.org/pmb21 and www.ecdpm.org/capacitystudy
3   For example, the 5Cs framework is being employed by the Inspectorate for Operations and Policy (IOB) of The Netherlands Directorate-General for International Development Cooperation (DGIS) as the basis for an evaluation of capacity development undertaken by some of the non-governmental organizations that it finances.
4   The following pieces of text are a selection and summary by the authors of the original ECDPM material. Large parts of it are, however, original formulations.

References

Baser, H. and Morgan, P. (2008) 'Capacity, change and performance: Study report', Discussion Paper 59B, European Centre for Development Policy Management, Maastricht

Kaplan, A. (1999) 'Organisational capacity: A different perspective', Development Dossier No. 10, Non-Governmental Liaison Service, United Nations, Geneva

Mintzburg, H. (1983) *Structure in Fives*, Prentice Hall, Englewood Cliffs, NJ

Recommended readings

The ideas and information provided in this chapter are woven throughout the other chapters in this volume. The following are some essential texts that help to deepen the basic notions of organizational capacity.

Morgan, G. (1986) *Images of Organization*, Sage, Beverly Hills, CA

A classic text still highly relevant today. Morgan introduces different ways of seeing organizations and stimulates critical reflection on what we think organizations are, how they work, and why.

Baser, H. and Morgan, P. (2008) 'Capacity, change and performance: Study report', Discussion Paper 59B, European Centre for Development Policy Management, Maastricht

This is probably the largest study ever undertaken on capacity development. The Synthesis report is accompanied by a series of 16 rich and detailed case studies and a range of theme papers. It provides the detailed foundation for the 5Cs framework.

Fukuda-Parr, S., Lopes, C. and Malik, K. (eds) (2002) *Capacity for Development: New Solutions to Old Problems*, Earthscan, London

This text takes a critical look at the way that asymmetries in the aid system impede capacity development, with proposals for how this can be remedied.

Mintzburg, H. (1983) *Structure in Fives*, Prentice Hall, Englewood Cliffs, NJ

This book is a milestone reading in organizational development and management science that helps in understanding different components and processes that shape an organization.

Kaplan, A. (2002) *Development Practitioners and Social Process: Artists of the Invisible*, Pluto Press, London

Using cases and stories, this volume deepens an appreciation of just how much is not readily seen in organizational processes. It provides a number of exercises so that a practitioner can self-equip to better see that which is not visible.

OECD (2006) *The Challenge of Capacity Development: Working Towards Good Practice*, OECD, Paris

An interesting summary of the perspectives of donors on capacity development and their views of what should be worked towards in terms of approaches, methods and responsibilities.

Thompson, M. (2008) *Organising and Disorganising*, Triarchy Press, Axminster

A recent, stimulating re-consideration of human organization that proposes a typology of five ways of organizing in a sort of ecology including typical civic, entrepreneurial and government strands. The book provides an additional perspective on the complexity of human organization which complements the frameworks described in this chapter.

2

Multiple Actors

Be it water out of a new tap or the practice of good governance, development is the product of relationships between stakeholders. Capacity exists not only within but also between them. Capacity and its development are therefore 'relational'.

This text by Jim Woodhill introduces multi-actor dimensions of capacity. He discusses features of the actors that are commonly found in aided development and then explores dimensions of working with relations between them. The chapter introduces an interesting model of three types of 'relating', then provides the reader with principles and approaches that can be applied to make engagement between multiple stakeholders more effective.

Capacity Lives Between Multiple Stakeholders

Jim Woodhill

Introduction

A society develops and solves its problems through its collective capacities. No matter how knowledgeable and skilled individuals or single groups are, if this type of capability cannot be coordinated for the common good, progress is improbable. This fact may be obvious. But, when planning for capacity development, it is easily overlooked. A key mechanism for creating a collective capacity is a national government. However, the world has become too interconnected and complex to rely on this solution. Developments in science and the economy are often beyond the influence or control of a state. Meanwhile, the web is opening a new world of collective engagement between people. In this modern world, government alone is often unable to marshal the collective capacity needed to tackle difficult issues facing a society. Consequently at local, national or global scales people are searching for new ways to create collective capabilities. As a result there are innovative forms of governance that try to create collective capacity through multi-stakeholder processes in which citizens, government, business and non-governmental organizations (NGOs) collaborate.

Box 2.1 The case of forest protection in Nepal[1]

Millions of people depend for their livelihoods on the Terai forests in the southern plains of Nepal, which are also an important source of national income. These forests are rapidly disappearing, however. Driven by poverty and corruption, people clear them to make way for agriculture or to sell precious timber. Outside national parks, wildlife struggles for survival in a few patches of remaining jungle. Meanwhile, downstream, people live in fear of the monsoon floods, which have become much more severe with the forest gone. Without any change there will be few trees left to harvest, shortage of firewood, scarcity of forest products and very little nature left to attract tourists.

All sorts of groups have a stake in the forests. For local villagers they are source of firewood, building materials, forest products and cash income. There are legal and illegal logging interests, including European logging companies seeking to engage in joint ventures. Environmentalists are concerned about the protection of the wide and exotic biodiversity. A further complication is that, until recent elections, Maoist rebels have also been active in the area. Central in these interests is the forestry department with the legal mandate to manage interests around these forests, and which is often powerless to ensure their sustainable management. Allocation of forest land and logging rights is closely linked with local politics and electioneering. Ultimately, if the forests are not protected, everybody loses. But in the short term conflicts between the different interests are rife.

In the late 1990s donors, NGOs and the Government of Nepal started to explore ways of dealing with these problems through a multi-stakeholder sector-wide approach. Large stakeholder meetings were held at district level and District Forestry Co-ordination Committees were established.

The challenge was to create a collective capacity to sustainably use and manage the forest resources. This collective capacity did not come from the knowledge or skills of any one group nor from the stakeholder process itself. Rather, the stakeholder process itself generated:

- a new, shared understanding of the situation;
- agreements about other, proven, ways of doing things;
- new formal and informal rules;
- new forms of trust; and
- new systems of reward and sanction to encourage or enforce different relational behaviours.

This is the capacity that lives between the stakeholders, offering a better starting point to tackle problems as they arise.

Over time, many innovations have occurred. These have included new cooperative partnerships between stakeholders, institutional reforms related to private forestry, new collaborative approaches to land use planning and an evolving understanding of the sort of rights and responsibilities that might lead to a more sustainable situation. These are all innovations that increase the collective capacity for sustainable forest management. They embed government processes within a wider network of stakeholder engagement and learning.

The problems of management in the Terai are far from fully resolved, and political instability in the country has been a major setback. Yet the multi-stakeholder approach that brings conflicting parties into dialogue with each other has endured. Sufficient gains have been achieved, demonstrating that the capacity to sustainably manage the Terai forests rests in the relationships and capacities that exist between the different stakeholders.

These efforts call for constructive interaction between many different parties. They depend on being able to direct people's energies and diverse types of capacity, distributed across a society, towards shared goals. But the parties involved – typically referred to as stakeholders or actors – differ in many ways. And differences are important because they can both enable or impede social change that seeks, for example, greater justice and ecological viability. Consequently, practitioners working to create collective capacities for change need to be aware of what makes stakeholders different, and why. This is an important starting point for becoming skilled in understanding the way relationships work and selecting appropriate ways of bringing stakeholders together. This chapter therefore examines why multiple development actors are distinctive, the types of 'relating' that practitioners need to be aware of and how connections towards joint results or objectives can be realized through multi-stakeholder processes. The practical example from Nepal illustrates these factors in real life.

Capacity through the lens of stakeholder interactions

This case from Nepal is one example of capacity being built because stakeholders interact to tackle a problem that one party cannot solve on its own. This process creates new, tested relationships that can not only add to every actor's individual effectiveness but also create a collective capacity to continue addressing forest management issues. This type of capacity-related outcome is seen in many multi-actor development efforts. In Recife, Brazil, local government works with many different community and business groups on a process of participatory budget monitoring that improves overall outcomes of the public means. In Uganda, the SNV Netherlands Development Organisation links farmers, business and government to improve their joint management and development of the oilseeds value chain. Across many countries governments have engaged a wide diversity of stakeholders in developing Poverty Reduction Strategy Papers (PRSPs) and sector-wide strategies in order to improve their formulation and implementation. In Australia a multi-level structure exists for involving farmers, environmental organizations, government, business and researchers in tackling land degradation. In Benin a community-based grass-roots initiative involving local traders has drawn together donors and government to improve the local market. At a global level the World Wildlife Fund has initiated a dialogue within the shrimp aquaculture sector to help create standards for a sustainable industry. Meanwhile, also at a global level, many players in the cotton industry are involved in the Better Cotton Initiative.

So what does all of this have to say about capacity arising from relationships? A conventional view sees capacity development as being about training a group of individuals, building skills, producing manuals and developing organizations. But behind the examples noted above lies a different sort of understanding of capacity development. It is an appreciation which recognizes that capacity in real life often exists at the interface between actors and it develops as interactions progress.

Capacity 'that works' is not just a matter of individual skills or internal organizational arrangements. These factors might be relevant building blocks – some would call these competencies or capabilities – but they do not constitute real capacity. Effective capacity is visible and exists when people identify and act on issues of shared concern. And thus real capacity lives between actors and in the ways that they deal with each other to solve problems or to realize their ambitions. In doing so, they build up relational competencies and generate trust which, for example, reduces transaction costs. If collaboration works well – and it is not guaranteed and is seldom conflict-free – stakeholders become less likely to treat each other according to general stereotypes with prejudices that cloud communication and reinforce wrong interpretations of behaviour. Seeing capacity as a living property of relationships is an important practitioners' lens.

This chapter therefore explores the notion of capacity development as an outcome of multiple actors or stakeholders working together to bring about change. It does so in stages to address practitioner-oriented questions. Who are these different stakeholders? What organizing principles do they follow? How do they see and understand when they are working and performing well? What are the dynamics and challenges of bringing them together? What are the implications for designing and facilitating such processes and what capabilities do practitioners need? What new capacity arises and remains from their interactions and why? Answers to these and other questions are accompanied by pointers to related chapters in this volume noted at the end.

Looking for answers is supported by two bodies of knowledge. One is by recognizing that capacity created by and between multiple actors relates to processes of 'governance'. The notion of governance does not equate to government alone. It is about how, collectively, communities, organizations, nations and the international community work together to make decisions for the common good. This perspective on combining capabilities and efforts is helpful because changes that matter to many people are not produced by active states and passive citizens. Instead, they can be better be understood as 'co-productions' (e.g., Mulgan, 2004).

A second support comes from substantial experience in connecting and engaging different actors in processes of collective social, economic and political change. Dialogue, social learning, round tables, learning alliances, communities of practice are but a few of the methods available. In this chapter, the term 'multi-stakeholder processes' (MSPs) is used as an overarching reference to these and other ways of collaborating. Selecting an effective MSP depends, amongst other factors, on the differences between stakeholders, as well as their reasons for collaborating. This type of competency is critical for professional practice.

Understanding stakeholders and why their differences matter

A stakeholder (or actor or player) is an individual, organization or group who has a role to play and/or is affected by the outcome of an issue, situation or process. In turn, what they do may influence the situation and how the situation changes will feed back to have some effect on them. This type of interaction is found in complex systems. While important for understanding MSPs, complexity is not covered in detail in this chapter, so a number of further readings are offered as a guide.

From a governance perspective, relational dynamics can be understood in terms of four main groups – citizens; private sector actors; government; and civil society organizations.[2] The inclusion of citizens, alongside the classic distinction made between government, business and civil society is important for three reasons. First, citizens, in how they vote, the products or services they buy and the way they engage with civil society are important actors in their own right. Second, individuals have roles as both citizens and as actors in all sectors of a society. An individual may well have different perspectives and interests depending on whether they are being a 'citizen' or carrying out a paid responsibility in, for example, government or business. Third, stakeholder processes at times fall into the trap of only engaging representatives from the three sectors and not considering how to involve 'non-organized' citizens, who self-organize in other ways to create a future for themselves and their families (Fowler and Biekart, 2008).

Beyond this most basic categorization of different actors, other distinctions can be made. Table 2.1 gives examples of how each of the four categories could be further characterized.

What is important in analysing stakeholders is not just knowing who the players are but understanding how they relate and where commonalities and differences lie. The essence of bringing different actors together is that they are *different*. The value-assumption of process involving connecting multiple stakeholders is that it

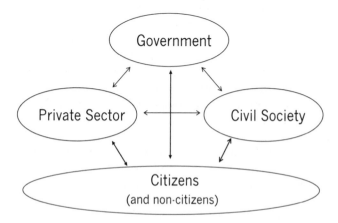

Figure 2.1 *Types of stakeholder*

Table 2.1 *Features in stakeholder characteristics*

Citizens	Government	Private sector	Civil society
• Identity	• Level: local to global	• Decision-maker	• Civil rights
• Wealth	• Public administration	• Employee	• Sport and
• Religion	and security	• Shareholder	recreation
• Ethnicity	• Role	• Local business	• Religious
• Education	• Minister	• Multinational	• Labour
• Age	• Parliamentarian	business	• Development
• Sex	• Policy-maker	• Associations	• Activisms
• Health	• Agency employee	• Professional groups	• Group identity
• Consumption	• Type of government		
• Ideology	ministry or agency		

will enable recognition of higher-order common goods, concerns and interests that motivate the overcoming of differences in pursuit of win–win solutions. If there is no common problem and no sense of some benefit for all engaged, then clearly collective effort has little point. From this precondition, combining respective resources, connections, technical capabilities, responsibilities, interests, perspectives and knowledge on situations, different forms of power and ways of driving change adds up to new types of capability. This newly established connectivity and experience is crucial for sustaining change.

The case of forest management in Nepal, cited at the beginning, illustrates how people's longer-term future is intertwined, even though they may have very different short-term interests. It also illustrates the very wide variety of stakeholders involved, with different and essential roles to play. In this case, they range from government forest workers and local communities through international donors and corporations.

Multi-stakeholder processes are not about a harmony model of change. Inevitably, processes of coming together start with varying degrees of conflicting perspectives, different interests, mistrust and misunderstanding. Table 2.2 illustrates five dimensions of difference that can be found between key actors that are potential sources of synergy, added-value and complementarity, as well as conflict in interests, rights, responsibilities, power and culture. Although a slight caricature of the four groups, analysing these aspects can provide a practitioner with useful insights about the stakeholder dynamics in a particular situation.

In any given setting, different stakeholders will have very different capabilities to share and thus different criteria by which they assess results and progress. What constitutes success or failure for one group may be quite different for another. For example, a business will look at profits; a donor might prioritize accountable use of funds; local communities may seek improved services; while a politician is perhaps focused on garnering voter support. Understanding the relationship between the various capacities and the types of results that different stakeholders are sensitive to can give practitioners an insight into potential sources of misunderstanding. Whether or not conflicts or synergies arise from collaboration depends on how stakeholders relate internally and externally.

Table 2.2 *Differentiating stakeholders*

	Core Interests	Rights	Responsibilities	Power	Culture
Citizens	• Livelihood • Security • Health • Meaning	• Human rights	• Obeying laws and social customs	• Electoral • Mobilizing • Consumer	• Diverse
Government	• Maintaining power • Stability	• Implement and impose laws	• Uphold constitution • Societal wellbeing • National security	• Legal • Military • Political • Financial	• Bureaucratic • Conservative • Risk-averse
Civil Society	• Improving situations • Wellbeing • Account-ability • Org. Survival	• As defined by law • Human rights	• Acting for constituency interests	• Mobilizing • Lobbying • Mindsets • Media	• Informal • Adversarial • Chaotic
Private Sector	• Profits • Viability • Image	• Carry out business within the law	• Profit making • Operate legally • Consumer safety	• Investment • Lobbying • Advertising • Resources	• Entrepreneurial • Pragmatic • Efficient

Understanding the way that people relate

The development sector is almost obsessive about defining, planning and evaluating 'results', often in a top-down, technocratic manner. Only a fraction of this attention is paid to creating the relationships on which achieving any sort of result hinges. Capacity development needs to focus not just on the capacities needed to achieve technical results but also on what it takes to build more effective and dynamic *relationships* that continue. Change in relationships not only provides results now, but should carry on in the future. This can be referred to as 'transformative capacity development' – that which enables people to collaborate and change situations in a profound, strategic and meaningful manner (see Box 2.2).

From the Tamil Nadu case we can see that real change happens in three interrelated types of relationships: with oneself; with others; and with the social (institutional) and environmental context.

Box 2.2 A story of change – relationships for impact[3]

The Tamil Nadu Water Supply and Drainage Board in India was in bad shape. Attempts by government to improve the situation through normal policy channels such as increased investments, better technology, organizational restructuring, privatization and decentralization had not been effective. A new head of the Board realized that a different approach was needed and embarked on an experiment. From January 2004 the usual formalized, bureaucratic processes of meeting and decision-making were replaced by the *Koodam*, a traditional cultural and social space. Here all persons are treated as equals (no hierarchies, no designations). There is an open, self-critical and transparent sharing of ideas generating democratic and consensual decisions that are collectively owned.

Through the *Koodam* the various stakeholders arrived at a shared vision and commitment – not something developed high up in the organization and handed down but something born from the heart of the organization. This then translated into a new set of relationships with local communities and water users. Then came the test of putting this into practice. In 145 villages the engineers took on the challenge of bringing about improvements and changes in a participatory way with local communities and water users.

The results have been astounding in terms of increased access to water, reduced costs and even the willingness of communities to pay for what has become a reliable service. Local communities invested themselves in water supply systems because of much better service delivery and a new trust in the Water Board. Investment costs in new systems were reduced by 40–50 per cent because of greater efficiency and reduced corruption. Operation and management budgets were reduced by 8–33 per cent. All this meant significantly expanded and more reliable water supply systems.

This change and eventual impact did not come about because of targets, indicators and external accountability mechanisms. It came about because of a new capacity embedded in the relationships between actors. First, the irrigation engineers looked at themselves. What was important for them? What were their values? Were their behaviours and practices something they would be proud to tell their children – or not? There were new relationships established between the engineers, between management and staff and very importantly between the representatives of the Board and water users. Finally, collectively, the engineers and the water users created a new relationship with their social (institutional) and physical environment – a new way of understanding what was previously seen as insurmountable barriers to improvement.

A new capacity had developed within the Water Board and water user groups. The capacity came about not through technical skills in water management, new management procedures or physical infrastructure. Rather, it was a capacity living in a new set of relationships – a new trust and collective capacity – between the actors involved.

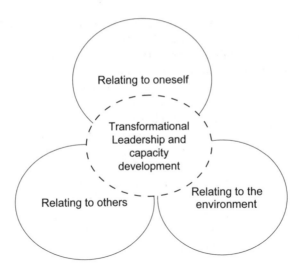

Figure 2.2 *Three different types of relating*

Relating to oneself

Ultimately the quality of human relations, human systems, leadership and process facilitation is linked with individual capacities for self-understanding, critical reflection and authenticity. In the Tamil Nadu example, the starting point was when water engineers looked deeply at what it meant for them as individuals to be part of a failed or a successful water board. They then began to ask themselves questions about the legacy they would bequeath to their own grandchildren. The answers to these questions came from within the *Koodam* space that was closely connected to their own personal and social-cultural identity.

Critical for aided development is not just what happens externally, but also what happens internally in people's hearts and minds. In practice, three aspects require attention. One involves investing in activities and processes that give people the time and space to develop themselves and their self-understanding. Another internal feature – also visible from the Tamil Nadu case – is including feeling and emotions as a normal part of discussion and exploration in collaborative processes of change. And it also means working to create trusting environments in which people can give and receive open and honest feedback.

Relating to others

Humans are equally capable of relating to each other in open, loving and compassionate or aggressive, violent and selfish ways. People are neither inherently selfish nor inherently altruistic. Rather we are 'conditional collaborators' and 'altruistic punishers' (Beinhocker, 2006). Essentially this means we have a strong inclination to collaborate with others *if* we feel we are being treated fairly and justly. If not, 'exit' or a fighting spirit easily springs up and we withdraw and 'silently' resist or go on the attack – even if such an attack is to our own disadvantage and may involve the ultimate sacrifice of losing life in war.

In small close-knit communities and organizations, the need to choose between 'flight or fight' is reduced because trust is built up through direct reciprocal relationships. In larger communities and societies, humans create all sorts of institutional arrangements to manage reciprocal relations, create trust and establish a minimal degree of fairness and equity. However, history shows that institutions are 'captured' and turned to the interests of powerful élites. And history also shows that societies with gross inequity and deep distrust eventually unravel, even if it takes a long time.

A strengthening of relational capabilities often arises from improved communication which enables people to enter into meaningful dialogue. In practitioner terms, this means developing deep listening skills, knowing how to give constructive feedback, knowing how to coach, developing patterns of leadership that create space for open communication, and understanding the dynamics of conflict discussed later.

Relating to the context

Self-understanding and good relations with others are in themselves insufficient for effective increase in capabilities. For this to happen in any particular context, actors with sufficient collective influence must share a common set of ideas about what is happening in their social or physical environment, how they would like to change it and how this can be done. In the Tamil Nadu case, a critical element of success was the shared understanding of the context built up between the different actors. This relationship with the setting enabled them to conceptualize issues and see innovative opportunities for improvement.

Development interventions often go wrong simply because the context is not well understood. Actions are taken on false and unchallenged assumptions about what is going on and how change happens. Developing capabilities that improve interactions with a setting, its history and present dynamics are critically important. This simply means getting good information on the table, enabling joint analysis and fostering effective strategizing. And, as noted before, because capacity is produced or reduced by complex backwards and forwards interactions across organizational boundaries, sensitivity is needed to the diverse ways that this plays out across different stakeholders that are trying to work together. For example, a major shift in exchange rate is likely to impact differently on government tax income, business profitability and a foreign-funded NGO's vulnerability. This is but one reason for a practitioner to be aware of the variety of ways in which diverse parties can be connected in order to produce new, relational and living capabilities.

Understanding stakeholder engagements and their facilitation

If stakeholders are diverse, so are the ways in which they can collaborate. For example, the ideals of more participatory forms of governance, ownership and development partnerships have logically led to the establishment of a wide variety of stakeholder processes, dialogues, learning alliances and round-table forums that can be found defining or operating within MSPs. Equally, practitioners need to be equipped with what it takes to facilitate across an array of collaborative arrangements and dynamics. This section serves as an introduction to both topics. Further readings provide greater detail.

Making connections: Multi-stakeholder processes and collaborative capacity

There are many variations in MSPs and the collective capabilities that they can produce. Table 2.3 gives some examples. The common aim is to get actors to work more 'productively' together. Some collaboration may be initiated and largely controlled by a state. Others are initiated by concerned citizens or civil society organizations perhaps frustrated by the failings of government. The private sector is increasingly engaged in establishing or being part of MSPs in response to demands for sustainable business strategies and corporate social responsibility. Some MSPs are initiated jointly between government, civil society and business actors (Waddell, 2005). The table shows a wide array of capacity development requirements that MSPs can bring to the fore.

The purpose of multi-stakeholder processes varies from simply stakeholder consultation about government policy through to joint decision-making and action by the involved stakeholders. Others are established to enable stakeholders to explore and learn about shared problems so they can use this understanding for taking action in their own domains of responsibility. MSPs also occur at and across different scales. Some are very localized, others work mainly at a global level, while many are set up to work across different levels of, for example, authority or responsibility. Across the diversity of the MSP landscape are the following common characteristics. A multi-stakeholder process:

- deals with a defined 'problem situation' or development opportunity (the boundary and focus may expand or contract during the process);
- involves the stakeholders involved in or affected by this 'problem situation' or development opportunity;
- works, as necessary, across different sectors and scales;
- follows an agreed yet dynamic process and timeframe;
- involves stakeholders in setting 'rules' for constructive engagement;
- works with the power differences and conflicts between different groups and interests;
- engages stakeholders in learning and questioning their beliefs, assumptions and previous positions;

Table 2.3 Types of multiple stakeholder process

Name	Issue / Purpose	Key Stakeholders	Examples of Capacities Needed	Examples of Collective Capacities Produced
Global Reporting Initiative (Waddell: 2005)	Limited mechanisms for global level reporting on environment and social performance by business Create workable and transparent reporting frameworks	• Global corporations • NGOs • Labour federations • Professional associations • Research organizations	• Managing multi-stakeholder processes between global NGOs and Corporations • Negotiating reporting criteria • Developing alliances • Marketing and communicating the concept	• Functioning clearing house and database for reporting on compliance with standards • Mutual understanding and rules between businesses and their upstream and downstream partners on environmental action.
Long-term vision for national unity in Mozambique (Pruitt, 2007)	Continuing poverty and low levels of growth after a long civil war To promote national unity through a participatory process of developing a long-term national vision and development strategy	• Government • Representatives of key sectors • Political groups • Civil society groups • Donors • Business leaders	• Dialogue skills for regional and sector working groups • Conflict resolution • Political negotiation • National planning processes • Economic analysis	• Shared perspective on and language for the future of society • Conflict early warning system • Public consultative forums • Culture shift to non-violent problem solving and negotiation
Participatory Budgeting – City of Pasto Columbia (Pruitt, 2007)	High unemployment, corruption and violence Better citizen participation in public administration and rebuilding social capital	• Mayor • Local government • Local citizens and rate payers • Local business	• Participatory leadership by Mayor • Citizens able to articulate their issues and understand budget processes • Facilitation skills for participatory budget planning	• Community forums with oversight on public expenditure • Application of performance standards to public services • Timely problem solving

Name	Issue / Purpose	Key Stakeholders	Examples of Capacities Needed	Examples of Collective Capacities Produced
Oilseed sub-sector Uganda (Mwesige, Chapter 14)	Oilseed production has great potential to reduce poverty of smallholder farmers in Uganda. The sub-sector has a set of challenges including lack of coordination and information sharing at all levels of the value chain To enhance growth, sustainability and competitiveness in the oilseed sub-sector in Uganda	• Producer organizations • Marketing Cooperatives • Processors and millers • Input suppliers • Traders • Private sector companies • Financial institutions • The government • Development partners • Donor agencies	• Value chain analysis • Multi-level MSP facilitation among the sub-sector players • Engaging private sector players • Brokering and negotiating business linkages • Policy analysis, lobby and advocacy • Action research • Stronger organization and representation of farmers	• Joint understanding, dialogue and priority setting • Improved deal-making with higher efficiency, lower transaction costs and better agricultural practices • Ability to attract new forms of finance • Influence on government policy • Improved working of value chain in terms of numbers of farmers profiting and import replacement

- balances bottom-up and top-down approaches;
- makes institutional and social change possible.

If these characteristics cannot be realized, a practitioner needs to consider other ways of gaining collaboration. Examples are less formal networks, consultative forums and other arrangements that call for less operational interaction and commitment. Collectively generated capacities, such as mutual responsiveness on a bigger scale, may still arise from looser set-ups.

And there is a 'deeper' dimension. Drawing on the section about ways of relating, a fundamental practitioner challenge is to help stakeholders really see and appreciate themselves, others and the context differently. This is the long-term basis on which capacities emerging from interactions will be sustained after a formal MSP or other time-bound collaborative efforts come to an end.

Key ingredients in designing and facilitating an MSP

Many capacity development efforts can be seen as MSPs or have elements of MSPs within them. Designing any type of multi-stakeholder process therefore requires clarity on many fronts. How do you get going? Who should you involve at the start? Are you dealing with major disagreements or big differences in power between the stakeholders? What sort of information and analysis is needed to move the process forward? Is a short-term or long-term process needed? What sorts of meetings, workshops and events will be appropriate? Importantly, the design must be flexible and adjusted as the process unfolds.

Although there is no simple recipe for a good MSP, drawing on practical experience enables us to identify some major ingredients. Figure 2.3 illustrates the stages of a multi-stakeholder process and some of the key considerations for success at each stage. For example, many MSPs go wrong because of false expectations and lack of initial understanding of different stakeholder interests. Having the wrong group of people involved on an initial steering committee can spell disaster for a whole process. When planning, it is important to work with stakeholders' visions of the future and not become bogged down in a mire of problems. Often processes fail because they do not move from the planning phase to implementation and interest and momentum is lost. If all those involved are not aware of how they will judge success and the process is not carefully monitored there is also a risk of failure. Thinking carefully about each of the checklist points can reduce these risks.

The less obvious challenge for practitioners is to facilitate relational processes that generate capabilities with effects that are beyond the scope of any one collaborating party. Typically, this calls for personal competencies that, for example, deal with differences in the capacities and power of each actor at inception and positively work with conflict. The recommended readings section provides details of what both can entail (see for instance, Wageningen International, 2009).

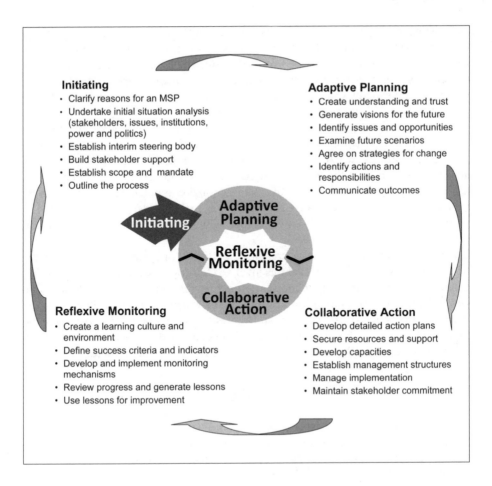

Figure 2.3 *A checklist for designing and facilitating MSPs*

Conclusions

Multiple stakeholders bring multiple combinations of capacities. And because they are time-bound, in MSPs practitioners need to work on two simultaneous capacity development outcomes. One is an increased capacity of each stakeholder. But just as important is the ability to facilitate interactions so that capacities arise which, for example, address social problems in new ways and with greater effectiveness.

In other words, in order to build effective capacity it is not enough to pay attention to individual skills or single organizations. Instead one also needs to develop capacities that live between multiple actors. Thus capacity needs to be understood as a dynamic 'energy' that lives in the relation of people to themselves, to others and to their environment.

Assisting this type of process calls on a practitioner's competencies in three ways. First is to have more than a generic or superficial understanding of the types and nature of stakeholders to be involved. While the labels may be the same, no two entities are. It therefore is important to delve into and respect their specificities, clarifying exactly what competencies need to be combined such that performance of the whole is more than the sum of the parts.

Second is an ability to 'unpack' and see how types of relating are playing out within individuals, within the organizations they work for and across towards other actors and the wider world. More often than not, this calls for sensitivity to and an ability to read the 'invisible' dynamics in relationships. Put another way, it involves applying a skill to identify the relational competencies that are critical for translating stakeholders' roles and assets into higher-order outcomes – such as reduced infant mortality or local economic value-added – that no one actor can achieve alone.

A third demand is selecting or creating the most appropriate form of collaboration as circumstances allow. Often this involves charting unknown waters in making connections where they were tenuous, perfunctory or did not exist. MSPs offer one way of thinking about and doing this. But MSPs are not a panacea. There may be deep conflicts of agenda, perceptions and interests, or deep-rooted mistrust where the premise of 'partnering' as the basis of aided change simply does not hold. Practitioners must be prepared for this. It pays to have a contingency option in mind.

Notes

1   Based on information provided by Frank van Schoubroeck and Jan Brouwers.
2   The term citizen is used here but in some situations there may be people who are stakeholders but not officially citizens – displaced people for example.
3   Based on information provided by Viju James.

References

Beinhocker, E. (2006) *Origin of Wealth: Evolution, Complexity, and the Radical Remaking of Economics*, Harvard Business School Press, Boston
Fowler, A. and Biekart, K. (2008) *Civic Driven Change: Citizens' Imagination in Action*, Institute of Social Studies, The Hague
Mulgan, G. (2004) *Politics in an Antipolitical Age*, Polity Press, London
Waddell, S. (2005) *Societal Learning and Change. How Governments, Business and Civil Society are Creating Solutions to Complex Multi-stakeholder Problems*, Greenleaf Publishing Ltd, Sheffield

Recommended readings

This chapter provides links to and is complemented by many others. The visible and invisible features of capacity are explained in Chapter 1, while multiple actors operating at different levels are described in Chapter 3. Chapter 11 concentrates on institutions as a source of collaborative principles for practitioners to bear in mind, while Chapter 9 explores and explains how situations and organizations can be read. The use of dialogue and the pressures for accountability that tend to accompany collaborations like MSPs are covered in Chapters 10 and 14, with the sources of conflict and their constructive management described in Chapter 6. The following is a short selection of useful resources as a starting point for further reading on this topic.

Hemmati M. (2002) *Multi-stakeholder Processes for Governance and Sustainability: Beyond Deadlock and Conflict*, Earthscan, London

Overview of stakeholder processes and governance at the international level with case studies and a clear process model.

Pruitt, B. and Thomas, P. (2007) *Democratic Dialogue – A Handbook for Practitioners*, CIDA, IDEA, OAS and UNDP, Washington DC

Comprehensive background to the theory and practice of establishing and facilitating dialogues.

Vermeulen, S., Woodhill, J., Proctor, F. and Delnoye, R. (2008) *Chain-wide Learning for Inclusive Agrifood Market Development - A Guide to Multi-stakeholder Processes for Linking Small-scale Producers to Modern Markets*, International Institute for Environment and Development and Wageningen University and Research Centre

An illustration of how to use stakeholder processes in value chain development. Includes a process model, methods and tools.

Wageningen International (2009) *Building your Capacity to Facilitate Multi-Stakeholder Processes and Social Learning*. http://portals.wdi.wur.nl/msp/, accessed 19 November 2009

Extensive resource portal on multi-stakeholder processes, participatory methods and tools and links to other useful sites.

3

Multiple Levels

For capacity to develop effectively one often has to work across different levels of human organizing. One may, for example, have to deal with capabilities of the individual, the organization, a network of actors and sector or national institutions. Another way of distinguishing levels is geographic or administrative units: communities (micro), districts and/or provinces (meso) and nation state (macro).

This chapter by Hendrik Visser discusses the real-life example of a capacity development initiative in road construction that consciously worked across both types of level. The story illustrates how additional capabilities were needed and developed at each level to achieve effective and sustainable results. The practitioner will find lessons on deliberately working with the 'multi-level' nature of capacity and implications for the place and role of change teams or advisers.

Capacities at Multiple Levels and the Need for Connection: A Bhutan Example

Hendrik Visser

The EFRC Project in Bhutan in a nutshell

This chapter looks at capacity development that began with a technical project and evolved to bring about change in a whole sector. This case will be used to discuss how capacity-development efforts often have to link to different scales of human organization and to different administrative levels in a country.

In 1999, the Royal Government of Bhutan received a first World Bank (WB) credit for the construction of rural access roads. Recently-enacted environmental laws and credit conditions required these rural access roads to be constructed in accordance with new environmental standards. The implementing agency, the Department of Roads (DoR), approached the SNV Netherlands Development Organisation for support in developing Environmentally Friendly Road

Construction (EFRC) methods and standards and designing and implementing a capacity-development component to the Bank-financed project. An EFRC project team was formed bringing together DoR staff and (inter)national advisers of SNV. Within its first three-year project phase, the project adapted existing proven technologies from Switzerland and Nepal to develop and test an effective innovative road construction method for Bhutan. It developed basic skills and organizational procedures within the DoR to scale up EFRC methods to all roads constructed by the Department. It also initiated capacity-development efforts towards various other actors relevant in road construction.

In March 2003 a second project phase was commissioned based on a broadened sector development vision, which brought all main road-sector stakeholders together. By then the project had made headway in embedding the new construction methods within the DoR and in facilitating various enabling regulatory and institutional arrangements. The project was also able to build on the good relationships it had established with stakeholders involved with the construction of district-level agricultural roads and community tracks. This allowed for capacitating and empowering local government engineering units at the district level vis-à-vis national agencies, thus creating better conditions for local performance. At the micro level the project was therefore also able to ensure that communities had a clearer role and better negotiation position in construction processes and in the maintenance arrangements around roads. Over time the project also provided support for improved capacity of policy bodies, the organization of contractors and the inclusion of EFRC methodologies and standards in national technical education.

By the end of its second phase in 2009, therefore, the project had succeeded in transforming road construction methods in the country, resulting in reduced environmental damage. It had also improved the physical durability of roads, resulting in long-term financial gains for the government of Bhutan, and achieved significant effects on capacities at different levels within the sector as a whole.

In this chapter we will analyse and discuss how such capacity results at different levels were brought about. We will then extract some important findings and lessons with regard to the role of the change team and the approaches it used. We will also provide conclusions on the 'multi-level' nature of capacity.

Working across different scales of human organization

Right from the start the EFRC project team had a fairly broad view of the road construction process and the actors engaged in it. Over time it continued to expand its scope and worked deliberately across different levels of capacity: with individuals, with teams, the DoR organization itself, with the network of other actors and with the road construction sector as a whole.

Improving individual skills and experiential learning

The SNV team invested a lot of energy in understanding the technical require-ments and constraints of implementing EFRC methods in the local context. Team members engaged key stakeholders in the analysis of the project cycle (Figure 3.1), which highlighted the main areas for improvement in existing construction processes and the appropriate sequencing of the development and introduction of new techniques.

Taking existing proven technologies from Nepal and Switzerland, the team helped to adapt these to the local physical and organizational realities of Bhutan. During the early stages, capacity-building support was provided directly to individuals and teams working on construction sites. This enabled experiential learning during adoption of the new construction technologies, while building on local knowledge and techniques.

A common perception in such change initiatives is that there will be winners and losers, which can create resentment and even outright sabotage. To win over scep-tics, the EFRC team understood it would need to demonstrate some quick results. Some of the new practices and skills provided good opportunities for 'quick wins'. At a very early stage, for instance, the team facilitated training for all DoR survey and design staff to improve their skills in survey data collection and the use of design software. This human resource investment facilitated a fast integration of environmental safeguards and design improvements that went well beyond the mandate of the roads project. This generated a positive atmosphere around the EFRC concept within the DoR organization and management.

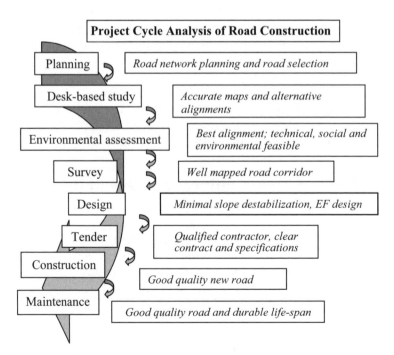

Figure 3.1 *Inclusion of environmental safeguards into the road project cycle*

A second example of a 'quick win' and 'win–win' situation, that also improved the relationship between DoR supervisory staff and contractor staff, was the introduction of new rock blasting techniques. These techniques substantially reduced environmental damage, resulted in stable rock faces above the road, facilitated faster excavation and easier work for the contractors. They also cost less for each cubic metre of blasted rock compared to existing techniques. The use of local vegetation to stabilize adjacent slopes (bio-engineering) is yet another example of a technological innovation introduced by the project. This measure not only provided a low-cost and therefore easily acceptable mitigation measure for damage caused during road construction, it also demonstrated the value of 'working with nature' rather than trying to 'control nature'.

Moving into the DoR organization

Parallel to the introduction of technical improvements by the project, a simultaneous process was underway to overcome opposition and build trust and credibility within DoR. The first EFRC road stretches built were used as demonstration sites to show that the new approach was both effective and feasible – an important step in overcoming resistance to change within the DoR, and among policymakers and the contractor community. Such awareness creation was further supported by mobilizing external 'buy-in' through newspaper articles, promotional brochures and an EFRC video to create sector-wide attention.

Over time, as new problems and constraints were encountered, 'project solutions' were translated into organizational improvements in DoR processes. Examples are enhancement of technical specifications and contract documents, tender and award procedures, site management instruments, quality assurance systems and human resource development plans. This resulted in a gradual and mostly implicit organizational development process within the DoR, which increased the acceptance and ownership of the EFRC innovation beyond the initial project actors.

Looking at these developments from the perspective of Allan Kaplan's explanation of seven organizational features described in Chapter 1, it is apparent that the EFRC team mainly worked on the lower levels of hierarchy within DoR. There were, however, also a number of subtle ways in which SNV helped the DoR develop more effective practices, which relate to the upper levels of the hierarchy. Supporting the formulation of an EFRC policy statement in DoR's Ninth Five Year Plan, which symbolized the leadership's commitment to the change, is one example.

The EFRC team also helped to strengthen and improve the quality of the professional (engineering) culture of the DoR. A strong professional culture can translate into pride and peer pressure to deliver good work, which can be an important driver for better performance and change. However, in this case, external pressure and the DoR management's 'executive culture' remained dominant factors. As in many bureaucracies, fear of punishment for mistakes, be it stemming from supervisors or external auditors, created a tendency to stick with formal procedures and a certain avoidance of experimentation, which slowed down learning. Chris Argyris (1991) lays out this basic problem of learning in organizations. He notes that most people in organizations are quite smart, but that to succeed, they have learned to find 'correct' answers in the eyes of superiors and cover up incorrect ones. The DoR's espoused goal was to be a responsive implementing organization, doing good work because of an intrinsic professionalism. However, externally and internally it was continuously subjected to higher hierarchical decision-making processes and judgements and that pattern never really changed. This made it all the more important for the change team to also work with external forces.

Engaging other stakeholders

Many organizations had a direct influence on the ability of the Department of Roads to construct roads using the new EFRC methods. Figure 3.2 illustrates various necessary components for EFRC, many of which are dependent on other actors. Consequently the first project phase was already marked by active engagement with these and other stakeholders at an operational level, notably the Geology Department and the Ministerial Quality Authority. However, sustaining the change process in DoR and ensuring broader system capacity called for more interactive involvement of the main actors. This became a central focus of the second phase, during which the following stakeholders were directly engaged.

- The Ministerial Quality Authority, the National Environmental Body and the Ministry of Human Resources and Labour, for the development of a sustainable EFRC policy framework and related regulatory systems

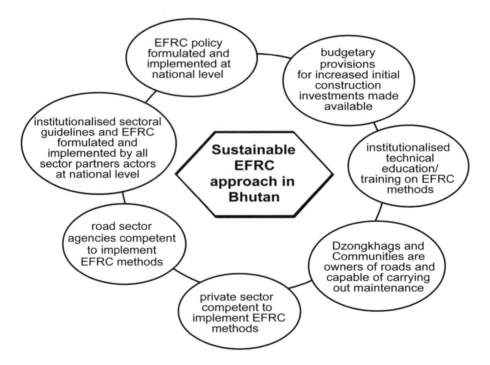

Figure 3.2 *Requirements for EFRC sustainability*

- The Ministry of Agriculture, the Forestry Corporation and District Engineering Units, for the introduction of EFRC to district-level roads and for increased community participation, amongst others for income generation through road construction and maintenance
- The Construction Development Board and the Contractors Association of Bhutan, for increased capacity with contractors in particular and improved policy within the construction sector as a whole
- The Royal Bhutan Institute of Technology and the Vocational Skill Training Centre, for integration of EFRC in the curriculum of technical training and university-level science education.

Including these stakeholders as formal project partners allowed for well-considered allocation of resources (including time of external advisers) to their capacity-development needs. In addition, it supported their formal participation in a stakeholder coordination platform and process. This step was important since many capacities required were located more in the inter-relationships between organizations than within individual entities (Morgan, 2005). The second project phase also saw the DoR allocated a leading role in broader sector development.

As we will discuss later, at first the DoR and World Bank were hesitant about incorporating such a broad scope of capacity-development efforts within the project as they feared it would dilute the EFRC team's attention to the technical challenges involved. With time, engagement with other actors such as the Ministerial Quality Authority and the National Environmental Body proved to be essential to the project's success as it helped institutionalize the EFRC approach across the sector.

As the understanding of such interdependencies increased, new possibilities for exchange of experiences and knowledge emerged. Ultimately a number of structural construction sector issues were identified and addressed, notably the poor linkage between national- and district-level planning processes and the structural capacity limitations of district engineering units (discussed later in this chapter). By acting together, several actors felt a greater sense of empowerment and courage to bring such structural constraints to the attention of the Minister. Such an action would have been impossible for an individual organization to undertake on its own.

Figure 3.3 illustrates the evolution of the project actor constellation and relationships over time. The initially 'isolated' project, with the EFRC team as key driver for change, gradually broadened to a sector-wide systemic change process, reaching out to an ever-increasing number of actors. System-level change eventually became driven and sustained by its own organizational and sector demand, allied to resonance with deeper values and institutions within society.

Working with formal and informal institutions

Sustaining new ways of working and capacities in a sector does also require embedding them in the 'institutions', the formal or informal rules of the game, norms and understandings that orient people's behaviour. One can distinguish between formal institutions, enshrined in government laws and regulations, and informal ones that are part of a society's culture, mindset and deeper value systems.

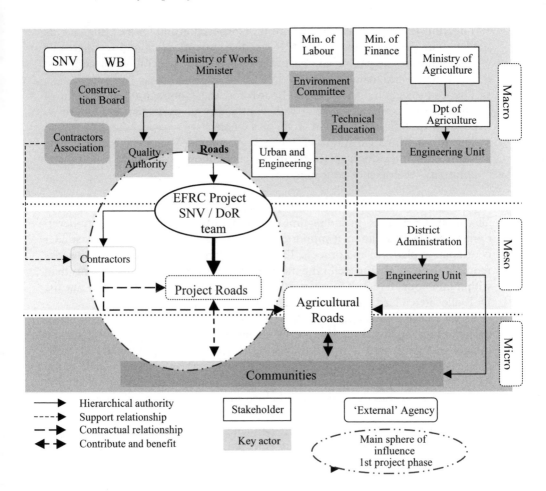

Figure 3.3 *Key EFRC project actors and main sector stakeholders*

In any major change process a coalition of supporters is necessary to generate political will and create required regulatory or legal backing. In the EFRC case, it was especially important for the EFRC team to work with the national environmental body. Regulations developed by the environmental body formed the basis for participation of stakeholders and underpinned the need for improved construction methods.

Another key actor which helped embed broader institutional change was the Ministerial Quality Authority. During the early years of the EFRC project this agency was a relatively weak external driver for systemic change. As the work proceeded, the DoR initiated new road standards. The Quality Authority formalized these and also strengthened the more formal instruments for monitoring and enforcing standards across the system. The EFRC team contributed to the development of a quality assurance strategy and framework, which was adopted as a compulsory set of requirements pertaining to both the work of the DoR and the construction sector in Bhutan as a whole. This ensured a gradual and lasting improvement in the performance standards of the construction sector. The Quality Assurance system and EFRC were also integrated in the curriculum of the Royal Bhutan Institute of Technology so that new graduates would have the right skills and competencies upon entry in the market.

Just as important as working towards formal regulatory frameworks and institutions was to work with the informal ones and to win over 'hearts and minds' for the changes that EFRC was promoting (Kotter, 1998). The EFRC team actively connected to the fundamental system of values and beliefs in Bhutanese society. The team underscored the inherent contribution of the EFRC approach to advancing Bhutan's development philosophy of *Gross National Happiness (GNH)*. The philosophy assigns a higher value to respect for the natural environment and embracing interconnectedness and compassion for others, as compared to conventional indicators of economic development. The team therefore used this cultural awareness as leverage for broader system change. In its public awareness activities, for example, emphasis was placed not only on the EFRC's contribution to nature preservation, but also its role in the protection of private property and places of Buddhist or historical importance as well. This emphasis was complemented by hard-nosed economic arguments, for instance a joint SNV/ WB economic comparison between EFRC and traditional road construction. The results convinced the DoR and the Ministry of Finance not just of the cost-effectiveness of EFRC, but also of its practical expression of environmental care. Consequently the DoR was given responsibility and the financial resources to introduce EFRC in all its operations.

The evolution described above was assisted by other transformations in Bhutan society. One example is the process towards democratization and the increasingly open and critical engagement of the public and media in assessing the performance of the public sector. This was especially noticeable in relation to highly visible construction projects. This public attention contributed to greater external accountability, acting as an important driver in stakeholders' acceptance of the need for improved sector performance, and the subsequent development of their capacity.

Working across another type of levels: Macro–meso–micro linkages

In applying EFRC methods to their 'own' roads, the DoR had already developed much more effective engagement with district authorities and the local population. This was an essential ingredient in achieving the improved alignment, construction and maintenance practices of EFRC roads. The importance of such linkages further deepened when the EFRC concept was expanded towards rural roads and tracks constructed under the responsibility of the Ministry of Agriculture and the districts, with increased involvement of communities.

The dynamics of agricultural road projects at national level had led to the common practice of project staff deciding on resource allocations with hardly any coordination with district engineering units. Project infrastructure works were subsequently delegated to respective districts for implementation, usually with unrealistic project plans. These preconditions made it almost impossible for district engineers to develop realistic annual work plans to make best use of the capacity and skills available.

An important focus area of the EFRC advisory team was therefore to create space for district engineering units to voice their concerns and capacity needs. By bringing different stakeholders together around a shared problem and by facilitating problem analysis and solution finding, the project created a strong driver for speedier action and more realistic solutions. This was triggered mainly by the realization that:

- the reality at district level was very different from perceptions at national level;
- there was a high interdependence of the national and district levels for each achieving results; and
- by working together the various stakeholders were better able to find structural solutions (for example in planning and budgeting procedures) that none of them could create in isolation. National-level staff therefore became more open to understanding and addressing meso- (district-) level realities.

The challenge of engaging effectively with the micro level became even more evident when the EFRC concept was expanded towards the construction of relatively small agricultural tracks for Power Tillers (small two-wheel tractors). These tracks are generally constructed by district engineering staff in collaboration with local communities. During the construction and maintenance phases, however, problems arose from a lack of clarity on the division of responsibilities, and insufficient capacity for a wide variety of tasks like planning and budgeting, routine maintenance and monsoon restoration works. In the past, community participation was generally seen as the provision of free community labour to implement district-level plans. Against this backdrop, the process of clarifying each stakeholder's role and responsibilities in road construction and maintenance empowered the communities to demand and set performance criteria for services delivered by the district. This, in turn, initiated pressure from districts for the adaptation of existing national procedures for agricultural road construction and the development of a road maintenance policy with clear implementation plans and capacity-development modules.

These examples demonstrate that this type of micro–macro divide can be bridged by empowering communities as 'rights holders' and by improving processes in which they can participate and engage meaningfully with district (meso) level authorities. This was especially important in Bhutan where organized civil society is still largely absent. At the same time, the district-level organizations needed different capacities to address the community (micro) realities and to influence national policies and the existing top-down infrastructure planning systems. And for system change to take place, there was a need to strengthen a sense of responsibility at the national level for meso- and micro-level problems.

The positioning and approach of the change team

Normally, finance for technical assistance to borrowers of World Bank loans is part and parcel of, and subject to conditions of, the loan agreement. For the EFRC project, SNV's services were financed separately. Hence, the SNV-led, capacity-building component of the project ensured relative independence from the WB roads credit, for which DoR took full responsibility and ownership. Based on previous experiences, the DoR initially expected the SNV team to be actively involved in implementation and execution of the WB project and subject to its edicts. But from SNV's point of view, the financing arrangement allowed for a more long-term, organization-wide vision on capacity building. It also allowed the SNV team to identify and stimulate developments in the broader sector and to monitor the effect of these broader system dynamics on the DoR organization. The dual funding set-up thereby prevented the emergence of the often criticized 'projectized capacity building', where project implementation efficiency is prioritized at the cost of a systems approach and sustainability. The tensions that stemmed from DoR's pre-conception needed to be acknowledged and managed, however.

Similarly, at the start of the project's second phase, the DoR and World Bank were, at first, hesitant about the broader scope of capacity-development efforts initiated by the EFRC team towards other actors in the sector. They feared it would divert the attention from the 'project roads' and attract too much additional work. The two key players were also lukewarm about allocating financial resources to other agencies. This resistance is entirely understandable, and highlights the tensions of trying to 'scale up and scale out' towards a more systemic change initiative.

But all in all it can be concluded that the fact that the change team was not strictly tied to the loan agreement had important advantages. It allowed the team to become a true adviser to the DoR and other actors (instead of having to play significant watchdog roles for the WB, for instance). It also allowed the team to use the (pilot) roads project as an entry point for influencing the wider DoR organization and to expand beyond the DoR organization to other critical actors and processes. Furthermore, it created the space for the change team and DoR to develop a flexible approach and to identify strategic and practical priorities more creatively than would have been the case had the team been narrowly tied to the credit agreement and document.

In working across different levels, as sketched in this chapter, the EFRC team used a set of essential starting points and perspectives.

- Right from the start the change team understood that road construction was much more than just a technical challenge. Also and maybe most importantly, this was seen as a matter of collaboration between different actors and ultimately of reshaping the patterns and rules that shaped their interaction. Though SNV had initially little technical experience in road construction, it brought to bear its extensive experience with rural development, local governance, engagement with line-ministries and participatory processes in Bhutan. It also sourced additional road construction expertise from Nepal and Switzerland by recruiting short-term advisers. The mix of context knowledge, change expertise and technical specialization thus developed was critical in the project's success.

- Though some vertical connections were present early in the process (for example the change team's connection with the environmental body that shaped essential regulations), the ability to work systematically with these partners evolved over time. The description of the case shows a somewhat gradual development from working on new practices on construction sites, to working with the whole DoR organization, and on towards working with multiple stakeholders, institutional patterns in the sector as a whole as well as with macro–meso–micro linkages. Clearly the team's ability to address capacity dimensions at different levels grew over time. Gradually the 'platform of change' was enlarged (EuropeAid, 2009).
- If there is any secret to successfully navigating change from within a complex, tiered system, it is in constantly reading the environment. This means being able to analyse for unanticipated, emerging events, and for people with informal influence who are ready to get involved in creating pathways forward. Looking back, we can conclude that the advisers in the EFRC team have had a special role in what one might call 'bridging leadership' (Garilao, 2007). Bridging is a method for harnessing and coordinating the energy, interests and resources of multiple and diverse actors and stakeholders in a system. This is done in a way that builds relationship capital and trust, thereby maximizing each actor's comparative advantage and making sustainable social change possible. It is particularly appropriate when a collaborative approach to solving complex social problems is required.
- Another striking aspect of the EFRC change story is how the EFRC team established ways to 'learn on the go'. This is essential since no matter how much training has been taken, there is never a manual, or a set of 'recipes' that perfectly suits a complex project. A lot has to be learned in the field and in the moment.

Conclusions

The case study discussed in this chapter clearly shows that solutions that make a difference usually require the development of adequate capacities at different levels rather than at one specific level of organization. The EFRC case has been used to discuss two types of level within systems. The first can be characterized as dealing with scales of human organization in terms of the sequence individual–organization–network–sector: the individual skills and working practices, the organizational arrangement within the DoR organization, the forms of collaboration between different organizations in road construction and finally the institutional rules of the game in the sector as a whole. Clearly these levels are interdependent. Each level cannot exist in isolation, but needs the other levels to function well. This is what systems theory calls 'nested systems'.

The case also illustrates the second type of level discussed, which is captured in the terms macro, meso and micro. These broadly equate to geographic or administrative distinctions: the national actors and institutional arrangements for road construction, the regional or district-level organizational arrangements, and the micro or community level where rural roads are built, used and maintained. Clearly, effective linkages were required to achieve adequate results across these three levels.

The experiences highlighted in this case suggest that to effectively link and work across levels, capacity development practitioners and change teams may make use of the following approaches and perspectives:

- create room to operate beyond a fixed implementation agenda or narrow project document;
- take a broad view right from the start, but be prepared to adopt a careful and phased approach to gradually build one's own capacity for dealing with wider organizational, network or institutional dimensions ('platforms of change');
- apply (informal) 'bridging leadership' that builds relational capital and maximizes each actor's comparative advantages and makes sustainable social change possible;
- hone abilities in systems thinking and 'learning on the go' in order to be able to deal with the complex connections across levels;
- work consciously with the formal institutions (for example, regulatory frameworks) and informal institutions (for example cultural values) that inform people's mindsets and behaviour across the levels.

References

Argyris, C. (1991) 'Teaching smart people how to learn', *Harvard Business Review*, vol 69, no 3, pp.99–109

EuropeAid (2009) *Toolkit for Capacity Development*, Brussels, available at www.capacity4dev.eu

Garilao, E. D. (2007) *Bridging Leadership at Synergos: Experience and Learnings*, Asian Institute of Management, www.synergos.org/knowledge/07/bridgingleadershipatsynergos.pdf, accessed 24 November 2009

Kotter, J.P. (1998) 'Winning at change', *Leader to Leader*, no 10, pp.27–33

Morgan, P. (2005) *The Idea and Practice of Systems Thinking and their Relevance for Capacity Development*, European Centre for Development Policy Management, Maastricht

Richter, I., Strobosch, P. and Visser, H. (2006) *Learning to Build the Road to Sustainability: Environmentally Friendly Road Construction and SNV Bhutan*, SNV Netherlands Development Organisation

Visser, H. and Richter, I. (2009) *Environmentally Friendly Road Construction in Bhutan, Multi-Stakeholder Sector Development and Complex Change Facilitation*, SNV Netherlands Development Organisation

World Bank (2005) 'Institutional and governance reviews – An evolving type of economic and sector work', Public Sector Prem Notes, World Bank

Recommended readings

This chapter builds on the introduction of multiple dimensions and multiple actors in capacity development in Chapters 2 and 3. Political and governance dimensions of capacity, accountability and micro–macro linkages are further discussed in Chapters 11, 12 and 13 respectively. The issue of (bridging) leadership is also touched upon in Chapter 16, and practices for ongoing learning are the topic of Chapter 21. The following are some other key readings on a systemic and learning approach to capacity development illustrated in this chapter.

Fukuda-Parr Sakiko, Lopes Carlos, Malik Khalid (2002) *Capacity Development. New Solutions to Old Problems,* United Nations Development Programme and Earthscan Publications Ltd, London.

The authors make a case for understanding development as a transformational process, an organic development process where building local capacity is essential. They analyse system capacity at the individual-organizational and institutional-societal levels.

Chambers, Robert (2003) *Whose Reality Counts? Putting the Last First,* Intermediate Technology Publications, London

Chambers provides valuable insights on how professionals and organizations create their own realities. He cautions about an inability and lack of motivation of professionals to understand the reality of 'poor people' and their complex livelihoods, thus creating a cycle of development activities that is based more on the (unconscious) needs and mental models of the professional and his organization than the need and reality of the poor.

Morgan, Peter (2005) *The Idea and Practice of Systems Thinking and their Relevance for Capacity Development,* European Centre for Development Policy Management, Maastricht

Morgan provides a concise and comprehensive overview of 'systems thinking' theory and its implications for capacity-development approaches. He highlights how systems behave, in terms of patterns and flows more than in individual actions and events. (See also www.ecdpm.org for other publications worth a look.)

Wilber, Ken (2001) *A Theory of Everything, an Integral Vision for Business, Politics, Science and Spiritualism,* Shambala Publications Inc, Boston, MA

Wilber offers an ambitious framework for understanding and navigating complex change. He analyses theories on the development of human consciousness and highlights three broad development stages: ego-centric (self), ethno-centric (family) and world-centric (whole). These stages are applicable for individuals as well as collectives like societies. He also makes a case for better understanding how informal systems (like values and beliefs) interact and are inter-dependent with formal systems in society. (See also: www.integralinstitute.org.)

Part II

Establishing your Practice

From the 'what' and 'what for' of capacity and its development explored in the opening chapters, the contributions in Part II move to doing it in practice. They discuss a range of key aspects, dimensions and competencies that a practitioner has to master. The seven topics that make up this Part help practitioners to develop quality in their work and shape their professional profile.

Chapters 4 and 5 open the section, homing in on the different roles that a capacity-development adviser can be called upon to play and the need to strike a balance between an understanding of the technical field(s) that one works in and the capacity change expertise that one brings. Chapters 6 and 7 explore the challenges of dealing with the inevitable power relations found in one's work and the ways that value differences express themselves. Chapter 8 discusses the history of the field of 'organizational development' as a source for capacity-development thinking and practice. Chapters 9 and 10 conclude with insights on the art of 'reading client situations' and an overview of useful skills and methods for engaging in substantive dialogue with clients and other actors in capacity development.

This group of chapters provides a substantive basis from which professionalism in capacity development can be understood and personally developed.

4

Advisers' Roles

Both external advisers and internal change agents can choose very different roles in capacity-development processes. Over the duration of an assignment or project, a competent adviser takes on a variety of positions in relation to different people or parts of the client system. This demands a critical awareness of types of roles and judgements about what is needed when.

In their article originally published in *Training and Development* journal February 1990, Champion, Kiel and McLendon identify nine possible roles and suggest key factors to consider in making judgements about which consulting role to take on. Their model helps advisers, change agents or consultants to improve the clarity of expectations between themselves and their clients. The article also explores factors that consultants may consider when adjusting their role towards a particular situation or phase of a project. Though it was written 20 years ago and not specifically targeted at the development community, this text is still highly relevant and addresses questions that will be very familiar to practitioners.

Choosing a Consulting Role: Principles and Dynamics of Matching Role to Situation

Douglas P. Champion, David H. Kiel and Jean A. McLendon[1]

Introduction

You have been asked to help an organization to manage a task force charged with designing some new procedures as part of an overall organizational development plan. The organization has never had a task force, but you've been told that your role is simply to 'sit in from time to time and make comments' as needed. You don't think that provides enough support to ensure success in this important aspect of the change process.

You have been asked to provide some 'listening training' to a work group with a history of conflict and dissension. You suspect that training at this point may not be well received by the group and that the causes of the problem are deeper than skill deficits.

Both of the above situations illustrate a common dilemma. In both, the consultant's initial view of the relationship and the intervention that will be effective differs from what the client thinks is needed or wanted. Such situations are likely to end up with disappointing results.

Consultants – internal and external – often talk about getting 'burned'. Usually it happens when the way the consultant's role has been structured leads to no-win situations.

Much good advice is available to new and practising consultants on how to be effective organizational development (OD) practitioners, but not much of it is focused on the special problem of role definition. There isn't much clear guidance for the consultant and client as to whether the role being played is the right one.

In order to do this kind of practical assessment and to facilitate collaborative agreements between clients and consultants, we need three things:

- a clear understanding of the purposes of a consulting relationship;
- a language for talking about consulting roles;
- criteria for determining which role is appropriate in a given situation.

Goals and roles

In any consultation, the clients will have two types of needs.

First, the need for results refers to concrete outcomes associated with a project. These might include changes in the bottom line, organizational structure, information transmitted, skills learned or behaviour and attitudes.

Second, the need for growth means increased capacity to perform new functions or behaviours on a continuing basis. In other words, if a high level of growth is achieved in the consultation, then the client will be able to do the job next time with less or no outside help.

The need for results and the need for growth will vary depending on the nature of the consulting project. For example, in performing a one-time service with which the client is unfamiliar, the consultant's major focus is likely to be 'getting the job done' for the client.

However, in helping the client perform an important and recurring – but new – task, the appropriate emphasis is on helping the client learn how to perform that task over the long haul, instead of merely producing an immediate result.

When project outcomes are specified in that way, it is easier to determine what services are needed from the consultant and what contributions are needed from the client system to bring about the desired changes.

Nine roles to consider

By constructing a grid model of consulting, using as the two axes consultant responsibility for growth and consultant responsibility for results, we can identify the specific consulting roles appropriate for the mix of services that the consultant is expected to provide.

The nine roles of the consulting role grid (Figures 4.1 and 4.2) reflect the options the consultant has in a given situation. Presumably, if a consultant correctly assesses the situation, he or she is likely to choose the role that will be most effective.

The consultant who takes on the hands-on expert role (9,1) actually undertakes the task on behalf of the client. In this role the consultant has most, if not all, of the responsibility for producing good results. The client is not expected to grow in capacity very much. He or she will need the consultant again next time in order to perform the task equally well.

The modeller role (9,5) implies that the consultant is highly responsible for results in the current project, but also that there is some value in the client system building its own capacity. The modeller carries out the task for the client system, but does so in a way that makes his or her approaches and techniques apparent. The consultant is available for answering questions about what he or she is doing, and why. The implication is that some time in the future the client may carry out the task.

The partner role (9,9) implies high responsibility for results and growth. It assumes that both the client and the consultant have the capacity to successfully perform aspects of the task and that both will share responsibility for the results. It

Counsellor	**Coach**	**Partner**
'You do it. I will be your sounding board.'	'You did well; you can add this next time.'	'We will do it together and learn from each other.'
Facilitator	**Teacher**	**Modeller**
'You do it; I will attend to the process.'	'Here are some principles you can see to solve problems of this type.'	'I will do it; you watch so you can learn from me.'
Reflective observer	**Technical advisor**	**Hands-on expert**
'You do it; I will watch and tell you what I see and hear.'	'I will answer your questions as you go along.'	'I will do it for you; I will tell you what to do.'

Source: Champion, Kiel and McLendon, 1985

Figure 4.1 *Typical role statements for the consulting role grid*

also assumes that a big jump in the client's capacity to do the task is an important goal. The partner role means that the client is ready to learn in a hands-on way and that the consultant can teach effectively in this mode, as well as guide the task to successful completion.

In the coach role (5,9), the consultant does not have direct responsibility for performing the task. Instead, he or she may observe the performance of the task and provide feedback. The coach uses highly directed instructional techniques to improve the client's performance; providing feedback, prescribing and observing practice sequences, and giving advice and support during actual job performance. The coach is indirectly involved in carrying out the task, but highly involved with the client and his or her growth.

The teacher or trainer role (5,5) is even more removed from the scene of the action. The trainer or teacher, unlike the coach, is concerned with general performance rather than performance in a specific situation. For example, the teacher is concerned that the client knows the basic principles and has mastered the skills of managing a meeting, while the coach may actually observe the client leading meetings and discuss the results afterward.

The technical adviser role (5,1) is a back-up role. In this role, the consultant has moderate responsibility for results; the client uses the adviser's expertise for specific purposes. The technical adviser may have close or distant personal relations with the client, but his or her concern is not the growth of client capacity, except in an incidental sense. The focus is on helping the client get over a specified problem that the technical adviser's knowledge and experience can solve.

In the counsellor role (9,1) the consultant's concern is almost entirely for the capacity of the client to perform the task. The counsellor tries constantly to help the client clarify and set goals, maintain positive motivation and develop and implement effective plans. The counsellor often is removed from the performance of the situation. He or she may have to rely on the client's data about what is happening in the project. Hence, much of the counsellor's skill is in helping the client to gather, analyse and develop conclusions from his or her own experience.

The facilitator role (5,1) consists largely of helpful but process-oriented activities such as convening, agenda building, recording, collating and displaying data, providing techniques such as problem analysis or brainstorming, and planning and leading meetings. Through the facilitator's intervention, clients may absorb the helpful techniques and processes the facilitator uses. That leads to moderate growth of the client's capacity in these areas. One main reason the consultant is an effective facilitator is that he or she has a low stake in the task at hand and is neutral within the client group. This is a low task-responsibility role.

With the reflective observer role (1, 1) the client is most responsible for the results and capacity building; the consultant is least responsible. The consultant's task is limited to feeding back observations and impressions. In spite of the low activity level of the consultant, this role can have a dynamic effect on a client system that is skilled in using such assistance. The reflective consultant can help clients monitor themselves on such ambiguous but critical indicators as trust, teamwork and openness.

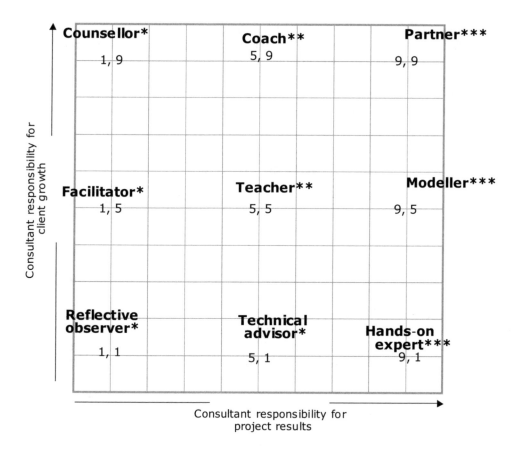

Source: Adapted from Champion, Kiel and McLendon, 1985

Notes:
*   low-intervention roles
**   moderate-intervention roles
***   high-intervention roles.

Figure 4.2 *The consulting role grid*

Roles versus jobs

We shouldn't proceed much further before distinguishing the nine consulting roles outlined above from job titles. A person may have the job title 'technical adviser' or 'trainer' but he or she may still take on any or all of the above roles on a temporary, situational basis. For example, a trainer may leave the classroom and 'coach' the student, or be the expert in designing a curriculum or course.

Similarly, a consultant may play multiple roles simultaneously within a client system, but with different clients. He or she might be counsellor to one manager, a trainer for the team the manager leads, and coach for a task force of other managers. In this framework, the consulting role is always defined situationally within a specific client or client group.

Ideally, roles will be well defined and clearly understood by both the client and consultant. Many consulting errors arise from the consultant's attempt to play more than one role simultaneously with the same client without a clear contract to do so.

How to choose

The process of role choice and transition is obviously a critical area of judgement and skill for the consultant. What guidelines can we go by to make informed choices?

We can identify four key areas building on Robert Tannenbaum and Warren Schmidt's classic formulation of criteria in determining behavioural choice for leadership roles ('How to choose a leadership pattern', *Harvard Business Review*, March–April 1958). These are the areas to consider.

The organizational situation The roles in column 9 on the grid (partner, modeller and hands-on expert), are likely to be appropriate in cases where there is immediate need for results and for client capacity development. If client capacity is already moderate to high, then the low-intervention roles (counsellor, facilitator, reflective observer and technical adviser) may make more sense.

Characteristics of the client In determining an acceptable role relationship, the client ought to ask the following questions. Will the proposed consulting relationship be likely to achieve the results that the organization needs? Will I be helped to grow in the process in a direction that is in my long-term interests? Will the skills that I already possess be used to their fullest extent? Are the skills that the consultant possesses being used in the best way?

Characteristics of the consultant The capacity of the consultant is the most obvious limiting factor in determining a consultant role. Consultants cannot take on the more results- or growth-oriented roles if they lack the experience, knowledge or confidence to do so. But if the consultant is competent to take on various roles, how should he or she choose among them? Willingness, interest and time are factors. The consultant needs to ask him- or herself, not only 'Can I do this?' but 'Do I want to serve in this role?' A role that is unwanted will probably not be well performed.

The client–consultant relationship A relationship of trust and openness permits collaborative determination of the appropriate client–consultant role. Too often, the client's unwillingness to ask for help leads to an insufficient consulting role, or the consultant's need for business results leads to an unhealthy dependency. But most relationships don't begin with the necessary trust to permit open discussion and negotiation of roles. The grid model, by providing a common language for clients and consultants, may help overcome some initial barriers.

Role negotiation

Here are five steps for effective role negotiation for the client and consultant.

1 Collaborative clarification of the organization's need for results and growth for each client or client group
2 Open discussion of the current capacities of the clients and consultants
3 Identification of an appropriate match between client needs and consultant capacities relative to the various tasks and client groups, using the consulting role grid
4 Assurance that all parties have the support they need in the situation to deliver on their accountabilities for results and growth
5 Commitment of both parties to their respective role responsibilities in the consultation

With those steps in mind, we can now go back to the two consulting dilemmas posed at the outset of this article. Let's examine how our framework can provide conceptual support for clients and consultants when negotiating the right consulting role which is crucial to success of the project.

In the task force situation, the needs of the system are relatively apparent to both the client and consultant, yet the role suggested for the consultant seems inadequate to bring about the results. In such a case, the consultant should discuss with the client the apparent discrepancy between the need for immediate results in the situation and low-results orientation of the observer role the consultant is being asked to take (step 1). That discussion would probably result in agreement on more active consultant roles, such as coach to the manager in question, and facilitator to the task force (steps 2 to 5). That would leave the organization and the client more protected against the consequences of project failure.

In the second case – in which the consultant is charged with training a divisive work group in listening skills – the consultant and the client are not in a position to collaboratively diagnose the needs of the organization. The consultant might point out that the training role assumes willingness to learn on the part of the group: a willingness that may not exist. It also assumes that listening skills would solve the problem: a claim that may not be true. The consultant cannot safely accept responsibility for results unless the group shows interest in learning. If the group does not, the client's relationship with the group – and the consultant's relationship with the client – could be seriously damaged.

The consultant could suggest an initial phone call or interview with group members. In it, the consultant would help the group clarify its need for results and for capacity-building by assessing the nature and causes of past conflicts and the group's willingness to engage in problem solving (step 1). With those data in hand, the consultant and client can more confidentially negotiate an intervention role (steps 2 to 5).

Successful outcomes

Consultants and clients can do a better job of negotiating roles and increase their chances for successful project outcomes. But that can only happen if both parties are clear about the outcomes the organization needs and the capacities they both have. The consulting role grid can help match needed outcomes with appropriate levels of consultant involvement. The five-step model of role negotiation can help ensure that the agreements reached can be successfully carried out.

By using this simple framework, consultants and clients may be able to avoid some of the game playing and misperceptions that can handicap consulting relationships from the early stages. The result is openness about what is needed and about how the client and the consultant can meet those needs. That openness can set the stage for a collaborative relationship for the duration of the project.

Note

1   The editors of this volume are grateful to the American Society for Training and Development (ASTD) for permission to republish the original article from *Training and Development* journal (February 1990). While the content remains unchanged, minor stylistic changes have been made to the text for consistency with other chapters in the volume.

Recommended readings

The reader is directed to a number of chapters in this volume that touch on the question of roles and capabilities that advisers combine in supporting capacity development processes. Chapter 5 explores the balance that advisers or consultants must strike between technical or 'hard' skills and 'softer' process capabilities, while Chapter 6 looks at the role of a practitioner in dealing with the inevitable conflict of interests that occurs when working with multiple actors. Chapter 24 takes a broader look at the field of capacity development as a whole and examines what a move towards professionalization of the field would mean for both practitioners and their organizations. In addition, the following publications offer further perspectives on advisory roles and how a practitioner may position him- or herself effectively in working with clients depending on the context, needs and client capabilities.

Schein, E. H. (1998) *Process Consultation Revisited: Building the Helping Relationship,* Prentice Hall Organizational Development Series, Addison-Wesley, Wokingham

Against the background of systems thinking, Schein offers very practical ways in which practitioners can position and clarify the different roles they play in various client situations. The main messages are complementary to those discussed in this chapter.

Divine Thaw and Warren Banks (2007) *Facilitating Development Processes: Working in the Unknown,* Olive-PPT, Durban

This is an eight-part series dedicated to a practitioner's work. Adopting a process approach it covers a number of angles which help to reflect on the roles to be played at different stages of engagement.

5

Thematic and Change Expertise

To be effective in capacity development one often has to combine specific knowledge of the client business with change expertise. This combination of capabilities seldom arises naturally from formal education. Gaining and holding the required balance therefore calls for conscious and continuous effort on the part of practitioners as well as the organizations they work for.

This chapter by Naa-Aku Acquaye-Baddoo analyses how these two different capabilities interact in practice, based on the experience of one development organization. In an engaging style, she explores how practitioners could improve their ability to combine the two in a balanced way and what organizational conditions help enable them to do so.

The Balanced Practitioner

Naa-Aku Acquaye-Baddoo

Introduction – the Diber story

Diber Region in the mountainous northeast of Albania is one of the poorest areas of the country. Most of the population of 200,000 earn their living from subsistence farming and herding; 63 per cent of the land is forests and pastures (half of these are communally owned). In 1996, the government started the Albania Forestry Project to rehabilitate the communal forests and pasturelands close to villages and to introduce participatory communal management of those areas. It also included a scheme to transfer usufruct rights to communes and their inhabitants (after these had been expropriated by the former communist regime). In the communist years no one felt responsible for 'state owned' land – abundant forests and pastures had become barren and desolate from unchecked soil erosion.

Between 1999 and 2004, a team of advisers from the SNV Netherlands Development Organisation, led by a senior forestry expert, worked with and supported the Albania Forestry Project to restore and manage communal forests and pastures in the Diber Region. Over this period, the SNV team developed trust relationships with key individuals and groups in the area: from village communes to regional and national actors, to representatives of international and bilateral donors (the World Bank and Swiss and Italian governments respectively). They immersed themselves in the dynamics of the nascent local organizations charged with restoring and managing communal forests and pastures, learning what the new User Associations meant to the communes who had only recently had their rights returned to them. They supported the development and consolidation of the User Associations by forging links with relevant networks at regional and national level. This entailed building their organizational and technical capabilities to protect and manage communal forests and pastures and engage with policy-makers at regional and national level to influence forest management approaches for the whole of Albania. Partly as a result of this positive example, up to 70 per cent of all forests in Albania today are managed by local communities.

Reflecting on the experience, a senior manager at the District Forestry Service later observed that: 'Six years ago the District Forestry Service was not convinced about the concept of communal forestry. Now more than half of the communes [9 out of 13 communes in Diber district] are practising it'. He emphasized the importance of collaboration between key players at different levels and the supportive role of the SNV team in the growth of transparency and organizational strength of the User Associations (Richter and Strobosch, 2006).

Towards tacit 'knowing': Achieving balance in everyday practice

The experience, expertise and wisdom of the SNV team and its leader at the centre of this practice story are clear. Collectively, they brought high level technical knowledge and experience of forestry, and deep understanding of the areas where the communal forestry associations were set up and developed. They imbued passion and commitment to the vision that informs the forestry project, and earned the respect of different actors. They supported ground-breaking, community led initiatives in forest management that have all the signs of sustainability and potential integration into the regular development policy of the area. How did this happen? It is clearly not down to the forestry expertise of the team alone, in spite of their evident project management skills. What happened stemmed from something additional – an ability to live and deploy two types of professional competence that, when aligned, contribute to increased capacity.

This chapter therefore explores the necessary connection between two types of expertise that are critical for professionals in the field of capacity development. One is the competent and responsive deployment of what will be called 'technical capabilities'; that is, the explicit knowledge or 'science' that informs development strategies, plans and expected outcomes in a specific sector (for example education, sanitation, health, micro finance, housing or agriculture). The other expertise is found in the 'softer' capabilities and skills required to increase and embed technical as well as social and political capabilities both in and between

---

Box 5.1 Creating relationships of trust

Observations by two consultants who researched and described the Albania Communal Forestry case shed more light on how the team worked, which possibly laid the foundations for the success of this project.

'It was a surprise to us to learn how much effort was focused on building the network of connections among the actors at the early stages of the initiative. And especially that these change process skills, such as multi-stakeholder engagement, were more primary than the technical forestry skills – at least initially. The forestry expertise was important in creating credibility and trust, but it was secondary until later stages of their work'.

'We were struck by the way that the team carefully tuned in to the deeply rooted local traditions and values in Albania (those which predated the communist regime). They wisely drew on traditional forms of solidarity and cooperation between families and villagers so that their clients could see how the change in forestry practices were consistent with deeply rooted traditions and values. This helped to ground the change and made it seem less "strange" or imposed by outsiders'.

'The team leader's ability to balance, "pushing" his expertise by gently and patiently inviting villagers to consider new ways of using their forests was masterful. His team members learned this from him. This art of balancing is often overlooked as an important competency in advisory work. When done well, it can be critical to the development of long term ownership and progress'.

'The team included Albanian advisers, whose knowledge of local decision makers, existing relations between individuals and groups, forms of cooperation, and key players, was very influential for SNV. We feel this combination of skill and local knowledge is not to be underestimated in facilitating complex change'.

---

the different types of institutions at different levels as described in Part I. Such skills are often underpinned by explicit knowledge of change management and organizational development concepts that a practitioner draws from and brings to bear in a specific situation. This quality of professionalism is evident in how practitioners bring actors together, supporting them to collaborate in ways that result in specific development or social justice gains, in enduring change in relations and in the way things are done. The challenge is to understand and describe how practitioners can combine and balance these two features of capacity development practice in ways that more effectively contribute to sustainable and self-renewable outcomes.

The professional problem is that there are more forces working against gaining the right balance, than those working towards doing so. Practitioners who attempt to achieve this balance often find themselves swimming against the tide. Why imbalance is 'normal', and what can be done about it, is the theme running throughout this chapter. The story is told in stages: the first is separating out and being clear about the 'knowledges' that professionalism in the field of capacity development relies on. These are hard and soft, explicit and tacit. Second, a relationship is explored between the five core capabilities described in Chapter 1, that together make up capacity, and the 'knowledges' that capacity development practitioners use. Capacity development practitioners who combine the two types of competencies described above are not easy to find. Yet both types of 'expertise' are necessary and complementary in capacity development. Both represent bodies of 'knowledge' and what will be called 'knowing' or applying knowledge in practice – in doing – as an active meaning of knowledge.

As an asset to be drawn on, this latter type of knowledge is continuous and evolving and therefore difficult to make static or stable. Practitioners gain knowledge all the time as they add to, contest, question and shift assumptions, and revisit previously accepted rules. The act of 'knowing' is both expressed in and shaped by action. It cannot be divorced from the interaction between the practitioner, the actors involved and the situation they are in at that time. However, what is not readily apparent in this view is that knowing and knowledge are developed and refined in almost opposite ways and at different speeds. Keeping them in tandem, deepening their substance and seamlessly merging them in professional behaviour, requires conscious and explicit choices about learning and reflection that play out at the level of an individual practitioner in an organization.

In the way described above, many capacity development practitioners are out of balance. This is not a coincidence. In education, professional development and a learning culture, attention is biased towards technical or hard expertise. Even when 'change' expertise is addressed, this is usually done in a way that values and develops explicit knowledge to the detriment of tacit 'knowing'. Figure 5.1 illustrates the interface between the two.

Technical expertise is unquestionably important – capacity development processes are not an end in themselves. They must lead to tangible gains for actors and for the beneficiaries involved. Human development outcomes – whether they stem from better access to or quality of particular services, or from removal of conditions that have perpetuated injustice or from increase in income or human rights – all rely on adequate technical capabilities and explicit knowledge.

However, experience shows that hard expertise and explicit knowledge alone is not enough to make complex capacity development processes effective and their results sustainable. Chapter 1 explains why it is that, when added together, the open and hidden dimensions of human relationships, and the multifaceted nature of capacity, call for an appreciation of soft dimensions of change processes – such as trust, and consistency between word and deed. Also needed is an appreciation of the forces and behaviours that arise from tacit knowing, for example, about power relations and dynamics in practice and not just in formal arrangements, and about 'real' feelings and perceptions not formally shared but influential nonetheless.

Key to finding a balanced approach to capacity development is to be clear about which capabilities rely to a greater or lesser degree on what types of knowledge and knowing. Box 5.2 (page 70) reminds us of five dimensions of capability which contribute to capacity and increase the likelihood of organizations, communities and wider systems sustaining, leading and renewing development gains achieved.

Table 5.1 (page 71) illustrates one way of connecting capacity development professionals to types of expertise and knowledges as a guide to this way of thinking about balancing. Each dimension of capacity has an illustration from the Diber story with a suggestion about the degree to which technical expertise (hard

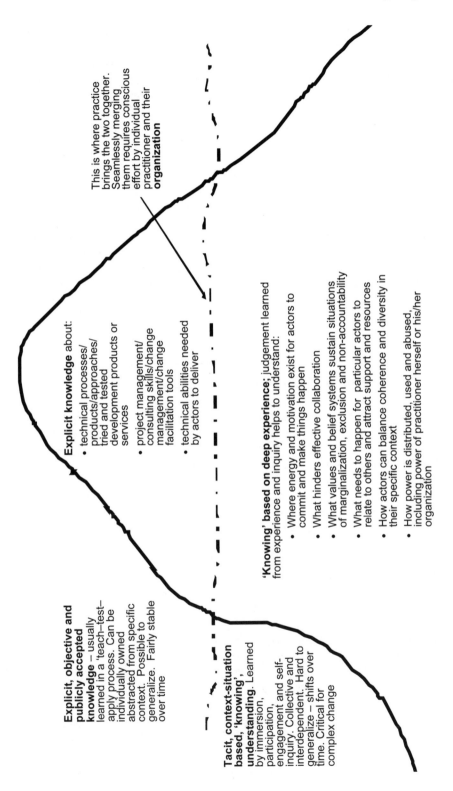

This is where practice brings the two together. Seamlessly merging them requires conscious effort by individual practitioner and their **organization**

Explicit knowledge about:

• technical processes/ products/approaches/ tried and tested development products or services

• project management/ consulting skills/change management/change facilitation tools

• technical abilities needed by actors to deliver

'Knowing' based on deep experience; judgement learned from experience and inquiry helps to understand:

• Where energy and motivation exist for actors to commit and make things happen

• What hinders effective collaboration

• What values and belief systems sustain situations of marginalization, exclusion and non-accountability

• What needs to happen for particular actors to relate to others and attract support and resources

• How actors can balance coherence and diversity in their specific context

• How power is distributed, used and abused, including power of practitioner herself or his/her organization

Explicit, objective and publicly accepted knowledge – usually learned in a 'teach–test–apply process. Can be individually owned abstracted from specific context. Possible to generalize. Fairly stable over time

Tacit, context-situation based, 'knowing', understanding. Learned by immersion, participation, engagement and self-inquiry. Collective and interdependent. Hard to generalize – shifts over time. Critical for complex change

Figure 5.1 *The interface between knowledges*

knowledge) or soft skills (tacit knowing) played a role in helping that dimension of capacity to come about. When Table 5.1 is considered alongside Figure 5.1, it can be argued that more attention needs to be paid to the balance between the top (explicit) and bottom (hidden) aspects of the iceberg of conscious and 'unconscious' knowledge. The more experienced and skilful a practitioner becomes at merging and balancing the two types of expertise, the more difficult it is to distinguish when one type of expertise is deployed in capacity development.

Getting in balance

To understand how the imbalance mentioned earlier can be righted, it is important to understand how the two knowledges are developed. The first, explicit technical knowledge, is gained in more traditional ways. In other words, it is more or less objectively abstracted, that is, separated from a particular context or indeed the experiences or intuition of the learner or expert-to-be. It is true that 'technical' knowledge is increasingly taught in more experiential ways with less strict objectivity. But by and large the assumption is that a rigorous process of teaching covers a certain amount of explicit

---

Box 5.2 Dimensions of capacity

The European Centre for Development Policy Management (ECDPM) study of capacity and change (Baser and Morgan, 2008, elaborated in Chapter 1) identifies five capabilities to explain capacity as a multidimensional phenomenon.

Capability to carry out technical, service delivery and logistical tasks Actors can generate development results in terms of substantive outputs and outcomes (e.g. health or education services, income opportunities or justice). Actors are able to sustain delivery over time and add value for their clients and beneficiaries.

Capability to commit and engage Actors are able to commit and create the space needed in their context in order to act. They demonstrate collective energy and agency and can mobilize and motivate others to act.

Capability to adapt and self-renew Actors are able to: adapt and modify plans and operations based on monitoring of progress and outcomes; proactively anticipate change and new challenges; cope with shocks and develop resiliency; and foster internal dialogue and incorporate new ideas.

Capability to balance diversity and coherence Actors can: develop shared short and long tem strategies and visions; balance control, flexibility and consistency; integrate and harmonize plans and actions in complex multi-actor settings; and cope with cycles of stability, change and innovation.

Capability to relate and attract Actors can: develop and manage linkages, alliances, and/or partnerships with others to leverage resources and action; build legitimacy in the eyes of key stakeholders; and deal effectively with competition, politics and power differentials.

Table 5.1 *Relating types of knowledge to five capabilities*

Dimensions of capacity (5 capabilities) with illustrations from Albania case	Degree of reliance on the two types of knowledge	
	Hard expertise (explicit technical knowledge)	Soft expertise (tacit knowing from practice)
Capability to carry out technical, service delivery and logistical tasks 70 per cent of forests in Albania are protected and managed by functioning User Associations. Forests are becoming productive. User Associations have capabilities to provide range of services and logistical tasks needed.	High	Low
Capability to commit and engage Newly formed User Associations were able to gain support and commitment from the communes they represented to shift and change old attitudes to forests. They stimulated a sense of collective responsibility and ownership to overcome historic tensions and lack of collaboration among key actors needed to make the project work.	Medium	High
Capability to adapt and self-renew Forest User Associations are moving from protection to sustainable utilization and possibilities for income generation for communes. At the level of the federations they are considering vocational training for User Associations and farmers. The federation of User Associations in the Diber region is now a registered NGO.	High	High
Capability to balance diversity and coherence User Associations now engage actively and collaborate in federations with other User Associations to contribute to district and national level policy on forest and pasture management.	Medium	High
Capability to relate and attract From individual commune based User Associations, Albania now has a nationwide network of associations that are organized in regional and national federations. Their collective influence stems from this relationship. The success of what became known as the Diber approach has attracted more resources from the Albanian government and World Bank.	Low	High

knowledge which then qualifies the 'expert-to-be' to apply and test this knowledge in practice in a particular context, with a reasonable expectation of results.

The second type – softer, often tacit knowing – is also offered to practitioners using traditional methodologies. Conceptual aspects that underpin the set of soft skills are taught, covering theories of individual growth and cognition, of learning processes and of organizational and system change. Acquisition of these areas of knowledge is accompanied by a huge range of possible tools, techniques and interventions that can be designed and applied in a particular context. But what does it take for a capacity development professional to be able to combine the two types of knowledge skilfully enough to do the following?

- Jointly identify an opportunity for development outcomes with interested parties (be they services, income or justice)
- Gain the interest and commitment of relevant actors, and
- Support them to work together to develop and/or unleash their collective capacity to effect meaningful change and tangible results, which they can sustain and adapt over time.

Achieving balance requires the combination of a number of things in a capacity development professional:

- the foundation of explicit knowledge probably learned in a 'traditional' teach, test and apply setting;
- immersion over time in a particular setting where grappling with technical problems yields contextualized and situational understanding about what may work and not work;
- participating alongside the different stakeholders and mediating, untangling and negotiating the different lines of conflicting interests and power differentials that inevitably exist;
- developing relationships with critical players and groups in a way that builds trust and enables more frank dialogue about the nature of real underlying issues that may help or hinder the end results expected;
- continually testing the publicly accepted explicit technical knowledge against what is discovered about the tacit, collective and unnamed knowledge and patterns that exist in the context;
- enabling different actors involved to become more self-aware about this complexity in a way that improves their capabilities, for example the five dimensions analysed in the ECDPM model.

Staying in balance – dancing between art and science, between individual and organization

Balanced practitioners do this merging and skilful blending of the two types of knowledge until the whole becomes so deeply tacit that it appears effortless to others. But arrival at this point depends not just on individual characteristics or personal predispositions; it can also be nurtured or stifled by the quality of the organization they are in. In other words, the dance resembles one of hard and soft competencies that become more and more in step and mutually dependent as in a tango but, to help get there, the organization needs to be generating the right rhythm. In the concluding sections, we examine these interacting factors in more detail. But before that, we need to look at the practitioner dance and 'listen' to the organizational tune.

The dance – practitioner disciplines and attitudes

It would seem that 'effortlessness' in professional balancing comes from a certain level or depth of expertise in both types of knowledge. But it is actually the interaction and iteration between what lies at the visible top of the iceberg and the hidden part that has become effortless. The effect is always contextualized and situation specific, responding to the social and political context in which capacity development efforts take place.

Let us go back to the five dimensions of capacity described above. With the exception of the capability 'to carry out technical, service delivery and logistical tasks', organizations can only be supported to develop the other four capabilities if there is sufficient understanding of and empathy for the historical patterns, relationships, power differentials and opportunities that will determine the potential for development and progress. The SNV advisers in the Diber story took the time to invest in relationships, with a genuine curiosity about the context and its history and potential for self-motivation. This earned trust and openness from different actors, contributing to a high level of collective commitment to engage and act.

Practitioners who 'dance' between the art and science of the two types of knowledge craft and hone their skilfulness over time, in context specific situations, drawing from and applying their explicit knowledge with judgement and responsiveness to the setting.

For some, tacit knowledge by its nature is not communicable (Polanyi, 1964). It is difficult for a skilful practitioner to explain step by step how this merging of the knowledges happens. But it is possible to identify some of the disciplines, habits and ways of being that help a practitioner to become more able to do this 'dance'. They stem from predispositions of an individual adviser as well as the (dis)enabling deeper nature of the organization.

Like everyone else, professionals in this field have predispositions towards and comfort zones in what they do. Experience suggests that there are a number of these that come into play when 'balanced practice' is the aim. What do they look like?

Self-knowledge

This refers to a professional's awareness of his or her own motives and mental maps, especially how they influence his/her perceptions of events and dynamics in a complex change setting. It is also about awareness of both the potential and limitations of one's power to act or influence others. Self-knowledge grows from open, critical engagement with others and a willingness to have one's assumptions challenged. It is also helped by regular self-reflection.

Curiosity and inquiry

A genuine curiosity about the setting and dynamics in which organizations, networks or multiple actors need to collaborate to realize development outcomes, drives practitioners to form relationships and to inquire beyond the immediate boundaries of a particular project. This contributes to a more holistic understanding of current and historical factors and relationships that may have an impact on the capacity development process or the sustainability of outcomes. Each context is treated as unique and approached with fresh eyes, although insights and wisdom from previous experiences are not abandoned. It demands an ability to listen in order to understand and not simply to know – to listen with suspended judgement and hear 'empathically' in order to understand the different 'truths' of the many actors involved.

Investing in relationships and dialogue

Paulo Freire (1970) describes dialogue as 'the encounter between "persons" [my term], mediated by the world, in order to name the world'. As Chapter 10 reaffirms, dialogue offers an important route to form the quality of relationships that are central to creating trust, generating shared meaning and common basis for action and collaboration. In trustful relationships it is easier to unearth underlying issues and understand where real energy or blockages may exist in a capacity development process. People are willing to take risks with those they know and trust.

Belief that capacity is inherent

If dialogue and trustful relationships are critical to effective capacity development practice with sustainable results embedded in the local context, practitioners must believe that local people, organizations and wider systems are capable of developing and demonstrating capacity in the first place. Freire writes about faith in people as a precondition for dialogue. It is not blind faith, though. He agrees that in dialogue one must also be critical and recognize that 'although it is within the power of humans to create and transform, in a concrete situation of alienation, individuals may be impaired in the use of that power'.

Practice of critical reflection and articulation

We all reflect naturally and very often, but not with the same rigour that is implied when we talk about a practice of critical reflection similar to that described in Chapter 20. This is an exercise designed to explore and/or interpret events we have participated in or observed, and to consciously draw learning or insights from them. Reflective thoughts may be articulated in writing or as a recording and may be shared with others or kept confidential. The process of articulating reflective thoughts itself helps to clarify ideas further and also invites comment and engagement from others. When gathered systematically over time, recorded or written reflective thoughts about events may reveal patterns and important linkages that would otherwise be missed.

Immersion in context

This dimension is about active participation and engagement alongside different actors in both formal project activities and informal and opportunistic events that offer the practitioner opportunities to learn more about underlying socio-political and cultural dynamics of the setting in which he or she is working. The SNV team in Diber developed relationships with different actors in the forestry sector ranging from users at communal level to district level actors to national and international stakeholders. These relationships were developed and nurtured in both formal and informal settings where appropriate. The team often organized meetings, workshops or discussions in the middle of communal forests. Stories and anecdotes told over lunch, during breaks and after meetings gave rare insights into the way people really felt about the proposed changes in land rights after the long years of communist state ownership. They learned about traditional systems of forest management that had not been forgotten and could inform the new forest management project, with a far greater sense of ownership and responsibility on the part of the communes.

Strategic thinking and linking at multiple levels

Balanced practitioners draw on both technical expertise and soft knowledge and understanding – as described in the bottom part of the iceberg in Figure 5.1, to make judgements about actions that will create the most leverage; timing for connecting parties or actors at different levels; when to intervene openly and when to step back. It demands an ability to see a particular capacity development project in its wider systemic setting and understand the critical interfaces and interactions needed to ensure the effectiveness of the project organization.

Recognizing and working with power and conflict

Capacity development practitioners cannot avoid the issue of power or conflict described, for example, in Chapter 6. Differences in rights and access to resources, services, justice, infrastructure or income, often lie at the root of the development issues that practitioners collaborate with others to address. It is important to recognize and understand the specific dynamics of power and conflict that exist between different actors involved in a particular situation. The different types of power held by various actors can be harnessed for action, as well as disruption in multi-actor capacity development (CD) processes. In addition, practitioners need to understand both the potential and limitations of their own power and how it is perceived by others.

The tune and the rhythm – qualities of organization

Practitioners who manage this harmony appear to do so in spite of, rather than because of, the organizational settings in which they work. Many organizations have systems, cultures and ways of working that often separate the two kinds of capabilities and value them differently. For example, organizational rhetoric may be positive about tacit soft skills but in recruiting and hiring, more value is placed on technical expertise and qualifications. Organizations express commitment to learning and reflection on one hand and, on the other, deploy monitoring, reporting and evaluation systems that are narrowly focused on describing and reporting activities and results against predicted or planned targets. Time for critical reflection with peers or clients is often squeezed out by pressure to increase 'productivity' by completing more tasks and activities per day or per client. Practitioners who consciously try to develop a balanced practice often find themselves fighting an uphill battle.

Figure 5.2 shows how conscious practice of 'soft' change expertise by practitioners, in a conducive organizational setting, can contribute to a balanced practice. The elements mentioned are based on observations from years of working on practitioner learning and development initiatives in SNV. On the practitioner side are some of the 'disciplines and attitudes' that appear common to those SNV practitioners who are widely regarded as highly experienced or talented. Their professional behaviour comes close to the seamless merging of the two types of knowledge. On the organizational side, the list reflects some organizational conditions and facilities that are supportive to the development of a balanced CD practice. While on each side, the different elements work iteratively with each other, neither list is exhaustive or prescriptive. They simply offer practitioners a way of reflecting on their own practice in the context of the organizations they work for. What, then, are helpful organizational conditions?

Organizational strategy recognizes and defines capacity as multifaceted
It is helpful if capacity development organizations make their understanding of capacity explicit and indicate that they subscribe to a view of capacity that recognizes its multiple dimensions and their inter-relationships. It is even better if there is congruence between this recognition and the strategies and approaches adopted for capacity development. Organizations can demonstrate recognition for both hard and soft expertise in a number of ways: by explicitly reflecting both types in the profiles of practitioners they attract and recruit; by setting both hard and soft change targets or expectation in the kinds of results that practitioners are judged on; by describing organizational results and achievements in both hard, tangible results – for example, number of hospitals built or number of people with an income stream from a micro credit project; and soft, less tangible results – for example, changes in relationships and power dynamics between actors.

Space for reflection with peers, clients and partners
This is one of the simplest things that organizations can offer to practitioners but it is also what many practitioners find elusive. There is always pressure to get things done, to show results and account for resources. More time is spent in descriptive reports than reflective narratives that also explore how results happened and what can be learned at both individual and organizational levels. If reflection is not separated from daily practice, it does not cost a lot of time. Joint reflection improves collective understanding (collective tacit knowledge if you like), of what works or does not work and why.

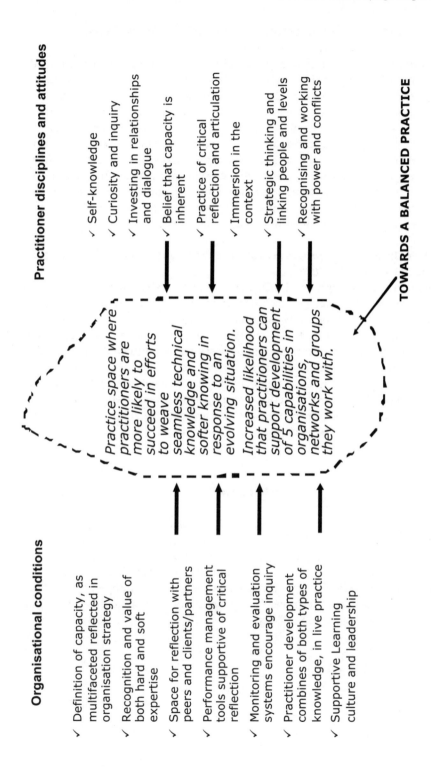

Practitioner disciplines and attitudes

✓ Self-knowledge

✓ Curiosity and inquiry

✓ Investing in relationships and dialogue

✓ Belief that capacity is inherent

✓ Practice of critical reflection and articulation

✓ Immersion in the context

✓ Strategic thinking and linking people and levels

✓ Recognising and working with power and conflicts

TOWARDS A BALANCED PRACTICE

Practice space where practitioners are more likely to succeed in efforts to weave seamless technical knowledge and softer knowing in response to an evolving situation.

Increased likelihood that practitioners can support development of 5 capabilities in organisations, networks and groups they work with.

Organisational conditions

✓ Definition of capacity, as multifaceted reflected in organisation strategy

✓ Recognition and value of both hard and soft expertise

✓ Space for reflection with peers and clients/partners

✓ Performance management tools supportive of critical reflection

✓ Monitoring and evaluation systems encourage inquiry

✓ Practitioner development combines of both types of knowledge, in live practice

✓ Supportive Learning culture and leadership

Figure 5.2 *Connecting organization and practitioner*

Monitoring and evaluation approaches encourage inquiry and seek understanding as much as measurement

The pressure to show quantifiable results and account for resources used, tends to push monitoring and evaluation approaches and methodologies to the measurement end of the spectrum with far too little attention paid to inquiry and learning. As argued in other chapters across this volume, measurement is typically conducted against a predetermined indicator of right or good results. It is usually the capacity development organization's own indicators which do not reflect how other actors or end beneficiaries may define 'right or good results'. Measurement approaches are definitely useful. But when emphasized alone, a whole world of insights and understanding about unpredicted results, what other actors or beneficiaries find significant, and how capacity development support actually contributed to the realization of results is often not appreciated.

Practitioner development processes combine both types of knowledge and are embedded in live practice

As mentioned at the beginning of this chapter, many capacity development practitioners have a highly developed technical expertise side and an underdeveloped soft change side. Indeed they are often recruited for their proven technical expertise and knowledge of project and change management techniques and tools. Organizations can invest in learning and professional development initiatives that help practitioners to recognize the need to redress this imbalance and identify ways of doing so over time. The design challenge is to create learning trajectories that are embedded in current practice, and to provide spaces where participants can take distance to reflect and share what they are learning about themselves and their practice with other participants.

It is not an easy dance!

References

Baser, H. and Morgan, P. (2008) *Capacity, Change and Performance*, Study report, European Centre for Development Policy Management, Maastricht

Freire, P. (1970) *Pedagogy of the Oppressed*, Continuum Publishing, London

Polanyi, M. (1964) *The Tacit Dimension*, Doubleday, Garden City, NY

Richter, I. and Strobosch, P. (with contributions from Kampen, P.) (2006) 'Cultivating a canopy of relationships: perspectives on change process facilitation', SNV, The Hague, unpublished

Recommended readings

The issues raised in this chapter are picked up in different ways in other parts of this volume. For example, Chapters 3 and 13 show how 'hard' and 'soft' knowledge and skills are successful in working with multiple dimensions in capacity development. Chapter 4 looks at possible roles of advisers and how these may be combined and matched to different client relationships and contexts. Finally, Chapters 22 and 24 look ahead and touch on aspects of practitioner capability and the professional field of capacity development that need further attention. Below are suggestions for further reading in relation to this topic.

Richter, I. and Strobosch, P. (with contributions from Kampen, P.) (2006) *Cultivating a canopy of relationships: perspectives on change process facilitation – a case study from a SNV communal forestry initiative in Albania*, SNV Netherlands Development Organization, The Hague

This is the original case study from which the Diber story is taken. Apart from the full story of how different capabilities of networks of user associations grew and evolved, the case study also offers the researchers' insights and observations of how the team developed its collective tacit knowledge and 'knowing' over time.

Kaplan, A (1996) *The Development Practitioner's Handbook*, Pluto Press, London

Allan Kaplan describes the phenomenon of development as a continuum with many different confluences and influences. This requires that a development practitioner develop an ability to see the whole even if one is only able to work with or influence a part. Chapters 6 and 7 deal with the practice and art of the development practitioner and explore ways in which practitioners may hone their ability to balance the types of knowledge and knowing touched upon in this chapter.

Schein, E.H. (1998) *Process Consultation Revisited: Building the Helping Relationship*, Prentice Hall Organizational Development Series, Addison-Wesley, Wokingham

In this stimulating classic, Schein offers a simple introduction to systems thinking and the concepts of personal mastery and mental models, referred to as 'core disciplines' in the book. It is a stimulating read and offers practitioners many different angles from which to critically reflect on their own practice. It is not a how-to book though there are plenty of practical examples drawn from Schein's own experience in different organizations.

De Caluwe, L. and Vermaak, H. (2003) *Learning to Change; A Guide for Organizational Change Agents*, Sage Publications Inc., Thousand Oaks, California

This lively and very readable book looks at why change processes are so complex and offers the reader different ways or lenses for looking at change. The use of colours as a metaphor works particularly well as one of these lenses and can be easily related to many capacity development situations.

6

Ownership, Authority and Conflict

Capacity-development practitioners commonly find themselves in work settings where different forces, interests and power asymmetries need to be dealt with. These factors can create potential sources of conflict over ownership, authority and the allocation of roles and responsibilities. This problem is poorly acknowledged and seldom explored in ways that are useful for practitioners.

This chapter by Joe McMahon draws upon work from the fields of consulting, facilitation and conflict resolution to expose the power dimensions that are inherent to capacity development. He delineates a number of practical, common-sense 'behavioural guides' for the practitioner that will help to adequately define one's own role, position oneself towards multiple actors and constructively deal with (potential) conflict.

Who is the Boss? Behavioural Guidance for the Practitioner in Complex Capacity-Development Settings

Joe McMahon

Introduction: Accepting complexity and power asymmetries as normal and key elements of capacity development

The professional brings to each capacity-development programme substantive knowledge and process skills which, for beneficial outcomes, must get traction in a complex environment. That environment usually contains a variety of diverse actors with differing world views and interests, substantial power asymmetries and existing or emerging conflicts.

The professional must accept this complexity and wide variation of power as 'the water in which he or she swims'.

The context in which the professional practises

Figure 6.1 is a sample relational schematic – showing the array of parties engaged in or affecting a capacity-building programme. The professional is one member in the circle of prime actors – but the professional is not at the hub. Outside the core circle of participants in Figure 6.1 are organizations or societal factors that influence the programme and the actors without being directly involved. Although these larger influencing factors (shown as partial large circles at the four corners) are not direct parties in the programme, they may nonetheless have great influence on those who are directly involved. In this example, such external factors include local social dynamics, the wider economic context, the higher level political land-scape, and perhaps the donor's agenda. The professional's interactions will likely need to consider all actors and forces – whether in the core group or affecting the work from the fringe.

Power asymmetries are inherent in capacity-building programmes

If Figure 6.1 is the 'playing field' in which the professional operates, she or he must be able to confront and respond to the power asymmetries present which, among others, may include:

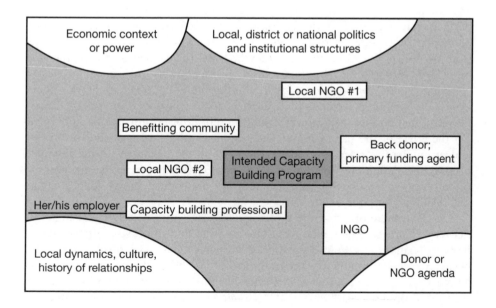

Figure 6.1 *Example of a relational context for the capacity professional*

- the back donor's perception that by underwriting and significantly funding the programme, it has the inherent right to 'control' the direction and delivery of the programme;
- the perception of the international non-governmental organization (INGO) that its long-term experience in development in other locations mandates that as the most experienced actor it should strongly steer the programme and evaluate its quality against its own standards;
- the local NGO's perception that its knowledge of local needs and capacities should be paramount to ideas developed, in some instances unilaterally, by the back donor or INGO that do not fully understand or respond to local realities and interests;
- national, district or local agencies' perception that capacity-building programmes undertaken in their domain are, or should be, properly under the control of those agencies.

Using Figure 6.1, imagine the interconnections among the participants in terms of power, resources, culture, use of language, manner of problem solving and communications. Although not drawn to scale, Figure 6.1 depicts the back donor and INGO in larger box shapes, indicating substantial resources and formal authority that they may have as compared with the local NGOs and benefiting community.

The centre of Figure 6.1 shows the actors engaged in actual programme implementation at the local or community level. Thus, although more powerful actors or forces may exist on the large scale, the power asymmetries will likely differ at the local level in day-to-day events. Larger national policies may give way to local expressions of power and the interaction among local actors. The inevitable presence of power asymmetries does not necessarily mean that the most powerful participant is 'in control'. In the face of such asymmetries, the less powerful participants may resist the controlling behaviours of the more powerful. The responses from the less powerful participants may be overt (challenges to power that stop or impede programme progress); more passive (non-compliance or closing communications); or flexible (using local influence to improve outcomes without overtly challenging power). As such, overt, passive or flexible responses by the less powerful may in fact shift 'power' from the more powerful to the less powerful. Yet the effect of the use of power and responses to it may well shift the reality and, in numerous cases, are reported to work to the detriment of the intended programme. Ambitions formulated at the start or at 'higher' levels of power are often simply not realized in practice: a sign of the counter power of local actors and relations (for good or for bad).

It is clear, therefore, that the professional's task is not merely to facilitate the delivery of programme content but also to build and improve the participants' working relationships. Full acceptance of one party's claimed control is an unlikely event in complex multiparty programmes. Even where all participants seem to 'agree' or at least accept that a lead actor has the control over the programme, a thoughtful professional knows that such agreement is thin, and divergence and conflict will likely later emerge. A quick fix by seeking the direction of the donor and/or lead actor is not likely to lead to a sustainable result.

Faced with this situation, the professional may be able to coach the more powerful party or her/his employer to engage more, if not all, participants in sharing their perspectives and reaching forms of consensus. Where this is not possible, the professional must decide how and whether to proceed, balancing what may be the competing interests of the participants. Where multiple parties have programme ownership, the professional must mediate among these parties to find action plans sufficiently acceptable to all (see 'dealing with conflict' below).

Do not confuse formal or contractual power with accountability

The setting of power asymmetries between multiple actors also plays out towards the practitioner him/herself. The professional's immediate accountability to her or his employer is a natural and legal consequence of their engagement. The professional is expected, and has agreed, to carry out the terms of her or his engagement according to the agreement reached with the employer-donor. Yet, accountability does not end there. Each participant in the programme has made explicit or implicit agreements of accountability to each other. Consultation expert Edgar Schein advises that '[a]ny helping or change process always has a target or a client … but in reality, the question of who is actually the client can be difficult' (Schein, 1999, p64). The question of who is the real client is even more complex because capacity-building processes evolve over time. Schein suggests that the question of 'who is the client' may be simplified and made more clear by asking oneself: 'with whom …[am I] trying to do what?' As such, the professional has a collection of 'clients' or 'owners' including primary clients, intermediate clients, ultimate clients and involved 'non-clients' (Schein, 1999, pp64, 65). A professional should pay careful attention to distinguish among the various clients and types of clients.

Figure 6.2 shows the two components of the professional expertise at the top. The first relates to substantive knowledge for programme content, and the second to the techniques and skills needed to deliver the content or improve working relationships. At the bottom it then shows the range of 'clients' he or she has to deal with. It may be that the professional must focus on the primary client and at other times, across the bottom of the pyramid, to the ultimate client and involved non-clients. The intended capacity development usually takes place across the entire spectrum of 'clients.'

The professional's relationship with the paying party (donor or his or her employing NGO, for example) may theoretically set forth the terms of the professional's work. Yet resorting to the contract of engagement or terms of reference alone does not usually provide all the needed guidance. 'Within the bare outlines of such a contract, there are large zones of discretionary freedom for both parties. The client may show more or less deference, more of less compliance with the professional's advice, may present a greater or lesser challenge to the professional's opinions' (Schön, 1983, p292).

The capacity-building professional must also look to her or his own professional standards when considering accountability. What if a powerful donor seeks to direct some of the programme in a direction that the professional does not think will benefit (or perhaps is harmful to) the benefiting community? No easy answer

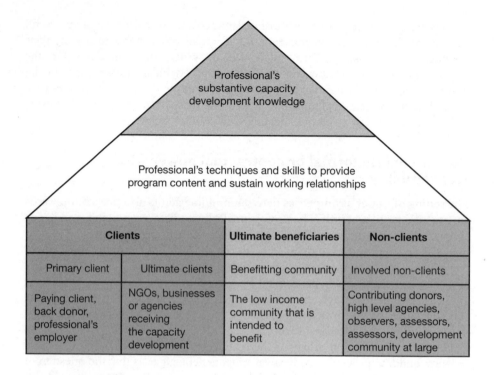

	Clients		Ultimate beneficiaries	Non-clients
Primary client	**Ultimate clients**		**Benefitting community**	**Involved non-clients**
Paying client, back donor, professional's employer	NGOs, businesses or agencies receiving the capacity development		The low income community that is intended to benefit	Contributing donors, high level agencies, observers, assessors, assessors, development community at large

Source: Concept based on Schein (1973) and Schön (1983)

Figure 6.2 *Applying the professional's substantive knowledge and techniques to deliver content and sustain relationships*

exists. Proceeding may bring about compromised outcomes, while stopping the programme could lead to even greater harm.

Fostering effective relationships among participants

No matter how knowledgeable the professional may be, in the light of Figure 6.2, his or her substantive knowledge can only be connected to various clients through the application of the professional's relational skills. If this is the case, what behavioural guidance can we think of?

The professional should be appropriately impartial to the process and participants, while also taking co-responsibility for progress

There is a debate among professionals about the usefulness of the concept of 'neutrality' or even whether neutrality is appropriate (Mayer, 2004, pp83–86).

Even if desired, full neutrality is often not possible. The professional in the capacity-building programme does have a vested interest in the outcome – he or she wants the programme to be successful. The facilitating professional therefore is not a neutral facilitator but a person with vested interests in success (Forester, (1999, p77). Nonetheless, the professional should work to be impartial towards both the process and its participants. The delicate balance is for respectful treatment of and impartiality among the participants, on one hand, while engaging in a manner designed to obtain the desired programme outcome. There is a danger of loss of impartiality when the professional becomes excessively involved in the programme details rather than the programme's broad vision of success. By taking too much responsibility for the process, the professional likely reduces the participating parties' sense of responsibility and becomes too much of a 'driver' of the process. By taking too little responsibility, the professional may not sufficiently influence the status quo, hence denying the parties the benefit of her or his good qualities, judgement and inputs.

Inclusion as a core operating principle; clarify roles and motives, including those of the professional

It is sometimes said that the weaknesses in any social system can be identified by what is excluded from its conversation. A strong collaborative system is difficult to maintain if relevant voices are excluded. The professional should strive to plan and undertake capacity-building processes so that the process is inclusive. This works to avoid conflict and becomes even more important when conflict arises. It precludes always using a 'problem solving' approach. Rather, one should ensure that space and time is available for considerations, deliberations and real-life stories. Let the group approach its challenges in its own way and, to some extent, at its own pace.

With multiple actors engaged, complex processes can be greatly aided by having early dialogue on each participant's roles and responsibilities, including those of the professional. Such a discussion would include how the process and participants will operate together. While clarifying roles, responsibilities and accountability, it is helpful to develop a set of operational guidelines for the capacity-building process, to include clarifying what are the actual and reasonable expectations of each participant about the professional's role and responsibility.

In developing a 'credo for facilitators', Peter Adler has described 'a three way good faith contract', which is an agreement among (a) the sponsor, (b) the professional and (c) other process participants (Adler, 2008). In this agreement, the sponsor or donor should be clear with other participants about the donor's intent and the degree of control retained by the donor.

Whether formal or informal, clear agreement among all participants about the professional's role and methods of operation increases trust and reduces misunderstanding. The 'agreement' described above can clarify the expertise that the professional brings, and identify areas that are beyond the professional's role and expertise.

A professional should be clear on what he or she can and cannot do, and should not permit the desires of one or more participants, particularly the paying party, to push the professional to undertake actions outside her or his expertise or professional limits. Having considered what is within and without their expertise and professional code before a conflict arises, the professional is able to signal when being inappropriately asked to depart from his or her limits.

Base process communications in dialogue and learning: The importance of effective communication

Effective communication will help the professional approach and effectively address both collaboration and conflict. When the professional conducts processes founded in dialogue, all participants see they are engaged in the planning and programme activity. Yet dialogue can be rare because so few people actually engage in it. Therefore, a competent professional will learn to teach, encourage and support dialogue.

Experts remind us that dialogue (the root being *dia-logos*) means 'working through meaning'. When engaged in dialogue, participants explore the root of the challenges they face, are open to real inquiry, explore ideas rather than debate and let a common meaning for issues arise from their shared willingness to explore (Bohm, 1991, p1). Dialogue is 'the art of thinking together' (Isaacs, 1999, p3).

When the professional encourages programme participants to work through dialogue, the need for any participant to be 'right' or to 'win' is diminished. Rather, all dialogue participants engage in self-reflection and seek shared learning. Thus, participants speak to bring about understanding rather than to persuade. They listen in order to understand other perspectives rather than to craft the next counter-argument. By reducing the incentive to 'win,' the professional helps the entire group better

---

Box 6.1 Case example: Clarifying intentions to minimize misunderstanding

In the early phase of an African capacity-development process, unexpressed tensions quickly arose about the nature of the paying party's real commitment to the process (for example, what payments would be made and for how long). Although the paying party had convened local NGOs and agencies to begin a capacity-development process, the paying party's real level of commitment was unclear. The capacity-development professional felt that, although an issue that may not have needed immediate resolution, it was appropriate to gently raise the issue in initial meetings. The professional guided discussion and helped parties find an approach that would ensure that all parties, at the proper time, were made aware of the level of commitment and funding from each (including the paying party). By scheduling and defining the topic, the professional ensured that an important issue was transformed from one that participants felt was difficult to discuss, to one on which open exchange and dialogue could happen. Consequently the matter of the paying party's real level of commitment was raised in a timely manner and confusion or misunderstanding was minimized. By gently pushing for payer confirmation of commitment and funding, local NGOs had better data with which to set their own levels of commitment and engagement. Clarity of intention and finances made decisions much easier for all parties.

function and address possibly conflictive issues. What had been debates intended to either change someone's mind or impress them, now become dialogues in which the group learns from one another. As such, all parties gain a deeper understanding of why their views differ, enabling them to find ways to complement each other.

The practical aspects of communication can also be very important. Both at the beginning of the process and as the process continues, it can be helpful if the professional encourages participants to draft summary documents that assess their joint work, describe their current plans and discuss how future actions will be undertaken. Also, during the process, clear documentation can support an atmosphere of openness and respectful dialogue. By documenting changes in direction and any new agreements, the chance for misunderstanding or conflict is reduced. Such summary documents might include formal documents as well as more informal and regular sources (such as meeting agenda and summaries, facilitator process assessments or the parties' self-assessments). Proper documentation involves a balance: A professional will seek to document and communicate well to ensure understanding by all parties while working to conserve programme budgets and time for other important tasks.

Working through conflict

Professionals working in the midst of participants with differing interests and power 'inevitably work in the face of conflict' (Forester, 1999, p61). Yet, in the challenges of capacity building and programme design and delivery, a professional should do more than chase after compromises. Rather, using well accepted approaches to managing and transforming conflict, the professional can support learning among participants and help them better address conflict on their own.

Power is often defined as the ability to cause another person or entity to take or refrain from action. As such, power is one method of resolving a dispute – meaning it is resolved in favour of the party with power. Naturally, the use of such power can cause resistance from the party over whom power is exercised. Besides the exercise of power in the relationship among the parties, capacity-building efforts occur in a context of culture, social dynamics, economics and politics. Such context may include, for example, great societal needs for change and improvement, low governmental capacity, or even armed conflict.

Although some 'conflict' may be obvious, conflict is often subtle and not so easy for the professional to detect. This chapter uses the Institute for Conflict Analysis and Resolution at George Mason University definition of conflict:

> Conflict is the product of unmet needs and unrecognized differences. Often, it is the result of perceived present or future incompatibility of plans, goals or actions. But conflict is also the product of unacknowledged issues as well. … Conflict is a normal product of human interaction, not good or bad… [and] the effects of conflict can be positive or negative.
>
> http://icar.gmu.edu/ICAR_philosophy.html, accessed June 2009

The capacity-building profession has an array of interventions and approaches that may help deal with conflict in a programme or better direct the programme to its intended goal.

Understanding is the key to progress and reducing conflict

When the professional shows a desire to understand the participants rather than direct them, a relational shift occurs. An understanding-based approach lets the conflict at issue sit unresolved while the participants seek to better understand each other's perspectives, interests, concerns and fears. Often, an increased understanding of perspectives and fears will lessen the conflict and open the way for solutions to emerge. Using the understanding-based approach to conflict entails first letting stories, views, interests and concerns be shared before attempting to create a new direction or decision.

When conflict arises, a professional moves the participants from positional debate to interest- and value-based dialogue

It is fully consistent with a capacity-building approach for the professional to help both individual actors and the entire group move from debate to interest-based discussions. In a capacity-building process, conflict could arise over programme control, the allocation and use of resources, views on how development should be undertaken, accountability, leadership practices, debates as to how gender or social inclusion is or is not being accomplished, as well as fundamental differences of world view. The professional can help improve the context by moving competing participants from arguing their 'positions' (for example, 'my position is that …') to discussing the real interests

---

Box 6.2 Case example: Stereotyping each other

In an environmental capacity-development process, the paying party (a government agency) was viewed by many programme participants as a party that used capacity-development processes to enforce its will while maintaining the appearance of being open to stakeholder input. The process was seen by some local interests as an attempt by the payer to appear to care about local interests while nonetheless imposing its will. The capacity-development professional needed to coach the paying party to be more open whilst, at the same time, meeting individually with participants to ask them to support a change by the paying party by avoiding stereotyping (it is difficult for the controlling party to reduce its need for control in the face of stereotyping and unexpressed accusations). The result of the coaching was partially successful: the stakeholders were able to develop and present ideas to the payer – although retaining in large part their suspicions. The paying party, which had a long history of domination, remained rather rigid in its approach and policies, but did in fact consider and adopt the stakeholders' ideas. As such, the intervention of the capacity professional was partially but not completely successful.

and values of each participant that need to be considered in any dispute. This approach is often called interest-based bargaining. A professional tries to lead conflicting parties to interest-based bargaining by, among others, helping participants:

- understand the difference between 'positions', 'interests' and 'values';
- identify the interests that are really important to you and those of the other parties;
- understand each other's values; and
- exchange ideas and proposals that will adequately satisfy the interests of all parties without causing any single participant to lose a fundamental interest.

Using this approach, conflict is reduced and outcomes tend to be those that work for all concerned participants.

At times a professional may be confronted with covert conflicts, such as in the case above, where moving directly to a group process is not feasible or practical. This may be true because a party does not feel confident to discuss the issue in a group format, or that such a large group discussion would be inconsistent with local culture or the sensitivity of the issue. The professional may therefore need to coach the individual or organization to clarify what is happening and to help the party to discuss the issue with the remaining participants. Individual coaching not only helps in addressing any conflict that has arisen but also ensures that a participant can know they were heard.

Encourage healthy and transformative approaches to conflict

In conflict situations a professional can help the process participants to go beyond conflict resolution to transformation. Conflict transformation aims not only to stop what is undesirable by resolving the specific issue at stake, but also to build a stronger relationship. Transformative processes help participants to both perceive and take on new views and perspectives, and to redefine their relationships. When used succesfully, conflict transformation helps participants address the present problem and also be prepared for future conflicts. Conflict resolution is content-centred. In comparison, conflict transformation is a suitable goal for capacity-building programmes for two key reasons: first, it aims at mid- and long-range change rather than the short-term relief of merely ending the conflict; and second, it accepts conflict, not as a crisis, but as part of dynamic relationships and a source for development and learning (Lederach, 2003, p35).

Model the behaviour you desire from participants

When a challenge arises, the professional can assist the participants by modelling the behaviour desired from them. This may include clear communications, working to increase understanding, discouraging premature decisions, discouraging the use of harsh language, including all key players in the discussions, reducing conflict through increased understandings, thoughtful consideration of available options, considered decision-making, and following through to ensure the planned actions are undertaken. It is natural for programme participants to closely observe how the professional responds to conflict and to take a cue from and reciprocate her or his behaviour.

Some possible radical choices available to the professional

A dramatic circumstance may present itself where the professional believes that continuing the programme without substantial change is ill-advised. This could arise where conflict between two or more participants is so great that damage to the participants is increasing; the programme is or is becoming dysfunctional; or important relationships are being damaged. In this circumstance and to prevent further damage, the professional may decide to suspend or propose the suspension

---

Box 6.3 Summary of behavioural guidance for working in multi-actor settings

Dealing with power and complexity

- Power asymmetries are omnipresent in capacity-development work. The facilitator should anticipate and be patient with their expression in a programme or capacity-development activity.
- Sustaining working relationships among different parties is a major part of the capacity-development practitioner's work.
- Role clarity is critically important hence the facilitator should continually work to ensure that all parties understand the roles and responsibilities of each party (see also Chapter 4).

Fostering effective relationships calls for:

- Continued impartiality to the process and the participants while promoting progress;
- The use of inclusive approaches to enable diverse voices to be heard by all parties;
- Encouraging the parties to be responsible for the process through dialogue, joint problem-solving and thoughtful action among all parties.

Dealing with conflict

- When conflict arises, first seek to promote understanding – conflict is often fuelled by misunderstanding.
- Do not just seek to resolve conflict. Rather, move beyond resolution to building stronger relationships among conflicting parties.
- When parties are in negotiation, gently move them from stating their 'positions' into disclosing their interests. Ask all conflicting parties to look for options that adequately address the interests of all parties.
- In your own actions and way of relating, model the behaviour that you seek from the parties.

---

of process activities until improvements can be made. Sometimes the threat of, or actual, programme suspension is needed to get the attention of one or more participants. The professional should use this extreme intervention rarely; nonetheless; it must be part of the menu options seen as being available to the professional, subject to his or her engagement limitations.

Conclusion

Although the professional works in a complex multi-actor environment with substantial power asymmetries, approaches exist that, when adjusted for the specific context, can give the professional ways to deal with the challenges inherent in these programme situations. A summary of the 'behavioural guidance' resulting from the discussions in this chapter is provided in the list of ten points in Box 6.3 above.

References

Adler, P. (2008) 'A Credo for Facilitators', www.mediate.com/articles/facilitation-Credo.cfm?nl=165, accessed June 2009

Bohm. D. et al (1991) *Dialogue: A Proposal,* www.david-bohm.net/dialogue/dialogue_proposal.html, accessed July 2009

Chrislip, D. and Larson, C. (1994) *Collaborative Leadership,* Jossey-Bass, New York

Fisher, S. et al (2000) *Working With Conflict, Skills and Strategies for Action,* Zed Books, New York, NY

Forester, J. (1999) *The Deliberative Practitioner,* MIT Press, Cambridge, MA

Eade, D. (1997) *Capacity-Building,* Oxfam Publications, Oxford

Isaacs, W. (1999) *Dialogue and the Art of Thinking Together,* Doubleday, New York, NY

Lederach, J.P. (2003) *The Little Book of Conflict Transformation,* Good Books, Intercourse PA

Mayer, B. (2004) *Beyond Neutrality, Confronting the Crisis in Conflict Resolution,* Jossey-Bass, San Fransisco, CA

Schein, E. (1999) *Process Consultation Revisited,* Addison-Wesley, New York, NY

Schein, E. (1973) *Professional Education,* McGraw Hill, New York, NY

Schön, D. (1983) *The Reflective Practitioner,* Basic Books, New York, NY

Schwarz, R. (2002) *The Skilled Facilitator,* Jossey Bass, New York, NY

Recommended readings

This chapter links to a range of others in this volume. Chapter 2 introduces the dimension of multiple actors. Chapter 7 focuses specifically on the challenge of working with the different 'values' that these actors bring to bear, including those of the capacity-development practitioner him/herself. Chapter 10 explores dialogue as a central skill for the capacity-development practitioner and discusses a range of dialogue methods available. Chapter 11 places the different interests of actors in a wider framework of politics, governance and institutions and Chapter 12 discusses an example of working with (public) accountability in capacity-development work. Chapters 3, 13, 14 and 15 also explicitly discuss situations and approaches in which the practitioner deals with power differentials between actors.

The following is a short selection of useful resources that may assist the practitioner in a deeper understanding of his/her role and how to best face dilemmas that arise in that role. Several thoughtful authors have written informative texts on the role of the professional or outside consultant. For detailed information on the sources, please refer to the references section.

Edgar Schein has written extensively, and a very useful summary of his thinking is contained in *Process Consultation Revisited: Building the Helping Relationship*, published by Addison-Wesley, New York, 1999.

Although written primarily for planners, John Forester's *The Deliberative Practitioner* (MIT Press, Cambridge, MA, 1999) is very helpful in aiding practitioners in obtaining stakeholder and citizen input in important decisions. That book draws upon the thinking contained in Donald Schön's influential text, *The Reflective Practitioner* (Basic Books, New York, 1983), which helps professionals move beyond their academic training to better encounter and solve real-world problems.

A useful supplement to the above is *Collaborative Leadership* by David Chrislip and Carl Larson (Jossey-Bass, New York, 1994). The concept of Collaborative Leadership can aid the professional in helping leaders and citizens to solve challenging social problems.

Working With Conflict, Skills and Strategies for Action, edited by Simon Fisher (Zed Books, New York, 2000), is a good reference text on conflict.

7

Whose Values Count?

The diverse actors engaged in a capacity-development process often have very different values and views. The fact that it is the dominant values and voices that determine the direction and outcomes of the process is a particularly pertinent issue in addressing exclusion and inequity.

Drawing on two local settings in India, this text by Rajesh Tandon demonstrates how some of these issues are played out in capacity-development processes. He highlights the need for a practitioner to be fully aware of how imbalances in interests and voice may reinforce or even worsen existing situations of disempowerment. He also discusses how a lack of awareness of a gap between the practitioner's own values and those of the client, or key stakeholders, can impact on the practitioner's relationship with his or her client.

Voice, Values and Exclusion in Capacity-Development Processes: Experiences from India

Rajesh Tandon

Introduction

Before diving into the issue of whose values and voices count, it may be helpful to locate the question clearly in the arena of capacity development. Capacity-development support here refers to the wide range of processes and interventions that in some way contribute to the 'ability of a human system to perform, sustain itself and to self-renew'. Much capacity-development work also aims to influence, in some way, the more structural issues that underlie those situations where 'human systems' are clearly not performing, sustaining themselves or self-renewing. The causes are many, interrelated and complex. It is widely acknowledged that some of the most intractable development challenges have to do with inequalities and situations of exclusion that are often rooted in deep-seated and entrenched values, beliefs and practices. They also have to do with social and political arrangements that result in the under-representation or non-representation of different groups and sections of society.

Many approaches to capacity development aim to redress these imbalances and help organizations – and the societies in which they are embedded – to extend the freedoms, services and level of well-being, that are taken for granted in some sections, to all groups including those previously marginalized. This necessarily involves the bumping together and shifting of power relations and practices that have hitherto been accepted as 'the way things are'. Practitioners are familiar with concepts that explain the complex relationship between values, beliefs and inequality in the societies they help. What are not discussed are the values and beliefs in our own practice and how they inform the choices we make about where and how to intervene and with whom. That is the subject of this chapter. How do the issues of conflicting values and unequal voice play out in daily capacity-development practice? How can practitioners develop a more acute awareness of them and how far is it possible to respond in a helpful way?

Using a simple story drawn from Rajasthan in India but which could take place anywhere in the world, the chapter shows how issues of voice and values are present in the client relationship, the wider client system and the assumptions made by practitioners and their organizations when they intervene. A second story, again from India, is used further on, to show how the values question may play out at the level of daily practice in a situation where there is a difference between the values that an individual practitioner holds and those of the client.

It is not the aim of this chapter to provide prescriptions, or even examples of 'best practice'. While practitioners will find some pointers and possible tips on ways in which they may approach these questions, our aim in this chapter is to shed light on what is going on beneath the surface of our capacity-development practice and to invite practitioners to reflect on three things. First, how conscious are they of the signals that a client system may give about the different power and value conflicts that underlie the issues that practitioners and their organizations have been called in to help with? Second, how do their own values and assumptions inform their intervention approach and does this in some way reinforce the very imbalances they seek to address? Finally, practitioners are invited to reflect on situations in which there is a direct conflict between their own values and those of the client.

The Ramnagar story – what did we do wrong?

Ramnagar municipality in Rajasthan comprises nearly half a million residents. Located on the eastern end of the state, the old settlement has long served as a business hub for agricultural produce. Over the past decade, it has grown enormously from a sleepy old town to a bustling city. In 2005, a new female mayor, a teacher and member of a respected middle-class family in the city, was elected into office.

Meanwhile, under a new national scheme, the Asian Development Bank (ADB) had made funding available for 'capacity strengthening' of medium-sized municipalities in Rajasthan. The new mayor was keen to tap into these funds to improve infrastructure services in Ramnagar municipality. A consultancy firm hired by the ADB was tasked with assisting the municipality to formulate a capacity-development plan. The mayor approved the plan proposed by the firm, and applied to the central government for funding.

One day several months later, the local newspaper carried a front page story claiming that the mayor had approved a city development plan with a middle-class bias that ignored the needs of shanty towns in and around Ramnagar and their residents. All hell broke loose: the majority of councillors distanced themselves from the plan; an emergency meeting called by the mayor was first boycotted by many councillors; and a planned presentation by the consultancy firm on the proposed plans could not take place as the town hall was surrounded by protesting slum-dwellers.

The young professionals at the consultancy firm were thoroughly confused by the developments. They believed they had done a good job in analysing the existing capacity gaps and making detailed recommendations on the way forward. So, why all this fuss and noise?

The mayor too was confused and irritated. She believed the proposed plans would enable the municipality to function better. She considered the report as very professional and focused. At the other end of the spectrum were the inhabitants of unplanned neighbourhoods who were excluded from many services. The number of slum residents was rising rapidly as new labour migrants came to the city in search of employment. These informal settlements were considered 'illegal' by some government officials, even though a number of councillors had been elected into office by local residents. Tired of demanding services from the municipality to no avail, many slum-dwellers perceived the new plan as an instrument to exclude them further from accessing municipal services.

This story brings into sharp focus the issues raised in the introduction to be tackled in this chapter. In a complex social system, with multiple actors and constituencies having differing – and at times conflicting – value-bases, how does the practitioner discover, understand and use these value differences to inform his or her intervention choices and approach? Which relations of power may exclude differing viewpoints in a process of social change?

Development processes everywhere, whether in relation to a smart new tram line in a city like Stockholm in Sweden or providing water supply services to slum residents in Ramnagar, India, involve conflicts of interests, values and power. The challenge for capacity-development practitioners is how to work with this unavoidable fact of life in the apparently 'neutral' process of clarifying a request from a client (such as the municipality in the case described above) and providing a professional service in response to that request. How does one take the underlying value issues into account at the start and during an intervention? What is the practitioner's role? How far can it go?

We now draw out some signals and possible pitfalls for practitioners from the Ramnagar story and ask what implications, if any, there are for practitioners or their organizations.

Understanding the client system

As noted above, capacity-development practitioners need to be well equipped to identify, understand and engage with exclusionary processes that may mask value differences and conflicts within a client relationship.

However, who the client is in a capacity-development assignment is often unclear. For example in the above story, the ADB hires the practitioners' firm and presumably pays them. The services are to be provided to the municipal government of Ramnagar with approval of the Central Government. Whether the services are the right ones or not has everything to do with whether the constituencies of the municipality feel that their needs are met. Hence, the consultancy firm signs one contract with ADB but clearly cannot ignore the interests of any of the parties mentioned. This is why it makes sense to refer to this cluster of interested parties round a specific contract as the 'client system'. It is the system that the practitioners have to engage with and whose interests and boundaries they have to take into consideration in the course of designing and carrying out their intervention. One of the important boundaries in the Ramnagar story was that between the municipal administration or government and certain sections of its constituency – residents of the informal settlements that had developed at the outskirts of the city. The practitioners in this case did not consider this question or encourage the municipal administration to ask itself this question. Opening up this subject may have made the difference or conflict in interests and values clearer. It might also have revealed that not all stakeholders felt fairly represented or even trusted that any undertaking by the municipal administration would reflect their needs. The mayor's enthusiasm and well-meaning vision was taken for granted. An examination of the relations of power between various stakeholder groups inside the municipality, and the city as a whole, may have provided an opportunity to bring these different voices into the discussion about how new resources in the form of infrastructure could be allocated more inclusively.

By their nature, the client systems in any development setting are embedded in social settings, and are often microcosms of the wider society, reflecting inequalities and imbalances of power which exist therein – a mosaic of conflicting values and world views. Hierarchies and inequalities based on gender, race, caste, religion and age get further reinforced in institutional hierarchies of power and authority. Practitioners of capacity development need to be aware of how this picture plays out in a client system and draw upon their insights in making judgments, choices and decisions about how and where to intervene. This does not mean that practitioners have to solve these issues – but they do need to demonstrate awareness and understanding of which voices, perspectives and values are unlikely to be heard on their own.

Practitioner blind spots

The first blind spot that this story highlights is that of assuming that professional expertise is neutral and universally applicable. The professionals involved in the Ramnagar municipality project had a management and accountancy background.

Their analysis of the managerial and accounting capacities of the municipality was informed by the values and world views of the professions in which they had been trained. Drawing on their past experiences and cumulative tacit knowledge gained therefrom, their definition of a well-run municipality was logically informed by the deeply-held assumptions of the accounting and management professions. As is often the case, these perspectives were deemed to be value-neutral and applicable to any institutional setting. Practitioners need to reflect critically on the value premises of their different professional backgrounds and disciplines so that they do not turn a blind eye to or inadvertently mask over value differences that often go to the heart of the very issues they want to help with. By assuming value-neutrality of capacity-development efforts and their expertise, the Ramnagar professionals in an unwitting manner contributed to 'suppression' of voices and values of the excluded and the powerless in the system.

The second possible blind spot highlighted by this story relates to the considerable power that practitioners themselves have within the client system they work in. The Ramnagar practitioners had the power to recommend a city-wide development plan to a major donor. On the strength of their recommendations, desperately-needed resources could be made available to the city, and hence could enhance or diminish the status and power of the mayor. The resulting fall-out serves as a cautionary tale on the need to examine the power relations of consultants vis-à-vis various constituencies inside and outside the client system. Power and values are intricately related. Our position in society strongly shapes our values. Similarly our position in institutions strongly determines our world views, and our role in institutions defines our relations of power with others. So practitioners may inadvertently use their power to exclude different voices and perspectives and impose their own. On the other hand, they could also use their power to open up spaces for the sharing of different perspectives, values and visions.

Finally, in a complex client system practitioners need to be aware of how they are perceived by different interest groups. The unheard voices and invisible conflicts in the client system tend to remain unarticulated, especially if the practitioner is perceived to be working in the interest of only one party: the paying party in most cases. The capacity to negotiate an open sharing of different voices and values may be a critical factor in establishing credibility with different interest groups.

We now look at a situation where a practitioner's personal and organizational values are in direct conflict with those of her client.

Another story – tiny steps

The conversation below took place between a capacity-development practitioner from the Society for Participatory Research in Asia (PRIA) and a workshop participant, against a backdrop of caste-based discrimination and exclusion. The elected head of the village *panchayat* (an elected village council) belongs to a lower-caste group. He has been elected as a result of an affirmative action quota system but the age-old beliefs and prejudices about his caste are still firmly in place. The social practices around caste differentiation are such that members of a higher caste do not share water and food with those belonging to lower-caste groups, and separate utensils are earmarked to be used by such lower-caste groups in public functions.

> Why is the *sarpanch* [elected village leader] [not?] having a cup of tea with us?
> Madam, he is not well.
> But, the tea might make him feel better?
> Yes, madam, I will send for a mud cup for him right away.

The facilitator quietly, but visibly, offers her own cup of tea to the *sarpanch* and starts a conversation with him. Concerned that the 'guest' from PRIA has not had tea, several village leaders rush to get her another cup.

With this seemingly minor action the facilitator takes a stand against the exclusionary and discriminatory practice she just witnessed. The meeting proceeds to discuss the agenda of the day. There is no further discussion of the facilitator's action. She continues to chat with the *sarpanch* after the meeting, explaining why she acted in that way – that she felt all people regardless of caste should be treated equally.

Encouraged and somewhat empowered, the *sarpanch* himself begins to take small steps in the village to demonstrate equality among households in providing access to public programmes. At the next meeting, the facilitator arranges the tea, in identical cups for all, and starts by serving the *sarpanch* first. The younger *panchayat* leaders begin an informal discussion on caste-based exclusion. Gradually, the facilitator encourages a more structured reflection among a handful of such young leaders about how they might help to build a stronger governing structure and do more to make the village a more equitable society.

On the face of it the action taken by the facilitator was a light intervention that created a tiny shift in 'the way things are'. Such tiny shifts may generate some ripples beyond the immediate setting (as in the *sarpanch* feeling encouraged to make his own tiny shifts in other areas of village life) or they may not. The facilitator did not accept caste-based exclusion as normal practice and deliberately, and publicly, acted against it. The facilitator also consciously demonstrated solidarity with the lower-caste *sarpanch*, and made it clear that respect for the leadership potential of all classes of society is a core value in her practice. This personal affirmation encouraged the village leader to consciously demonstrate his own values of inclusion, despite the possible disapproval of the dominant caste groups. Thus the facilitator chose to 'walk the talk' by demonstrating her stated values through her actions. Of course it is not always possible to do this and practitioners have to judge for themselves when a situation offers the opportunity to act in this way.

The second thing the facilitator did was to encourage critical reflection among a category of potential change agents within the system – the young leaders. This was 'lightly', yet intentionally, facilitated by linking the discussion to issues that were of interest to the young leaders – the effectiveness of local government institutions and the well-being of the village society as a whole. This approach overcame inhibitions to critically and openly discuss such issues as caste discrimination, and made it possible to consider ways that things may be done differently.

It may well be that all that can be facilitated is improved understanding among different constituencies of differences in values and their implications, and that no resolution may be possible, or even feasible. In such a situation, the practitioner has to learn to live with the tensions within, because sharpening of value differences can also heighten a practitioner's own value dilemmas. Learning to live with conflicts of values may be an essential capability for practitioners of capacity development.

Conclusion

The two stories discussed in this chapter have highlighted how issues of equal voice, conflicting values and contested interests are intricately interwoven with the capacity-development process. These issues should be constantly 'on the table' in all stages of capacity-development practice, and are already well discussed in the literature that is aimed at organizations and actors in developing societies at large. It is time for those that seek to support capacity development – donors and capacity-development organizations and their practitioners – to confront these issues more thoroughly in their intervention approaches and daily practice. A more systematic process of including these questions throughout the process, from analysis, through intervention design to implications for interaction within the client system, is needed. Many of the initial analyses carried out by practitioners when called upon to provide-capacity development services, do indeed point to likely conflict of interests and values. However, the thread gets lost when it comes to translating into intervention strategy and approach. The question of what it means for the practitioner as an individual is particularly fraught and may probably never be raised in the discussion. In addition, the training skills-development of practitioners needs to include more reflection on the issue of values. It does not matter what the technical background of practitioners is: so long as they practice in the development sector, they are bound to be confronted with these questions. Clearly, this area needs further work and it is our hope that the issues raised in this chapter will stimulate readers to take this forward.

Recommended readings

Two other chapters in this volume may be of interest to readers, in relation to this topic. Chapter 6 explores power dimensions inherent in capacity development and provides some behavioural guidelines for the practitioner. Chapter 11 unravels a complex web of politics, power, formal and informal institutional norms that interact to influence processes of capacity development and change. Readers may also be interested in the following:

Rajesh Tandon (ed.) (2002) *Participatory Research: Revisiting the Roots*, Mosaic Books, Delhi

Readers who want to explore this theme further will find the theoretical papers and practical methods in this book very useful.

John Gaventa (2006) 'Finding the spaces for change: A power analysis', *IDS Bulletin*, vol 37, no 6

This is a helpful and interesting article on power and how it plays out in the settings in which practitioners often work.

Schein, Edgar H. (1992) *Organizational Culture and Leadership*, 2nd edition, Jossey-Bass, San Francisco

Schein's description of culture, values and mental models is highly relevant to the discussion in this chapter.

Chadha Prem, Jagadananda and Lal Gayatri (2003) *Organisation Behaviour*, Centre for Youth and Social Development, Bhubaneshwar, India

This publication is targeted at development NGOs but is highly relevant to different organizations and settings. It explores issues such as values, value analysis and professional practice.

8

Organization Development as a Source

The professional field of organizational development (OD) is a major source for thinking about and practising capacity development. Capacity-development (CD) practitioners will therefore benefit from a good understanding of this rather eclectic discipline.

In her insightful contribution, Ingrid Richter traces the evolution of OD and describes the multiple influences that have shaped it. She draws on her own experience and that of other OD practitioners to show how much convergence there is between OD and CD practice, especially with regard to approaches and methods for supporting long-term change. This convergence is a growing resource for the work of CD advisers. Practitioners will find this chapter illuminating in locating the roots of some capacity-development practices and approaches with which they may be familiar.

Riding the Pendulum Between 'Clocks' and 'Clouds': The History of OD and Its Relation to CD

Ingrid Richter

Introduction

According to the scientific philosopher Karl Popper (1972), all complex systems fall on a continuum between clouds and clocks. He described cloud systems as irregular and unpredictable and clock systems as regular and predictable. Over the years the practice of organization development (OD) might be described as riding the pendulum between activities driven by 'clock' thinking assumptions and activities driven by 'cloud' thinking assumptions. In this respect it has much in common with the swinging pendulum of assumptions behind capacity development (CD) practice. Both sets of activity are focused on facilitating change in complex systems.

Organization development, while rooted in human relations and social sciences, has evolved into a field which is truly cross-disciplinary. Historically it has deep roots in social psychology and social change, but has increasingly been focused on improving the effectiveness and productivity of organizations in general, and workplaces in particular. It is important to acknowledge that there are many practitioners, especially in the Southern hemisphere, who have always been committed to the support of organizations and social movements by applying OD and capacity development practices in an integrated way.[1]

Organization development grew out of the human relations traditions of the 1940s and 1950s, and it has had enormous influence on management practices and thinking about how organizational effectiveness can be achieved. Many of its original proponents would have agreed that there is a significant overlap between OD and CD, as defined earlier in this volume:

Capacity is the ability of a human system to perform, sustain itself and self-renew.

(SNV, 2007)

This chapter stimulates further thinking and debate about what OD brings to capacity development thinking and practice in three ways. Firstly, it provides a historical overview of the roots and branches of OD and some of the 'pendulum' of ideas that it has shaped it over time. Secondly, it suggests and points to what OD offers to our understanding and practice of capacity development as the evolution is traced. Finally the chapter proposes some implications, trends and future perspectives that seem to draw the two practices closer together.

The roots and evolution of OD

In this section, the aim is to trace a history and evolution of the field showing the different strands of psychology and social science disciplines it has drawn from. As this story unfolds, connections, overlaps and similarities with capacity development will be highlighted. The section is divided into broad chunks, each of which loosely describes a major trend or set of developments that contributed to the OD field as it is today.

The psychology of groups and social change

The story starts a bit on the 'cloud' side of things. The Polish-born psychologist Kurt Lewin is considered to be one of the intellectual fathers of contemporary theories of applied behavioural science, action research and planned change, or OD. In the 1920s and 1930s, he worked with others to research WWI German soldiers with brain damage and examine how their immediate experience (the here and now) is influenced by their subjective reality (as influenced by needs and feelings). From here they developed 'Psychological Field Theory' which explains how perceptual experience is determined by things like feelings, intention, needs and tensions.

The roots of Lewin's work are very much embedded in questions of social change, and have strongly influenced the practice of OD. Lewin was troubled by social conditions and conflicts in 1930s Germany and turned his attention to their resolution. His investigations were grounded in his desire to stop the growth of anti-Semitism, to see the democratization of German institutions, and to advance the position of women in society. Driven by the realities of the political situation, he emigrated to the USA. At the time, much of the seminal research in social psychology was focused on human behaviour in warfare and post-warfare contexts. These included exploring the morale of the fighting troops, psychological warfare, and reorienting food consumption away from foods in short supply. Lewin conducted a great deal of research on group dynamics, and in 1944 one of his dreams was realized with the founding of the Research Center for Group Dynamics at the Massachusetts Institute of Technology.

Another of Lewin's many lasting contributions to the field of OD and CD was his model of Action Research (research directed toward the solving of social problems) which evolved from a number of significant studies into religious and racial prejudice. While Action Research has been a core theory and intervention model for OD practitioners in corporate contexts, it has also gained a significant foothold in community-based and participatory action research, especially as a form of capacity development practice oriented to the improvement of educative encounters (Carr and Kemmis, 1986).

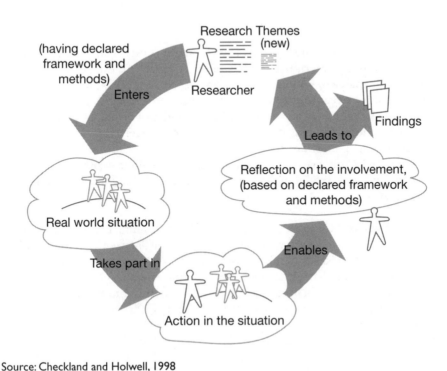

Source: Checkland and Holwell, 1998

Figure 8.1 *The action research cycle*

In 1946, the notion of 'T groups' (laboratory training groups) emerged out of Lewin's work with community leaders and group facilitators. A central feature of the T-group labs was intensive 'basic skills training,' in which an observer reported on group processes at set intervals. The skills developed in these labs were intended to help participants function in the role of 'change agent'. A change agent was thought to be instrumental in facilitating communication and useful feedback among participants in group and organizational settings. A change agent was also to be a model or example who could identify the need for change, diagnose problems, plan for change, implement the plans and evaluate the results. To become an effective change agent, an understanding of the dynamics of groups was believed necessary. Skills in facilitating group dynamics and group processes are a core competency of OD professionals today.

From the psychology of groups to planned change

An important strand of OD thinking and practice arose from Gestalt theory (the word has German origins and refers to the notion of 'wholeness'). Gestalt approaches seek to explain how a whole situation is experienced and perceived rather than to analyse its constituent parts.[2] Gestalt therapy and OD were proceeding more or less independently of each other up to the early 1950s, when Nevis and Wallen integrated Gestalt therapy into Lewinian systems theory (Nevis, 1987). The similarities between the Gestalt approach and the thinking and practice traditions in capacity development are striking. Carter (2008, p50) offers the following summary of Gestalt thinking:

> Gestalt Organization and Systems Development (OSD) consultants prefer non-expert, non-prescriptive models of practice since these (a) imply that people are capable of addressing their own issues, concerns, and problems, and (b) focus on developing the competencies and capacities of the organization and its members above all. Rather than identify what is 'wrong' with an organizational system, the Gestalt OSD intervener takes an appreciative approach. This is not simply a positive stance. It means focusing on the strength of the system and supporting the individuals involved to play with all fifty-two cards in their deck and to acknowledge the jokers and the wild cards.

However, post-World War II, there was also a strong emphasis on the need for business to become efficient, especially in the face of international competition. With this more 'clocklike' trend in management, OD practitioners were called upon to plan and implement strategic change interventions. Over time, particularly in North America, OD practices gradually branched into specializations that concentrated on specific organizational issues: strategy, leadership development, team-building, culture change, and so on.

In the 1960s and 1970s, largely under the leadership of the American psychologist Richard Beckhard, a very pragmatic approach to OD was emerging and evolving. It became synonymous with long-term, planned change (Beckhard, 1969). Organization development was fundamentally connected with strategic planning, and was undertaken through rational, controlled, orderly processes of diagnosing needs, engaging all levels of the organization, and facilitating participatory interventions. There is, however, broad consensus that in practice the change process is far more chaotic and 'cloudlike', with shifting goals, discontinuous activities, and unexpected turns in direction. Core competencies of OD practitioners include the ability to assess (or 'diagnose'), design, facilitate and navigate change across all sizes and types of organization. They are also able to address power struggles that emerge, and work with the dynamics of covert and overt conflict between various individuals and groups throughout a planned change process.

In today's tumultuous times, the widely held assumption that long-term, systemic change can be planned and managed is increasingly being brought into question. This will be discussed later in this chapter; however, it is important to point out that this assumption is paralleled in the field of capacity development: many approaches are based on the deep belief that with the right actors engaged, and with a long-term commitment to the time and energy required to maintain engagement, social change can be achieved, and in a measureable way.

Through the 1980s and 1990s, OD continued to straddle the domains of psychology and management, but practitioners in the field increasingly brought an emphasis on how to increase efficiency. Business consultants with strong analytical ('clock') orientation drove methodologies for organizational performance. One of the most well-known was business process re-engineering – an approach aiming at improvements by means of elevating efficiency and effectiveness of the business processes that exist within and across organizations (Hammer and Champy, 1993). This approach and others similar to it had important results in terms of organizational efficiency, but often pitted the priorities of the organization against the perceptions and expectations of workers. To adherents of the values espoused by the OD founders, this trend towards 'engineering' or 'managing' change conflicted with the humanistic and participatory underpinnings of OD. This dynamic created additional streams of professionals: one stream emphasizing structured, linear approaches to outcome-driven 'change management'; the other (OD) stream concentrating on the 'people side of change', which emphasized understanding how the human dimension of an organization could be brought into alignment with strategic directions and new business modalities.

The focus of OD practitioners during the 1980s tended to swing between rational tools and techniques for diagnosing and facilitating change in organizational structures and internal systems, on the one hand, and more holistic views on human relations, influenced by deep-seated organizational cultures on the other. During this era there were grand hopes for OD, and the idea was that by helping organizations of all types become healthier, society would also become more productive and healthy. But the relationship between planned change and organizational performance and/or effectiveness was (and is) not well understood. In particular, the often substantial time required for complex change initiatives to achieve results was under-appreciated and frequently led to weak evaluations of OD interventions. Many organizations launched programmes of change but ran out of energy or money before all the stages of the change initiative were completed.

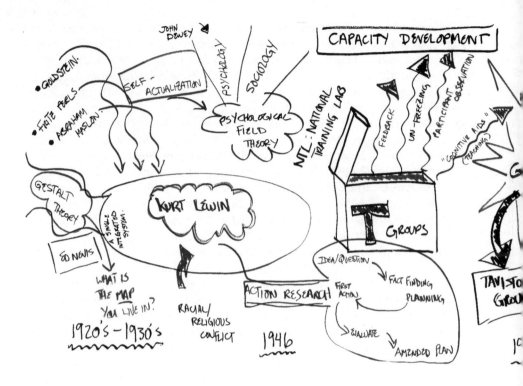

Source: Ingrid Richter

Figure 8.2 *Evolution of OD through the decades*

As Schein (2005, p135) explains, the 'combined effect of these trends [towards tools and techniques] were loss of ability to design large-scale systemic interventions, lack of skill in working with complex systems, and (most important) lack of understanding of culture and its impact on individuals and groups. In fact, one could say that OD in the 1980s and 1990s was culturally naïve'.

Towards systems views of change

Through the late 1980s to the present, the impacts and complexities of globalization on national economies, ecological systems and human life conditions have become increasingly obvious; but in these complex conditions there is still little or no consensus on the most successful and appropriate ways for OD and CD practitioners to conceptualize, approach and facilitate change. Nevertheless, there have been promising developments. More systems-oriented ('cloudlike') theories of change originating some decades earlier have slowly been infused into OD and CD practice. Focusing on relatively narrowly defined 'organizations' as the realm of intervention has become less relevant. With the growing awareness of

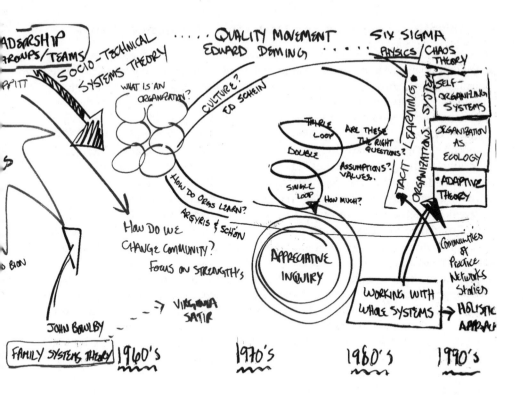

interdependencies between systems, the importance and power of working with the dynamics of the multi-faceted relationships between partner organizations, customers, suppliers, citizens and other stakeholders has become increasingly critical. New and more holistic ways of thinking about the nature of systems and how to intervene in them were needed. The foundations of holistic and systems-oriented approaches to complex systems change arose from several important theoreticians and practitioners.

Eric Trist of the Tavistock Institute was also heavily influenced by Kurt Lewin in his research into human behaviour in groups and systems at the Tavistock Institute (Trist et al, 1963). Lewin and Trist shifted the focus from research on groups to research on systemic change in and between organizations. They emphasized direct professional–client collaboration, and affirmed the role of group relations as the basis for problem-solving. Both were avid proponents of the principle that decisions are best implemented by those who help make them. As the 1970s progressed, the thinking of researchers evolved, bringing environmental and contextual factors into sharper focus as determinants of successful organizational change.

Organizational learning and leadership of systemic change

Donald Schön made a number of important contributions to the growth and development of a systems-oriented approach to OD. His ideas on learning systems (learning organizations, societies and institutions); double-loop and organizational learning (in collaboration with Chris Argyris); and the relationship of reflection-in-action to professional activity were a bridge between the 'efficiency' mindset of re-engineering and the 'development' mindset of OD. Argyris and Schön (1974) proposed that people have individual and collective mental maps which guide their actions in organized settings. The mental maps are largely unexamined, and often at odds with the 'theories of action' people talk about when asked. In other words, there is a split between what people *say* they care about and do, and what they *actually* demonstrate through their actions (Argyris and Schön, 1978). This way of thinking taught us that our picture of reality is always incomplete – people are continually working to add pieces and to get a view of the whole, largely to know their place in the organization.

Of course these decades also saw the emergence of unprecedented pressure for change (broad technology implementation, downsizing, mergers, acquisitions and globalization) that challenged every aspect of the definition of 'organization', as well as across networks of organizations, (such as industries, markets, supply chains). Questions arose about how 'knowledge' was acquired and transmitted, and this naturally led to questions about facilitating organizational learning on a macro scale. As a result, the late 1980s and 1990s saw a rapid expansion of thought and practice on systems thinking, organizational learning and approaches to leading change systemically (Senge, 1990; Lave and Wenger, 1991; Easterby-Smith et al, 1999). These trends challenged OD practitioners to understand organizations, sets of organizations and entire sectors (private, profit and non-profit) as complex living systems, which are capable of thinking, learning, and actively adapting to contextual shifts. This in turn contributed to a new wave of OD practices and interventions, essentially because OD practitioners began to understand the focus of intervention as a wide web of intersecting, complex relational dynamics, rather than more narrowly defined organizational groups, or business units. OD practitioners in this branch of practice began to shift away from 'designing' change, towards mapping systemic learning, creating systems for reflection on practice, and stimulating adaptive learning, all with a view to releasing or unblocking a system's natural inclination to adaptation and change.

Organizational culture and change

Another tributary in the development of systemic views of OD theory and practice is connected to the work of family therapists, especially the Italian group that built its entire therapeutic framework on understanding families as tightly interlocking systems (Campbell et al, 1994; Palazzoli et al, 1970). Schein's work (1992) gained much greater attention during the 1990s as he was able to show that culture is the most difficult – yet often the most influential – organizational attribute to change, outlasting organizational products, services, founders, leaders and all other physical attributes of the organization.

He pointed out that at the deepest level, the organization's tacit assumptions and 'unspoken' rules often exist without the knowledge of organizational members, and are in fact the underlying and driving elements often missed by organizational behaviourists.

Spectrum of OD practices

The increasing and sometimes overwhelming complexity of challenges in organizations over the 1980s and 1990s led to a trend towards specialization among OD practitioners. It could be argued that by the end of the 1990s OD had splintered into a broad mix of practices, each of which had specialists, including those who concentrate on:

- strategic planning;
- facilitating the development of mission and vision;
- organization design (especially designing structures for distributed and outsourced work);
- corporate culture (assessing it, changing it);
- leadership development of every stripe;
- coaching (at all levels);
- knowledge management and the links to 'informal knowledge' (communities of practice);
- organizational learning structures and processes;
- change and transition process design and facilitation;
- individual and team group assessments;
- talent management and succession planning;
- team interventions – including how to change dysfunctional teams;
- addressing conflict, managing diversity and other values alignment needs.

By the end of the millennium, with the impact of rapidly accelerating globalization, and the exponential growth of technology, new forms of enterprise and systemic connections were both called for and enabled. With these developments, there was also an increasing need for OD practitioners to be able to convene and facilitate broad stakeholder engagement processes in order to realize systemic change. This is yet another form of specialization and possibly the one that has the most in common with capacity development practice.

Trends and influences of the last decade

The theoretical work on systems from earlier decades is now being translated into practice. This includes systems theory, mentioned earlier (Senge, 1990; Checkland and Scholes, 1990); as well as complex adaptive systems theory (Lorenz, 1993; Prigogine, 1980; Wheatley, 1992), complexity theory (Waldrop, 1992; Capra, 2002), social network theory (Milgram, 1967; Granovetter, 1982), integral theory (Wilber, 1999) and many other 'cloudlike' ways of thinking about complexity in relationships and systems. These lenses offer both OD and CD practitioners new ways of understanding the complex systems and societies they work within.

OD practitioners have typically been trained to be 'neutral' process experts, while capacity development practitioners are often engaged to bring specific expertise or 'technical' knowledge to a situation although they will work in participatory and inclusive ways. As OD practice has diversified, and as the issues facing organizations and systems have become more complex, there is an increasing need for both OD and CD practitioners to recognize that their work is not 'neutral'. There are strong and distinct values that accompany the ways in which systems are analysed, how actors in the system are engaged in decisions about change and the ways in which change is enacted. With the complexity of the times it is also becoming clear that skilful OD practitioners need to have both process expertise, and an in-depth knowledge and understanding of the sector or organizational type they are working with: health, education, non-profit, religious or commercial, for example. OD and CD practitioners may be focusing on different types of organizational, sectoral or social systems, and have some differences in terms of the outcomes they are seeking, but there are many opportunities for OD and CD practitioners to open up a fresh conversation about how human interaction can be more thoughtfully linked with social, economic and environmental challenges.

Organization development and capacity development: Towards convergence?

The growing need for whole-systems approaches to change has spawned a number of methodologies, which can be applied equally well to organizations and stakeholders as well as to sectors, communities and societies. Variously known as 'large scale', 'large group', or 'multi-stakeholder' methods, this is a growing body of knowledge and practice committed to involving stakeholders at all levels (particularly the historically disempowered) in decision-making about system change. A key principle of these methodological processes is that participants collectively co-create the future, rather than collectively focusing on how to solve problems that are rooted in the past. Trist et al (1963) and others have carried out ground-breaking work in this area. More recently, Bunker and Alban (2006), as well as Holman and Devane (2007), have synthesized it and brought it together more comprehensively.

Depending on the method, literally hundreds of people can participate in creating the agenda for change. Large Group Methods are now part of the core practice repertoire of many OD and change practitioners, and increasingly part of the repertoire of CD practitioners as well. Many CD and OD practitioners have already developed creative ways of combining and adapting these methods as part of long-range change in complex, multi-actor settings.

While it is not possible to go into detail here, the following are some of the better-known breakthrough methodologies for readers interested in this topic: *Future Search* (Weisbord, 1987*), Whole-Scale Change* (Dannemiller Tyson Associates, 2000)*, Open Space* (Owen, 1997), *World Café* (Brown and Isaacs, 2005) and *Appreciative Inquiry Summit* (Cooperrider et al, 2005, and Ludema et al, 2003). This brief scan of the latest OD/CD approaches indicates that there are more similarities than differences between the two. The work of both types of practitioners increasingly focuses on system abilities, collective capabilities and individual competencies. They are concerned about what is needed to support the system's (or organization's) abilities to endure and perform over the long term. They seek to engender the system's ability to master change and determine its own need and capability to continue to change and adapt. Both CD and OD practitioners' relationships with clients require content expertise, but can also be distinguished by the in-depth knowledge that they bring in the 'participatory how to' or *process* expertise. OD and CD work involves helping organizations define and clarify values and goals, manage and solve problems, make informed decisions and develop and effectively use human resources. In recent years, there has been an increasing and shared concern about fully understanding the unique aspects of the context within which change or capacity development is envisioned, and a shared emphasis on developing integrated and networked ways of working across systems, interests, and narrowly defined ambitions. There are also fresh perspectives developing on how to understand systems better, and what is meant by 'responsible progress', adding for example, ecological and cultural criteria to the elements that must be taken into account in designing and facilitating systems change.

In terms of methodological principles, too, the overall approaches of CD and OD are quite compatible: both work collaboratively with various levels and actors in a system. They emphasize inclusive, democratic processes and are guided by concepts, theories and approaches, drawn from social and behavioural science as well as culture and anthropology. Both OD and CD practitioners maintain a collaborative relationship of relative equality with client organizations, groups and individuals. They work in tandem with a system, acknowledging that the actors in the system possess perspectives, knowledge and skills that are critical to positive change, but that the OD/CD professional brings other perspectives, knowledge and skills that can enrich and support what is being done. Indeed, both types of practitioners are also *participants* and *co-learners* in the process of change. They are face-to-face, and in conversation, with the realities of it.

Implications, trends and future perspectives

There is well-established evidence demonstrating that OD interventions lead to improved organizational effectiveness and health, and facilitate collective problem-solving and the achievement of shared goals by members of an organization. At the same time, critical voices, both in the OD field and outside it, have argued in recent times that due to its relatively narrow focus on a humanist view of change, OD has failed to evolve and to adequately address today's complex and rapidly shifting environments. In order to retain its relevance there are at least two important questions that the field must address (Bradford and Burke, 2005).

- What can OD do in terms of facilitating strategic, scaleable change within complex, interdependent systems (within organizations as well as across organizations, systems and societies more broadly)?
- Where is the evidence that OD interventions contribute to effectiveness? OD

practitioners need to be more rigorous in evaluating change processes and their outcomes.

As we face the challenges of the next decade, there are a number of topics which could form a shared agenda and a new field of convergence between CD and OD. Here are some examples.

- 'Up-scaling' change. What does this mean? How does it work in various contexts? How can societal innovations be accelerated?
- CD/OD practitioners as 'idea' innovators (or social entrepreneurs): what approaches need to be taken to stimulate innovative thinking, discourse, knowledge-creation, social interaction, resource expenditure and allocation, and policy and/or legislation shifts?
- The practitioner as a leader: what are the critical elements of leadership by OD/CD practitioners? Possible components might include questioning the strategic context and/or directions of decision-makers in all sectors at the community/organization level and beyond. Practitioners could also help to identify key innovations at local level and help to promote these to key decision-makers, drawing on their judgement to determine the best approach for this.
- Fostering leadership: What do OD/CD practitioners need to bring in order to enable leaders and other actors and/or stakeholders to address conflict (especially deep-seated values conflicts) productively; take up appropriate roles in various phases and processes of change; and collaborate constructively in networks and other forms of loosely-coupled organizations?
- Developing improved ways of monitoring and measuring change as it happens, to understand who and how much has changed as well as to understand why. Here, capacity development practice already has some notable innovations and approaches that OD could benefit from.

Given the number of complex and intractable issues that need to be addressed on our planet, it is time for these two 'strands' of change practitioners to rediscover their shared interests and skills, and to explore how they can bring their strengths into alignment. The case for coming together is further strengthened by the recognition that sustainable solutions for some of the big issues societies face require more collaboration and innovation across historical boundaries like private, public or civil society. The development sector recognizes this and it opens up new possibilities for OD and CD to learn from each other's experiences and bring their collective experience of these sectors together to support the level of collaboration and innovation required between and across the different organizational types.

Notes

1   The work of Rick James at INTRAC (www.intrac.org) as well as of Allan Kaplan, (www.proteusinitiative.org/ProteusIntro2.aspx), Doug Reeler and others who have been associated with the Community Development Resource Association (www.

cdra.org.za) offer inspirational examples of integrated approaches to organization development, capacity development and social change.

2   A *Gestalt* is a coherent whole; it has its own laws, and is a construct of the individual mind rather than 'reality'. Gestalt theorists were intrigued by the way our mind perceives wholes out of incomplete elements. To Gestaltists, things are affected by where they are and by what surrounds them. Things are described as 'more than the sum of their parts'.

References

Argyris, C. and Schön, D. (1974) *Theory in Practice. Increasing Professional Effectiveness*, Jossey-Bass, San Francisco

Argyris, C., and Schön, D. (1978) *Organisational Learning: A Theory of Action Perspective*, Addison-Wesley, Reading, MA

Beckhard, R. (1969) *Organization Development: Strategies and Models*, Addison-Wesley, Reading, MA

Bradford, D.L. and Burke, W. (2005) *Reinventing Organization Development: New Approaches to Change in Organizations*, Pfeiffer, San Francisco

Brown, J., Isaacs, D., World Café Community and Senge, P. (2005) *The World Café: Shaping our Futures Through Conversations*, Berrett-Koehler, San Francisco

Bunker, B.B. and Alban, B. (2006) *The Handbook of Large Group Methods: Creating Systemic Change in Organizations and Communities*, Jossey Bass, San Francisco

Burke, W. (1982) *Organization Development: Principles and Practices*, Little Brown & Co, Boston, MA

Campbell, D., Coldicott, T. and Kinsella, K. (1994) *Systemic Work with Organizations*, Karnac Books, London

Capra, F. (2002) *The Hidden Connections: A Science for Sustainable Living*, Random House, New York

Carr, W. and Kemmis, S. (1986) *Becoming Critical: Education, Knowledge and Action Research*, Deakin Press, Abingdon

Carter, J.D. (2008) 'Gestalt organization and systems development and OD: A past, present and future perspective', *OD Practitioner*, vol 40, no 4, pp49–51

Checkland, P. and Scholes, J. (1990) *Soft Systems Methodology in Action*, Wiley, New York

Cook, S.D.N. and Yanow, D. (1996) 'Culture and organizational learning', in M.D. Cohen and L.S. Sproull (eds) *Organizational Learning*, Sage, Thousand Oaks, CA

Cooperrider, D.L., Whitney, D. and Stavros, J. M. (2005) *Appreciative Inquiry Handbook*, Berrett-Koehler, San Francisco

Dannemiller Tyson Associates (2000) *Wholescale Change: Unleashing the Magic in Organizations*, Berrett-Koehler, San Francisco

Easterby-Smith, M, Araujo, L. and Burgoyne, J. (eds.) (1999) *Organizational Learning and the Learning Organization*, Sage, London

Hammer, M. and Champy, J. (1993) *Reengineering the Corporation: A Manifesto for Business Revolution*, Harper Business, London

Holman, P. and Devane, T. (eds) (2007) *The Change Handbook: Group Methods for Shaping the Future*, Berrett-Koehler, San Francisco

Granovetter, M.S. (1982) 'The strength of weak ties: A network theory revisited', in P.V. Lave and E. Wenger (1991) *Situated Learning: Legitimate Peripheral Participation*, Cambridge University Press, Cambridge

Ludema, J.D., Whitney, D., Mohr, B.J. and Griffen, T. (2003) *The Appreciative Inquiry Summit: A Practitioner's Guide for Leading Large Group Change*, Berrett-Koehler, San Francisco

Lorenz E. (1993) *The Essence of Chaos*, University of Washington Press, Seattle

Milgram, S. (1967) 'The small world problem', *Psychology Today*, (May), pp60–67

Nevis, E.C. (1997) 'Gestalt therapy and organization development: A historical perspective 1930–1996', *Gestalt Review*, vol 1, no 2, pp110–130

Owen, H. (1997) *Open Space Technology: A User's Guide*, Berrett-Koehler, San Francisco

Palazzoli, M.S., Boscolo, L., Cecchin, G. and Prata, G. (1970) *Paradox and Counterparadox*, Jason Aronson, New York

Popper, K. (1972) 'Of clouds and clocks', in *Objective Knowledge: An Evolutionary Approach*, Clarendon Press, London

Prigogine, I. (1980) *From Being to Becoming*, W.H. Freeman, San Francisco

Schein, E.H. (1992) *Organizational Culture and Leadership*, 2nd edition, Jossey-Bass, San Francisco

Schein, E.H. (2005) 'Organization Development: A Wedding of Anthropology and Organizational Therapy', in D.L. Bradford and W.W. Burke, (eds) *Reinventing Organization Development: Addressing the Crisis, Achieving the Potential*, Pfeiffer, San Francisco

Senge, P. (1990) *The Fifth Discipline: The Art and Practice of the Learning Organization*, Random House, London

SNV (2007) *Strategy Paper 2007–2015, Local Impact – Global Presence*, The Hague, The Netherlands

Trist, E., Higgin, G., Murray, H. and Pollock, A. (1963) *Organizational Choice*, Tavistock, London

Waldrop, M.M. (1992) *Complexity: The Emerging Science at the Edge of Order and Chaos*, Viking, London

Weisbord, M. and Janoff, S. (1995) *Future Search*, Berrett-Koehler, San Francisco

Westley, F., Zimmerman, B. and Patton, M. (2006) *Getting to Maybe*, Random House, Toronto

Wheatley, M.J. (1992) *Leadership and the New Science: Learning about Organization from an Orderly Universe*, Berrett-Koehler, San Francisco

Wilber, K. (1999) *The Collected Works of Ken Wilber: Integral Psychology, Transformations of Consciousness, Selected Essays*, Shambhala, Boston

Recommended readings

This chapter has links to various others in this volume. In particular, it is complemented by Chapters 1, 5 and 24. Chapter 1 introduces the notion of multiple capacities of organizations from two complementary perspectives, while Chapter 5 looks at how practitioners may balance the combination of technical knowledge and change and OD skills needed for effective capacity development work. Chapter 24 explores the future of capacity development as a professional field. For those interested, the following are some of the best readings on OD and its connections to capacity development.

The Barefoot Guide to Working with Organisations and Social Change. (2009)
www.barefootguide.org

This is a practical, do-it-yourself guide for leaders and facilitators wanting to help organizations to function and to develop in more healthy, human and effective ways as they strive to make their contributions to a more humane society. It has been developed by the Barefoot Collective (www.barefootguide. org).

Block, P. (2008) *Community: The Structure of Belonging*, Berrett-Koehler, San Francisco

Block's latest book focuses on direct efforts to bring into conversation those groups of people who are not in relationship with each other. He offers powerful and provocative ideas as well as simple tools and strategies to invite new possibility, accountability and commitment to the work of engaging citizens and their communities.

Westley, F., Zimmerman, B. and Michael Q. Patton (2006) *Getting to Maybe: How the World is Changed*, Random House, Canada

Getting to Maybe applies the insights of complexity theory to specific stories from a wide range of people and organizations – including the micro-credit story of the Grameen Bank, and the efforts of a Canadian clothing designer to help transform the lives of aboriginal women and children. It offers new ways of thinking about making change in communities, in business and in the world.

Gamble, J. J. (2008) *Developmental Evaluation: A Primer*, J.W. McConnell Family Foundation, www.fondationmcconnell.ca/utilisateur/documents/ EN/Initiatives/Sustaining Social Innovation/A Developmental Evaluation Primer - EN.pdf (accessed 27 November 2009)

When both the path and the destination are evolving, how do we evaluate progress? Developmental evaluation is an emerging approach to evaluation, best applied when working in situations of high complexity, and when working on early stage social innovations. Based on the work by Michael Quinn Patton, also worth reading: www.scribd.com/doc/8233067/Michael-Quinn-Patton-Developmental-Evaluation-2006 (accessed 27 November 2009).

Holman, P. and Devane, T. (eds) (2007) *The Change Handbook: Group Methods for Shaping the Future*, Berrett-Koehler, San Francisco

This textbook gives basic descriptions of over 18 different methods for getting many people to collaboratively make a plan for system-wide change in their organization. The language and examples are written mostly from a Western business management perspective, although they do include references and useful insight for community organizations as well.

See also: 'Appreciative Inquiry Commons: A comprehensive listing of publications on Appreciative Inquiry and Positive Change', Sponsored by the Weatherhead School of Management at Case Western Reserve University, http://appreciativeinquiry.case.edu/research/bibPublished.cfm, accessed 27 November 2009.

9

'Reading' Situations

Advisers or change agents always enter and intervene in living dynamic processes. Accordingly, a critical competence is the ability to see and make sense of what is going on in and around a client organization. Organizational assessments are one way of doing this, but they often focus on predefined and rather standard elements of an organization. A different but complementary approach is what is called 'reading situations', that is, to try to discover the story and dynamics of an organization in a more open and creative way.

This chapter by Catherine Collingwood describes how to 'read an organization', with a special focus on understanding the less-visible dynamics that occur within civil society organizations and their contexts. This exploration reveals the limitations of conventional organizational assessment approaches, leading to the conclusion that these may be complemented by 'readings' to unravel the unique context and history of an organization. Finally, Collingwood considers what this approach may mean for practitioners wanting to apply it across different types of organizational settings.

Looking to See the Whole

Catherine Collingwood

The real voyage of discovery consists not in seeking new landscapes but in having new eyes.

(Marcel Proust)

The novel's spirit is the spirit of complexity. Every novel says to the reader 'Things are not as simple as you think'. That is the novel's eternal truth, but it grows steadily harder to hear amongst the din of easy, quick answers that come faster than the question and block it off.

(Milan Kundera, *The Art of the Novel*)

Introduction

The notion of *reading* an organization suggests that organizations are like novels, in the sense that they too have characters, themes and plots. To find the narrative thread running through a novel is no mean feat, however. So, too, is discerning the core purpose and energy threading through an organization. In a novel there is usually a cast of many, who cause and experience the twists and turns of various events and with whom the reader engages to discover the essential message around which all the events swirl. When applied to an organization, this idea of reading reveals otherwise hidden and unarticulated aspects, such as the core messages that lie underneath all the busy activities. Organizational reading also reveals and explores great themes of organizational life like purpose, power, community and leadership. They are intriguing themes, requiring contemplation rather than a simplistic assessment to determine whether the organization meets the standards of what makes a 'good' or a 'bad' organization.

Many capacity-development processes, especially when targeted at organizations, begin with some form of assessment or diagnosis. There are many different methods for conducting organizational assessments and over time, they have evolved to become more and more holistic, but they all involve some way of determining how far the organization meets or falls short of certain performance criteria. They tend to have as a primary objective the identification of gaps in efficiency, or effectiveness in relation to goals and available resources. They generally involve building a picture of an organization by first examining different parts in great detail – for example, structure, finance, human resources, strategy, culture and leadership, and then piecing the information together to come to a judgement or conclusion about how the organization (seen as a sum of its parts) measures up. In addition, many organizational assessment methods involve an external person or team, making sense of the information and inviting the organization to corroborate or validate it.

An organizational reading, by contrast, involves the organization itself in the process of making sense of its own evolution and articulating what emerges as the essence of the organization. It results in a deeper self-knowledge within the organization, with greater confidence to accept both its potential to excel and difficult issues that must be confronted.

Assessing an organization against some agreed benchmarks or criteria for performance is in itself not a bad thing. This chapter does not argue against conventional organizational assessments. It does make the case, though, that they are limited and lead, at best, to a partial understanding of an organization as a dynamic, complex and highly contextual entity. It also makes the case that a different approach, namely 'reading', creates a greater likelihood that the reader and organization members will understand 'the deeper processes of change and adaptation that lie at the heart of the system and how it continues to respond to both internal and external influences. Such an understanding improves the quality of judgement when it comes to asking how the organization can best be helped' (Morgan, 2005).

This chapter offers an approach to organizational reading that enables the practitioner and members of an organization to use multiple lenses to reflect on and apply to the work of reading organizations. The approach consists of a fairly extensive exploration exercise to create an organizational 'biography' and a number of perspectives (lenses) from which the results of the exploration (the biography) may be interpreted or read in order to 'see' the whole organization. From here, it goes on to explore the implications for practitioners.

The art and practice of reading civil society organizations

The chapter focuses on civil society organizations (CSOs) because of the unique role they play in the development and well-being of their communities. Emerging from, and often embedded in, their local communities, CSOs weave and help to hold together the social fabric, providing services, picking up where state or decentralized provision marginalizes or does not cover particular groups, and agitating for change on specific issues of social injustice and inequality. They are also unique because many of them do not start off in a form that fits in with the conventional notion of an organization. They tend to start off informally and often grow into more or less structured entities as they start engaging with different actors and agencies who demand more formality. Formality, structure and form may also develop from expansion and demand for the services a CSO provides. Using CSOs as a backdrop, this chapter demonstrates that a holistic understanding of how a particular organization has come to be where it is – and therefore how it can best be helped – requires more than a seemingly objective 'checklist-based' assessment. It must be stressed, however, that the ability to 'read' situations is equally important when one works with other types of organization.

When reading civil society organizations, we are not simply assessing an organization in relation to its ability to manage particular projects but reading a complex and unique phenomenon. Reading involves looking at organizations as organic and alive, rather than inert vehicles for delivering particular services or projects. To illustrate the difference between looking at organizations as inert vehicles and looking at them as organic phenomena, Table 9.1 below describes the different responses or understandings that each way of looking might generate. It demonstrates that the view one takes of an organization directly informs the resulting assessment one makes of that organization's capacity and consequently how it can be helped to develop.

Facilitating an organizational biography: A sense of history and how the present came to be

The complexity and uniqueness of organizations means that one cannot use one model or frame to carry out an effective reading. We need rather to draw on an approach that uses as many angles or perspectives as possible. This involves

Table 9.1 *Assessing the capacity of an inert and a living phenomenon*

Assessing a vehicle (an inert object)	Assessing an organization as if it were a vehicle (an inert object)	Assessing a plant (a living being)	Assessing an organization as if it were a plant (a living being)
Does the clutch work?	Is the HR system functioning effectively?	What is dying and what is coming to life on this plant?	How vital is this organization?
What makes this car go?	What is driving this organization?	What is sustaining this plant?	What is keeping this organization alive?
Who is driving this car?	Who is leading this organization?	Is this plant at seed, sapling or flowering phase?	At what phase of leadership development is this organization?
How old is this car?	How old is this organization?	How deep are the roots of this plant?	How strongly rooted is this organization in its landscape?

Source: based on Patton, 2003, Guijt, 2008, and Rogers, 2008

rigorous reflection and observational processes that the practitioner undertakes together with the members of the organization that is being 'read'. The character, including the capacity and flaws of the organization, emerges through this process as the practitioner helps members of the organization to make a collective sense of the insights generated. Understanding how things came to be, what choices were made and how that influenced direction and action, helps the organization to move forward from a position of self acceptance to one of self awareness.

An organizational biography process is one where all members contribute their knowledge and experiences of the major milestones in the organization's development. This process can support an organization to connect with its founding vision and character, and help to explain how subsequent chapters of its story came to be. It is a valuable way of understanding the present.

An organizational biography may simply consist of a chronology of events where each individual or small group is assigned a time period and asked to list the internal and contextual events in those years on cards. The cards are then put up in chronological order on the wall. It may also be done through a reminiscence of turning points where each individual or small group is asked to recall what they believe was pivotal for change. It may also be a chronicle: an account of 'turning points' where each individual or small group is asked to remember significant moments in the organization's history. The facilitator may consider dividing the group up to work simultaneously on chronology and turning points. The results – each event or moment – are then written on cards and added to the timeline on the wall. In this way you would have both a list of events (everything that can be remembered) as well as moments in the organization considered as being particularly meaningful. Two visual images may be generated from these separate or combined exercises: a 'river' of significant organizational moments and shifts as well as a timeline of organizational events (Figure 9.1 and 9.2 respectively).[1]

Source: N.D. Mazin

Figure 9.1 *River of life: Example of an organizational chronicle*

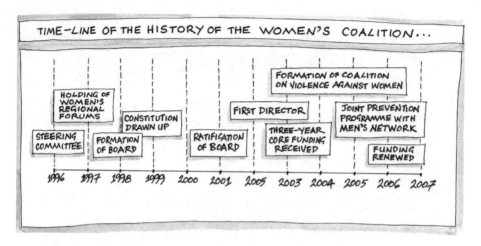

TIME-LINE OF THE HISTORY OF THE WOMEN'S COALITION...

FORMATION OF COALITION ON VIOLENCE AGAINST WOMEN

HOLDING OF WOMEN'S REGIONAL FORUMS

CONSTITUTION DRAWN UP

FIRST DIRECTOR

JOINT PREVENTION PROGRAMME WITH MEN'S NETWORK

STEERING COMMITTEE

FORMATION OF BOARD

RATIFICATION OF BOARD

THREE-YEAR CORE FUNDING RECEIVED

FUNDING RENEWED

1996 1997 1998 1999 2000 2001 2005 2003 2004 2005 2006 2007

Source: N.D. Mazin

Figure 9.2 *Timeline of organizational events: Example of a chronology*

A clear *narrative thread* of the organization may emerge through such an exercise as recurring patterns become apparent through a reading of milestones.

Phases of organizational development

One helpful model distinguishes three main development phases of an organization: Pioneer, Differentiated and Integrated. The three phases are illustrated in Figure 9.3.

Pioneer phase
In many civil society organizations, this phase is characterized by a small number of people relating informally, driven by a shared vision for change and inspired by a strong founder and dependent on him or her to give direction.

Differentiated phase
This phase is often triggered by the growth of the organization, in response to demand for its services and the inevitable need for more formal systems and role clarification. At this point, the staff members have more independence and are guided by their particular job descriptions and organizational policies rather than relying on the discernment of the founder for every decision. It is at this phase that the scope of work may be further differentiated into programmes or services. Each of these programmes is usually overseen by a manager and so the structure of the organization becomes more hierarchical. This second phase may reach a crisis when too much specialization and differentiation leads to a sense that things are fragmented and staff realize that they have lost sight of the original purpose of the organization.

Integrated phase

The final phase in this model emerges as the organization begins to connect the different parts of itself more consciously by forming teams around common tasks and spreading leadership for different parts of organizational life and programme work. The members begin to relate to one another interdependently, bound more by a common vision than by a set of rules and regulations.

Interpreting the narrative of an organization in terms of its phases of development can help us to gain deeper insights about the capacities it may need either to reach the milestones necessary to fully move through that phase, or to abandon one phase altogether to move on to the next. Here, 'crisis' is read as a sign of an imminent growth surge instead of a problem to be eliminated or solved although there may well be problems to deal with as part of this growth and development.

Organizational aspects revealed by a biographical exercise

We now consider some aspects of organization that may be revealed or 'seen' through a biographical exercise. These are: sovereignty, resilience, leadership and the organization's relationship with its external environment. Each of these aspects may be better understood if examined in terms of the particular phase of development the CSO is at.

Sovereignty

By identifying and confirming their narrative, members of an organization may come to see themselves more clearly as a collective with a consistent message and mission, expressed in a way that is unique to them. It may help an organization to shift away from a narrow self-perception as a 'vehicle' for projects and better appreciate the projects they undertake, as a means to a higher end – their mission or purpose as a collective and not simply as an implementing entity. This contributes to what may be referred to as the organization's sense of 'sovereignty'. Sovereignty in a CSO is its sense of self-reliance and local ownership; decision-making out of consciousness and free choice; and freedom from outside interference, domination or exploitation.

'Sovereignty has to do with the "deeper" capacity that forms at the core of the system – its ability to bring about its own transformation, to engage the energy and commitment of its own staff, to reflect and learn, to maintain its own integrity, and to treat itself as a human community' (Morgan, 2005, p18).

The Community Development Resource Association (CDRA), South Africa, considers the following factors to be important in determining the degree to which an organization is sovereign (Reeler, 2008):

- the extent to which there is a home-grown resilience and an 'inside–out' identity;
- the extent to which the organization is an expression of the free will of its constituents; and
- the extent to which the organization is open to collaboration, support and solidarity.

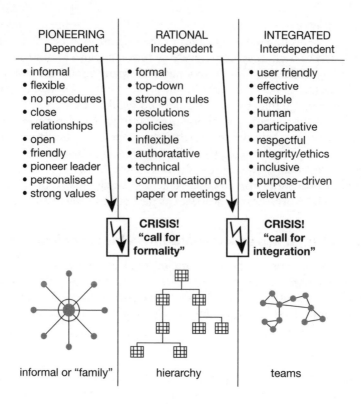

Figure 9.3 *Phases of organizational development*

The notion of sovereignty is important in a reading of civil society organizations which often start up as a small collective usually with a strong and central leader or leaders, driven by a desire to change a particular situation of social injustice, lack of access to basic services or to advocate for the needs of a marginalized group to be recognized or better met. This is the 'inside–out' identity referred to by Reeler, above. As time goes on CSOs acquire more 'conventional' features of organization, often in response to pressure from potential funders and the legal framework needed to operate. The initial energy that drove everything they did may come under quite some pressure and the organization may find itself responding to external influences and actors for pragmatic reasons of survival. Maintaining sovereignty and ensuring organizational choices are congruent with what members believe they are working for, requires conscious effort and critical reflection from time to time. Factors that may make it difficult for CSOs to hold this balance include:

- constant pressure to raise funds for organizational survival rather than to invest in innovation for better impact;
- internal monitoring processes that become routine and tend to serve funders' demands for reports. They do not sufficiently link the organization's activities to its overall purpose and intended impact;

Figure 9.4 *Key stages of organizational positioning*

- rushing from one deliverable project to the next without taking time to reflect on the significance of the organization's interventions.

The authentic voice of the organization may thus become trapped under all the entrenched practices that it has adopted over time in order to survive, which no one enjoys but which are difficult to shake off. In such contexts, an organizational biography process can help the 'reader' to understand how the events in an organization's life – and its response to them – have shaped its identity, and particularly how past choices have led to the organization's positioning in this broader context.

Resilience

Another dimension that may be revealed through an organizational biography is the CSO's *resilience*. Identifying significant moments in the organization's history can help participants in the exercise to gain a sense of its strength and the flexibility of its 'backbone'. Organizational resilience is sometimes a defensive response to challenges, not drawn on to expand its options in the world but rather to stave off perceived threats to its existence. The quality of resilience mentioned here refers to an organization's ability to generate options for itself when faced with challenging situations and come through on the other side. It is about the organization's ability to weather periods of crisis, be they internally or externally triggered.

Leadership

The organizational biography may also throw light on the nature of leadership issues that may have emerged from the narrative. Complaints about 'the difficult leader' or 'staff who do not want to take responsibility' are familiar. The type of leadership (and followership) being experienced will be strongly influenced by where the organization is in its development.

For example, the concentration of leadership in one person lessens from the end of the pioneer phase onwards. In the pioneer phase, leadership, typically direction setting and decision-making about strategy and operations, is concentrated in one person. In the differentiated phase, authority for some decision-making is decentralized to various managers, although it still defers to the top for final decisions that affect the whole organization. In the final, integrated phase, the organogram becomes more flexible and may begin to resemble a network rather than a hierarchy, with staff from across the organization forming teams to undertake certain time-limited tasks or to fulfil certain organizational mandates for a time with some degree of self-leadership or decision-making power.

Gaining an understanding of the dilemmas of the leadership and how the organization is dealing with them will give insights about the extent to which the organization is moving in a healthy direction, or is stuck in a rut. It is also an opportunity for the leader to gain a broader perspective on the impact of his or her leadership approach and what this means for the organization.

Reading the leader's influence on the organization is a delicate matter requiring respect – and sometimes respectful battle – as the practitioner shares insights and observations and helps the organization members to articulate their experiences and feedback.

Relationship with context

The biography reveals both the dynamics within the organization and those between it and its world or context. It has to do with how an organization relates to and is perceived by the variety of actors and stakeholders who are relevant to its purpose and mission. It is also about how the organization has responded to events and trends in its environment, consciously or unconsciously. Of particular importance is the pattern around what an organization or CSO says to itself internally and what it actually does or is perceived to do from the outside. Practitioner and CSO members are required to adopt a systems-thinking perspective – perhaps in the way that we might study a living organism like a plant or animal in order to understand how it both adapts and is adapted by its environment.

The narrative will shed light on the organization as a relational being. This is different from analysing each of the different relationships an organization may have. It has more to do with how the organization 'sits' within a particular environment of forces, trends, opportunities – and other organizations. It is also about clarifying the specific intention of the organization in its context and how this comes across to others. What is the nature of the space that the organization occupies in this context? What does it bring to this space? What unique role, if any, does it play in the complex web of relationships that exist there? This is not a definitive list but an attempt to describe the message that the organization sends to the world about itself.

Finally, practitioner and organization may stand back and try to describe a coherent story of the organization as a purposeful being. The idea is to look for and articulate the essence of the organization – the creative idea or force underlying the very being of the organization. Depending on how thoroughly or intensively the biography exercise has been done, there will be some convergence in the group about what this essence of the organization could be. This is at once extremely simple and difficult, because the essential character and contribution is not one activity that best represents what the organization is about, but rather the idea or energy which drives the organization. When there is convergence on this, it is crystal clear to all present. When there is not, it is almost impossible to generate it from outside the group.

Practitioners of this approach will say that this last insight may not emerge at all. If it does, it is a gift. As Peter Morgan says,

> Knowledge can come from an analysis of the parts. But understanding comes from synthesis. There is a risk that people will begin to treat emergent properties as discrete elements or parts. This will return the process to fragmentation from a place of synthesis and result in the loss of attention to the whole. But a full understanding of the whole escapes us. It will always be partial and subjective. (Morgan, 2005, p12)

Implications for practitioner stance and capabilities

To develop and hone the ability to see in 'wholes', a practitioner first needs to be able to listen and observe deeply. Listening for the core message of the organization and its identity, rather than measuring the fitness of its parts, is what is required of us if we want to help organizations to develop their adaptive capacities. Listening and observing deeply helps a practitioner to identify patterns in an organization's narrative, guide members to those issues that may need further exploration and encourage them to confront issues that seem to be glossed over as the story unfolds.

There are different ways in which a capacity-development practitioner may develop the capacity to see and listen in this way. One of them is by writing reflectively; 'writing is thinking on the page' (Schuster, 2009). As we write, our own practice and authorship as facilitators becomes clearer to us. As we describe the organizations we support on the page, we start to gain some perspective, to be able to differentiate between them as autonomous organisms and ourselves as interveners. We become more aware of where our ideals are obscuring what may be best for that organization. We also begin to *experience* 'emergence' through our own creative process of writing – what we eventually end up with comes after many iterations. When we experience this capacity to write developing in ourselves and accept the uncertainty and discomfort of this process, it becomes a little easier to facilitate learning around emergent processes with others.

Facilitation is an obvious skill required for many capacity-development processes. But a systems-thinking or emergent approach to reading organizations and supporting others to do so requires particular facilitation ability – the ability to 'portray' instead of 'explain'. Instead of a practitioner explaining what he or she has discovered about an organization to its members, an ability to portray means he or she finds ways of letting people experience actual reading and makes the process by which greater understanding and insights emerge quite explicit.

Conclusion

A co-creative reading of all types of organizations is engrossing and absorbing – just like a good book! Reading an organization is best done in a co-created manner, where the organization reads as much of itself as possible and where the perspective, questions and *way of seeing* that the practitioner brings enables an organization to appreciate its own complexity. Bringing a range of angles to the task ensures that a dynamic view of the organization will emerge and that the living essence of the organization will be respected.

Antoni Gaudi touched on this notion of the living essence at the heart of all social endeavours when he wrote of his participation in the development of La Sagrada Familia in Barcelona (the expiatory church now 127 years old and still being built with funds drawn entirely from donations – therefore developing through the voluntary action of citizens):

> There is no reason to regret that I cannot finish the Church. I will grow old but others will come after me. What will always be conserved is the spirit of the work, but its life has to depend on the generations it is handed down to and with whom it lives and is incarnated.

In relation to CSOs the key question is why a reading approach is particularly pertinent and what this means for capacity-development processes. It is because CSOs are embedded in and responsive to dynamic social and community settings. They develop many informal and often intangible ways of getting things done, making judgements about when to intervene, working with and around other complex social structures and cultural practices, and influencing and making change happen in small but significant ways. Their processes, their achievements and the forces that come together to bring these about are often not visible when measured against a checklist of whether they have certain organizational parts working as expected. Often, such expectations are set by external parties like donors, local government, international NGOs who work with them as so-called partners, and so on. A reading approach may help to make these complex processes and abilities of CSOs more visible and understood by both themselves and the parties who are interested in helping them perform better. More intelligent judgements might then be made about the capacity development of this unique group of development actors.

In applying a 'reading approach' to other organizations, practitioners will need to explore and respond to the specific relationship that the organization and its type has to its context and how its evolution has contributed to what it currently is. The story is never standard: each organization is uniquely individual though it may share common elements and trends with others similar to itself.

Note

1   All drawings used in this chapter have been kindly provided by N.D. Mazin, Social Change Communicator based in Cape Town, South Africa.

References

Guijt, I. (2008) *A Word about 'Complexity' to Locate the Work on 'Right to be Heard'*, Learning by Design, Randwijk, The Netherlands

Morgan, P. (2005) *The Idea and Practice of Systems Thinking and their Relevance for Capacity Development*, European Centre for Development Policy Management, Maastricht, The Netherlands.

Patton M.Q. (2003) 'Qualitative evaluation checklist', The Evaluation Centre, Western Michigan University, Evaluation Checklist Project

Reeler, D. (2008) 'Shaping our world: Making a case for sovereign local organizations and social movements', Paper presented at INTRAC Conference, UK

Rogers, P. J (2008) 'Using programme theory to evaluate complicated and complex aspects of interventions', *Evaluation*, vol 14, no 1, pp29–48

Schuster, A. (2009) 'Moments of Being', Creative Writing Course, Cape Town

Taylor, J. (2009) *Organizations – The Melting Pots of Social Change*, The Barefoot Guide to Working with Organizations and Social Change, www.barefootguide. org

Recommended readings

There are links between this chapter and Chapter 1 on the issue of multiple perspectives. Readers will also be interested in Chapter 8, which provides a broad overview of the field of organizational development and Chapter 15, looking at the unique position and potential of civil society organizations in development. For those who want to explore this topic further, the following are some additional readings.

Shaw, P. (2002) *Changing Conversations in Organizations: A Complexity Approach to Change,* Routledge, London

This book portrays a methodology for working with complexity. Through the stories Patricia tells of her encounters (specifically *conversations* and not structured engagements) with organizations, the reader can grasp what it means to practise, not only theorize from, a complexity perspective.

The Barefoot Guide is a practical, do-it-yourself guide for leaders and facilitators wanting to help organizations to function and to develop in more healthy, human and effective ways as they strive to make their contributions to a more humane society. It is freely downloadable on www.barefootguide.org. This is a good resource for understanding organizations as complex organisms and contains diagnostic tools as well as appealing cartoon illustrations.

Soal, S. (2004) *Holding Infinity - Guiding Social Process: A Workbook for Development Practitioners,* Community Development Resource Association, Cape Town, South Africa

This guidebook provides facilitation process outlines for use in diverse unique situations. The processes are all designed to allow for emergent and unfolding, rather than predictable, change.

Morgan, G. (1986) *Images of Organization,* Sage, Beverly Hills, CA

A classic text that is still highly relevant today. Morgan introduces different ways of seeing organizations and stimulates critical reflection on what we think organizations are, how they work, and why.

10

Dialogue

Dialogue is an essential ingredient of any intervention directed at changing a situation and is a vital competence for any adviser. While it is not easy to facilitate true dialogue, it is a capability that can be developed in its own right. Real dialogue can create collectively shared and owned understanding and an agreed direction of effort as well as clarity about divisions of tasks and responsibilities.

This chapter by Marianne Mille Bojer reviews factors critical to the success of capacity-development processes that use dialogue as a key philosophy. Her excellent menu of dialogue tools and approaches shows the reader what is on offer and how to choose between them. She also provides concrete examples of how some of these methods have been used.

The Place of Dialogue in Capacity Development

Marianne Mille Bojer

Introduction

Dialogue is an essential ingredient of successful capacity development interventions. The intention of this chapter is to explore the power of dialogue in supporting sustainable change, to look at some of the critical elements of effective dialogue processes, and to offer a menu of possible dialogue tools and approaches for practitioners to draw on.

Dialogue is essentially a practice and discipline of *creative* conversation. The word 'dialogue' is often used very loosely to denote any kind of conversation between two or more people. At the same time, we often hear people making statements like 'that was not a real dialogue'. This is usually because the conversation was not participative and creative, but rather a competition between points of view, or simply a transfer of knowledge from one actor to others. What makes a dialogue *real* is the emphasis on listening, questioning and thinking together that makes it a genuinely creative process.

In 2007, I was invited to work with my colleague Busi Dlamini on a capacity development programme in Alexandra township in South Africa. Our partner organization had noticed that there were many good community-based service providers, but that they were duplicating services, rarely collaborating, and not managing to refer people on to each other where necessary. During the first workshop, we explored with the group what capacity means and what capacities the programme was intending to build. What emerged was that the most crucial capacities the group needed were the capacity to collaborate with one another, and the *capacity to build their own capacity*. Both of these objectives became central to the process over the ensuing months. Neither was about pre-defined skills that could be trained but rather about collective results that could only be reached through an emergent and experiential group process with continuous dialogue. The experience greatly deepened our understanding of community capacity and the importance of dialogue as an essential ingredient.

There are a number of reasons why facilitated dialogue is such an essential ingredient of any intervention designed to increase the power of a social system – any inter-dependent web of actors, be it an organization, a sector, a multi-stakeholder team, or a community – to perform, sustain and self-renew. Dialogue enables the system to *perform* because it generates *movement*. Often groups or collective efforts get stuck because they have lost sight of where they are going; roles and responsibilities are not clearly defined or fairly distributed; or underlying relational dynamics are getting in the way of taking decisions. Dialogue processes can enhance shared and collectively owned vision, purpose and direction, as well as role clarity, and the ability to take decisions, thus releasing energy to perform.

Dialogue enables the system to *sustain* itself because it generates *health*. A system may be unhealthy and therefore unsustainable if it is fragmented because its different parts are not communicating with one another; if people are afraid of contributing or saying what they think; or if conflicts and tensions are consistently brushed under the carpet. As participants in a dialogue process listen to one another, the process increases trust, openness, connectivity and understanding, and participants learn how to resolve conflicts. This value is something that may be difficult to measure and is not necessarily about transfer of knowledge or practical skills, rather about the more intangible but extremely influential field of relationships.

Finally, dialogue enables the system to *self-renew* because it generates *learning* and *creativity*. It creates spaces for the system to see itself, its strengths and weaknesses, and its context more clearly. It can create opportunities to pay attention and learn from past experiences and opens space for the diversity of voices, including the younger or less powerful ones, to be heard and harnessed, thus creating new paths that weren't apparent before.

It is important to understand that in relation to capacity development, dialogue is both process and substance. This means that a capacity development intervention will be far more successful and sustainable in its impact if the facilitator manages not only to create dialogue and apply dialogue methods *during* the intervention, but also to embed dialogue practices that are relatively easy for the system to *continue* applying after the intervention. So the intervention must not only use dialogue in its approach but also include dialogue in the capacities to be developed. This can be done by explicitly articulating what is going on when dialogue capacities are being worked on, creating time for reflection on how these capacities and processes may be useful to the group beyond the current intervention, and allowing participants to take over the process and facilitate themselves at times while the facilitator plays more of a coaching role, providing supervision and feedback.

Critical elements of successful dialogue programmes

Fortunately, a vast and rapidly increasing number of dialogue tools, handbooks and case studies are available to practitioners seeking to increase their emphasis on dialogue in capacity development. This chapter gives just a taste of these approaches. Each one has its own set of guidelines and underlying principles and specific types of situations in which it is most helpful. Regardless of the specific choice of tools or methods in a given situation, though, there are certain critical ingredients to the success of any dialogue intervention. These include:

- clarity of purpose;
- alignment of purpose, people, and process;
- good questions;
- safe space;
- competent, helpful and empowering facilitation.

Clarity of purpose

In designing and facilitating a dialogue intervention, it is important to be clear, thoughtful and transparent about the intention: the answer to the question 'why are we here?' This answer helps to identify the appropriate methods to apply and process to follow, and it helps participants to feel safe to open up to one another and move into uncharted territory.

Alignment of purpose, people, and process

The three core design questions to answer are the why, who and how of the process. It is important that these three are aligned; they are based on the questions of purpose, who needs to participate, and what process we should follow. For the intervention to be effective these three questions need to be answered together, so we do not end up with a beautiful purpose and process but the 'wrong people' in the room. Once the people are in the room, it makes sense to adjust purpose and process if necessary to fit the people we have to work with. This may seem obvious, but it is a common limiting factor to success.

Good questions

Strong questions provide fuel to a dialogue process. They need to be questions that are relevant to those involved, that cannot be answered by one expert and therefore require collective attention, and that are formulated in such a way that they energize the participants, encourage their curiosity and open up their thinking.

Safe space

In order for participants to engage in a truly creative conversation, they will need to acknowledge what they don't know, which in many cases makes people feel vulnerable. The safe space that allows people to be vulnerable and engage with not-knowing depends on clear communication about the purpose and principles of the process, on the 'groundedness' of the facilitator, and on the culture the group is able to create together. In most cases, it's useful for the group to create 'ground rules' or principles together, so they can voice what they need in order to feel safe.

Competent, helpful and empowering facilitation

Given that dialogue is generally not the normal way of working for most groups, the role of the facilitator becomes extremely important in holding the space and the process that allows people to shift into a more collaborative and creative way of operating. The facilitator affects the group in many visible and invisible ways. Important qualities of the facilitator include: strong listening skills, a sense of service, flexibility and responsiveness without losing track of the purpose, self-awareness and authenticity, asking good questions, and the ability to empower the group.

A brief menu of dialogic tools and approaches

The variety of tools, methods and approaches to assist in creating successful dialogue interventions has proliferated over the past 20 years or so. What most if not all the creators of these approaches have in common is an awareness that traditional models of training and of hosting conferences and meetings have not managed to generate systemic changes where needed. All of these approaches help groups to solve their problems and develop more from within, in ways that make sense to the people participating, build bridges among diverse players, and build capacity of the systems involved. Here is a taste of some of these approaches.

Appreciative Inquiry

Appreciative Inquiry is a methodology and process that focuses on identifying the best of what is already there in a system, and finding ways to grow and support that, thus engaging 'possibility thinking' instead of 'deficit thinking'. The Appreciative Inquiry work can be used in shorter- or longer-term interventions. It includes specific methods for stakeholder interviewing, conference designs and community organizing. It is particularly powerful in situations where people are focusing too much on deficiencies and need to wake up to their strengths and potential (http://appreciativeinquiry.case.edu).

Change Lab

The Change Lab is a holistic approach to working with multi-stakeholder (usually cross-sector) groups to create transformation in a given system. In the change lab, participants gain a whole-system perspective, clarify their roles and commitments to addressing systemic challenges, build new partnerships, and design and incubate creative solutions. Through the process, the Change Lab builds leadership, relationships and capacities. One of its strengths is that it follows through to the action stage, rather than finishing at the point of ideas. The Change Lab approach is specifically designed to address complex, social challenges that no one actor can resolve on her or his own and usually runs over several months or years (www.reospartners.com).

Circle

There are many variations on Circle dialogue practices, but generally they are based on a recognition that sitting in a dialogue circle helps to level power structures, distribute leadership and responsibility, and support listening, questioning and sharing. Sometimes a talking piece is used – an object passed around the circle or back and forth between participants to help with the flow of meaning, which can be very helpful especially to invite more silent voices to speak. The Circle is rooted in ancient practices, and is particularly useful when a group needs to slow down to really listen and think together, develop shared vision, and in situations where a few voices otherwise become dominant (www.peerspirit.com).

Deep Democracy

Deep Democracy is rooted in process-orientated psychology, and is based on the idea that a system is unhealthy if roles are 'stuck', and if minority voices are not being expressed. If a few people are holding on to certain positions, opinions or emotions on behalf of the whole group, or if conflicts are being suppressed under the surface, it is difficult for the system to grow. The role of the facilitator is to help make roles in the system more fluid, and to help the system become more aware of itself and its wisdom. Because this role is very challenging, it is generally important to have a trained Deep Democracy facilitator. Deep Democracy includes methods for decision-making, awareness-raising and conflict resolution. It can help release energy in situations where difficult things are going unspoken and blocking a system from moving forward (www.deep-democracy.net).

Dialogue Interviewing

The dialogue interview is a form of stakeholder interviewing that is not based on a set of fixed questions but rather takes the form of a dialogue in the sense that the interviewer's questions follow the energy and content of the interviewee's story. The dialogue interview is not purely about data collection, but also about building a relationship between the interviewer (the intervener) and the interviewee, and about generating motivation and insight for a collective project. It is particularly useful at the beginning of an intervention as a way of designing in a context-sensitive and flexible way and as a way of building energy and finding allies for the process (www.presencing.com/tools).

Dynamic Facilitation

Dynamic Facilitation is a facilitation technique whereby the facilitator follows the natural dynamic flow of the conversation, rather than trying to direct it. It is aimed at facilitating a co-creative process by inviting in the group energy and allowing it to flow. A key feature of the approach is the use of four flipcharts – for problems, solutions, concerns and data. The facilitator uses these four areas to guide the group in creating a common picture of their situation and their proposals for change. This is a highly creative process that requires an active facilitator and a pre-existing group energy (www.tobe.net).

Future Search

A Future Search is a structured process designed to work with stakeholders on a given theme to look at the past and the present, and to design the future. It works on the principle of getting the 'whole system' represented in the room. The process moves from story-telling about the past through mapping current trends, stakeholder groups owning their actions, developing ideal future scenarios, identifying common ground and planning actions. The historic perspective, the emphasis on stories, and the use of visuals in Future Search are particularly helpful in working with local communities that have a common history and need to move towards a common future (www.futuresearch.net).

Open Space

Open Space is a simple and easy to apply process that allows a group to create its own agenda and enables participants to self-organize around the topics they are passionate about and willing to take responsibility for. It helps a group move forward quickly when passion and engagement are present. While it doesn't necessarily guarantee dialogue, it does tend to lead to highly creative conversations because of the emphasis on people taking responsibility for their own learning and ideas (www.openspaceworld.org).

Scenario Development

Scenario Development processes enable groups of people to create possible pictures of their shared future. The scenarios enable participants to think deeply about their context and to challenge their assumptions and mental models about the world. Scenario processes always create multiple pictures of the future, and as such help to create choices that make sense within multiple possibilities and so create more resilient systems. It is very useful in situations of high complexity, where a longer-term perspective is required, and where there is uncertainty about how the context will affect the system. (See for example, www.gbn.com/about/scenario_planning.php.)

Story Dialogue

Story-telling is an under-utilized but powerful tool in encouraging dialogue. Story Dialogue uses stories as a way to bridge theory and reality and to recognize the expertise that is present in people's lived experience. In this approach, participants are invited to tell their stories around a particular theme, and then to identify connections and differences across their stories. The ensuing dialogue is based on the questions:

- 'what?' (what was the story?);
- 'why?' (why did events in the story happen as they did?);
- 'now what?' (what are our insights?); and
- 'so what?' (what are we going to do about it?).

This approach is powerful for creating shared understanding, relationships and a sense of grounding for change initiatives (www.evaluationtrust.org/tools).

World Café

The World Café is a methodology that allows even large groups of people to have in-depth dialogues about certain questions, and to network the emerging ideas. The room is set up like a café with small tables, each for four participants. After a first round of dialogue on a certain topic, participants are asked to move to new tables and make linkages between the conversations, while one table host stays behind at each table to represent the previous conversation. The World Café is designed to bring out the collective wisdom of the group. Its success depends on the facilitators designing strong questions and a safe and hospitable space, and supporting mutual listening and a spirit of inquiry. It is a strong dialogue tool especially helpful to engage large groups of people, open up possibilities, equalize power structures, and identify emerging patterns among ideas (www.theworldcafe.org).

Several handbooks are available and referenced in the key references section of this chapter which give much more detailed suggestions on the strengths and limitations of each of the tools mentioned here as well as many others.

Choosing dialogue methods

If there are so many diverse methods and approaches available, how does one go about deciding which one to apply in a given situation? None of these methods are recipes that should be applied universally. As stated earlier, dialogue is both process and substance in this field, and so it is helpful to use a creative and dialogue-based approach to designing the dialogue intervention itself. Any longer-term intervention for capacity development will most likely combine several different dialogue methods at different stages.

The ability to assess the relevance of different methods for different situations depends primarily on an understanding of several factors. First, what is the purpose of the intervention? Is it primarily to share knowledge and build relationships, is it to create shared vision, develop strategies, and take decisions, or is it to resolve conflicts and solve problems? Second, what is the context of the intervention? Is it dealing with a highly complex problem, with severe power imbalances, with high diversity or with high levels of conflict? Third, who are the people and/or the stakeholders that need to be involved in order to meet the purpose? And finally, what is our capacity as facilitators? What do we have the competencies and resources to do?

One practice that can be extremely helpful in this upfront reflection on choice of approaches is to engage in dialogue interviews with participants. This serves multiple purposes. It helps the facilitators or interveners to deepen their answers to the above questions, but it also develops allies and creates an early sense for participants that this process will be different and that they will be listened to, which means they take part in the dialogues with a more open approach.

To give an example, in the capacity-building programme mentioned earlier in Alexandra, we applied a number of these methods over the course of the intervention. We drew much inspiration from the Change Lab process in designing the overall flow. We used Appreciative Inquiry early on in the process to uncover the community's assets, as the group was too focused on deficiencies and not on their own strengths. We facilitated a process whereby participants did Dialogue Interviews with each other to create understanding and build relationships around their visions. We drew on a scenario project that had been done previously for the HIV/AIDS situation in South Africa as well as some creative visioning exercises to develop a long-term perspective, nurture a sense of unity, and make apparent the importance of choices made today. We frequently sat in Circle Dialogue to check-in with the group and get every voice into the room, as it was a group with an unbalanced power structure. We used the World Café at different stages when we needed to create shared meaning while ensuring everyone was participating. And in the final workshop, when it turned out that a underlying conflict was preventing the group from really getting to action, we facilitated a Deep Democracy conflict, in which group members got so engaged until 10.00pm that they forfeited watching South Africa win the World Cup in rugby! The next day one of the participants said, 'I thought conflict was about fighting, now I know it's a way to cross the bridge'.

The capacities developed in this intervention were not possible to predict exactly from the outset. Through a process of dialogue and collaboration over four months, we uncovered the capacities being developed. At several checkpoints, we asked the group to talk in small groups and name what capacities they felt they were developing, and at times we were surprised by the answers.

When choosing to engage with dialogue methods, it's important to realize that everyone changes through these processes, including the facilitators, donors and organizers. It's a different type of posture from much of traditional development work, which focuses on the problems outside us. Sometimes it's difficult and requires courage to hear what people truly have to say, and sometimes it requires acknowledging that we ourselves are a part of what needs to change. With these more emergent approaches it becomes harder to predict results, and at the same time we are consistently surprised by the unplanned positive outcomes. We need to be open, agile and willing to change our plans, allowing the collective process to unfold together with the participants.

Figures 10.1 and 10.2 *Dialogue processes in Alexandra township*

I once read in a recipe book a quote by one of France's most famous pastry chefs, who said if he could trade everything he knows about pastries for everything he does not, he would do so in an instant. My sense of the development field is similar – that what we do not know dwarfs what we do know. I think this is a healthy attitude with which to enter any dialogue-based capacity-building intervention: with a respect for, and an artist's approach to, the methods we bring in our backpack combined with an infinite curiosity about what we are about to learn.

References

Bojer, M.M., Roehl, H., Knuth, M. and Magner, C. (2008) *Mapping Dialogue*, Taos Institute Publications, Chagrin Falls, OH

Brown, J. and Isaacs, D. (2005) *The World Café: Shaping Our Futures through Conversations that Matter,* Berrett-Koehler, San Francisco

Cooperrider, D., Whitney, D. and Stavros, J. (2007) *Appreciative Inquiry Handbook*, Lakeshore Communications

Holman, P., Devane, T. and Cady, S. (eds) (2007) *The Change Handbook: The Definitive Resource on Today's Best Methods for Engaging Whole Systems,* Berrett-Koehler, San Francisco

Owen, H. (1997) *Open Space Technology: A User's Guide*, Berrett-Koehler, San Francisco

Weisbord, M. and Janoff, S. (1995, 2000) *Future Search: An Action Guide to Finding Common Ground in Organizations and Communities,* Berrett-Koehler, San Francisco

Recommended readings

Many chapters in this volume touch on issues and situations that call for more or better quality dialogue. Readers are invited to look particularly at Chapters 2 and 6, which identify different actors and stakeholders with competing or conflicting interests that need to be aligned in capacity development processes. Dialogue has much to offer in these situations. Another topic of interest is found in Chapter 7 where the question of values and how this may play out in CD practice is explored. All chapters in Part III have important dialogue components. Finally Chapter 22, in taking stock of the whole volume, looks at the implications of the topics treated here, for practitioner capabilities and competencies. For further readings on topics related to dialogue as method, the following may be helpful.

Peggy Holman, Tom Devane and Steven Cady (2007) *The Change Handbook: The Definitive Resource to Today's Best Methods for Engaging Whole Systems*, Berrett-Koehler, San Francisco

A wonderful resource for practitioners who want to increase their repertoire of methods and ways of engaging large groups. It provides a background to the different approaches and for each one, practitioners are guided through how to prepare and adapt to suit the situation they are faced with.

Adam Kahane (2004) *Solving Tough Problems: An Open Way of Talking, Listening and Creating New Realities*, Berrett-Koehler, San Francisco

This is a lively and readable account of rich experiences from all over the globe, through which Kahane invites readers to reflect on how seemingly intractable and complicated problems may be resolved thorough more or better quality dialogue.

The Barefoot Guide to Working with Organisations and Social Change, www.barefootguide.org

Here is a down-to-earth introduction to working with organizations and groups with dialogue and engagement built in at all stages. It is targeted at development practitioners so the language is accessible, but what makes it unique is that it is illustrated with evocative drawings and cartoons that use humour to make quite serious points and to illustrate some of the issues that practitioners confront on a daily basis. It also provides many guidelines and tips.

Part III

Working with Connections

Where Part II focused on a range of personal abilities and aspects of capacity-development work that a practitioner will have to master, Part III moves further into the 'how' with a range of specific intervention angles and approaches. Most of these are illustrated using real-life cases. The need to work with connections (between capacity dimensions, actors and levels) is a recurrent theme across these seven chapters.

Chapter 11 sets the tone with an exploration of the 'political' dimensions of capacity development and the role played by contextual factors and dynamics. This is followed, in Chapter 12, by examples of working with public accountability mechanisms. Chapters 13 and 14 demonstrate the importance of bridging gaps between macro policies and implementation at the micro-level, with a practical example of how capacity development can be undertaken with multiple actors along a value chain. Chapter 15 shows how, without care, the distinct quality of community-based organizations – as the ultimate vehicle for capacity-development change on the ground – can be undermined rather than increased by external interventions. Leadership as a connecting and essential force in capacity development is the focus of Chapter 16. And finally, Chapter 17 discusses connection by means of knowledge networking as a powerful capacity-development approach.

11

Institutions, Power and Politics

Any capacity-development activity takes place within the wider setting of institutions, governance and politics. This reality poses for practitioners critical and difficult questions that are too seldom confronted in the open. For example: how can one best tackle the complex webs of power and informal relations that surround organizations? How does capacity development relate to governance dynamics? How can one explore, and maybe even widen the space for capacity development by working with 'political' forces and factors?

Traditionally, most attention is directed at capacity development from the 'inside out'. In this compelling contribution, Nils Boesen shows that a focus on governance and stakeholders opens additional perspectives on how change can be and often is stimulated from the 'outside in', or demand-side. He also discusses the political dimensions that shape capacity and the importance of change management – particularly the political tasks that it entails – is stressed.

Looking for Change Beyond the Boundaries, the Formal and the Functional

Nils Boesen

The power to change

It is not breaking news to claim that the capacity of many United Nations (UN) organizations is constrained. Or that the same is true for, say, the European Commission (EC). Over several decades, such organizations have been labelled as bureaucratic, politicized, costly and inefficient – far from the modern ideals of lean organizations where performance and excellence is driving behaviour rather than career manoeuvring, formalism and risk avoidance.

The calls for reforms have been loud. For example, the UN Reform process has been ongoing for years, and some things are surely changing. But why is it apparently so hard to develop the capacity of – that is, to change – organizations like the UN or the EC?

Surely, such organizations have executives as smart as any other public entity? And a lot of devoted staff that want change to happen so that they can deliver to their worthy mandates?

Of course they have smart executives and devoted staff. But they also operate in a context of powerful, multiple and conflicting interests of their stakeholders that may talk about reform, but walk against it by promoting their own geopolitical interest and their own nationals. And resistance to change may also be tremendous inside the organizations – after all, who wants to lose a well-paid job in New York or Brussels?

This chapter will argue that the UN and the EC are not unique. Organizations and systems in developing and developed countries face the same set of external and internal 'political factors' influencing current capacity and the prospects of change. These factors may be less visible than in the case of the UN and the EC, but capacity and capacity development is always shaped by the power and interests of stakeholders, as well as the more subtle pattern of institutional norms and values in which organizations and people are embedded.

This is often overlooked in many well-intended approaches to capacity development which only focus on 'functional' aspects like skills, systems, technology, leadership, and so on. Making organizations and people 'right' in these areas through training, revised organizational structures, clearer mandates, new business processes and technology can be important – but it often does not work well.

Such improvements only work if they do not threaten the interests of the powerful stakeholders in and around an organization. If there is no pressure on an organization to change, then it is unlikely that functional considerations alone will make it do so. And if there are very good – that is, powerful – reasons not to change, then change is only likely to happen if change agents can build a coalition strong enough to overcome resistance through a smart combination of accommodation, appeasement and, in the last resort, the defeat of opponents.

How can practitioners grasp this nettle of politics, power and formal as well as informal institutional norms? How can they explore, and maybe even widen the space for capacity development working with these 'political' factors? First, let us look at some basic notions about capacity, capacity development and change. Then we will explore how capacity can be influenced by 'working from the outside'. We will bring this together through a look at three essential elements that have to be considered for change to happen, before offering a short conclusion.

Performance by force, or by argument?

According to the Development Assistance Committee of the Organisation for Economic Co-operation and Development (OECD/DAC), 'capacity is the ability of people, organizations and society as a whole to manage their affairs successfully' (OECD, 2006). Importantly, capacity is an attribute of people, individual organizations and groups of organizations. Capacity is shaped by, adapts to and reacts to external factors and actors. It includes skills, systems, processes, ability to relate to others (internally and externally), leadership, values, formal and informal norms, as well as loyalties, ambitions and power.

Thus, capacity development is a change process modifying some of these factors, or their configuration. If the energy of a team is low, it may need a powerful 'pusher' to regain its edge. If capacity to think 'out of the box' is restrained it may require a less authoritarian leadership to unleash creativity. If an organization has become inward-looking and self-serving, it may need the pressure of competition to serve clients rather than itself. People and organizations can have strong or weak incentives to change, develop and learn, as a result of their environment or because of internal factors. Like learning, capacity development takes place in people or organizations, and, like learning, it cannot be forced upon them.

As a logical consequence, change processes must be owned and led by those who develop their capacity – otherwise it simply does not happen. Outsiders can teach, and shape incentives for learning – but no more than that.

This view on capacity and capacity development is well captured by the open systems view on organizations, a mainstream approach in organizational development literature. This approach is illustrated in Figure 11.1.

The open systems framework underscores the following key points about organizations and capacity.

- Organizations operate in a context with which they interact all the time, through formal as well as informal mechanisms. Think of organizations as living organisms thriving – or suffering – in the social and institutional 'ecosystem' to which they relate. The boundaries of an organization are permeable, permitting energy and information to enter and leave through multiple channels, and organizations use their capacity to relate and exchange with actors in the environment when they perform.

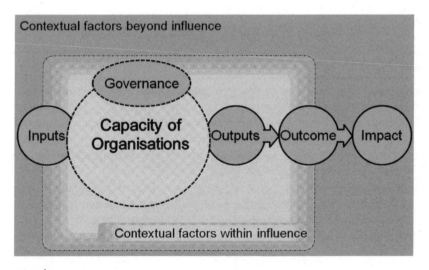

Source: author

Figure 11.1 *Analytical framework – organizations as open systems*

- Performance leads to outputs. When people, organizations or systems perform they are at least formally expected to produce certain outputs. Particularly in the public sector, outputs (services or regulations) are intended to lead to outcomes (e.g. children learning) and impact (e.g. ability to cope successfully with life).

As underlined above, capacity is an attribute of people, organizations or systems, but whether and how capacity develops is mostly determined by the 'demand-side' or 'ecosystem factors'. The power of the external pressure – or demand in a broad sense – from citizens, clients, politicians and other stakeholders for performance and accountability is the most important incentive to performance and to capacity development. The power of values, expectations, norms and other factors in the 'ecosystem' will underpin or undermine this performance.

Thus, organizations cannot be understood by looking only at official mandates and goals, formal procedures and structures, and other 'functional aspects' inside the organization. Organizations have this 'functional dimension', but they also always have a 'political' dimension as described in Table 11.1.

So, clearly, the 'political dimension' is a trouble-maker. Should capacity development therefore aim at giving the 'functional dimension' more room to dominate? Organizations should function by virtue of reason rather than by force, shouldn't they?

The answer is no to both propositions. All organizations have both dimensions, and a well-functioning organization needs both. The political dimension – the power, the incentives, the tensions, and sometimes conflicts – provides energy that brings motion, direction and change to an organization, for good or bad. The functional dimension ensures technical and economic efficiency and professional quality.

Table 11.1 *Two dimensions of organizations*

Change element	Functional dimension	Political dimension
Main unit of analysis	Focus on functional task-and-work system	Focus on power-and-loyalty systems
Driving forces	A sense of norms, intrinsic motivation	Sanctions and rewards, incentives
Image of man	Employees caring for the organization	Individuals caring for themselves
How change happens	Participative reasoning, finding best technical solution, orderliness	Internal conflict, coalition with powerful external agents, unpredictable
What change focuses on	Internal systems, structures, skills, technology, etc.	Incentives, change of key staff, promotions, outsmarting opposition, modifying symbols and values

Source: adapted from Mastenbroek, 1993

The challenge is to keep a balance between the two dimensions. If loyalty and narrow vested interests dominate, then the organization may end up serving private or partisan goals only. If functional dimensions dominate, the search for the perfect technical solution or product may go on for ever, while the interests of customers and stakeholders are ignored.

The functional aspects of organizations are often formalized in manuals, organizational charts, job descriptions and so on. But the formal may not correspond well to how things are really done: there are informal ways of behaving that can actually be very useful when formal systems become stiff and rigid. Part of the political dimension is also codified: formal hierarchy and authority is well defined, and official values and mission statements may hang in every office. But how real power is distributed in an organization is rarely formally described, and informal 'old boy networks' may be known by everybody although they do not appear in organizational charts.

In extreme cases where public organizations have been 'captured' for the narrow purposes of a powerful elite, they may thus have a formal façade with a mission, vision, plans, budgets, structures and systems. The informal capacity behind the formal façade may serve totally different purposes and produce hidden outputs unrelated to the formal purposes of the organization.

The open systems approach and the dimensions just outlined allow practitioners to assess present capacity and the dynamics that explain present capacity and output levels. Table 11.2 shows the four dimensions of the framework.

The four dimensions framework is useful for getting a 360-degree view of an organization or a group of organizations. It also indicates four areas from which to promote capacity development: internally (often called a 'supply-side approach') or by modifying context parameters ('demand-side approach'), and with a focus on functional or political aspects, respectively.

Table 11.2 *Four dimensions shaping capacity*

	Functional	*Political*
Internal	**Internal, functional dimension**	**Internal, political dimension**
	Strategy, systems, structures, work processes, internal relationships, etc.	Leadership, power distribution, material and non-material incentives, rewards and sanctions, possible vested interests, conflicts
External	**External, functional dimension**	**External, political dimension**
	Legal framework, timeliness and adequacy of resources, performance targets, oversight bodies, formal accountability requirements	Political governance, possible vested interests, pressure from clients, customers, competitors, media attention

What is most important for performance? Working on the supply- or the demand-side, on reason or on power? The answer is – yes, all of them! Traditionally, however, the focus has been on the internal side and on mostly functional aspects. A devoted change champion – typically a senior executive – can achieve an impressive turnaround of her organization applying this focus in a stable and developed society. In many countries the room for reformers is small, however, and internally-focused approaches to capacity development have not worked well. So let's look in the next sections at how change can also be supported by forces from the outside, and how to work with the political dimensions of capacity development.

Working from the outside: Appreciating the context, getting stakeholders right and governance better

The open systems model (Figure 11.1) distinguishes between context factors within and beyond influence. For simplicity, let's say that factors within influence are those that individuals can affect over the short to medium term, while those beyond influence are those that change slowly, and largely by processes that cannot be ascribed to one or a few persons' deliberate decisions. So, changing a culture of high acceptance of and respect for formal authority ('the boss is always right') to a culture of creative exploration of viewpoints ('help me, guys, with some new ideas of what to do here') may happen by wilful action in small groups, but in a larger system is only likely to become the broad norm for behaviour over a long period of time.

Such institutional factors simply do not change by decree! Still, they deeply influence how organizations perform, and they set the parameters for how and how quickly organizations can change. They include factors such as to what degree policies – and the laws that formalize policies – are really driving actions of senior executives, civil servants and front-line service providers, or to what degree the budget process is policy driven or driven by entrenched interests of influential groups and persons. On the organizational level, the incentives to performance are also influenced by informal institutional factors: in some places, a public office is widely regarded as a reward for loyalty, rather than an obligation to work. Civil servants that are not able to use their office to provide benefits for the extended family may be considered disloyal to the family – or outright incompetent.

Trying to change organizational capacity in the short term by addressing these factors head-on is unlikely to yield success unless there is some strong domestic pressure on the organization to deliver better.

The good news is that organizations can deliver better, also despite the web of institutional constraints they are facing. The bad news is that it takes time to improve performance, and that there are limits to how far improvements will go even in the medium term if the context is less than enabling.

To explore these opportunities we must look at the context within more direct influence. In practice, this 'context' means the stakeholders: all those with an interest in the performance of an organization or a group of organizations. They may be stakeholders either because they are customers or clients – or want to become so – or because they are policy-makers, or a labour union organizing the staff, or politicians, or local governments, NGOs and private actors that have certain ambitions or interests, and so on.

A useful way to approach stakeholders is to focus on their role in the governance of an organization or a sector. Governance is broadly the relation between one or more 'governors' and an 'agent' (an individual or one or more organizations). Through formal authority, through the market mechanism or through informal mechanisms of different kinds (patron–client relations, traditional authorities, etc.) the 'governors' direct the actions of 'the agent' (one or more organizations), who then in turn is accountable to the various governors for the performance of the agency.

Figure 11.2 displays a model for looking at the existing governance mechanisms or 'rules of the game' in a sector, or in a district or other social unit, with some degree of complexity. It shows that governance is not determined by a single framework or set of rules but actually takes shape through a web of formal and informal governance and accountability relations.

The governance assessment framework permits us to look at the questions of who decides priorities, how resources are distributed, how authority is exercised, and who, formally or informally, is accountable to whom. It allows a systematic scanning of the stakeholders: do users of public service effectively have a say – either as voters, or through scorecards, or by having a choice between different service providers so that they can 'vote with their feet'? Are there effective check and balance mechanisms (auditors, supervisory agencies, appeal boards or complaint mechanisms)? Are core public agencies helpful to frontline service providers with

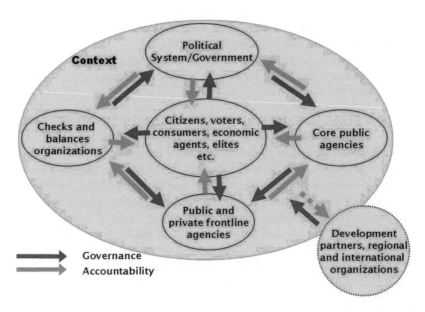

Source: EuropeAid, 2008

Figure 11.2 *Governance assessment framework*

policies, regulations and resources enabling performance at this level? To whom are actors accountable, formally and informally, for their performance?

Looking closer at stakeholders in the various arenas, you can examine their interests, the power and resources they command for influence, and the importance a certain performance level of an organization or a sector has for them. The present performance level of a sector or an individual organization is likely to benefit some and punish others. A run-down health system that is only able to deliver very basic services in rural areas is likely to foster dissatisfaction among the rural poor, but poorly paid health staff may tolerate this if they are not expected to work much for their meagre salary and if they are allowed to sell private services on the side. Taxpayers – often a small, but powerful group in developing countries – may prefer low taxes to better rural health care.

These stakeholder preferences or interests can thus be mapped in relation to the existing situation: what is the balance of interests at present? Who is winning, who is losing as things are? Who has a voice that is heard, and who has no voice?

This is the first step. The next is to consider whether the governance around an organization or a sector could be modified: can some actors get a stronger voice? Will scorecards – and, say, media attention to the results – provide incentives to frontline providers to perform better? Will giving vouchers to poor people create effective demand for better educational services? Will advocacy by civil society make policy-makers react? Should oversight and accountability be strengthened, and can poor performance be sanctioned?

These options are all examples of working from the outside to influence capacity and performance. The focus on stakeholders' interests is a practical way of discussing the power in and around organizations, and the focus on stakeholders' role – or lack thereof – in governance enables a facilitator to go through a series of options that would strengthen the pressure on, and incentives for, an organization to perform and strengthen its capacity.

But having identified 10 or 20 options does not mean that change will actually happen. So the next section will turn to the politics of change.

What it takes to make change happen

When, then, is change and capacity development likely to take place? It depends on the scope of change. The more comprehensive the change, the more likely that conflicts and resistance will arise. Capacity development and change are most often not a tea-party! Therefore, three essential ingredients must normally be present.

First, in the current situation, dissatisfaction must exceed satisfaction: some stakeholders inside and around an organization or sector must find the current capacity to be too low, or misdirected. And because others may think that the present capacity and performance level is good enough, those wanting change must carry more weight – have more power and willingness to use it – than those who are satisfied. The discussion of stakeholders and governance in the previous section looked at this aspect.

Second, there must be a shared vision about the future. Dissatisfaction with the present, however acute, is not enough. If there is no idea of and belief in a realistic, better future with enhanced capacity, then pressure to change will only lead to frustration and passivity.

Third, a credible change process must form the 'bridge' from the present situation to the future vision. Those who are supposed to change must be confident that sufficient leadership, competence and resources are behind the intended change. If change management is poor or poorly prioritized, then few will invest energy in joining the process. They will prefer to wait until the bad weather disappears and things continue as usual. Even if everybody can see that capacity and performance could improve, they will not buy in to change processes unless they see a credible way forward.

These three basic elements: the level of dissatisfaction in the current situation, the vision of change and a credible change process, are dependent on each other and they must be balanced. If the power behind dissatisfaction is limited, then a very ambitious vision may be beyond what actors will support. If the capacity to manage change processes is limited or not credible, then even strong dissatisfaction will not be enough to achieve an inspiring vision.

The elements are not static: dissatisfaction can be nurtured, for example, by data about the existing situation. Most actors will be satisfied with some aspects of the situation and dissatisfied with others, and this will change over time. An over-ambitious vision can be tempered so that it becomes a realistic offer to those who have to support it in order for things to happen. Capacity to manage change can be strengthened. We will briefly look at these three elements.

Assessing the current situation

We have already introduced stakeholder analysis as a means to gauge satisfaction and dissatisfaction. It sounds simple, but is in practice quite demanding, not least requiring a detailed insight in who's who, and who connects to whom, and how dynamics of interactions between various groups and individuals play out. The wider set of institutional and cultural norms and values also influences how dissatisfaction, satisfaction and power are expressed and played out. Knowledge of these dynamics is often tacit in nature, meaning it is invisible to the external eye and can be inappropriate to share and discuss openly. Nonetheless, it has to be done. Poor assessments (or none) here are one of the key reasons that so many technocratic approaches to reform have failed miserably.

The vision and design of capacity development processes

A second element is the vision and the results that are expected after a successful capacity development process. How comprehensive and ambitious will the vision be? Is it to be big scale reform or incremental capacity development? How will the vision be expressed? Will a detailed results framework up front serve the process best, or will it create a straitjacket, fitting nobody? What should the time horizon be? Can capacity development be sequenced, tackling some 'basics' first and then increasingly addressing complex or controversial issues? How much do the answers to these questions depend on the complexity of the desired capacity development? Enhancing capacity to deliver high-quality classroom teaching in thousands of schools is, for example, notoriously more complex than managing the fiscal policy.

There are no blueprints to help stakeholders shape a vision for capacity development, but there are a few emerging lessons of experience that may give some good pointers.

- Capacity development should be integrated in the broader vision of sector or organizational performance. That is, it should not be a separate vision and plan, but a consistent focus embedded in the efforts to achieve wider outcomes and impact.
- Capacity development should lead to demonstrable changes in the outputs (services, regulatory functions) of a sector or organization in a relatively short time.
- Capacity development requires flexibility, and rigid results and indicator frameworks are unlikely to be helpful. Respecting the dynamic – and political – nature of change is essential.

Change processes and change management

Is there a credible change process that can convince sceptics, overcome resistance, accommodate losers, seek win–win situations, forge alliances, keep capacity development on the agenda, drum up additional financial support, ensure adequate technical quality, and manage the daily business of implementing capacity development or reforms? Who and what will appease public officials standing to lose influence, or even their job? Who will keep a powerful senior minister informed so that she continues to support the capacity development process? Do those in charge have sufficient capacity to manage the process? These are the kind of questions that come out of a focus on change management.

Change management includes three sets of tasks: political tasks, technical tasks and managerial tasks. The change team needs capacity in all three areas. Crucially, it needs the ability to reach up to senior executives; horizontally to other organizations that must contribute, and to customers or clients; as well as downwards within its own organization.

Is a special change or reform unit a feasible way of ensuring buy-in, oversight and strategic guidance from higher levels, or will it isolate the change agents from those whom they should help change? What role – if any – should external consultants play? Should donors, if they are supporting the process, keep at arm's length, including when progress is less than impressive?

These questions have to be addressed as part of the preparation of capacity development processes. Often, the technical and managerial tasks are discussed, but the political tasks are not given much attention. That is a pity. Negligence of the political tasks of change management is likely to lead to failure. Checking whether these tasks can actually be performed is a litmus test as to whether there is sufficient commitment and capacity to change, and whether change can be sustained.

Conclusion

This chapter has argued that capacity development is much more than a technical process – power, politics and stakeholder interests shape what can be done, and how. The open systems framework usefully captures how organizations are embedded in an ecosystem that shapes both capacity and prospects of change. The double perspective on functional as well as political dimensions of organizations allows a fuller diagnostic and broader discussion of entry points for capacity development.

Because most attention has traditionally been given to 'capacity development from within', in this chapter emphasis was put on describing how a focus on governance and stakeholders helps to draw additional perspectives on change from the outside, or demand-side, and with full attention to the political dimensions that shape capacity. Finally, the importance of change management – particularly the political tasks that it entails – was stressed.

All this adds to the complexity of promoting capacity development, but also to the fun and the energy it can release when it deals not only with the dry technicalities, but also with the multiple aspirations and the passion that are, in the end, what drive change and development.

References

EuropeAid (2009) *Analysing and Addressing Governance in Sector Operations*, EuropeAid, Brussels

Mastenbroek, W.F.G. (1993) *Conflict Management and Organization Development*, Wiley, Chichester

Organisation for Economic Co-operation and Development (2006) *The Challenge of Capacity Development: Working Towards Good Practice*, OECD, Paris

Recommended readings and resources

This chapter links to several others in this resource volume where power, politics, engagement with stakeholders and governance issues come to the fore. Chapter 2 introduces multi-stakeholder engagement while Chapter 3 discusses capacities at different levels of human systems and also touches on the importance of formal and informal institutions in achieving capacity at scale. The present chapter builds on these and sets the scene for the following chapters that all touch on multi-actor and multi-level capacity development approaches and experiences. Chapter 12 gives examples of working with accountability relations. Chapter 13 discusses the macro–micro gap and capacity development focuses that may help to overcome this. Chapter 14 gives an example of the use of multi-stakeholder partnerships in value chain development. The personal challenges for a capacity development practitioner to deal with power, conflicts and differences in values are treated in Chapters 6 and 7. The following is a short selection of useful resources as a starting point for further reading on this topic.

There are a lot of operational toolkits available, too many to list. However, this section draws heavily on EuropeAid's *Toolkit for Capacity Development* (Brussels, 2009), available at www.capacity4dev.eu and developed by the author of this chapter. It provides for a number of practical tools that help the practitioner to map and deal with political and informal dimensions of a capacity development situation.

A thorough and comprehensive introduction to the open systems approach is found in Harrison and Shirom (1999) *Organizational Diagnosis and Assessment*, Sage, London.

Gareth Morgan's *Images of Organisation*, Sage, London, 1986, is still an excellent reader on different perspectives on organizations. Particularly on the public sector, Christopher Hood's *The Art of the State*, Oxford University Press, Oxford (2000) is indispensable for bringing fads and fashion into a historical perspective.

With regard to politics and power, W. Richard Scott's *Institutions and Organizations*, Sage, London (2001) provides a great overview on the fundamentals of institutions and context. Colin Hay does the same for political analysis – though mostly at the macro level – in his *Political Analysis: A Critical Introduction* (2002) Palgrave, New York.

On change and change management, Nils Brunsson's *The Irrational Organisation (2000)* Fakbogforlaget, Stockholm, vividly explores how irrationality is a basis for organizational action and change. The classical comparative volume on public sector reform is Christopher Pollitt and Geert Bouckaert's *Public Management Reform*, Oxford University Press, Oxford (2004).

12

Public Accountability

Being held to account is a driver for performance and capacity development. However, accountability to local constituencies is often weak in many 'aided-development' programmes, with negative consequences for results and the ownership of such programmes by their intended beneficiaries. Increasing mutual and public account-ability can therefore be an important force for enhancing the overall performance of actors around an issue of collective concern.

In this chapter, Rakesh Rajani sketches various ways in which a Tanzanian NGO deploys information and public media to boost citizens' demand for accountability in the provision of education and other public services. These experiences have inter-esting implications for expanding a practitioner's repertoire of capacity develop-ment beyond discrete organizations. They also stimulate thinking about how capacity development is connected to activism.

Capacity is Political, Not Technical: The Case of HakiElimu in Promoting Accountability in Education in Tanzania

Rakesh Rajani

Introduction

There is no shortage of initiatives to build capacity in Tanzania; for almost 50 years governments, donors and NGOs have established thousands of schemes and spent billions to enable people to know more, gain skills and perform better. But ask virtually anyone today, and the lack of capacity will appear in the top set of challenges facing the country. If nothing else, the persistence of this problem should give us pause to reflect on the soundness of the premise on which the capacity-building enterprise is built, and whether we need to look for an elephant in the room.

Capacity development in Tanzania is fraught with at least three key challenges. First, a great deal of time is spent worrying about capacitating actors to improve laws and policies – and develop strategies, plans and budgets – and very little on grappling with what actually happens in practice. This imbalance is particularly worrying because the gaps between policy and/or plans and implementation and/ or practice are known to be quite substantial, and yet there is little problematizing of the ability of planning and policy change to deliver progress. Capacity building that is squarely situated within the policy–planning domain can therefore quickly become an artificial or phoney exercise because its participants know that its value is limited from the outset.

Second, regardless of the phraseology of 'participation', 'bottom-up', 'ownership', and the like, capacity-building efforts tend to be supply-driven. This is not to say that there are no willing participants – there are – but rather that the agenda and the analysis underlying the agenda are shaped and motivated by well-meaning actors in government, donor agencies or NGOs. One implication of this supply-driven bias is an exaggerated sense of the influence of donors and aid in bringing change,[1] despite emerging evidence to the contrary. Another is that issues are framed in apolitical, technocratic terms; technical gaps are identified and interventions designed to fill them. The basic presumption is that the targets of their capacity-building interventions are keen to perform their roles, and will be able to do so better with more awareness, training and skills-building. Where this turns out to be insufficient, more of the same is offered, as if more vigour or improved technique will bring the desired change.

Third, there is little informed lesson learning or interrogation of the lessons it is claimed have been learned. Since capacity-building efforts are organized through short-term projects, designed by donors or programme officers on short-term contracts and undertaken by roving consultants, there is limited historical perspective on what has been done before and on its effects. Approaches undertaken today are invariably labelled new and innovative, even when the same things may have been tried decades before. It does not help that evaluations of capacity-building projects are themselves ahistorical, and further compromised by uneven quality and lack of independence. The operating incentives are such that the key players or consultants hired to do the job are told to think within established frames, and quickly learn what can be said and which red lines cannot be crossed. As a result much of what is generated, often at great cost, adds little understanding and reinforces a lack of accountability.

The sum effect is a lot of activity with little result and even less learning.

Underlying these three challenges is a split in motivation. Because many capacity-building efforts do not lead to real change, and therefore have not convinced their participants of their intrinsic value, external inducements (understandably) assume increased importance. Hence people have to be offered multiple incentives (sitting allowances, travel allowances, top-up pay, per diems, meals, accommodation, and so on) to participate in efforts to build their own capacity. Enormous effort is expended in negotiations about benefits, such as holding meetings outside official city limits in order to qualify for larger per diems, or crafting reasons to make new claims, such as the need to be given mobile phone airtime units. The true incentive to engage in capacity building is often these external incentives (without them no one shows up) but people need to pretend otherwise, and maintain the façade necessary to keep the inducements rolling. In this sense, by offering 'easy money' and goading people into unproductive work, capacity-building initiatives can have a corrupting effect.

What would capacity development look like if conceptualized from the other – demand-driven – end? Would it be better achieved by creating a different set of incentives, whereby, through public awareness and pressure, the relevant actors were *compelled* to figure out how to do the right thing?

A basic premise informing this view is that sustainable change needs informed and active citizens. Informed and active citizens can better negotiate their rights, and create pressures that hold governments and service providers to account. People in positions of authority will do the right thing (or less of the bad thing) not in the face of solid evidence, good policies or effective lobbying, but because it pays to do so or there is no way out. Capacity and accountability are in this sense relational and political, not technical.

The work of HakiElimu — an independent citizen engagement organization focused on education in Tanzania – provides a useful case through which to explore the contention that public engagement can contribute to greater accountability and capacity. Below I outline concrete examples of how HakiElimu has involved citizens in government accountability and describe the effect they have had. I then briefly speculate from this experience on how one might usefully re-conceptualize capacity development for change.[2]

Illustrations of HakiElimu's work

Media investigations

The Primary Education Development Plan (PEDP) is arguably the largest reform programme in Tanzania in terms of scale, scope and budget. Its centrepiece is the capitation grant – a flat $10 per pupil per annum to be disbursed to the school level for non-salary, quality related improvements.

Early in the first year of PEDP implementation (2002) there was emerging information that the capitation grants were not reaching the school level on time. The precise problems were uncertain, but there was some evidence that the funds were being diverted to other uses. HakiElimu enjoyed good relations with the Ministry of Education then and tried numerous ways to relay that information to the authorities so that corrective action could be taken. Over a period of 6–8 months these included:

- sharing the information at high level consultation with the decision-making body;
- sharing it informally and formally with various senior government leaders;
- informing key donors and asking them to use their influence to make something happen;
- informing the 'impartial' reviewers of PEDP of the problem.

Despite these concerted efforts little happened. The problem was not explicitly denied but there was little follow-up and few consequences. The situation, however, took a different turn when HakiElimu subsidized journalists to investigate PEDP disbursements in five regions and independently report on the situation. Their findings were splashed in papers, radio and TV, showing that indeed PEDP funds were often stuck in district accounts. Suddenly this was 'news'. In response, the government hurriedly undertook their own missions. The Education Minister breathed fire on local officials and personally visited four of the five regions covered in the news. Disbursement of the capitation grant now merited political and administrative action.

Since then, HakiElimu has facilitated over 100 media investigations. It has also passed on key reports, evidence and other information on public matters that comes its way, and brokered connections between editors, journalists and credible sources. These actions have led to coverage of issues that were 'known' to most policy-makers, but had stimulated little debate or corrective action prior to their being covered by the media.

Media advertisements

HakiElimu's advertisements on radio and TV have addressed different issues over the years, but the basic approach is the same: identify key challenges from research and government documents, depict a typical scenario that illustrates that challenge in human terms, and raise questions (not preach or give solutions). The advertisements are professionally made, interesting to watch, entertaining and provocative (so not at all like typical NGO 'development-speak').

Among other issues, these adverts have addressed procurement, a key focus of capacity-building efforts in Tanzania. In one advertisement a shopkeeper approached by school committee members asks: 'Do you want your personal price or the school price?' When asked why this matters, his somewhat exasperated response is of course the school price is higher because of the cut the education official requires. In another, a head-teacher has no patience for 'impertinent' questions from school committee members whose job it is to hold him accountable. A new series being finalized (in cooperation with the national anti-corruption agency PCCB) shows how, by diligently doing their job, 'ordinary' junior staff succeed in thwarting questionable practices that would have otherwise sailed through with the blessings of their bosses.

Virtually everyone who has access to radio and television knows about these advertisements. Some of the characters have become household names, with iconic symbols even working their way into everyday language.[3] The issues have been widely debated, and in some cases have led to practical action (e.g. timely payment of teachers' salaries). A government ban on the advertisements late in President Mkapa's term, just before the general elections in late 2005, only served to make them more popular, and the subject of wide public debate, spurring thousands of ordinary citizens to speak out.[4]

Simplifying information

Providing information to citizens is seldom sufficient because reports are often complex and difficult to understand. Readers are overwhelmed by the volume of information and unable to discern the key data or main points. This is even more difficult where the information is dispersed across different reports. Furthermore, many documents are available only in English, a language not familiar to most Tanzanians.

In response, one of HakiElimu's activities has been to compile valuable information, organize it systematically, identify the key points (see the forest from the trees), render it in a simple format, translate it into Swahili, publish a large number of copies and distribute it countrywide.

Two examples

In its first three years, PEDP had been reviewed numerous times under government-led processes, but little had been done to deal with the findings and recommendations. Many of the same issues would arise repeatedly every half year but led to little corrective action. Furthermore, the reviews showed that progress often fell short of targets, and several key areas were neglected. HakiElimu compiled this information in accessible text, published it in Swahili, and launched it at a press conference with key points in a two-page handout.[5] The event made the headlines and forced the government to respond (in a manner far more robust than previous consultations, sector dialogues, and so on). The Minister's public dismissal of the findings did not hold sway when it was pointed out that the HakiElimu report was sourced *entirely* from government documents. To the contrary, it sparked further public interest, and a report that would have otherwise only been read within policy and research circles was serialized in a national newspaper.

A second example concerns the National Audit Office. Its annual reports consistently unearthed large amounts of unaccounted public funds, but the information was not widely known, difficult to access, and not easy to understand. A new initiative, Tanzania Governance Notice-board (TGN), an initiative of the local think tank, Research on Poverty Alleviation,[6] had usefully made the information available online, but this too was yet to constitute broad public access or ignite national debate.

In 2006 HakiElimu worked with TGN to convert its information into simple leaflets in English and Swahili.[7] The leaflets ranked the audit performance of ministries and districts, listed amounts of questioned expenditure and provided other highlights. The leaflets were launched with media events, and circulated as inserts in national newspapers. In 2007 the National Audit Office requested HakiElimu to produce updated leaflets. These were presented at a national meeting that involved many members of parliament and government leaders and were widely covered in the local press. President Kikwete, in an unprecedented move, convened a national meeting to discuss the audit reports.[8] Thereafter, the audit reports became available online in full for the first time.

While causality is difficult to establish, it is interesting to speculate on the extent to which the public availability of the reports may have contributed to greater executive attention.

Public competitions

HakiElimu conducts public essay and/or drawing competitions in which ordinary citizens countrywide submit their views and suggestions. In 2004 it invited ideas on types of corruption in education, and what could be done about it. There were 3000 entries which were analysed and the key findings summarized; the best entries were published in a booklet. The booklet and views received wide media coverage, and attracted considerable public response, including letters to the editor. After apparently hearing about the report on BBC radio, President Mkapa became personally concerned and instructed the Minister for Education to investigate further. The Ministry issued full-page newspaper advertisements dismissing the initiative as 'unscientific' and misleading, and a vibrant debate ensued. While the government was resistant then, the issues raised by participants are now openly acknowledged by the highest levels of government leadership as major public concerns.

Simple monitoring

HakiElimu has developed and experimented with simple tools to enable citizens to monitor everyday realities against policy and budget commitments; undertake basic analysis; share and discuss the information at the community level; and finally forward it for compilation, national comparison and analysis. Two tools have been used to monitor PEDP and citizen access to information. They allow citizens to collect information on issues such as the degree to which they have access to information about how much funds reached the school and about policies regarding the use of these funds, how people access information, where they can take complaints, and so on. The tools are deliberately kept simple so that they can be used easily without training or supervision, and take relatively little time to administer. The involvement of a diverse group in undertaking the exercise is encouraged to verify the information gathered and foster quality assurance.

Feedback on both tools typically demonstrates that citizens and local leaders alike have found them to be 'practical', 'revealing', 'helpful', and 'useful to spur changes'. The tools generate information that can immediately inform community discussion. The national analysis also reveals interesting findings, for instance that additional funds are reaching school levels but vary widely between schools and generally fall far short of policy targets; teachers are often not teaching, and attendance is far lower than enrolment. This type of information is rarely captured in national surveys, and allows for useful disaggregated analysis that can unearth inequities that would be otherwise missed. The tool also represents a concrete manifestation of the core idea of citizens holding government to account beyond elections.

Friends of Education

People across Tanzania care about education, but their concern often remains at a private level, and is unable to translate itself into public action. The essence of HakiElimu's approach is to enable ordinary citizens – including historically excluded groups such as people with disabilities, women, and the rural poor – to devise options in which private concern can be turned into public action. A main vehicle to do this is the Friends of Education initiative through which any concerned citizen can join with others, free of charge, to pursue their own agendas and interests and effect change. Friends receive a quarterly mailing of materials in Swahili (such as policy documents, leaders' speeches, simple summaries, popular materials, news clippings, and a newsletter profiling views and actions of other citizens). They also receive a handbook describing practical actions they can take (such as participating in a school committee or writing a letter to the editor). These inputs then spur local actions by Friends, which in turn are shared to inspire cross-learning and action by others in similar situations.

At the time of writing (mid-2009) there are about 30,000 Friends (individuals and groups) across every district of mainland Tanzania. The concept is fraught with challenges, though, and many Friends often assume a passive role and expect HakiElimu to organize seminars and dish out allowances (the 'corrupting' effect of capacity-building initiatives described above). Nevertheless, there are examples across the country of ordinary citizens taking actions to make a difference in governance. For example, a Friend in Ukerewe district has used his own funds to build a shack that serves as a community library. In Kibaha district, a Friend has organized community notice-boards and serves as a local journalist and information hub. Another in Songea district successfully convinced the local authorities to ensure that his daughter could continue with her education (after becoming pregnant). In Tabora district, a group was organized to stop the forced collection of fees and contributions contrary to education policy. These examples have been replicated across the country.

Conclusion

Each of these illustrations of HakiElimu's work has its own limitations, and there is a long way to go before fundamental social and political arrangements can be transformed. Nonetheless, the examples show that large-scale public engagement and action is possible, and that it can both stimulate citizens to hold government accountable and also generate greater government responsiveness in return. While none of these interventions were conceptualized as 'capacity development' (nor does HakiElimu characterize itself as a capacity-building organization), they constitute some of the most potent examples of capacity in action in Tanzania in recent years.

What is at play here? Might it be the case that understanding and getting the political dynamic right – including having incentives align in a manner that can promote greater accountability – is central to the development and exercise of capacity?

In HakiElimu's case, and perhaps more generally, broad public access to information, including the public pressure effect of media coverage, was an essential feature of triggering public awareness, debate and action. This appears to have been equally important for local community action as well as at national and policy levels. Importantly, the *manner* or *style* of communication matters; far from being development oriented or offering solutions, HakiElimu's approach uses a combination of solid evidence, humour, creativity and contradiction to stimulate the public imagination.

A second critical feature is the emphasis on open-ended exercise of agency by citizens. While there was no lack of guidance, materials and tools, the core idea is to stimulate demand-driven actions that are not centrally determined or coordinated. In the best examples, citizens are stimulated by what they get from HakiElimu, but choose to act when and how and to what extent they please, with the freedom to relate to HakiElimu (and other agencies) as and when they see fit. Crucially, in this conception citizens act on their own behalf and name, unencumbered or lured by sitting allowances and other distortional incentives.

In a context where the paraphernalia of 'development' is so alienated from the daily lives and aspirations of people, capacity development talk, however differently articulated, may come across as more of the same: as boring, a variation of a discredited discourse that has time and again failed to live up to it its promise. In contrast, HakiElimu's rhetoric appears to be characterized by the twin notions of citizen agency and imagination, each informing and energizing the other, fuelling a virtual spiral of possibility and action.

In other words, the best way to do capacity development may be *not to do capacity development*. Instead, the real task may have more to do with fuelling aspirations and citizens stretching the boundaries of what is possible, which is the business of the political imagination.

Notes

1   Andrew Lawson and Lise Rakner, 'Understanding patterns of accountability in Tanzania', Final Synthesis Report, August 2005, www.gsdrc.org/docs/open/DOC98.pdf, accessed 15 September 2009.
2   This paper is a revised version of a working paper first published by HakiElimu, and is based on a presentation made at an anti-corruption workshop organized by U4, The Anti-Corruption Resource Center (see www.u4.no, accessed 15 September 2009). Earlier drafts of this paper have benefited from comments and editorial support from Mai Amundsen, Ruth Carlitz, Daniel Luhamo and Geir Sundet, but the final responsibility rests with the author.
3   See HakiElimu and Research and Education for Democracy (REDET), 'What can people know? Access to information in Tanzania. Findings of a nationwide opinion poll', May 2006, www.hakielimu.org/hakielimu/documents/document42brief_what_can_ppl_know_en.pdf, accessed 15 September 2009.
4   The government banned HakiElimu adverts on education, so the organization promptly developed others on poverty, broader development and freedom of expression issues. See HakiElimu Inapotosha Elimu? www.hakielimu.org/hakielimu/documents/document98hakielimu_inapotosha_elimu_sw.pdf, accessed 15 September 2009.
5   HakiElimu, Three Years OF PEDP Implementation: Key Findings from Government Reviews, July 2005, www.hakielimu.org/hakielimu/publicationdetailusers.php?publicationid=86, accessed 15 September 2009.
6   See www.repoa.or.tz/content/blogcategory/10/34/ (accessed 15 September 2009). Note that for the first time, in 2007 the consolidated report of the Controller and Auditor General was available online at www.nao.go.tz, accessed 15 September 2009.

7   See HakiElimu, 'Is Central Government Managing Money Well?' October 2006, www.
    hakielimu.org/managing_money_2.pdf, accessed 15 September 2009; and HakiElimu,
    'Are Local Governments Managing Money Well?', October 2006, www.hakielimu.org/
    managing_money_1.pdf, accessed 15 September 2009.
8   The meeting was held on 15 April 2007, and was widely covered in the media. Refer to
    Statement by Hon. Zakia Hamdani Meghji (MP), Minister for Finance of the United
    Republic of Tanzania, at the Launch of the General Budget Support Annual Review
    2007, 29th October 2007, www.mof.go.tz/mofdocs/GBS/GBS%20Launch%20state-
    ment%20by%20MF%20final.pdf, accessed 15 September 2009'.

Recommended readings

This chapter has links to various other chapters in the volume. Chapter 3
introduces the relevance of governance and formal institutional arrangement
for capacity development. Chapter 11 provides a clear explanation of the
relevance of governance, politics and accountability to capacity development.
Other examples of the use of media, information and knowledge networking
can be found in Chapters 17, 14 and 13. The importance of accountability
relations with local constituencies in monitoring and evaluation is discussed
in Chapter 18.

The following is a short selection of useful resources that provide a starting
point for further exploration of this subject.

Boyte, H., *Everyday Politics: Reconnecting Citizens and Public Life*, University
    of Pennsylvania Press, 2005

Harry Boyte shows how ordinary citizens can make and have made a difference, through public work and civic engagement, all along educating one
another and transforming everyday politics. Most references relate to the US
context, but they have relevance for a broader context.

Calland, R. and Tilley, A. (eds), *The Right to Know, The Right to Live: Access to
    Information and Socio-Economic Justice*, ODAC, 2002

This is one of the first primers to make a compelling case of why access to
information is essential to the exercise of freedom and the attainment of well-
being. It comes with a film showing the work of the MKSS (Mazdoor Kisan
Shakti Sangathan) movement in India in using social audits for change.

Fowler, A. and Biekart, K., 'The civic driven change (CDC) initiative', see
    www.iss.nl/Portals/Civic-Driven-Change-Initiative, accessed 15 September
    2009, and 'Twaweza, Twaweza: fostering an ecosystem of change in East
    Africa through imagination, citizen agency and public accountability, 2008'
    downloadable from www.twaweza.org

The first – CDC – is an interesting group effort led by Fowler and Biekart that makes the case for re-conceptualizing change as civic driven; the website provides essays, notes from meetings and blogs. The second – Twaweza – is an initiative that the author is involved with that seeks to enable large-scale change in Kenya, Tanzania and Uganda by promoting access to information and citizen agency, using an unusual theory of change.

Ginzburg, O., *The Hungry Man*, Hungry Man Books, May 2004; and *Here You Go!*, Hungry Man Books, March 2005

These simple illustrated books should be required reading for everyone doing development. Cheeky, irreverent and wickedly funny, they poke fun at the hypocrisies we are all so familiar with, but somehow cannot get out of.

Kaplan, Allan, *The Development of Capacity*, CDRA 1999, downloadable from www.cdra.org.za/articles/The%20Developing%20Of%20Capacity%20 -%20by%20Allan%20Kaplan.htm, accessed 15 September 2009; and *Development Practitioners and Social Process – Artists of the Invisible*, Pluto Press, 2002

A critique of dominant ways of conceptualizing capacity development and a presentation of an alternative perspective that emphasizes practice and a process of open facilitation, and resourcefulness over resources. Kaplan emphasizes the need to embrace complexity of change rather than reduce it down to technocratic formulas.

Shirky, C., *Here Comes Everybody: The Power of Organizing Without Organizations*, The Penguin Press, 2008

A savvy observer of how new technology and new politics are reshaping citizen organizing, Shirky catalogues the many ways in which individuals and small, loose groups of people are making a personal and social impact. Particularly important is to note how new tools can reduce the heavy transaction costs of traditional forms of organizing, as well as accelerate the speed of change.

13

The Micro–Macro Gap

It is not uncommon to find that public policies formulated and promulgated at national, or macro, level are not effective locally. Conversely, local development needs and interests seldom enjoy a supportive policy environment. These types of disconnects are referred to as the micro–macro gap. In programmes of some scale, therefore, capacity-development processes often need to establish and nurture linkages between actors and systems operating at different levels.

In this contribution Ubels, van Klinken and Visser describe three cases of sector development in which conscious efforts were made to create this type of connectivity. They extract five specific capacity-development focuses that will help practitioners engaged in any capacity-development initiative of some scale, to avoid perpetuating or reinforcing micro–macro disconnects.

Bridging the Micro–Macro Gap: Gaining Capacity by Connecting Levels of Development Action

Jan Ubels, Rinus van Klinken and Hendrik Visser

Introduction

Recent years have seen significant changes in development cooperation. For example, bilateral and multilateral donors have moved away from the direct implementation of projects and programmes towards sector-wide approaches (SWAps) and budget support to governments.

There is some evidence that these new aid modalities have stimulated institutional reform at macro or national level. They have helped improve policy coherence and planning capacity, strengthened the quality of public financial management and expanded the volume of public services. However, SWAps and related forms of donor support continue to face a broad range of structural challenges in achieving real impact on the ground. These include their:

- focus on public sector actors, which often neglects civil and private actors, who also play major roles in providing services, especially for the poor;
- underlying assumption that decentralization always leads to effective service provision, while in reality that is often doubtful;
- vulnerability to spending pressures and demands for quick results;
- reliance on centrally formulated performance frameworks and standard-ized notions of capacity development, often at the expense of improving their responsiveness to local specificity;
- tendency to strengthen upward (donor) rather than domestic accountability;
- inability to address power issues within the existing service delivery systems.

A common result of these structural weaknesses is that macro intentions do not often translate into intermediate or local impact, hence the macro–micro gap. Commonly used strategies to counter this gap include: making use of policy dialogue processes; improving institutional analysis; monitoring performance and results; funding mechanisms that support local development; and redirecting donor support to capacity development at the local level (van Reesch, 2007).

Yet while such recommendations generally hold true, they are to some extent also 'more of the same'. They reflect dominant development thinking, main-taining a top-down, funding-driven, central government-centred and technocratic approach. It makes it sound as if development itself – as much recent donor-driven aid language seems to suggest – is primarily about 'implementing the right policies'. Should it rather not (also) be about supporting the creativity, ambitions and abilities of local actors that give shape to their own processes of change? When seen from the bottom up, the challenging question stemming from the macro–micro gap is: how can national policies and programmes better respond to and create space for local solutions and innovations, rather than follow global prescriptions?

Each of the cases discussed in this chapter describes a major policy change in a sector and related efforts to make it work in practice. All cases focus on activities that require strong involvement of communities: the construction of rural roads, the management of community forests and the provision of primary health care. In the description of each case special attention is paid to the way that local practices changed and to the interaction between macro-level policy processes and micro-level experimentation and application. As we will see, the capacity-development lessons across the three cases have strong similarities.

Case Study 1: When macro dynamics limit local effectiveness

The first case is about the health sector reform in Mali. The original case study was prepared by Sonia Le Bay, Boubacar Dicko, Dramane Dao (SNV Mali) and Thea Hilhorst (KIT).

It presents a situation where aid provision and a combination of institutional reforms created both obstacles and opportunities for effective local service delivery.

Decentralization and developing partnerships for health in Mali

In Mali, most people depend on community health centres (Centres de Santé Communautaire – CSCOM) or traditional systems for their health care. Each CSCOM serves a population of at least 5000 people in several villages within a radius of roughly 15 kilometres. They provide basic health care, vaccinations and health education. Community health associations (Association de Santé Communautaire) are organizations of health users and are formally responsible for managing the health centres. This includes recruitment, acquiring drugs, overseeing planning and monitoring. In practice, however, most decisions are made by the CSCOM staff.

Sector planning and decentralization

Tied to a policy of 'deconcentration' since 1990, Mali has pursued a sectoral approach to administer its public services. The focus at the national level is on policy-making and regulation, while the CSCOMs and the districts undertake implementation. Planning is an upward process, starting at health centres and passing through meso levels of district and regional authorities to central government, where final approval is given and budgets are allocated. Aggregation inherent in this process often results in a loss of local priorities as well as long delays between budget allocation and the funds arriving at local level.

The establishment of elected local government in 1999 brought a major change in Mali's institutional landscape. Local governments became co-responsible for planning and managing public health in their areas, including the construction of health centres as well as funding equipment and staff. However, the Ministry of Health's planning system was not well integrated with local planning and funding mechanisms, so the two existed side by side. This disconnect resulted in poor use of meagre resources, duplication of activities and failure to adopt a more integrated approach to health care. National level actors were not ready for change. Workshops addressing the problems simply recommended new studies, which were then discussed at subsequent workshops.

Using action research to bridge the micro–meso–macro gap

At the municipal and district levels, however, health stakeholders who had to live with the frustration and waste stemming from lack of integration were more willing to move forward. Two development partners, the Netherlands Development Organisation (SNV) and the Dutch Royal Tropical Institute (KIT), had been actively involved in Mali's health sector and decentralization programme. The two organizations helped initiate an action research and learning process in the Koulikoro region with the aim of facilitating multi-stakeholder partnerships around primary health care. The programme was coordinated by the regional and district health service staff.

Working towards establishing a 'level playing field' and building trust, the process started with an exchange of information, ideas and experiences between the municipalities, the staff of the centres and user associations. Local platforms began informally and were gradually institutionalized around formal planning, monitoring and evaluation procedures. The approach established an understanding of each other's views, roles, policies and mandates, while making sure that all parties had timely access to all information. Joint planning and monitoring helped build shared vision, values and ownership. This process contributed directly to the 'decompartmentalization' of different types of actors and of different levels.

Results and advocacy

The programme has significantly changed actors' perceptions and attitudes, helped clarify roles and convert this into joint action. Ministry of Health staff have become increasingly supportive of local governments' engagement with public health. The partnership that has gradually emerged since 2004 has generated results that go well beyond what each could have achieved on their own. Here are some examples.

- Greater accessibility of information enables non-experts to participate in discussions and actions on health services. In the pilot municipalities, health indicators have started to improve. In one municipality, for example, the vaccination rate for tetanus has reached 100 per cent since the mayor led the community health association's mobilization campaign.
- Pregnant women experiencing complications during childbirth are now usually taken to hospital by ambulance. When they learned that the ambulance system was under threat because of arrears in funding, women pressed their local authorities to take action. After discussions between municipalities, the district and the Ministry of Health, the system's viability is now assured and municipalities understand their responsibility for paying their annual contributions.
- Community health centres rely for regular funding on the Ministry of Health, but unforeseen expenditures for emergencies are increasingly covered by local governments. Local governments have also mediated in conflicts between the CSCOMs, the health associations and villages.
- The Ministry of Health now takes local government planning into account in its own planning, and mayors attend planning sessions to defend their municipalities' priorities.

Results of this process have been communicated regularly to the regional and national level. The deconcentration and decentralization support unit (Cellule d'appui à la Déconcentration et décentralisation) at the Ministry of Health is now facilitating roll-out to other regions. The unit will also play a key role in institutionalizing the approach in the Ministry.

Key observations

This case highlights several barriers to good micro–meso–macro level connections.

- Macro plans for improved delivery based on institutional reform and shifting roles and mandates often exhibit implicit (and possibly unrealistic) assumptions about the capacity of local actors to develop new relationships and practices. Local communities often need assistance and support in meeting these challenges.

- Different institutional and policy developments can interfere with each other, creating contradictions and tensions that can become quite unworkable for local actors.
- A lack of open communication and collaboration between hierarchical levels is often a major obstacle for achieving effective results.

Key factors that enabled the new institutional arrangements to overcome such obstacles were:

- acquiring a much deeper understanding of local situations and collaboration of various local actors to find practical solutions to the problems faced;
- working explicitly to change dynamics between hierarchical levels;
- improving planning, budgeting and disbursement practices.

Case Study 2: A different story of micro–macro dynamics: Successful innovation and up-scaling

The following case from Albania shows how adequate attention to vertical and horizontal connections worked out well in terms of generating capacity for disadvantaged communities and groups. The original case study was prepared by Peter Kampen, Sheza Tomcini and Hamit Salkurti (SNV Albania).

While there are challenges still to be overcome, the case allows us to look at elements that may help to overcome a gap between macro intention and reality as it unfolds on the ground.

Innovation in the forestry sector in Albania: Using macro-level opportunities to build and up-scale local practices

Albania has a population of 3 million people. It was governed by a Communist regime for 40 years, transforming into a democracy and market economy after 1990. About 1 million hectares – 50 per cent of the country – is covered by forest. Forests surrounding villages are traditionally used by local communities. During the Communist era, the lower-level forests in particular were severely over-exploited and during the transition period there was illegal logging in large forests at higher altitudes.

Communal forestry was proposed in the 1990s as a policy response to problems of erosion and degradation. A government forestry project, funded by the World Bank (WB), entailed giving communities the right to use and manage degraded forests close to their villages. Local governments helped set up Forest User Associations. With support from SNV, such associations were established first in 5 communities, and later expanded to 30 locations. Ministry officials and other macro-level players were consulted during the development process. The experiment led to improved practices and guidelines for communal forestry.

The Forest User Associations and the surrounding communities began by investing in protection and regeneration. Through improved management, degraded forests gradually started to regenerate and provide and/or generate 'services' (erosion control, land stabilization, water management) and 'products' (firewood, fodder, sticks and poles, fruit, herbs and timber). Large areas of degraded forest have been regenerated and with the rise in productivity, household incomes have improved.

Due to the positive response from communities in the selected areas and a supportive policy environment, the number of communal forests and User Associations gradually increased. Regional associations, known as Communal Forest Federations, were established and, finally also, an umbrella National Communal Forest Federation, representing local associations at national level. This process allowed community users to be actively represented in national policy and decision-making processes. Regional and national federations now play an important role in reforming forestry legislation and influencing the policy process. At the regional level and below there is strong cooperation between the regional federations, local government and the Forest Service. This facilitates the up-scaling and horizontal dissemination of communal forestry practices.

The success of the project has resulted in a focus on communal forestry in the second phase of the forestry reform programme. Of the national forest area 70 per cent has now been transformed into communal ownership involving two-thirds of all local governments in the country, and currently supporting one-third of the population.

The positive results were achieved by providing flexible capacity development support at local and regional level, thus bridging the gap between these levels. Donors such as the World Bank and the Swedish International Development Cooperation Agency (SIDA) provided funding and, at times, pressure and accountability to move forward with the reform process. As the main capacity-development support provider at the local level, SNV had continuously to balance (a) technical forestry expertise, (b) facilitating interactive processes and local initiative, and (c) organizational and institutional development.

Key observations

Based on this Albanian case a few key observations can be made on how a new institutional pattern evolved and the importance of allowing adequate time for multi-actor engagement.

- Based on evidence of good local practice, actors at the meso-level (the associations and later the federations as well as local governments) began to adopt and spread the changes.
- The bottom-up process resulted in more support and accountability between the local, regional and national levels. This capacity gain provided the impetus for improvements to policies and regulations and the downward transfer of property rights. Gradually, micro and meso forces started to drive macro dynamics, rather than the other way around.
- Long-term commitment was crucial. Key individuals among forest users, and also within the Ministry, made the necessary changes possible.

- Overall, knitting together linkages between micro, meso and macro levels and across actors made a valuable contribution to the project's success.
- Key elements of the SNV capacity-development approach were: (a) a responsive form of support to building local practices with special attention to multi-actor engagement; and (b) development of meso-level structures capable of supporting, spreading and advocating effective practices.

Case Study 3: Trying to make a new policy responsive to local realities

This third case concerns a new road construction policy in Bhutan. The original case study was prepared by Hendrik Visser (SNV Bhutan). It shows how in a government-driven process deliberate efforts were undertaken to overcome the macro–micro gap.

Finding a new balance between micro and macro in a new concept of rural road construction

In the Himalayan kingdom of Bhutan, providing access to rural communities is one of the government's highest priorities and a key prerequisite for socio-economic development. Traditional construction methods cause considerable environmental and agricultural damage and require high investments for maintenance and restoration. In 1999, because of its track record in building capacity for district infrastructure in Zhemgang district, the Department of Roads (DoR) asked SNV to help develop and mainstream environmentally friendly road construction (EFRC) methods and standards.

After a number of local pilot projects had provided experience, an improved building method proved to be relatively successful and over time was formally adopted within the Department. Early in 2003, when the second phase of the EFRC project started, the focus of the programme shifted from technical innovation to organizational capacity building at the Department of Roads, and the institutionalization of the EFRC approach within the broader construction sector.

District engineering units had a keen interest in applying EFRC on district roads. However, since the units have a very diverse portfolio of public works responsibilities, they found it difficult to cope with their workload. Although they generally managed to start up construction works, there were often delays, budget lapses and inadequate quality control. Two main constraints were insufficient staff and a lack of necessary skills. However, the EFRC team also discovered a more fundamental institutional problem: the district engineering units played little or no part in the infrastructure planning process, from community or sub-district level up, or from national sector level down. For donor-funded projects, ministry staff decided on resource allocations and hardly coordinated with district engineering units on implementation planning or required capacity. This made it nearly impossible for district engineers to develop realistic annual work plans to make effective use of capacity and skills available.

One area that the DoR–SNV team focused on in the second phase was to create the space for district engineering units to voice their concerns and capacity needs. Workshops were conducted with sector ministries and the Ministry of Works to discuss structural constraints. Bringing stakeholders together, for problem analysis and solution finding, created a strong driver for action. It was realized that both levels – district and national – were highly interdependent when it came to achieving results. Central-level staff acquired a better understanding of meso-level realities. Increased communication boosted their motivation to address the issues. The national Department of Urban Development and Engineering Services, which represented the district engineers, played a critical role in this process.

Another interesting factor emerging during the second project phase related to community voice in infrastructure planning and quality. In the past in Bhutan, community participation was essentially seen as a matter of providing 'free' labour to implement district plans. Now, during construction, communities at times refused to take over the roads until they were satisfied with the quality and assured of funds for maintenance. The process of clarifying roles and responsibilities in road construction and maintenance gave communities the power to set criteria for the quality of services delivered by the district.

Key observations

This case illustrates a number of key elements for enhancing micro–meso–macro linkages.

- It reinforces some of the pointers of the earlier cases for capacity-development support to pay attention to building local practices, multi-actor engagement, changing dynamics between hierarchical levels, strengthening accountability and planning–budgeting–disbursement practices.
- It shows in particular that new policies need time to develop and mature. The credibility, products, experience and expertise acquired in a three-year pilot phase were essential in successfully achieving scale later on.
- The case also illustrates that if partner country ownership is strong, project management can create an incubator for a new approach and can stimulate broader sector change. Going to scale requires project management to develop sector-wide, multi-actor, inclusive ways of working, after which its own role can be gradually reduced.

Analysis: Lessons on developing more effective micro–macro dynamics

All three examples discussed in this chapter relate to situations where capacities need to be developed in a large number of local settings in order to realize a new policy or national programme. Though they are very different in sector and country conditions, the cases provide a number of remarkably clear lessons.

Effective policy implementation requires time to experiment and develop realistic new practices

Whether it is innovations in road construction in Bhutan, new forms of forest management in Albania, or decentralization of Mali's health sector, the three cases show that the policies initially formulated at the national level were not by themselves 'implementable'. Top-down standards do not create local solutions. Developing effective practices is indeed done locally. New policies and changed mandates require various actors to develop new roles and practices, indeed new capacities. Only through repeated practice does it become clear what it takes to actualize a new policy or a set of technical innovations. To this end, across the three cases, SNV practitioners applied principles of action-learning to assist local actors in developing effective solutions. This requires renewed appreciation that sources of innovation are found on the 'work floor', the periphery or edges of a sector rather than in the centre. Documentation, use of evidence and lobbying became important elements later in the process when the challenge was to spread and anchor practices in the larger system.

Local solutions require flexible and responsive capacity development support to local levels, with strong attention to multi-actor relations

In common across the Bhutan, Mali and Albania cases was the availability of sufficient support to develop new practices at the local level. Instead of spreading standard knowledge, prescriptions and training modules, the forms of capacity development provided were highly flexible and responsive in helping local actors to explore local solutions. They used generic knowledge, indeed, but applied this to local issues and dynamics. Their focus was not on 'transferring knowledge' but on working with local actors to adopt new insights and develop better working practices. Working sessions were tailored to the issues in each locality. Capacity-development support did not mean the roll-out of standard training modules only, but also entailed accompanying actors in addressing their issues and in their engagement with each other. In practice many sector programmes do not provide such support sufficiently, if at all. It is important too to understand that finding local solutions usually requires collaboration among various actors. Therefore practitioners must be able to (help) facilitate multi-actor engagement and interactions as a key part of their work.

To serve local requirements, significant attention is needed to changing the dynamics and working practices between hierarchical levels

Another cross-cutting theme emerging from the cases is the difficulty of effective communication and collaboration between hierarchical levels, even within one agency. Local actors needed support to get their voice heard at higher levels. Higher levels needed to learn to really listen and understand local problems, and not resort to the typical command and control 'instruction mode'. Actors at each level need to develop more trust and an appreciation that they have to work with other levels in the hierarchy in order to be successful. For this the quality and direction of information flows often need to change from top-down to much more bottom-up: action-learning processes, cases, field data and practical evidence appear to be essential in all cases to get a better quality of interaction and improve the quality of policy implementation. Notably processes for planning, budgeting and disbursement appear to be an important factor in the initial creation of the macro–micro gap. Adequate changes in these can strongly help bridge this space so that local priorities are better respected, planning is workable and resources are allocated on time.

Capacity-development practitioners can often play important roles in improving connections between levels in a system. Although it may be required in certain phases, the challenge is not to become too dominant as an intermediary oneself, but to facilitate the interaction between actors to be more open and effective. This places demands on the inter-personal, political and coaching skills of the practitioners involved.

Horizontal spreading is a key element in achieving scale

A common (implicit) perception is that 'policy implementation' is a top-down process. In reality it appears that horizontal spreading is an important mechanism for successful policy realization and scaling of effective practices. The Albanian regional forestry federations provide a particularly strong example of capacity development and scaling-up propelled at the meso-level. No higher-level government official can match the quality of information and convincing power provided by local actors and their representatives that have already realized a certain improvement on the ground. The source is as important as the message. Significant elements of this feature of communication are also visible in the Mali health and Bhutan roads cases. Central government units can play an important role in creating the conditions for such exchange. Practitioners can often make use of horizontal spreading mechanisms quite easily through, for example, organizing peer visits or inter-personal exchanges of information. However, the importance of such mechanisms is not often recognized in more formal policy processes or institutional dynamics.

Building effective micro–macro linkages is also about politics and power

At the start of the chapter we alluded to the fact that the macro–micro gap usually has much to do with politics. This is true for all the cases examined here. To achieve changes in road construction in Bhutan, develop forestry associations in Albania and improve health services in Mali, the key actors faced vested interests that either shied away from, or actively opposed, change. Practitioners involved in building capacities for such changes have to understand the forces at play and navigate the political dynamics. The capacity development focuses that we have identified here help to do so. Providing time for experimentation, support for realizing local practices, changing working relations and procedures between hierarchical levels, and fostering horizontal exchange all played a role in each case. These elements are not only functionally required for effective change to happen, but they also are strategies to carefully work with issues of power. Together these focuses help to shift relationships and strengthen downward accountability. Practitioners would do well to actively expand their understanding of the interests and political dynamics in their environment. They may also hone methods designed to see and analyse political and power dimensions, a capability that is underexposed in regular capacity-development discussion.

Conclusion

The macro–micro gap has been identified as a phenomenon reducing aid effectiveness. At the start of the article we raised the question: how can national policies and programmes better respond to and create space for local solutions and innovations? From the cases of micro–meso–macro dynamics that we have reviewed, five important capacity-development focuses can be extracted for use by practitioners:

- create adequate time to experiment and develop realistic new practices, document these and spread them on the basis of real-life experiences (not policy prescriptions only);
- power and politics need to be understood and worked with constructively to shift dynamics and accountability logics;
- provide responsive and flexible capacity-development support to local actors (rather than standard training), with strong attention to multi-actor engagement and facilitation of change dynamics;
- pay significant attention to changing dynamics and working practices between hierarchical levels, particularly communication and information flows and procedures for planning, budgeting and disbursement;
- foster horizontal spreading by representatives of local actors as an important motor for effectively achieving scale.

Our analysis suggests that these five focuses will help practitioners, when engaged in any capacity-development ambition of some scale, to avoid perpetuating or reinforcing processes where macro policy or programme objectives do not sufficiently translate into local solutions and micro results. Because it is there, at the local level, the rubber eventually has to hit the road.

Recommended readings

This chapter has direct links with explanations about different types of 'level' to be found in Chapter 3 and the discussion on governance and politics in Chapter 11. It also touches on multi-stakeholder engagement described in Chapter 2 and illustrated in Chapter 14. It further links to the conversation on 'balanced practice' in Chapter 5 (which also uses the Albanian forestry case) and on the challenges of dealing with power asymmetries between stake-holders in Chapter 6.

A starting point for writing an earlier version of the present chapter has been Van Reesch, E. (2007) 'Bridging the macro-micro gap: micro-meso-macro linkages in the context of sector-wide approaches', in *Rich Menu for the Poor*, Directorate General for International Cooperation (DGIS), The Hague (www.minbuza.nl/dsresource?objectid=buzabeheer:48068&type=org, accessed on 13 November 2009). That paper discusses the experiences with the sector-wide approach that has been adopted as a preferred aid modality by the Netherlands and other donors. Van Reesch identifies and discusses the 'macro–micro gap' as a key bottleneck and proposes ways to address it.

For a sharp critique on the planning and government orientation of most development assistance, see William Easterly (2008) *Planners vs Searchers in Foreign Aid*, Asian Development Bank, Manila (www.adb.org/Economics/ speakers_program/easterly.pdf, accessed on 13 November 2009). This paper is a fundamental critique on the planning fetishism that often still continues to determine the design and implementation of development policies and programmes. Easterly's concept of 'searchers' helps to elucidate the dynamics of 'social entrepreneurs', both in the context of social change and/or civic action as well as in more private sector and/or commercially driven dynamics. Easterly is also the author of the famous book: *The White Man's Burden: Why the West's Efforts to Aid the Rest Have Done So Much Ill and So Little Good*, Penguin Press, New York (2006).

On the role of donors, *Helping People Help Themselves: From the World Bank to an Alternative Philosophy of Development Assistance*, University of Michigan Press, by David Ellerman (2005) is an interesting perspective by another former senior adviser of the World Bank. This book discusses the fundamental shifts in dynamics required for the development sector to better enable inno-vation by local actors, ownership and empowerment. The book is particu-larly strong in drawing from a broad set of disciplines, such as economics, philosophy, psychology, management sciences, sociology and mathematics to develop other 'ways of seeing' the relations between aid organizations and recipients. Amongst others, Ellerman discusses the concept of 'decentral-ized social learning' that helps to elucidate why and how effective innovations spread horizontally rather than vertically.

Chevalier, J. and Buckles, D. (2008) 'SAS: a guide to collaborative inquiry and social engagement', co-published by International Development Research Centre, Ottawa, Canada and SAGE Publications India Pvt Ltd (www.sas2. net/en/sas2-guide, accessed on 14 November 2009). This book explains various participatory processes and techniques and highlights the extraordinary capacities of people to be collaborators in development research and activities. It also highlights five important skills for practitioners: mediating, grounding, navigating, scaling and interpreting (sense-making). It provides a challenging (new) view on already present micro-level capacities waiting to be embraced by macro-level policies.

Rondinelli, Dennis (1993) *Development Projects as Policy Experiments: An Adaptive Approach to Development Administration*, Routledge, London. This is a classic textbook on the design of development policies (and projects). Going beyond rational and linear planning models, it is a very useful guide on how to deal with the complex and uncertain institutional settings of development interventions and has practical suggestions and case studies.

Another interesting book is: David Mosse (2005) *Cultivating Development: An Ethnography of Aid Policy and Practice*, Pluto Press, London. Based on a detailed case study of a DFID project in India, the book critically questions the link between (macro-level) policy and (micro-level) development interventions. It argues that in practice, policies do not often generate the appropriate interventions for implementing them, but rather interventions look for the right policies to justify them.

14

Working with Value Chains

Understanding and developing value chains is receiving more attention as a systems-based approach for accelerating and scaling-up development processes. By their nature, value chains involve and connect multiple actors. A value chain approach is, additionally, applicable across economic as well as social domains.

In this interesting case, Duncan Mwesige describes a capacity-development intervention in an agricultural value chain in Uganda. He shows how particular multi-stakeholder processes (MSPs) were pivotal in helping chain-connected actors to develop new forms of cooperation that strongly improved efficiency, trust and pro-poor results at many levels. The practitioner will also find a number of practical lessons on the application of MSP methodologies.

Using Multi-Stakeholder Processes for Capacity Development in an Agricultural Value Chain in Uganda

Duncan Mwesige

Introduction

This is a description of a capacity-development intervention in an economic value chain in the Ugandan oilseed sector. It is an intervention that engages producer organizations, small, middle and large sized processors, input suppliers, traders and warehouse owners, government agencies, research organizations, higher institutions of learning, financial institutions, business development service providers, donor agencies and development organizations.

The article focuses on the effectiveness of multi-stakeholder processes (MSPs) and related methodologies in helping to improve capacities in the value chain as a whole. Often this will concern 'joint capacities' of several actors rather than capacities of individual actors only.

In the context of this chapter, multi-stakeholder processes are defined as 'bringing together different stakeholders (actors) who have an interest in a problem situation and engaging them in a process of dialogue and collective learning that improves decision-making, action and innovation'. The core role of MSPs in this case is to improve coordination and collaboration along the value chain, resulting in more efficient and equitable linkages that benefit the economically active poor.

Where market linkages are weak, such as is the case in many rural areas in Uganda, small and medium sized producers, input suppliers, traders and millers, are forced to depend on scanty and skewed information and business opportunities. They tend to have a narrow picture of their sector, which breeds suspicion and mistrust among the various actors and contributes to overall stagnation of the entire sector.

In such situations MSP approaches are a potentially relevant intervention. They seek to change the unproductive market dynamics and stimulate actors to take a broader view of the chain beyond the self interest of individual positions.

As we will show in this chapter, the development of multi-stakeholder processes in the Ugandan oilseed sector was the pivotal intervention that helped various changes to happen: existing relations were deepened as trust increased; new collaborations developed as new actors came into play; and overall coordination and information-sharing within the value chain improved tremendously. The MSP methodologies applied were part of a broader range of interventions that also included: improvement of rural information systems; strengthening of producer groups and service providers; innovations in value chain financing; and supporting effective public policy management initiatives. Together these interventions helped to increase growth and competitiveness for all actors and contributed to increased income for poor farmers in particular.

Initiating the multi-stakeholder process: A brief overview

A multi-stakeholder process to bring together various stakeholders in the oilseed value chain was initiated and facilitated by SNV Netherlands Development Organisation in 2007, and to date is still functioning.

The first concrete step in establishing the oilseed MSP was the carrying out of a sub-sector analysis and stakeholder mapping exercise. The analysis noted that while the sector had high potential for growth and a capacity to generate increased incomes at household level, it equally had a collection of constraints which, unless addressed, would remain a road block to prosperity. During the mapping exercise, therefore, time was taken to sensitize the respective actors and solicit their 'buy-in' to engage in transforming and streamlining the sector based on the identified challenges. Following the conclusion of the study, SNV convened a stakeholders meeting to agree on the analysis results and to prioritize the sub-sector challenges. Participants at the meeting set up a national platform to guide the process and, later in the same year, appointed task force committees to handle the different priority challenges. The main steps in the MSP intervention are described in more detail below.

Steps in the multi-stakeholder process

The situational analysis

The vegetable oilseed sub-sector is one of the seven strategic commodities selected by the Ugandan government within the policy framework of the Poverty Eradication Action Plan (PEAP). The sub-sector directly influences livelihoods of over 12 million Ugandans (all actors along the entire vegetable oil chain and their beneficiaries) mainly in north-eastern, south-western and central parts of Uganda. Oilseeds account for over 60 per cent of vegetable oil production in the country. Of the total vegetable oil consumed in Uganda, 60 per cent is imported as crude palm oil which is refined and blended with the locally produced sunflower oil (Bindraban et al, 2006).

Sunflower is the lead domestic raw material for vegetable oil. Annual production has increased from 70,000–80,000 metric tonnes (MT) per year in 2005 to 150,000 MTs in 2007 and was projected to increase to over 300,000 MTs by 2009/10, providing a livelihood for more than 500,000 farming households.

Sunflower is produced from both hybrid and open pollinated variety (OPV) seeds. Since Uganda is not able to produce hybrid seeds, they are currently imported from South Africa by a large private sector company, Mukwano Industries Uganda Ltd. Sunflower production is exclusively done by smallholder farmers, while processing is carried out by a range of small, medium and large scale processors with varying capacities (Vellema et al, 2007).

Oilseed prices have continued to increase from as low as 300 Uganda shillings per kilogramme (shs/kg) in 2005 to around 500shs/kg in 2008, and currently stand at 600shs/kg. The domestic demand continues to increase because of higher local per capita oil consumption. In addition, regional demand in the Democratic Republic of Congo (DRC), southern Sudan, Rwanda, Kenya, Tanzania and Burundi have further opened up markets for the Uganda vegetable oils (Ton and Opeero, 2009).

Over the past ten years the growth of the oilseed sub-sector has been supported by concerted efforts: enabling policies by the government, including macro-economic stability and human resource development, and privatization and liberalization with support from donors.

The situational and value-chain analysis also identified many constraints that could potentially limit the sector's capacity to generate the desired productivity, incomes and employment, including:

- inadequate access to high yield planting seed;
- lack of market information throughout the entire chain;
- poor input supply system;
- weak producer organizations and unequal power relations in the market;
- poor price setting mechanisms;
- poor bulking and post-harvest handling facilities and technologies;
- poor access to finance at various levels in the chain;
- poor innovation and technology transfer;

- lack of coordination and collaboration among actors in the chain;
- weak sub-sector policies and regulations.

Despite these weaknesses, the analysis found that there was sufficient potential within the sector, particularly with respect to improving household income and food security for poor smallholders. The restoration of peace in the main growing areas and the increasing household incomes from this chain meant there was room for further expansion in the number of producers. In addition, seedcake from milling could be used for animal feed and in the production of bio-fuels. Other possibilities included the potential to serve Uganda's domestic, regional and export markets, and to add value to oilseed value-chain activities by establishing links with the education sector for vocational training of producers and processors.

Establishing the national platform

Following the completion of the situational analysis, SNV facilitated a national meeting at which stakeholders discussed and validated the findings. The actors concluded that there was need to form a national oilseed sub-sector 'platform' to address sub-sector constraints and to simultaneously identify and strengthen capacity of the stakeholders, especially producer organizations, to actively participate in this process. It was also agreed that since most value-chain activities took place at the farmer (district and sub-national) levels, similar processes may be facilitated at that level. This would address specific local constraints and also support national-level initiatives with grass-roots based evidence. It was agreed to hold national platform meetings every quarter and regional platforms three times during the oilseed growing season (pre-season, during the growing period and at marketing).

After prioritization of key challenges, a task force was put in place to define the mandate, vision, objectives and activities of the platform. Additional task forces were established to convene processes to resolve the different sub-sector challenges. Eligibility for the various task forces was based on the role of each stakeholder organization in the chain and the potential contribution they could make. The task forces met every month to agree on strategies and undertake steps to engage stakeholders and address the specific issue.

The national platform also commissioned an 'oilseed value chain pro-poor development action research project', which was implemented by Makerere University and Wageningen University from the Netherlands. This project focused on two domains: market coordination and institutional arrangements; and innovative capacity and technological upgrading. The goal of the project was to support the task forces in defining a policy agenda and proposing workable solutions based on research evidence from the field. Two additional studies to enhance the evidence-base of the platform were undertaken by SNV Uganda, namely: a detailed oilseed value-chain financing analysis, and a study on the availability of quality planting seed in Uganda.

Box 14.1 Participants at the national level

These participants included:
Mukwano Industries, UOSPA (Uganda Oil Seeds Producers & Processors Association), VEDCO (Volunteer Efforts for Development Concerns), VODP (Vegetable Oil Development Program), UNFEE (Uganda National Farmers Federation) UIRI (Uganda Industrial Research Institute), USAID–APEP (Agricultural Productivity Enhancement Program), Wageningen University and Research Centre, Centenary Bank, Post Bank Uganda, ACDI/VOCA, Oikocredit, UNADA (Uganda National Agro-input Dealers Association), Victoria Seeds Ltd., Stanbic Bank, NPA (National Planning Authority), SNV-Uganda, DANIDA ASPS (Agriculture Sector Program Support Program), MAK-DFST (Makerere University, Department of Food Science and Technology), NARO/NASSARI (National Agricultural Research Organization) and NAADS (National Agriculture Advisory Services).

The regional MSPs

Much of what happened at national level was fed by information and experiences at regional level, and in turn national-level achievements benefited the actors at regional level. The regional actors involved in the platform were drawn from the major oilseed production and processing areas in Eastern Uganda, West Nile, Middle North and the Ruwenzori regions. As noted earlier, regional platform meetings were held at the beginning of the growing season, in the middle of the season and at the end of the season.

At the beginning of the season, regional-level actors were brought together to coordinate and plan the sub-sector activities for the entire season. Producer organizations were linked to input suppliers and facilitated to determine the expected demand and supply, identify the different distribution points for the inputs, agree on the prices, and so on. Financial services providers were invited to participate at these meetings to assess the extent of finance required during each phase in the growing period, and to discuss the criteria that actors needed to meet in order to access the financing.

During the growing period, actors came together to review the production targets set at the beginning of the season, and to assess the level of extension services and all the other requirements. Farmers at this point were linked to extension and other service providers. Processors were brought in at this moment to assess the expected level of production and start planning for the warehousing, transportation, buying and processing requirements.

At the end of the season, all the actors again came together to agree on bulking points and transportation arrangements, to negotiate the prices and agree on how to coordinate the marketing period. Action research took place during these platform meetings but also in between, led by individual actors.

The interactions at the regional level provided key evidence for the lobby activities and sub-sector growth strategies at the national level.

Box 14.2 Participants at regional level

Participants at this level included:
Mukwano Industries Uganda Limited, Cotton CN/Nile Agro Industries and donors such as USAID's Agricultural Productivity Enhancement Program (USAID-APEP), Agriculture Sector Program Support from Danida (ASPS), other small and medium sized processors, producer organizations, input stockists and distributors, traders, financial institutions, local government agriculture departments, extension services providers, local researchers, business development service providers, transporters and warehouse owners, among others.

Key achievements of the multi-stakeholder processes

Direct results of the MSP task force activities

The various task forces set up by the national platform developed strategies for both short- and long-term results. The following are some results of these collaborative processes.

- To ensure the availability of quality planting seed to all farmers, the platform presented a memorandum signed by all stakeholders to the Seed Variety Release Committee of the National Agricultural Research Organization to immediately release the seed varieties that had been undergoing trials for a long time but had not been released due to bureaucracy at the ministry. The seed varieties were released within two weeks of the request.
- The platform engaged in discussions with the largest processor and seed importer in the oilseed value chain (Mukwano Industries Uganda Limited) to increase the amount of hybrid seed they imported into the country to ensure sufficient quantities for all the farmers in the sub-sector. Several negotiations yielded positive results with the company agreeing to import seed worth US$1 million every planting season. The platform further negotiated for a guarantee scheme from the Danish International Development Agency – Agriculture Sector Programme Support (DANIDA-ASPS) for the Uganda National Agro-input Dealers Association (UNADA). The financing enabled the association to access the seed from Mukwano Industries and distribute it to farmers using its nationwide input distribution network. These actions led to about 70 per cent of the total oilseed-producing households gaining access to high quality hybrid seed. As a result, yields per acre increased from 600kg in 2007 to the current level of 1000kg. This increment has also been attributed to the improved agronomy practices resulting from skills acquired using the oilseed demonstration sites (see below).
- To further increase production, the platform members negotiated additional support from the United States Agency for International Development, through its Agriculture Productivity Enhancement Project (USAID-APEP), as well as the earlier-mentioned DANIDA-ASPS. This funding enabled the setting

up of demonstration sites in all the oilseed growing areas in order to improve agronomy practices.

- The national platform also carried out a policy study that recommended the establishment of a Seed Policy and Certification Act to regulate the activities of research and development, breeding, multiplication and distribution of planting seed. During a policy dialogue in 2009, the government of Uganda and the International Fund for Agricultural Development (IFAD) committed themselves to prioritize funding for the production of local hybrid varieties as well as maintenance breeding of the open pollinated variety. As part of the same efforts, the platform successfully lobbied for the mandate of monitoring and evaluating the implementation of the oilseed sub-sector policies and activities.
- Taking advantage of DANIDA-ASPS leverage funds, the platform negotiated an agricultural loan guarantee scheme with the Stanbic Commercial Bank, in which all oilseed farmers would have access to loans for purchasing ploughing implements on the basis of a 50 per cent guarantee from the donor. To date, 50,000 oilseed producers have benefited from the scheme.
- On the issue of market coordination, the action research carried out at the beginning of the partnership had recommended bulking at production level as a means to improve market coordination. Bulking is the collection of produce from different farmers at one spot. Two bulking best practices were recommended for up-scaling; producer organization-led bulking and processor-led bulking. The platform further facilitated producer organizations to access grants for warehouse construction and trade finance from financial institutions to purchase raw materials from farmers for bulking. The bulking practices helped to eliminate middle men, reduced post-harvest losses and increased the prices received at the farm gate. In addition the producer organizations were empowered to negotiate much better deals with the processors. This helped farmers to earn higher prices: rising from some 400 Uganda shillings (shs) in 2007, to between 550 and 700 shs/kg of raw material in 2009. This price increase has attracted more farmers to adopt sunflower production, with the number of producers rising more than three-fold in three years to around 500,000 currently. Coupled with increased yields, this has led to a very significant increase in the production of oilseeds in Uganda.
- The increased production has also attracted an influx of investments in the value chain. Recently, for example, a US$30 million processing plant was commissioned by Mt. Meru Millers Ltd. The growth in investments means there is competition for raw materials from producers, which is expected to result in improvements in the prices offered to farmers, as well as the quality of services across the value chain. The rise in the number of processors – from 25 in 2007 to 34 in 2009 – and the growing number of producers further reflect increased employment within the sub-sector. This drive to enter into the sub-sector is an indication of the oilseed value chain growth, business attractiveness and likely profitability.
- The action-research phase identified the role of government and donor agencies in encouraging bulking through establishment of the warehouse receipt system located closer to the production areas and guaranteeing agricultural loans through the existing commercial financial institutions. The policy dialogue held

---

Box 14.3 The Rural Information System (RIS)

This is an ICT-enabled market-information programme developed by SNV Uganda in partnership with the Uganda Commodity Exchange to support the collection, storage, processing, retrieval and dissemination of information on agricultural commodity markets. The programme provides organized farmer groups with business-development capacity building, communication equipment in the form of a computer and accessories, an email/internet link and a specially tailored database for information management.

---

in September 2009 resulted in the government committing to prioritize bulking through the IFAD-funded oilseed sub-sector support programme. Uganda's Minister of State for agriculture–crop production and IFAD representatives participated at the dialogue and signed an aide-memoire for a five-year US$30 million support to the development of the vegetable oil sub-sector.

- The government of Uganda and the main sub-sector donor (IFAD) have requested the oilseed platform to take the lead in the development and implementation of the long term Uganda vegetable oil sub-sector master plan. This is a sign of appreciation and confidence in the multi-stakeholder process and the results that have been achieved to date.

The MSPs as motor for other types of interventions

It was mentioned earlier that the MSPs were used as a pivot for implementing other interventions. Through the MSPs, producers were stimulated to strengthen their organizations, enabling them to have a collective and strong voice during the platform discussions, articulate their challenges and negotiate for better terms and conditions. Organizational-strengthening support helped farmers to gain confidence, trust and meet the criteria for conducting business with or receiving services from other chain actors. This helped producers to manage and have control over certain chain activities. Thus producer group strengthening was strongly stimulated by MSP dynamics.

The interactions in and around the platforms also formed a basis for working on improving value-chain financing. The SNV advisers brokered interactions, for example facilitating processes where the financial services providers developed products that would suit the needs of the chain. On the other hand SNV advisers facilitated the chain actors to meet the criteria for accessing the financing. Initially many actors didn't know what financing was available or how to access it. But empowered by growing interactions and information, gradually farmers and other chain actors started accessing these products on their own.

A lot of information that was used and shared during the MSPs was generated from the market intelligence studies and subsequently made available through the work on the rural information systems. Certain activities could not have been implemented smoothly without that information, analysis and intelligence. It empowered actors to understand options, take decisions and make deals with others.

In general one can observe that the use of MSPs has not only improved relationships between processors and farmers, but has also resulted in more equitable relations in the sector. Large processors have been able to negotiate with empowered producers on issues of prices, bulking points and access to other services during the regional MSPs. This has increased the trust and relationship between the different chain actors. The willingness of a highly capitalized large corporation to sit around the table to discuss and negotiate with small and relatively weak farmer organizations and small scale processors, is another indication of the leverage power of MSPs in ensuring more equitable relations across the entire value chain.

Box 14.4 Results of the MSP intervention

Outputs

A   Better communication and information sharing
B   Increased trust among actors
C   Better joint analysis and priority setting
D   Joint action on specific issues
E   Increased interactions with external actors such as government and donors

Outcomes

A   *Ability to act and self-organize*: Improved confidence, engagement and mutual understanding of actors in the chain, translating into various kinds of new actions and partnerships between value-chain actors
B   *Ability to cohere and integrate different dimensions:* Improved ability to think beyond specific actor interests and see overall perspectives, negotiate between different interests and develop joint positions
C   *Ability to relate and create operating space:* Increased effectiveness of engagement with government, donors and financial institutions to influence policy development and seek and use improved financing options
D   *Ability to learn and adapt:* The ability to create joint understanding and identify new solutions that subsequently translate into concrete actions and results mentioned under A, B and C
E   *Ability to produce relevant development results:* Increased ability to organize and improve the primary process in the value chain, resulting in increased engagement of farmers, processors and others and in improved effectiveness and efficiency of many links in the chain

Impacts

A   Increased productivity, incomes and employment of actors across the chain
B   More efficient and profitable production and processing
C   Reduced imports of palm oil, savings on foreign exchange

A summary of outputs, outcomes and impacts

The results of the MSP intervention in combination with the information, organizational, finance and policy interventions are summarized in Box 14.4. We use the so-called 'five core capabilities' (5Cs) logic to describe and group the outcomes. Developed by researchers at the European Centre for Development Policy Management (ECDPM), the framework is described in more detail in Chapter 1 of this volume. All five dimensions are considered to be required for an organization that shows effective capacity. Here we apply it to the capacities of the value chain as a whole.

Insights and lessons for the practitioner

This case shows that, when combined with other interventions, MSP methodologies can be successfully applied in the context of economic value chains, engaging actors with potentially opposing economic interests to produce pro-poor outcomes.

MSPs have the potential to be the pivotal intervention that also helps to stimulate and bring together the success of other interventions. In this case these other interventions were: strengthening of specific producer and service provider organizations; improving rural information systems; boosting innovative value-chain financing; and strengthening public policy management.

The outcomes of the interventions can not only be described in terms of improved capacities of individual actors, they can also be seen as contributing to increased capacity of different actors together, the value chain as a whole, and the actor-network around oilseeds. That improved capacity has been described in this case in terms of the 'five core capabilities'. The continuation of MSP types of dynamics without the engagement of external facilitators shows that indeed such processes start to form part of the collective capacity of the chain (Box 14.4).

Facilitating MSP interventions requires the use of a range of methods and approaches. As sketched in this case, SNV advisers employed various approaches and methods that included process facilitation, action research, focus group discussions, stakeholder analysis, training, organizational development, relationship brokering, scenario analysis, participatory rural appraisal, participatory learning and action and consensus building.

In addition a number of practical lessons on doing MSPs have been learned.

- Doing a good value-chain analysis early in the process is essential in helping everybody to understand the context/situation better.
- The personal competence to directly facilitate MSP activities or to lead the participation of a particular stakeholder group in an MSP is essential for the facilitating institution. As a facilitator(s) you should have a clear vision of what you are trying to achieve; a set of theories, assumptions and values about how to bring about change; a set of methodologies that will guide your action; a set of techniques and tools to put the methodologies into practice; and the personal qualities and skills to take on a facilitation role.
- MSPs, once properly organized and facilitated, can independently attract

Figures 14.1 and 14.2 *Benefits at the farm level include access to high quality seeds and collection facilities*

financing either from the private or public sector.

- The benefits of an MSP to the stakeholders should be made explicit. What do they expect to gain from participating in this complex and time-consuming process? What could your organization offer to the process and what does your organization expect to gain? And is there sufficient balance between 'give and take'?
- Factors related to behaviour and personalities are crucial to the success of an MSP. The human factor has to be very seriously taken into account. The working group for this MSP gives particular attention to the construction of mutual trust.
- The MSP approach proved to be a very stimulating concept for the stakeholders, but is also a complex approach. The identities, objectives, interests, organizational cultures, roles, etc. vary strongly between participants. A good MSP takes these differences into account and has to be flexible in its process. This also bears consequences for the facilitators who have to observe and deal with organizational differences as mentioned above and essentially need to be seen as non-partisan by the various actors.
- Effective MSPs will define both short-term wins and long-term strategies to keep the stakeholders interested and motivated.
- An effective MSP will try as much as possible to deal with issues that cut across the sub-sector and affect every stakeholder, as opposed to addressing issues that affect just a section of individual stakeholders. Once the big picture has been dealt with, the smaller issues can come into consideration.
- Since MSPs are loose networks of like-minded actors who come together to understand and solve specific constraints within the value chain, it has been observed that they should always remain action oriented, less bureaucratic and focused to maintain interest among actors. Time 'value for money' should be emphasized.
- Overall we can conclude that MSPs can indeed work very well in a setting of strong economic interests. They can help to make other particular interventions in the chain more effective. In the case described in this chapter, producer group strengthening, market information, value chain financing and influencing public policy yielded more results in an MSP set-up and thus proved more effective in fostering economic efficiency and pro-poor impact. The MSP work strongly helped to embed these specific interventions. The capacity of value-chain actors to work together increased, creating not only specific gains for themselves but also increasing overall capacity and development results.

References

Bindraban, P., Mutunga, J., Kamuhanda, R., Muyinda, G. and Agong, R. (2006) *Weaving the Oilseed Web: Report of a Scoping Mission,* AgriProfocus, Arnhem, The Netherlands

Ton, G. and Opeero, D.M. (2009) *Upscaling Oilseed Bulking Arrangements in Uganda,* Study conducted as part of the DGIS-WUR Pro-poor Oilseed value chain Action Research Project, Oilseed Subsector Uganda platform (OSSUP)

Vellema, S., Nakimbugwe, D. and Mwesige. D (2007) *Addressing Competitive*

Pressures, Instabilities and Uncertainties in Uganda Oilseed sector: Perspectives for a Multi-stakeholder Platform Strategy, presentation for the Third Sunflower Symposium for Developing Countries, Entebbe, Uganda

Recommended readings

This chapter builds upon the introduction of the multi-actor dimension of capacity development in Chapter 2 (which also has an interesting set of further readings). It also links to multi-actor dimensions in Chapter 12 on public accountability, Chapter 13 on micro–macro linkages and Chapter 17 on knowledge networking. The 5Cs model used to describe capacity outcomes is discussed in detail in Chapter 1. The following are some interesting readings on MSPs and especially on value chains.

Minu Hemmati et al (2002) *Multi-stakeholder Processes for Governance and Sustainability Beyond Deadlock and Conflict*, Earthscan, London and Sterling, VA

This book deals with governance and sustainability, which are important elements to consider when using MSPs to build value chains. The whole issue of chain governance is clearly articulated as are the ways in which the reader can apply it not only to deal with value-chain governance issues but the sustainability of MSPs as well.

Agriculture and Food Council of Alberta (2002) *Value Chain Handbook: New Strategies to Create more Rewarding Positions in the Market Place*, AFC, Edmonton

This handbook focuses on how to position particular value chains to achieve competitiveness in the market. It also discusses various strategies and approaches in value chain development. It helps one understand how to analyse value chains and the entire process of developing and implementing value-chain development strategies.

Bedford, A., Blowfield, M., Burnett, D. and Greenhalgh, P. (2001) 'Value Chains: lessons from the Kenya tea and Indonesia cocoa sectors', *Focus*, no 3, Resource Centre for the Social Dimensions of Business Practice, London

Using several examples, this article explores approaches and strategies for the implementation of value chains, drawing out valuable lessons for the practitioner. The reading also links value chain strategies to pro-poor development.

Lundy, M., Gottret, V., Cifuentes, W., Ostertag, C.F., Best, R., Peters, D. and
    Ferris, S. (2004) 'Increasing the competitiveness of market chains for small-
    holder producers', *Manual 3: Territorial Approach to Rural Agro-enterprise
    Development*, Rural Agro-enterprise Development Project International
    Centre for Tropical for Agriculture (CIAT), Colombia

This is an interesting reading because it examines how smallholder farmers
can be empowered and integrated into value chains. Some of the experiences
narrated here closely mirror the Ugandan case, especially in showing how
addressing constraints at the lower end of the value chain helped enhance
farmers' competitiveness.

Lusby, F. and Panliburton, H. (2005) *Promotion of Commercially Viable Solutions
    to Subsector and Business Constraints*, Action For Enterprise, Arlington, VA

This story provides lessons for practitioners on how to approach value-chain
development from a sub-sector or business point of view.

15

Engaging with Community-based Organizations

This chapter, by Schirin Yachkaschi, draws on practical experience and a study with urban community-based organizations (CBOs). It shows that if certain basic principles are not employed with integrity, a common outcome is the undermining of the distinct value of CBOs in aided-development processes.

Her evidence challenges the practitioner to step out of pre-conceptions associated with formal organizing. Only then can one properly appreciate the true contribution of community-based organizations in coping positively with the unstable, impoverished environments in which they operate.

Lessons from Below: Capacity Development and Communities

Schirin Yachkaschi

Background

This chapter addresses the question of how to strengthen community-based organizations (CBOs), which should be – and in theory are – at the centre of most development efforts, in order to take their rightful place in the development process. It is built on the assumption that the development of organizational capacity would be crucial in order to reach that aim. There is a long, well documented history of proven community development principles and practices to draw on which point to the value of a process-oriented approach for reaching this outcome. Yet this type of orientation has not been widely applied. Instead capacity development for CBOs tends to be about short-term (skills) training for individuals and 'packages' offered in various fields by different non-governmental organizations (NGOs) and donors. Such methods often reflect deeper forces and imperatives that reinforce aid-driven 'disempowerment' of CBOs. Avoiding this outcome calls for a practitioner's critical attention in selecting from present-day methods that respect the integrity of the principles and philosophy that lie at the roots of community development.

This contribution draws on experience of one type of contemporary process approach, namely the implementation of organizational development (OD) processes within three case CBOs. It also brings experiences from work with the South African NGO, Community Connections, as well as findings from PhD research in the townships of Khayelitsha, Mbekweni and Valhalla Park, Cape Town (Yachkaschi, 2008). The aim of the research was to analyse the current environment and the situation in which CBOs find themselves. This understanding allowed a practical evaluation of whether and how OD can provide a suitable way to build their capacity towards becoming independent and sustainable organizations; put another way, for CBOs to evolve as strong civil society organizations that actively participate in the development of their communities and are seen as valuable partners.

The following sections briefly set out the concepts and history of community development, CBOs and capacity development. After 'setting the scene' I discuss CBO capacity as it is widely perceived in the aid system. This review then draws on my work and study to offer suggestions about OD principles and approaches that have been inspired by experiences of community development, which practitioners could apply at a grass-roots level. The discussion stems from a particular grounding and so may not directly apply in other countries or more rural settings. However, it highlights dynamics in a local practice of capacity development which can be relevant in an international, aid-related context.

Community development, CBOs and capacity development – some definitions

CBOs, community development, participatory development, empowerment and similar terms labelling key principles to bring about change have been in use since at least the early 1980s. Today 'grass-roots' actors and concepts are entwined in the theory and practice of the development profession. Community development promotes human development by 'empowering communities and strengthening their capacity for self-sustaining development'. The basic principle is 'collaboration in life-sustaining activities', which has historically been practised by local communities since the existence of human societies (Monaheng, 2000).

Community development became a popular approach to social improvement during decolonization in the 1950s and 1960s. Influenced by experiences in the United States and Britain on social welfare programmes, its principles were based on self-reliance and cooperative action through popular bodies. Subsequently, governments were seen as the 'delivery machine' of development with hierarchical relationships (functionary vs. beneficiary) and political élites as results. Consequently, the concept of community development was abandoned in the late 1960s, but regained attention from the late 1980s as a solution to persisting social and economic issues in disadvantaged areas.

An understanding that development cannot be implemented by outsiders, and that the social capital of people at ground level needs to be tapped and enhanced, is increasingly informing development theory, even if the principles do not always translate into applied practice. However, critics see this approach as a way of depoliticizing development by co-opting grass-roots development organizations into a national or global agenda. They argue that the lack of focus on underlying causes, while aiming at producing short-term results, might rather worsen issues than remedy them.

For our purposes, CBOs are defined as voluntary associations of community members who reflect the interests of a broader constituency. They are generally small, informal organizations; often membership-based, initiated by local residents and located within the communities they serve. Thus, building the organizational capacity of CBOs could have a direct impact both on their involvement in communities as development agents, and as active citizens.

Capacity development can be located in a bottom-up approach to community development. In the context of this chapter, community is either understood as locality or neighbourhood, or can refer to an interest community forming the constituency of a particular organization. Such communities are not homogeneous. Particular sensitivity is needed towards issues of power and domination within communities regarding gender, class and ethnicity.

CBO capacity development – working against disempowerment

The following section takes a closer look at CBO capacity development, specifically, who determines which capacities are to be developed at a CBO level and towards what ends?

Views on CBO capacity and the importance of practitioner positioning

Fukuda-Parr et al (2002) challenge underlying assumptions that inform the practice of the capacity development profession. They object to the premise: (a) that developing countries lacked important skills and abilities – and that outsiders could fill these gaps with quick injections of know-how; (b) that it is possible simply to ignore existing capacities in developing countries and replace them with knowledge and systems produced elsewhere – a form of development as displacement, rather than development as transformation; and (c) that it is possible for donors ultimately to control the process and yet consider the recipients to be equal partners. These systemic issues also apply to development of CBO capacity which takes place within the development mainstream. Capacity development of community-based organizations is largely directed by those more powerful in the sector, such as donors, NGOs and local government institutions.

Community-based organizations are openly valued for capacities they have, becoming the target of many development interventions. They are seen as central to development efforts, since they are closest to and reflect the dynamics of poor communities. They are often embedded within social relationships at this micro level of interaction, which makes it easier for them to articulate concerns and drive local development processes. There is, however, a contradiction in the kind of capacity meant to be developed in order to execute their role as development agents, so working towards the historical task of eradicating poverty.

In interviews with CBO members, as well as leaders of the communities they are part of, there seemed to be general agreement regarding the areas of capacity that CBOs need to develop. Next to sectoral capacity relating to the particular technical field of work each CBO offered, suggestions relating to organizational capacity included:

- operating independently and accessing resources, including formal non-profit registration;
- financial management, project planning and management;
- writing of minutes, reports, funding proposals and reports.

Most CBOs that requested OD support from Community Connections asked for assistance in strategic planning; fundraising support including proposal writing training; help in formalizing their organizational structure, including registration as a non-profit organization; and policy development. Other requests related to training of committee members, analysing obstacles to organizational effectiveness, support for report writing, action learning and capacity building. Members wanted to professionalize in order to raise or maintain funding. However, since the need usually arose through external requirements, the capacity development process frequently lacked a living vibrancy and immediacy. Often there was no real commitment to work through the support asked for. It was difficult to tackle CBOs' actual needs, as the funding issue dominated.

The capacities listed above resemble the capacities expected in the more established NGO and (to a certain degree) the private sector. Having worked voluntarily for long periods, CBO members were expressing a wish to enter the development system and be rewarded for their activities. 'NGO-ism' became the role model to do so. One needs to seriously question whether those types of 'capacity' would have been requested by CBOs had they not been imposed on the sector. Under conditions of extremely unequal educational background, knowledge can be used to make CBOs subjects of those providing assistance, justified by their 'knowing better'. In such contexts, capacity development gets caught in a kind of politics of (un-) truths: donors and NGOs claim to know what capacity is needed by CBOs, which, in turn, play along to avoid jeopardizing future support. In a similar vein, capacity educational materials for CBOs and community workers promote capacity development relating to formalization and addressing basic community needs; but most do not address larger questions of power.[1]

The issue facing practitioners is that, often, the value stated behind capacity development is 'empowerment'. Yet no real shift in power results from such interventions when the original principles of community development are subordinated to the exigencies of aid agencies and their measures of performance.

Consequently, CBOs are more likely to be co-opted into the strategies of donors and governments, who use them as cheap implementers of programmes.

Hence, the 'for what' question is critical in capacity development. For what do you need capacity as a CBO? Is it to take on your own development and accept the 'empowerment by privatization' route where you have to take more responsibility for yourself? Or would you see it more in contestation and (rights-based) claim-making on the state systems that are supposed to be ensuring freedom from want by redistributing and re-allocating, and so on? My experience inclines me to say that, though they are not mutually exclusive and both capabilities are often needed, the latter makes you stronger than the former, and the former doesn't allow you to be stronger at the latter.[2]

While working with case study CBOs, answering the 'for what' question remained a professional dilemma, and one which challenges a practitioner to take a position. Should one try to enable a more authentic approach and ignore aid sector demands? Or should the practitioner help CBOs play by the rules of the game, risking the suppression of local needs and priorities? In one case, a CBO was promised funding by a local government authority to implement a home visit programme. This initiative was designed by the government to provide advice to several thousand people infected with and affected by HIV and AIDS. The amount to be provided for the programme bore no realistic relationship to the work involved. Moreover, the CBO was expected to deliver an audited financial statement for the received amount. The auditor's costs might easily have equalled the funding amount promised. The CBO would have been coerced into a contract that could have dragged it into debt. At the same time, after having tried for a long time to gain support from local government, members initially hesitated in rejecting the money, in the hope that they might be able to raise more reasonable amounts in future. Should time and resources be spent on capacity development to satisfy funders' demands? Wouldn't this be counterproductive to development and activism? In complying, might the CBO lose embeddedness in the communities or become incapable of challenging the agencies that they would depend on?

For all CBOs studied, closeness to the community was of vital importance for their existence as well as for the relevance of their activities, where governance requirements often became a burden. Donor demands put CBOs under a tension between wanting to meet such requirements while staying true to their purpose and accountable to the community they serve. On one hand, ignoring the need for finance in community organizations may romanticize poverty. On the other hand the current model of external donor control often reproduces the dependency and subordination that people in poor communities are already experiencing. Without care, supporting CBOs to become eligible for donor funding may contribute to their disempowerment. This occurs, for example, through disconnecting from community, as well as depoliticizing activities. An issue for practitioners, therefore, is to decide if and how to develop CBO capabilities which better enable them to navigate and steer around this type of tension without losing coherence and becoming 'un-rooted'.

At the same time, it is not often acknowledged that CBOs have capacities that donors or NGOs lack. Examples include: experience and rooting in their social context; having access to the intended constituency; language capacities; flexibility and adaptability; the ability to respond to crises as they arise; and the capacity to deal with tragedies and injustices. Those capacities seem to count for less and not empower CBOs towards equal status or an openly acknowledged interdependence in the sector. Beyond that, such acknowledgement may threaten those who currently hold power in an aided development process, as it would question their legitimacy. A 'neutral' stance or position of advisers in this common, structural, condition of CBOs is hard to describe as being neutral in practice. As an overview, Figure 15.1 describes the situation encountered in working with case CBOs.

Existing capacities – the importance of leading and relating

The concept of CBO-capacity development needs a thorough, close understanding of existing capacities, as well as deeper engagement with each individual organization. The results of my study point to a priority focus on two sets of capabilities: leadership and the ability to relate.

Leadership capacity in the case CBOs was expressed through strong pioneers. They were the main driving forces of the CBOs but could also tend to dominate the organizations. This condition raised questions about ethical and collective leadership styles. The leaders' personal history, and their sense-making of their circumstances with the members of their organizations, provided the collective

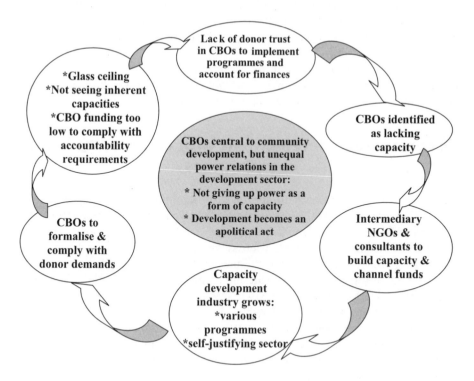

Source: Yachkaschi, 2008, p164

Figure 15.1 *CBO capacity development cycle*

story, which gave rise to the vision and identity of the organizations. In other words, they determine how the organization understands and stays true to itself and sustains its legitimacy within the community. Volunteerism plays an important part in the functioning of CBOs, which was described as a strength. But energetic commitment is also a threat for leaders and members because of the risk of burnout and personal deprivation in a context of material poverty and insecurity.

Maintaining relationships and networks formed a core capacity of CBOs. Knowledge and maintenance of network connections often were their leaders' main strength. Relationships in this context need to be understood from a complexity perspective, specifically looking at relationships within CBOs, between CBOs and their communities, as well as with the broader development situation. Here, power asymmetries needed particular attention, including the relationship with the OD facilitator or adviser.

From my experience, supporting the development of ethical, collective leadership as well as constructive relationships and networks, and the capacity to interface with more powerful stakeholders, may form important areas for capacity development. In this context, power and politics in the sector, and a resulting dependency of CBOs, need to be made more visible in order to work towards a more conscious approach which acknowledges asymmetric interdependence. As a facilitator or supporting organization, one needs to consciously choose whether to support a CBO-driven process, by engaging with and challenging the current structural contradictions at various levels, or to reproduce a capacity development sector where the rules of the game are directed by those with financial or positional power through hierarchy.

Against this critical background, the following section provides more specific principles and suggestions of how to work with CBOs in a way that encourages CBO members to maintain their own power in the process.

Organizational development with community-based organizations

Is an organizational development approach at community, or micro, level suitable for CBO strengthening? The case studies involved action-research reflections based on principles of OD, understood in this chapter as interventions that were purposefully facilitated in a people-centred way. The collective learning and decision-making which followed within the participating CBOs proved this type of process to be appropriate.[3] The ultimate aim of this style of intervention was geared to supporting development and growth at organizational, not just at individual or programme, level as described in Chapter 3. A prescriptive approach, where the consultant is seen as expert, was consciously avoided as much as possible.

The degree of existing structures and processes varied in the three CBOs, which affected their ability to remain committed to the OD process. It is important to recognize that in a CBO context organizational boundaries are 'porous' and weak. They necessarily shift with the movement of their setting. This gives them the flexibility needed to manoeuvre and respond to inevitable crises as they arise. But at the same time it makes it difficult for them to take control of their situation and act more proactively to change it. In this way it remained difficult to stay faithful to agreements with the facilitator: other issues need attention as they occur.

Many CBOs' practice of reacting to crises as they arise requires an open and contingent OD process similar to their way of operating. Instead of seeing it as chaotic or disorganized, a capacity development process should acknowledge the organization's contingent approach at community level as a key factor in effectiveness. Put another way, capacity development support takes place on a continuum between fieldwork, action learning and more structured OD (Kaplan et al, 1994). Training and imparting skills can prove to be useful additions. They may form part of the OD intervention, or be offered separately.

Ways of seeing CBOs – testing assumptions and embedding in context

When starting to work with a CBO, one needs to ask oneself the questions: What are my assumptions about what CBO capacity is? What lens do I use when assessing a CBO? If we try setting standards comparable to more established NGOs, that is, organizations with a high level of formality and differentiation, then most CBOs will look deficient and underdeveloped. A more appreciative approach, enabling the facilitator and organizational members to really understand the organization and its driving forces, may in turn lead to more self-empowerment of the CBO. This includes enabling the CBO to see and diagnose itself, which forms one of the most difficult tasks.

A more intuitive, deeper way of seeing enabled the facilitator to connect with the organizations' coming into being, their unfolding on a different level that appreciates their aliveness.[4] More specifically, what supports a deeper seeing is appreciating the context that the organization is working within and understanding CBOs as a product of and with it. This stance fosters an awareness that locally emerging CBOs are typically better or 'naturally' equipped to deal with unanticipated events than more formal NGOs that come from another context. It also heightens sensitivity to the fact that, as Part I of this volume illustrates, many issues exist at a larger, systemic level, and cannot be resolved by CBOs alone.

The OD principles and approaches recommended in the following sections therefore start from a view of CBOs within their context as complex, self-organized social systems. This perspective, also applied in other chapters, promotes a sense of humility in the face of unpredictable futures that can neither be fully understood through analyses nor resolved through strategic plans.

A developmental approach and fostering ownership

Organizations need to understand they do not need to be empowered, as in being given power by a seemingly more powerful person or organization. Instead, they can empower themselves and become more resourceful, with or without support from an outside facilitator. Instead of acting as an expert, a facilitator needs to work in a collaborative way to foster collective learning – which includes the facilitator as described, for example, in Chapter 20. An OD approach may enable CBOs to gain more control in an 'out-of-control' environment. While acknowledging flexibility and embeddedness as important strengths, an appreciative approach can raise awareness through inquiry about root causes of issues internally and externally. These insights can enhance the quality of an organization's decisions about adequate responses. In this way, the CBO's reactiveness may be guided towards a more conscious *response-ability* to issues.

Traditional OD does emphasize the notions of participation in problem analysis and solution finding. When combined with a people-centred, developmental approach, however, it goes beyond people's 'participation' and seeks to develop 'capacity to exert authority over their own lives and futures' and promotes a 'strongly developed civil society ... in which the power of the state, of capital and of transnational capital and transnational "aid" organizations, is held in balance by a plethora of competent, independent and self-reflective community-based and non-governmental organizations' (CDRA, 1999; Kaplan, 1996).

Effective development calls for the 'ownership' of processes of change by those who will embody them in the future. However, the power asymmetry of donor–recipient relationships has negative implications for a capacity-development intervention because it often leads to a lack of ownership. In the absence of strong ownership on the side of CBOs, it is tempting for the facilitator to take over rather than remaining 'developmental' by accepting the CBO's own pace of growth. A resulting facilitator-driven process may go beyond what the CBO is ready to engage with and, thereby, (re-) create dependency. Furthermore, a CBO-owned process would only be transformative if it was driven and self-organized by internal forces and dynamics of change.

Simplifying OD processes and language

The complexity of OD may also contribute to a lack of ownership since the approach is widely unknown at grass-roots level. Consequently, a facilitator must be able to deconstruct the OD language into simple questions that make sense in the local context. This can be done by avoiding jargon and using basic language, as well as by drawing on examples and metaphors that each participant knows from their own daily life. A simple example is the 'bus activity' as an analysis of the organizational structure and internal relationships. Here, members are asked to imagine their organization as a bus to then constitute that bus in the room collectively. When the bus is complete, each person reflects which part of the bus they play, how they relate to other parts, which parts are missing, etc., which is then translated into an organizational analysis.

Acknowledging different time frames

Often, donor-driven time frames, or other imposed time commitments, become a trap for the facilitator, which makes it difficult to allow for a CBO-driven process. This and other mismatches discussed in Chapter 19 are often augmented by the facilitator's personal need to be 'successful' and able to show results in order to feel that she has contributed meaningfully to the CBO's development.

To avoid or minimize this disparity in time frames, OD processes must remain flexible. Flexibility is also called for in order to respond to CBOs' changing needs and responses to shifts in external conditions. Inflexibility invites facilitators to question their own and third parties' agendas. This reflection often means clarifying and then adapting agreements previously made with CBOs. Too often this adjustment does not occur, forcing forward a process that has lost its relevance for the CBO's own measures of time and standards. Any OD process should be 'governed' by the CBO and foster independence of the organization. Signs of ownership are when CBO members take full responsibility for the process, by ensuring that it takes place, relevant people participate, logistics are prepared and there is enough time commitment for a meaningful process. Realistically, poverty-related and other crises and responsibilities at community level mean that not all CBOs can afford such a commitment. Nonetheless, a shift of ownership has taken place once CBO members actually drive their own change and identify areas of work themselves, instead of expecting the facilitator to deliver.

A repertoire of concepts and approaches

The previous text has stressed the importance of staying true to the lessons, inspirations and philosophy of community development in its early years. The practitioner's art with CBOs is to employ today's approaches that embody this history. And there is a wide repertoire to choose from. Those summarized in this section were applied in the research and proved useful. The references and readings provide additional sources and evidence of their efficacy. They also offer suggestions for working in ways which promote and apply the values and principles guiding a people-centred approach which is CBO-driven. Needless to say, any general techniques need to be adapted to be suitable at grass-roots level. While seeming disparate, each approach or method listed – which cannot be explained in detail here – is connected by a view of organizations as complex social systems and their emphasis on a developmental approach and learning.

- Appreciative Inquiry (AI) techniques: AI can enable CBOs to reflect on existing strengths, assets and energizing forces; and what areas they would like to enhance.
- Concepts of learning organizations and organizational learning: when viewing CBOs as complex social systems, the way of understanding and engaging with their dynamics shifts. Senge (1990) introduces the laws of the fifth discipline (systems thinking) and the practice of dialogue in organizations.
- Culture change approaches and methods: organizational capacity development can help members surface their basic assumptions in order to more consciously read and respond to environmental changes and internal dynamics.
- Concept of Communities of Practice: CBOs can be compared to Communities of Practice, which 'are about content – about learning as living experience of negotiating meaning – not about form' (Wenger, 1998).
- Concept of Presencing: an approach incorporating many elements of the above examples (Magruder-Watkins and Mohr, 2001).

Power and in(ter)dependence

The above suggestions offer guidance about how to engage with CBO capacity in a developmental way. However, CBO development does not take place within a neutral setting. Consequently, the methods and approaches noted above may not, in themselves, sufficiently address power imbalances inherent to the development industry. For CBOs to fully reach their potential and contribute to meaningful development the aid system needs to be turned on its head in terms of which processes count most where. Instead of CBOs remaining at the bottom of the aid chain, processes on the 'periphery' need to move to the centre. For example, a movement should take place such that socially embedded and trusted methods and rules of mutual support amongst people who are poor become a normative guide and measure for donor practice (Wilkinson-Maposa, 2009).

Further, in a context marked by power inequality, development cannot remain an apolitical act, which assumes that all the parties involved could cope with the more equitable society that they strive for. This perspective also has implications for practitioners who need to carefully reflect their own power in the relationship with CBOs. By accepting the status quo in the aid sector, where donors and larger NGOs exert power over CBOs, professionals contribute to the reproduction of a system marked by inequality – and therefore need to question their own political role in it.

Obviously, the changes argued for above should not simply turn around power imbalances, so enabling new leaders to exert power over others. Instead the shift needs to acknowledge interdependence and relationships. Such an understanding may enable development challenges to be addressed in a more holistic and sustainable way than has so far been possible in disconnected and often polarized contexts.

As previous chapters show, bringing stakeholders together will not level power imbalances or create a sense of interdependence per se. Hence it is necessary for CBOs to develop capacities to relate to and network with stakeholders who currently appear as more powerful. Dialogue – in the sense of fostering a deeper understanding of interdependence and the need for collaboration – may be a powerful way of overcoming polarizations and power asymmetries in society. However, where a genuine will to open up to each other and risk one's own power base is not present, contestation may be the only means whereby change can happen. Hence, all the above-mentioned approaches need to entail a political understanding, enabling each organization to analyse the context in which it operates and therefore decide where to position itself and whether and how to act upon contextual issues.

For a practitioner this means, on the one hand, establishing their own stance on the relationship between power and development and, on the other, equipping themselves with the tools and competencies needed to engage in the power dynamics of OD within CBOs as well as their relationships with the wider world. Figure 15.2 illustrates this perspective on CBO capacity development, by combining the capacity development approach with a consciousness of and engagement with power asymmetries.

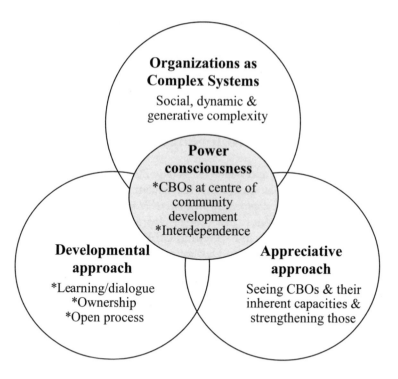

Source: Yachkaschi, 2008, p206

Figure 15.2 *Elements of CBO capacity development*

CBOs seem to live in a different world from other development actors and they are usually the ones expected to cross the threshold towards the other side. If they do not speak the language of donors and government structures they cannot be heard easily. Since CBOs are acknowledged for their relevance in development, the question remains whether the crossing of borders cannot be reversed and, in the process, provide a source of learning about real grass-roots development.

Notes

1 Examples are: Swanepoel, H. and De Beer, F. (1998) *Community Capacity Building. A Guide for Fieldworkers and Community Leaders,* Oxford University Press, Cape Town; Symes, C. (2005) *Mentoring Community Based Organisations. A Companion to the New Tool Box – A Handbook for Community Based Organisations,* The Barnabas Trust, South Africa. An exception is offered by Hope and Timmel (2002) who raise political inequalities using Paulo Freire's approach. Hope, A. and Timmel, S. (2002) *Training for Transformation: A Handbook for Community Workers,* Book I–IV, third edition, Training for Transformation Institute, Kleinmond.
2 Interview, Alan Fowler, 26 June 2006.
3 Definitions of OD include: 'the strengthening of those human processes in organisations which improve the functioning of the organic system so as to achieve its objectives'

(Lippitt, 1969, cited in French et al, 1989, p6); or 'the facilitation of an organisation's capacity to self-reflect, self-regulate, and take control of its own processes of improvement and learning' (Kaplan 1996, p89). These definitions are in line with the OD approach applied.

4   For example Goethe's way of seeing in Kaplan, A. (2005) 'Emerging out of Goethe. Conversation as a form of social enquiry', *Janus Head*, vol 8, no 1, pp311–334.

References

Fukuda-Parr, S., Lopes, C. and Malik, K. (eds) (2002) *Capacity for Development: New Solutions to Old Problems*, UNDP, Earthscan, London

Kaplan, A. (1996) *The Development Practitioners' Handbook*, Pluto Press, London

Magruder-Watkins, J. and Mohr, B. (2001) *Appreciative Inquiry: Change at the Speed of Imagination*, Jossey-Bass/Pfeiffer, USA

Monaheng, T. (2000) Community Development and Empowerment. Unit 9, in *Introduction to Development Studies*, 2nd edn, De Beer, F. and Swanepoel, H. (eds), University Press, Oxford, pp124–135

Schein, E. (1991) *Organizational Culture and Leadership: A Dynamic View*, 10th edition, Jossey-Bass, San Francisco

Senge, P. (1990) *The Fifth Discipline. The Art and Practice of the Learning Organization*, Doubleday, New York

Wenger, E. (1998) *Communities of Practice: Learning, Meaning and Identity*, Cambridge University Press

Wilkinson-Maposa, S. (ed), (2009) *The Poor Philanthropist III: A Practice-relevant Guide for Community Philanthropy*, Centre for Leadership and Public Values, University of Cape Town, Cape Town

Yachkaschi, S. (2008) 'Towards the development of an appropriate Organisational Development approach for optimising the Capacity Building of Community-Based Organisations (CBOs): A case study of 3 CBOs in the Western Cape', PhD thesis, University of Stellenbosch, South Africa

Recommended readings

The topics in this chapter have interesting connections to others in this volume. Readers may wish to look at Chapter 6 which places a practitioner in the power relationships that come with the work as well as the conflicts commonly arising. Chapter 7 addresses a practitioner's positioning in terms of values. The developmental significance of CBOs appears in Chapter 13 in relation to the gap between macro policy and micro action. Leadership is the topic of Chapter 16. The following is a short selection of useful resources as a starting point for further reading on this topic.

Kaplan, A. (1999) *The Development of Capacity*, NGLS Development Dossier, United Nations, New York

Kaplan (1999) divides organizational capacity into elements, which are listed in a hierarchy of complexity. The more complex levels of capacity, like the conceptual framework and reading of the context, are at a higher level of organizational capacity than organizational structure, skills or material resources. Kaplan suggests that the more complex and significant elements at the top of the hierarchy need to be developed before others. He points out that many capacity development efforts are too narrowly focused on skills development.

Gubbels, P. and Koss, C. (2000) *From the Roots Up: Strengthening Organizational Capacity through Guided Self-Assessment, Field Guide No. 2,* World Neighbours, Oklahoma City

This manual seeks to strengthen organizational capacity by providing tools and methods for self-assessment. It explains key areas for organizational capacity building, such as: decision-making; communication systems; collaboration with other groups; negotiation for services; clarity of vision and purpose; and monitoring and evaluation.

Galvin, M. (2005) *Survival, Development or Advocacy? A Preliminary Examination of Rural CBOs in South Africa,* Avocado Working Paper Series 1/2005, Olive ODT, Durban,; Ndlovu, N. (2004) *The Cinderellas of Development? Funding CBOs in South Africa,* Interfund, Johannesburg

Galvin and Ndlovu examine the CBO sector in South Africa based on empirical research. Ndlovu focuses on funding CBOs, whereas Galvin provides an overview of rural CBOs. Both have developed definitions and reflected on the roles of CBOs, and Galvin further provides a typology of rural CBOs in South Africa.

Wilkinson-Maposa, S., Fowler, A., Oliver-Evans, C. and Mulenga, C.F.N. (2005) *The Poor Philanthropist. How and Why the Poor Help Each Other,* Compress, Cape Town.

The monograph presents the comparable experience, patterns and living reality of community philanthropy across four countries in southern Africa. It offers a deeper understanding of why and how people who are poor help each other and questions the universal relevance of philanthropic orthodoxy and convention.

Yachkaschi, S. (2009) *Towards an Organisational Development Approach with Community-based Organisations. Findings from a PhD-study,* Community Connections, Cape Town.

This publication summarizes some of the major discussion and findings of doctoral action research into organizational and capacity development. It explores the capacity development sector and CBO capacity, leadership and relational capabilities, and relevant OD approaches applied during the study.

16

Leadership Development

Leadership is an important factor in fostering connections and guiding change. In development processes it can play a key role in governance, accountability and effectiveness of specific programmes. Given its pivotal role, practitioners need to pay attention to leadership as a critical aspect in capacity-development strategies and work.

In this chapter, Dia and Eggink use a West African case to illustrate how individual and collective leadership development complements and provides leverage for capacity-development efforts. Of particular interest is the combination of individual and collective approaches. The authors also show how engaging in leadership development processes can enhance the capabilities of practitioners themselves.

Leadership, the Hidden Factor in Capacity Development: A West African Experience

Brigitte Dia and Jan Willem Eggink
with contributions from Lucia Nass

Introduction

From the moment he took office, following Niger's first-ever local elections in 2003, the young and dynamic mayor of one of the districts of the capital Niamey, struggled to manage and influence a district council of 23 members. Almost all were older and more experienced than him and had very different political ambitions!

Like the mayor, Niger's national government and the community of development partners were keen to make a success of the new decentralized government, which comprised two levels, regional and municipal. They initiated a wide array of technical and organizational capacity-development interventions to support the newly-elected local councils. However, while these were appreciated, none of them addressed the organizational and personal leadership issues faced by key players like this young mayor. With limited financial, as well as human resources, municipalities were confronted with an enormous challenge to organize and deliver all the services that they were now directly responsible for. The mayor wondered if he had the ability to drive and bring about change in the face of deeply entrenched traditions, power dynamics and ingrained ways of doing things.

How could this mismatch between a clear need for leadership support on the ground and policy momentum for 'doing things differently' be bridged?

This chapter makes a case for leadership development as an integral part of capacity-development processes by describing a successful leadership development initiative in the West African region, facilitated by the SNV Netherlands Development Organisation. The programme targeted leaders of local government, civil society and other non-governmental organizations (NGOs) that were already involved in SNV-supported capacity-development programmes, and provided them with additional leadership support in order to increase the potential for results and strengthen the foundation for sustainability and local ownership. We do this in four parts: first we look at leadership as an important link in the capacity-development 'puzzle'. We then provide a brief background to the SNV initiative and the target group for the programme. In the third part we take a closer look at the design of the programme, starting with the programme ambitions and constraints followed by an overview of various leadership theories or assumptions that informed our approach. A description of the resulting design is provided, tailored as close to the specific country as possible. Finally we describe the key factors that contributed to the success of the programme and show how the different elements were combined in practice. We also provide some perspectives on the potential for making leadership development a more integral part of capacity development.

Leadership – an important piece of the capacity-development puzzle

Leadership is important in almost all human endeavours that involve two or more people, whether they are civil, public or private actors. The recognition that leadership is critical to development success is not new. Two recent, large studies by the Global Leadership Initiative (2007) and the European Centre for Development Policy Management (ECDPM, 2008) underscore the importance and relevance of leadership development in capacity-development processes. Similarly, a review of successful rural development programmes in the 1990s by Uphoff, Esman and Anirudh (1996; 1998) highlighted the crucial role of key individuals in initiating change and guiding innovation.

There is no shortage of leadership support programmes today. The United Nations Development Programme (UNDP) has supported more than 700 initiatives, providing access to leadership programmes in more than 30 countries (2005). The World Bank Institute's leadership development programme (2008) offers customized support to high- and mid-level decision-makers and emerging leaders at national and sub-national levels in developing countries. In addition, many development organizations have promoted and financed some form of support to the leaders of organizations that they work with or support. This is a positive trend and there are many more that are not mentioned here. In this sense, the West African initiative described here is not unique. What makes it interesting is the fact that the programme was embedded in local capacity-development processes in a specific country and sought to develop both individual and collective leadership abilities. It combined introduction to concepts and skill-building with peer feedback, experimentation in real-time, real-life leadership situations, and coaching over a significant period of time to building in action-reflection cycles. The programme was also actively supported by capacity-development practitioners (SNV advisers) who took on the role of coaches and were themselves mentored by skilled programme facilitators to deepen their abilities to work effectively with leaders as part of their practice.

It must be mentioned that apart from West Africa, SNV initiated leadership development in Asia (Laos) and the Balkans (Albania) as well. The experiences across the three regions were regularly shared and discussed across the organization. SNV advisers involved in the leadership development initiatives also interacted with, and learned from, other organizations, such as the World Bank, UNDP and IBIS Education for Development (a Danish development organization). With time, it was possible to distil the following tentative conclusions or insights about what constitutes effective leadership in a development context. Such leaders:

- work in complex settings, where collective leadership is needed;
- achieve results in the face of uncertainty and ambiguity; they show the flexibility and fortitude needed to achieve tangible results along the way to broader social change;
- keep learning and guide others in ongoing learning – change is constant;
- manage people through an understanding of their motives and behaviours, that is, they have a good understanding of the reasons behind their actions and behaviour in the context of the wider culture and cross-cultural relationships in which they operate;
- provide vision and meaning and direction, and inspire, motivate and mobilize others, drawing inspiration from global development and change movements (such as gender equality, rights of minorities, or more inclusive approaches to business);
- take initiative to (co-)create the future, instead of defining oneself as a victim of circumstances;
- demonstrate personal values that are congruent to the values espoused in their leadership;
- serve the benefit of the whole, of others, the team, the organization, society – going beyond one's mere self-interest;
- demonstrate credibility and the courage to address value conflicts and exclusion even when these are embedded in deeply traditional attitudes and practices.

Background to the Leadership for Change Programme (PLC)

Before 2005, there was no systematic training and coaching of leaders of the local organizations and networks that SNV was supporting in its capacity-development work, although SNV advisers did provide support to individual leaders and were aware that, while often informal, such support was both effective and highly appreciated. It also became increasingly clear that such mentoring relationships did play a critical role in the effectiveness of capacity-development support to the wider team, organization or network that SNV was supporting.

As mentioned earlier, from 2005 onwards, three separate initiatives took root in different SNV regions: West Africa, Albania in the Balkan region and Laos in South-East Asia. In each of these locations, SNV advisers with the support of senior managers experimented with different programmes to incorporate leadership development into their capacity-development approach in an effort to respond to recurrent issues around leadership that kept coming up in different processes, especially at the sub-national level.

In West Africa, a small task force was set up to look at practical ways of supporting the leaders of local organizations that were existing SNV clients. This effectively became the design team for the new Leadership for Change Programme (PLC) programme. The programme started in Niger and over a period of four years it had spread to include seven countries in the region (Niger, Mali, Benin, Burkina Faso, Cameroon, Guinea Bissau and Ghana).

One of the first questions that PLC addressed was which type of leader to target in order to provide a focus for the programme. The leaders that SNV advisers encountered in their practice fell into different categories. Figure 16.1 illustrates

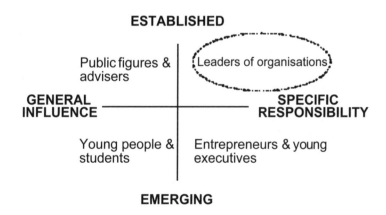

Source: Eggink, J.W., 2005

Figure 16.1 *Typology of leaders*

the typology that gradually emerged from numerous discussions on this question. The typology helped to clarify that the programme would be for more or less established leaders with specific responsibilities in the organizations that SNV served. These included heads of municipalities or districts within the Niger local government structure, heads of departments responsible for delivery of basic services such as health, education, water and sanitation, and leaders of local civil society organizations (CSOs) and networks who were key players in the sectors that SNV focused on.

Responsive design

As a team, we were not interested in simply developing a standard, albeit good quality leadership programme. We wanted a design that would help participants to begin to confront and address the leadership issues they currently faced in their roles. We wanted a design that would develop leadership capabilities but also act as a resource; tackling real-time issues by drawing on the collective knowledge and experience of participants, facilitators and coaches alike. The PLC design had to bring 'the world of participants into the room'. Instead of starting with what the programme could contain, we began by posing two sets of issues the design would have to respond to: the programme ambitions: what we wanted the programme to contribute to the nature and quality of local leadership, and the anticipated constraints: aspects of the context and culture that we knew could be problematic if not redressed or accounted for in the final design.

Programme goals and target group

We wanted to help individual leaders to increase their self awareness, develop their flexibility in using particular leadership styles, and be more open to feedback (both direct and indirect) about the quality and impact of their leadership style. The leaders we worked with were certainly aware of the power that came with their positions, especially in a culture where hierarchy was important. They were, however, less aware of themselves as individuals and the impact or effect they had on others and the organizations they led. They did not show awareness of the potential for using their power as a force for change and often did not realize that they had different options when faced with difficult situations. Would they be prepared for example to drop the common 'leader decides it all' approach and give more space to others to contribute and collaborate?

One of the persistent issues that come up in practice is the loss of momentum when leaders and their immediate teams have to follow through on some of the more challenging change processes needed to achieve effective coordination and delivery of services. A fundamental goal of the programme was thus to provide a space where leaders could be challenged by their peers to take some risks and show results, boosting their confidence to keep going at the end of the programme. In addition, the programme also aimed to help leaders demonstrate some early results as this would enhance their credibility within their organizations and wider communities and further improve their potential to influence others.

Although SNV worked with some of the organizations individually and with others as part of multi-stakeholder networks, the development issues in a particular area were so interconnected that within this group, it made sense to stimulate a sense of joint responsibility among participants. We felt that collectively, the leaders involved in the programme had the potential to influence and drive significant shifts in performance and culture at the sub-national level. We also understood leadership in capacity-development processes to be broader than training and coaching of leaders to improve their individual leadership skills. It also touches on the spaces where rules and norms about governance and mechanisms of accountability are created, negotiated and practised.

In summary, we wanted the design of the PLC to combine a focus on helping individuals to play an influential and helpful role in the performance and sustainability of their different organizations, on the one hand, and helping the collective to drive development processes that required complex collaboration beyond single organizational borders on the other. We asked ourselves such questions as: How will the design support the emergence of a community of leaders that share a vision for change and can call on each other for support and feedback? How can the programme sustain their motivation and focus on deeper change possibilities while they are constantly called upon to address daily worries of their constituents and employees?

Constraints

Right from the outset, we also anticipated a number of constraints that needed to be mitigated in the resulting design and approach of the programme. Addressing the behaviour of a group of high profile leaders in a setting where 'face saving' was an important motivation, especially for public leaders, would not be an easy task. Would they be interested in organized self-reflection? How would we handle direct feedback in a cultural context where the opposite was the norm in social relationships? Did we, as facilitators, have the right competencies to guide them and provide them with enough valuable insights?

We also had concerns about how the design could be implemented in such a way that it would also build the capacity of SNV advisers who would act as coaches to improve their ability to work with leaders in a more systematic way.

Resulting design and programme structure

The design that emerged from this soul-searching combined different elements to create a truly responsive programme. PLC was an innovative and intensive training and coaching programme that took place over a period of ten months, combined residential group workshops with practical projects on-the-job and follow-up and coaching that ensured the principles learned at the workshops were internalized and applied to real-life situations. Although the programme introduced new concepts and skills relevant to leadership in the residential workshops, it drew heavily on participants' experiences of being leaders and the dilemmas they needed to resolve. This made it highly relevant to them at a practical level.

Table 16.1 *Main blocks of the PLC curriculum*

Module 1 – Leading yourself	Module 2 – Leading your organization and context	Module 3 – Leading people and teams
Main aim was to increase self awareness in context of leadership styles and quality. Topics included concepts of leadership / personality types / leadership in Africa / time management	Aim was to improve strategic leadership within and across organizations. Topics included visioning / values and paradigms / strategizing / leadership and the Millennium Development Goals / external communication / public relations	Aim was to develop understanding of groups and dynamics from individual level to teams. Topics included situational leadership / conflict management / change and resistance / leading teams and meetings.

Cross-cutting elements and recurrent themes in each module
Preparatory readings to provide framework and language
Introduction of some theoretical concepts and application to context
Exercises to ground theory and build underpinning skills that relate to leadership practice
Real-life cases brought in by the participants for peer reflection
Individual reflection (diary) and action planning.

The main elements of the programme itself were not new or unique – they are well known and widely used. What was distinctive was the way they were combined over the duration of the programme and consistently used to address questions and needs of participants as they arose. Participants did not experience a break in the programme so motivation and momentum was sustained throughout, although the intensity of interaction obviously varied.

Figure 16.2 captures the main features of the programme in chronological order. The preparation phase involved personal intake interviews with each participant and a '360-degree' feedback exercise to create a baseline for assessing results and impact of the programme and to guide aspects that individuals might want to focus on.

Each of the three PLC four-day workshops provided an intensive interaction space for experiential-based introduction of new concepts, skill building, peer coaching and reflection. In between the workshops participants benefited from one-to-one coaching from senior SNV advisers as they formulated and implemented action plans for change in their respective organizations, based on the personal leadership and organizational goals they had set themselves. By keeping the workshops three months apart, we allowed enough time for participants to take meaningful actions in their organization and observe some short term results. They also kept in touch informally with each other. The relationships formed in the residential workshops made it easier for participants to call on each other for

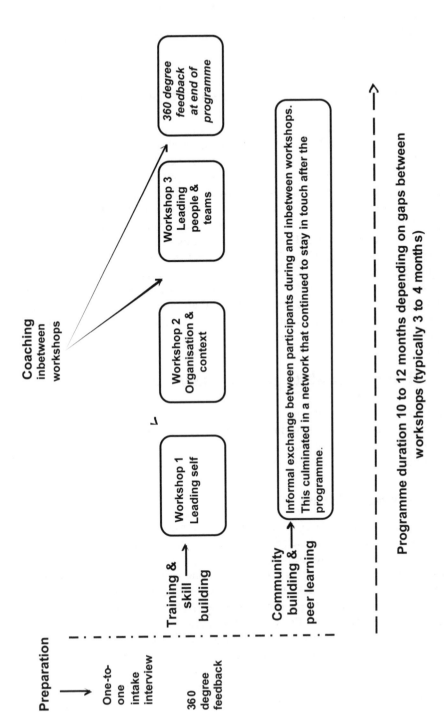

Figure 16.2 *Structure of the Leadership for Change Programme (PLC)*

help and also to start collaborating where they would previously not have done so. Coaching continued for a while after the programme, and participants repeated the 360-degree feedback exercise three months after the closure to assess the progress made.

Notions of leadership in the programme

Leadership theories and conceptual frameworks are plentiful and have evolved over many years. We did not define leadership in abstract terms or propose one theory that explains leadership in a coherent manner. Just as there are many definitions of leadership, there are many different approaches to the development of leadership. Each of them is informed by particular assumptions or theories of what leadership is and how it comes about. The simple classification provided in Table 16.1 (page 216) gives some idea of this evolution. The theories listed are a product of their time. They all serve to explain some aspects of leadership and ignore or downplay others. While we did not propose one 'grand' theory that explains leadership in a coherent manner, we made a conscious choice to work with leadership development interventions that reflected behavioural, situational and participatory views of leadership. We felt that these would help participants to develop the capabilities and attitudes demanded by the complexity of issues they had to deal with in work situations.

Bringing it all together – key success factors

On reflection, it was the combination of a number of major as well as very small design and process choices in direct response to our context that contributed to the PLC's success. The major design choices showed their value during implementation in a number of ways, which are now described.

Choice of participants

PLC participants were carefully chosen. The first criterion was leadership of an organization or network to which SNV was already providing capacity-development support. The aim of the programme was not only to develop individual leaders but also to contribute to the effectiveness of ongoing capacity-development projects by boosting the quality of leadership. The organizations represented in the PLC were seen as key actors with the potential to bring about significant change in their respective sectors and areas. Participation was restricted to the very senior level of leadership in these organizations. This helped participants to open up and accept others as peers who understood the specific challenges at that level of seniority and from whom they would accept feedback. This criterion also had the added value that participants in the PLC pilot attained a certain status in the community of local leaders. Choosing the name 'Leadership for Change' made clear from the start that we were in search for participants ready to look in the mirror, to face what they would encounter and to act upon that and improve their performance.

Table 16.2 *Broad classification of leadership theories and related interventions*

Classification of leadership theories or concepts	Main assumptions upon which interventions are based	Relevance/helpfulness for West Africa leadership development programme
Trait	Leaders are born with certain characteristics and personality traits. These 'traits' are inherent - a person either has them or not. Main aim of interventions would be identify rather than develop these traits.	None
Behavioural	Leadership is a set of behaviours that can be learned. People can be taught these leadership behaviours and apply them to good effect. Interventions are heavily skill based and tend to be in training programmes	High
Situational or contingency	Style of a leader depends on the context, situation, types of relationships, tasks, staff willingness and capability. Interventions aim to help leaders to identify the combination of factors in their particular situation and choose appropriate styles to match. Often hand in hand with training on how to 'use' a particular style.	High
Transformational/ charismatic	Relationship or bond between leaders and followers is important. Leaders inspire others to go beyond their own self-interest for the good of the group or organization. Leaders show desire to serve others Interventions promote social awareness and how to understand values and motives of others to be able to influence them	Medium
Dispersed or distributed / collective	Leadership is informal and emergent – there is a leader in all of us. The collective as a whole is leader, starting with shared beliefs, emerging out of a situation and process is in which we all influence each other Interventions tend to be with whole group together	Medium to low
Participative	Leadership relies on input from followers and encourages participation. Emphasizes collaboration and shared power. Interventions stress leaders' understanding of diverse views, and address how to communicate and how to stimulate others to participate	High

The fact that no dependency relations existed within the group also made it easier for the participants to take a vulnerable position during the training.

Clarity of expectations and commitment at intake

Taking time to conduct individual intake interviews before the programme paid off. Participants received dedicated attention and could freely explore the implications and demands of committing to such a programme. The PLC intake team gained significant insight into each participant's professional situation and motivation for participation. It also established early trust between individuals and the facilitation. Selected participants contributed the equivalent of about US$67 as a way of showing their commitment and were required to confirm their participation at all three workshops before starting the programme. To facilitate communication about the programme within the participating organizations a tri-partite contract had to be signed by SNV, the participant and his/her organization. The '360-degree' feedback exercise (a method of gathering feedback on an individual's behaviour and performance from multiple sources including peers, subordinates or direct reports, and managers) at the start and at the end of the programme was instrumental in determining leadership challenges for the participant as well as setting a baseline for measuring the effect of the programme. Participants gathered feedback about their leadership styles and effectiveness from peers at work: those senior to them and some junior. The feedback questionnaire was based on the leadership skills and abilities that the programme aimed to help participants to develop.

Coaching on the job

The decision to combine a series of workshops with on-the-job coaching proved to be the most important design element in the programme. Coaches helped the participants to reflect upon their experiences while experimenting with new behaviour, perceptions and projects in their daily leadership roles. Assigning a coaching role to senior SNV advisers who were already working with these organizations, sparked off a very interesting mutual learning process. The relationship between SNV-adviser and the leader he or she was coaching became much more personal and behaviour-oriented. SNV advisers working as coaches alongside the senior facilitators of the programme underwent a training-of-trainers programme before the programme started and continued to have access to the senior coach throughout the programme to reflect on their coaching practice and enhance the quality of coaching they provided. As they developed in their coaching skills and demonstrated more maturity, they earned more credibility with the leaders they coached. In all countries where the programme has been adopted, SNV-advisers now routinely receive extra training on coaching skills and leadership development. Furthermore, based on our early experiences, we have learned that it is worthwhile to invest in making the coaches well acquainted with the content of the workshops and in briefing them at the end of each workshop before they meet leaders for coaching.

Another role played by the coach is providing support to the leader in his or her effort to realize the organizational change project (formulated during the second workshop). Although the quality and intensity of the coaching may differ considerably in the different coach–leader pairs in successive evaluations of the programme, participants invariably name the combination of coaching and training as one of the key factors for success of the PLC.

Programme embeddedness in participants' leadership practice

This was another strong aspect of the PLC programme. Participants' own organizations provided a relatively safe setting in which to start to consciously practise leadership of a change process. Each participant had to identify improvements or changes they wanted to initiate and lead in their organization or department. The length of the programme (one year) allowed for this and enabled participants and their peers to track their own and each other's progress over time. The time allowed the development of meaningful relationships between participants and the level of trust that developed between them, as a result, meant that they could give each other truthful and critical feedback. The relationships built here were sustained beyond the duration of the programme. A year after the completion of the programme, more than half of the participants were still in touch with each other.

Peer learning and reflection

The targeted participants of the programme were men and women with many years of experience. Their situation and practice differed, their individual questions differed and their personal strengths and weaknesses were not the same. So the most practical way to help them become more effective leaders was not to offer a one-size-fits-all explanation of effective leadership behaviour. It made much more sense to help each participant become better aware of their own leadership behaviour; help them reflect about more effective ways to reach their goals; and then monitor them as they put their self-designed new behaviour into practice.

Peer relationships were an invaluable resource in this process. PLC participants brought a wealth of experiences and diverse perspectives but also found strong common threads in their stories and cases. This action-learning approach underscored the whole philosophy of the PLC. Cut off for four days from the daily fuss and the claims of their subordinates, the members of the group started to share their personal worries and pre-occupations among each other, especially during breaks and in the evenings. The programme also induced reflections on personal values, democracy and accountability of the leadership towards its employees or citizens. Ultimately, all participants had end responsibility for an organization or department and felt personal pressure to deliver: leadership development had immediate, not future relevance

Creating a network of leaders for change

The last design principle was the creation of a network of PLC alumni, with the goal of maintaining relationships and providing mutual support over a longer period of time. The alumni network was based on the simple idea of drawing on the common experience and background of the ex-participants to connect leaders with a shared passion for good governance.

In Niger and Cameroon an official association of 'Leaders for Change' has been created.

SNV supports these organizations as they fit in well with emerging insights on the importance of knowledge networks in building capacity. It is hoped that these associations may yield new initiatives for improved accountability of leaders and continue to empower their members in their often lonely fight against prejudice, vested interests and culturally-ingrained leadership constraints.

Participants' perspective on results

The evaluations held at the end of each training cycle have shown an invariably high appreciation among participants with regard to the content and style, as well as the set-up, of the programme. On content, PLC participants have consistently highlighted the focus on individual behaviour and practical management issues. On style, they welcome the personal atmosphere and the opportunity to freely exchange their experiences and concerns with 'colleague-leaders' who are in the same position but often from completely different sectors of society. They also value the interchange of training and coaching in the trajectory, which allows them to gradually grow and learn on the job and which is complementary to other SNV interventions in their organizations, for example conducting an organizational analysis.

What better way to conclude than to give the last word to the newly elected young mayor we encountered at the beginning of this chapter.

The Programme '*Leadership for Change*' (PLC) came for me as a gift from heaven. The modules on psychological types and feedback have opened my eyes on how perception and behaviour, including my own, determine the quality of processes in my organization. Participating in the PLC has given a boost to my self-confidence. It helped me defeat my fear of speaking in public. I have also learned how to handle delicate feedback of my colleagues in a constructive way. The modules on non-defensive communication, situational leadership and management of team-performance have been very helpful to embark upon a process of joint analysing, visioning and strategizing. This has taken away blockages for development. My district is now the most successful in Niamey; we have become a district of reference for all the country.

New developments

After some years of experience with the Leadership for Change Programme, new forms of leadership programmes are emerging based on the classic PLC approach. For example, in Mali, SNV advisers have designed and implemented a leadership programme in a local language, selectively picking from the content and methods of the PLC those aspects which seem relevant for peasant-leaders, like personal style of communicating, empowering people and organizing for collaborative action. In Benin a mayor of a commune has approached SNV to facilitate a leadership programme similar to the PLC for the local leaders he depends upon for achieving his local development plan. This programme is run with the help of a trainer based in Benin. In Niger SNV is supporting the National College for Administrators (ENA) to implement a leadership programme inspired by the PLC. The UNDP has also shown interest in developing in-company leadership programmes based upon the 'Leadership for Change' concept.

Box 16.1 Some personal reactions and perspectives from PLC alumni

I now dare to speak out and put the fish on the table….I am able to present my view to external parties.

I do not talk all the time during meetings any more, but I listen more and ask people what they think we should do.

I trust others to do their job and now I have more time, my collaborators have more fun and our organization is much more efficient.

We have analysed together what actions to take and tax-incomes have increased 20 per cent in a month!

The course made me aware of my own leadership style, which is rather domineering. As a result, I began to have more confidence in my colleagues and have started delegating jobs to them. The results have been amazing. My colleagues are much more motivated, and I go home at 6 pm with the job done.

Thanks to the support of the group, I persisted in trying to find funding to put my plans into action. I used to lose heart whenever money was short, but this time I succeeded in finding a backer.

Now I can see that once I have delegated a job to someone I have to follow it up, otherwise there may be unwelcome surprises.

Looking ahead – integrating leadership development as part of capacity development

Most leadership programmes in the development sector are one-off events or a series of events within specific agendas of funding organizations. While capacity-development practitioners, their organizations and an increasing number of donor organizations fully recognize the need for, and potential of investment in leadership development, there are simply not enough providers at local or sub-national level. Good quality leadership programmes require specialist trainers and coaches and a level of investment that is often not available below the national level. Initiatives like the West Africa programme and those offered by UNDP and World Bank require substantial investments. Many capacity-development organizations are not able to commit to developing and running such programmes – it not part of their core business and they are often not funded in ways that allow them to invest in this way. There are, however, interesting possibilities for enhancing collaboration among Southern-based institutions to develop leadership programme methodologies that are flexible enough to adapt for particular groups of participants within a capacity development context. It is not enough to provide 'off the shelf' leadership programmes, no matter how high the quality. Our experiences in West Africa show how much leverage can be gained by situating the programme firmly in the daily lives of practitioners where their immediate dilemmas are up for discussion and where they can take risks and get immediate feedback. Collaborating with and helping local institutions and consultancies to become established providers of leadership programmes and interventions would strengthen the supply in a particular environment making it more accessible to a wider range of leaders at the sub-national and community levels.

Although this chapter has focused on leadership support through well designed programmes, we realize that it is not always possible or feasible to access the resources required to implement an initiative like the Leadership for Change Programme. Yet the issues of leadership quality and leader development remain. Leaders of local organizations and key players in multi-actor settings can be supported as an integral part of capacity-development intervention. It requires methodical analysis of the types of leadership issues and challenges that occur in different capacity-development settings in order to identify the most appropriate forms of support. There are implications for practitioner understanding of leadership dynamics and the skills to use the different intervention methods available to support and develop leaders and leadership teams. This may be addressed in professional learning programmes for practitioners. Within the sub-practice of leadership development there are smaller scale interventions, for example peer-to-peer learning, that can be effective with small group of leaders and which do not require the in-depth preparation or training of practitioners.

If leadership is such an important link in the capacity-development and sustainability puzzle, its provision has to be scaled up but not in a way that separates leadership support from the substantive capacity-development processes that targeted leaders are involved in. It also requires more consistent attention to the way practitioners understand leadership and their skills in working with leaders.

References

Annan, J. and Ofosu-Koranteng, B. (2005) *National Development Planning and Implementation Strategy Note and Guide: The Answer Lies Within*, UNDP HIV/AIDS Group, United Nations Development Programme, New York

Baser, H. and Morgan, P. (2008) *Capacity Change and Performance*, European Centre for Development Policy Management, Maastricht

Krishna, A., Uphoff, N. and Esman, M.J. (eds) (1996) *Reasons for Hope: Instructive Experiences in Rural Development*, Kumarian Press, West Hartford, CT

Uphoff, N., Esman, M.J. and Krishna, A. (eds) (1998) *Reasons for Success: Learning from Instructive Experiences in Rural Development*, Kumarian Press, West Hartford, CT

World Bank Institute (2008) *Focus on Leadership*, World Bank, Washington DC http://siteresources.worldbank.org/WBI/Resources/213798-1253552326261/backgrounder_leadership_web.pdf (accessed on 30 November 2009)

Recommended readings

Chapter 3 of this volume, which describes a practical case demonstrating the need to connect capacities at multiple levels, also touches on the roles of practitioners, including support to key actors and leaders. Readers may also take a look at Chapter 15, which calls for a fresh look at the role of community-based organizations and their leadership, and Chapter 23, where the potential for stimulating local provision of capacity-development services (including leadership development) is explored. Finally, Chapter 20 offers creative ways of using evaluation for personal learning and reflection. For those interested in deepening the topic of leadership, the following are interesting entrances from different angles.

Covey, S. R. (1989) *The Seven Habits of Highly Effective People. Restoring the Character Ethic*, Simon and Schuster, New York

Covey's bestseller is very good background reading for people interested in self-reflection. His models of time management and the circle of influence were used to great effect in the Leadership for Change Programme.

Hannum, K.M, Martineau, J.W, and Reinelt, C. (2007), *The Handbook of Leadership Development Evaluation* – Center for Creative Leadership, Jossey-Bass, San Francisco

This handbook is a comprehensive resource filled with examples, tools and the most innovative models and approaches for evaluating leadership development in a variety of settings.

Kouzes, J.M. and Posner, B.Z. (2003) *The Leadership Challenge,* third edition, Jossey-Bass, San Francisco

The five leadership practices discussed by Kouzes and Posner provide a solid cross-cultural base for discussions about what leadership is. The 360-degree feedback test we use within the Leadership for Change programme was based upon their theory.

Olivier de Sardan, J.P (2003) *State Bureaucracy and Governance in West Francophone Africa: Empirical Diagnosis and Historical Perspective* (Revised version of a contribution for the colloquium of CODESRIA), Council for the Development of Social Science Research in Africa, Dakar

In this brilliant article, Sardan depicts a vivid picture of the dilemmas of modern African leaders finding themselves between the 'Scylla and Charybdis' of traditional patronage and modern demands of efficiency and transparency.

Senge, P.M. (1990) *The Fifth Discipline: The Art and Practice of the Learning Organization,* Currency/ Random House, London

There is probably no better introduction to systems thinking for managers than this book. This is especially so because the link is made with four other important aspects of effective leadership: personal mastery, mental models, shared vision and team learning.

Zigarmi, D., Blanchard, K., O'Connor, M. and Edeburn, C. (2004) *The Leader Within: Learning Enough about Yourself to Lead Others,* Prentice Hall, Upper Saddle River, NJ

Another book we used a lot on the programme, this includes a concise description of the model of psychological leadership dispositions. It treats the subjects of values and perception and it contains a renewed description of Blanchard's old but still relevant theory of situational leadership.

17

Knowledge Networking

Knowledge networking has started to be recognized as a valuable method for capacity development. If applied well it can have advantages of cost, scale and speed over more conventional methods such as training and expert advice.

In this chapter Geoff Parcell helps us understand three key elements of knowledge networking: the community of people participating, the knowledge topic or focus and the organizing processes used. These are illustrated with concrete applications in AIDS response networks, SARS research and organic farming. He shows that application of knowledge networking techniques can be beneficial for capacity-development results. This requires practitioners to shift an understanding of their own role away from the conventional expert model.

Learning Together: Knowledge Networks in Capacity Development Initiatives

Geoff Parcell

Overview of topic

Learning together is essential for any capacity development effort that goes beyond the individual and tries to influence performance of a team, an organization, a group of organizations or even a sector. Knowledge networking can play a key role in such joint learning. In fact it becomes essential in a fast changing, fast moving world. The knowledge networking we are referring to here is primarily about the human collaboration process, rather than the computer networking that underpins and enhances it. Knowledge networking is largely common sense yet, incredibly, not common practice.

Why is this the case? There are a number of reasons – we are too busy, too proud to learn, tied to hierarchy and formal conceptions of organization, or with outdated ideas on knowledge as power and competition for resources. So we have lots of excuses. However, should someone go hungry or become sick because they do not have access to knowledge that already exists?

In this chapter we will look at knowledge networking as a technique for capacity development. We will examine how people connect and collaborate to exchange and develop knowledge and the processes required to enable knowledge to flow and grow. We will further discuss some concrete examples that illustrate successful knowledge networking practices. We will then distil strengths and possibilities that knowledge networking has to offer to those involved in capacity development as well as challenges that one may need to deal with.

The world is changing rapidly and as we will see in this chapter there is much to be gained from networking. This is true for the individuals that are engaged in networking, for their organizations, and especially for people who seek to influence processes and capacities at a larger scale.

Context

In today's highly connected world, the need to go to a wise man or sage, dial up an expert, or to hire a consultant, either to find knowledge or address an insurmountable problem, has diminished. Instead we are learning to trust in the 'wisdom of crowds', to learn together with others and to look to our peers for shared experiences. Improved communications in the guise of mobile telephones, email, internet and cheap air travel means that more than ever before we can learn from, and share with, others who are doing or have already done what we are about to do. These modern means do not only allow us to exchange information and explicit knowledge, such as with books and magazines. They also allow more personal and informal contacts that facilitate a much wider exchange also of tacit knowledge, of that which people know by experience but have not laid out in formal texts. In other words, we all share knowledge. In our working and social lives we are now exposed to a variety of knowledge networking practices. For example:

- a shared working space for colleagues in a project team;
- an e-community of like minded organizations collaborating on a lobby agenda;
- social networking sites such as Facebook, MySpace or Bebo to keep in touch with friends and family;
- a network of partners in a donor-financed programme;
- a specialist network based on a technical or professional domain;
- a network of participants in a professional development programme;
- professional networking sites such as LinkedIn and Xing; and
- the use of interactive features on a website.

Some of these examples are explicitly supported by e-tools, but essentially they are social networks supported by technology. Even 'old' forms of networks such as one's study friends or the alumni of a school or university are now supported and enhanced by electronic platforms.

Networks are varied and can be large or small, internal or cross-organizational, co-located or distributed, spontaneous or deliberate, broad or narrow in their topic, informal or structured. All provide a conduit for knowledge to flow freely, horizontally, to where it is needed most.

British Petroleum (BP), the energy company where I worked, recognized two classes of networks: delivery networks that are focused on delivering value to the organization, and enabling networks, which build the capacity of individuals to do their job better. Some networking centres on a common interest – supporters of a football team or the fan club of a rock band for instance, while other communities focus on a shared practice such as agriculture, AIDS prevention, or even knowledge management.

To stand a chance of being effective long term, such networks need first to build momentum and then to sustain themselves. Effective knowledge networks share three common elements: a community of people who collaborate; a focused topic of knowledge; and organizational processes that ensure effective and meaningful connections.

Firstly, a network comprises a group of people or a community, who interact, learn together, build relationships and develop a sense of belonging and mutual commitment. Together they agree (implicitly or explicitly) on which methods work best, and how and when they are most useful. They build, agree and apply common practices together.

Secondly, one of the most salutary lessons I have learned about knowledge networking is to identify what knowledge is worth sharing. What is the topic and the relevant and useful knowledge? Knowledge networks require a clear focus that addresses the goals of the participants or their organizations.

Finally, all networks need effective processes to help members connect and collaborate. They need to develop adequate means of facilitating the discussions, a regular rhythm of interactions, certain practices in packaging the relevant knowledge and some form of understanding or statement of the purpose and 'rules of the game' of the group.

The following case study demonstrates how these three dimensions fit together in practice.

Knowledge networking to respond to AIDS: The Constellation for AIDS Competence

The following example demonstrates how knowledge networking can work to build capacity to reduce the spread of HIV and care for those living with AIDS.

The 'Constellation for AIDS Competence' is a small international NGO that I work with, which has global reach. A recent programme in six Asian countries brought together approximately 20 NGO staff in each country who between them visited more than 500 local communities.

AIDS Competence is an approach that enables communities (in villages, neighbourhoods and organizations) to use their own resourcefulness to jointly develop their capacity to respond to AIDS. The Constellation recognizes that the mobilization of information, technology and money is necessary but not sufficient, and offers to stimulate and connect local responses to HIV as a strategy to release potential. With few paid staff, the Constellation largely comprises people who work for other organizations, and who form a network bound by common beliefs and ways of working. At the core of this is the belief that every community has the inner strength to envision, to act and to adapt. The name of the organization draws on the image of stars that traverse the sky and occasionally cluster together to create something more than the separate stars. Participants in the network share a powerful vision of a world where AIDS Competence spreads faster than the virus.

The approach

The Constellation was sponsored by the Asian Development Bank (ADB) to build the capacity of Asian NGOs in six countries over a two-year period, to work alongside and support local responses to HIV/AIDS. NGOs from Cambodia, India, Indonesia, Papua New Guinea, the Philippines and Thailand received training on the AIDS Competence process and formed national networks and eventually an Asian network. The communities they work with were in turn encouraged to network with neighbouring communities, to share their local response to HIV/AIDS, and to learn from each other.

In each country an NGO network, called a 'National Facilitation Team' has been established. This team transfers the AIDS Competence Process to communities and other local organizations; learns from its community immersion and updates its practice; and shares its experience and inspiration with others. The national teams work closely together, calling upon each other for support and sharing experiences in-country and across the region, because they realize they cannot tackle the pandemic alone. With time, the NGOs have begun to take ownership of the approach and are actively collaborating to sustain their efforts. Working together as a facilitation team has helped the NGO facilitators to improve their understanding of the approach. There is a sense of solidarity and support for one another as they share their experiences.

In order to share these experiences of local responses more broadly, good practices are synthesized and captured into 'Knowledge Assets'. This step in the process was the focus of the International Knowledge Fair that took place in February 2009 in Chiang Mai, Thailand. There, representatives of the six countries exchanged their experience on various practices of AIDS Competence. They discussed the 'principles for action' that came out as a lesson from these experiences. These experiences were captured either as a 300-word written story or as a 3-minute video presentation to enhance their sharing capacities.

In order to continue the connections and the exchange an electronic collaboration space has been provided [http://aidscompetence.ning.com]. Participants are continuing to connect with new friends and peers on the electronic platform where they share their experiences in blogs and discuss issues in the forum. Many of the stories are available here too.

Networking for impact

This case study demonstrates the success of the application of the three key networking principles: creating a community of people who collaborate; a focused topic; and developing organizational processes to sustain connections.

We can see communities working together for the common good of the people in that community. These coherent communities have self-assessed their strengths and weaknesses in their response to AIDS and learned from their own experiences and those of other communities and countries. They have gone on to develop their own action plans and acted to tackle the issues of prevention and treatment together. At the Knowledge Fair in Chiang Mai, Thailand, Prabakar from India shared how sex workers in Periyackulam district raised an emergency fund to tackle inconsistent condom use and reduce vulnerability. Kalana, from Sri Lanka, explained that tuk-tuk (auto rickshaw) drivers in Mattakkuliya offer free rides to voluntary HIV testing centres. Andry, from Indonesia, reported that people living with HIV continue to work in their company without fear of being fired.

This approach is empowering communities to act on their own solutions. It enables a lot of spontaneous, lateral and low-cost learning and problem-solving. It helps to achieve scale. It also creates a more grounded and articulated demand for the services of local and international agencies and it is allowing those most affected to influence policy and practice. After two years, the programme has trained 437 facilitators (far exceeding the 108 planned); at least 543 communities have completed a self-assessment, facilitated by local NGO staff; 375 communities have developed their own action plans; and several communities have already conducted a second self-assessment to measure progress. ADB is currently assessing the impact of the programme with a view to extending it.

Learning

NGOs in the network have strengthened their capacity in dealing with communities and changed their way of working. The programme encourages the NGO participants to shift from being service providers to people who facilitate communities to determine their own response and then support them to do that. Participants self-assessed their facilitation skills at the start of the programme and repeated it at the end. Participants had a much better understanding of the practices and some showed improvement. One practice that shows clear improvement is teamwork, something observed in practice as facilitators support one another across NGOs to learn and apply the various tools and techniques. Here's what some of the participants have to say.

> The villagers told me I'd changed. I used to work the 'sausage way': trying to stuff all kinds of things into the community. And I used to talk a lot. Now, I am listening more, reflect more, and encourage the villagers to reflect and to express themselves more.
>
> (Anuwat, Thailand)

> People are changing their approach from working alone to teamwork. We are now working as a community.
>
> (Cambodian participant)

The coaches of the Constellation have also learned a lot. They have learned to let go of the process and give ownership of the process to those who apply it.

Participants follow the steps at their own pace and use or adapt the tools as applicable to their situation. Rather than train the participants, the coaches shared their experience of facilitating while accompanying and mentoring the facilitators.

The AIDS Competence approach unites people. AIDS Competence like the virus does not make a distinction in gender, race, economical status or country boundaries. At the knowledge fair, language did not stand in the way of learning. Participants felt related. Sanghamitra from India translated the stories from her team into English. And someone else translated them into Thai. I watched as a group of participants from Thailand hung on every translated word. Then the conversation and sharing continued.

Bearing this example in mind, let us look in more detail at the three dimensions of knowledge networking.

Dimensions of knowledge networking

A community of people

A knowledge network comprises a group of people who interact, learn together, build relationships and develop a sense of belonging and mutual commitment. Networks and communities do not stand still; the mix of people is always changing; the external environment changes, and hence a community's response to that environment also changes; and, over time, the culture itself changes.

All knowledge networks essentially share the following attributes: diversity, trust and reciprocity.

A diverse membership avoids the risk of 'group think'
Diversity goes beyond race, creed and gender and incorporates diversity of roles and thinking. Too much diversity, though, can lead to lack of common values and principles and could limit networking. In *The Tipping Point*, Gladwell (2001) talks about Connectors, Mavens and Salesmen. Each has a unique role to play in ensuring the free exchange of knowledge. Conscription doesn't work and participation is voluntary; after all, success depends on personal passion. Invite different levels of participation; expect and encourage a healthy turnover of people. It will keep the community healthy and refreshed.

Knowledge exchange relies on trust
Human beings do not like to admit ignorance and inability to solve a problem. They are also naturally reluctant to share as they think their experience is not relevant or 'good enough'. It takes trust and appreciation to share that vulnerability. That trust must be earned and is built by increasing the connections between individuals. People are also reluctant to share if the boss is in the room unless his or her behaviour is exceptional. Knowledge flows more easily between peers.

Reciprocity, social capital
As trust grows, people share more, expecting nothing in return except appreciation for their contribution and a validation of their expertise. Participants make

an investment of time, energy and emotion and there is potential for reciprocity. People recognize that one of the key resources of an organization, or community, is its social capital. This social capital takes a while to build up and can easily be destroyed by clumsy reorganization.

People share best when they feel part of the larger group, connected and not excluded by a small group of experts who dominate the exchanges. People participate when responses to their queries are timely. They are then more willing to reciprocate.

A great example of networking to share knowledge and create innovative solutions is described in James Surowiecki's book *The Wisdom of Crowds*. When the SARS (Severe Acute Respiratory Syndrome, a respiratory disease that was killing people in Asia) outbreak occurred in 2003, the World Health Organization (WHO) asked laboratories from around the world to work together to identify the cause. Each day they shared all the relevant knowledge they had gathered. Laboratories were then free to pursue their own most promising lines of investigation, and to share what they had learned the following day. Through this collaborative approach, the research team succeeded in isolating the virus in a matter of weeks, something which individually might have taken months or even years.

A focused topic of knowledge

Networking requires a focused topic of knowledge and a means to package and reuse the knowledge. Networking efforts can falter because the topic is too broad and esoteric. Some of the earliest networks were craftsmen's guilds. Craftsmen formed associations based on their trades: fraternities of masons, carpenters, carvers and glassworkers for example. These guilds controlled their secrets jealously and shared the art and technology of their crafts with each other.

It is important when determining the topic of the network that it is focused on addressing specific techniques, content or policy issues, and is not too general. The role of the community is to establish a common baseline of what is known and to act as guardians of this knowledge, both the explicit captured knowledge and the tacit (or 'how-to') knowledge which can be passed on to other members. The community is then free to build on what exists, in other words it is future-focused. So the knowledge of the community grows and keeps fresh.

While working for BP, we focused first on the processes of knowledge sharing and were happy to share knowledge about almost anything and everything. When we asked managers what their most important topics were we generally heard what their most urgent issue of the day was, or what they thought we wanted the answer to be. After a while three main themes emerged – Operations Excellence, Capital Productivity and Health & Safety. These were the primary focus of the business. Broad networks were formed to address these three issues, and sub-groups sprung up to address the more specific practices under these themes. A key lesson here is that it is important to identify a topic that is focused on specific practices.

Agreeing this common focus is a good starting activity for knowledge networking. A useful tool to enable this is to get the community to assess themselves on their current strengths and areas where they want to build capacity. The use of a self-assessment framework helps build a common focus and a common language for

---

Box 17.1 Organic rice farming in Thailand

In Suphan Buri province the Khao Kwan foundation educates farmers to shift to organic farming methods. They mix formal teaching with networking amongst peers. The focus is on three concrete practices: pest management without insecticides, soil management without chemical fertilizers and seed selection. The student farmers of all ages take turns to host a visit to their district, at their home or in a Buddhist temple. On one occasion they captured insects on the farm to identify and study their life cycle to distinguish between useful and destructive varieties. Then they shared their knowledge of how to remove the destructive ones. The students learn together for about 18 months but this has been so successful that the farmers continue to meet and share together after the course has finished. Through sharing their knowledge with each other the farmers have achieved higher yield, better health and less time working in the fields.

(Contributed by Professor Vicharn Panich, KMI Thailand)

---

the conversation in the community. *No More Consultants* (Parcell and Collison, 2009) provides examples of the application of this technique to build capacity for AIDS response, malaria prevention, knowledge management and analytical capability.

Networks are well placed to capture 'what we already know'. An active network embodies collective understanding of the knowledge that exists and collective experience in applying it. They have the practical experience and also know where to find references to 'captured knowledge'. So they have both the tacit and explicit knowledge, and through the sharing and connection to application, they usually have a good sense of what is worth sharing.

Organizing for networking

What processes can we put in place to ensure a network functions effectively?

We need a mechanism to help members connect and collaborate, a statement of the purpose and 'rules of the game' of the group, an adequate means of facilitating the discussions, a regular rhythm of interactions and a process for packaging the knowledge.

Connecting and collaborating

Knowledge networking is a social activity. Communities need connections in order for knowledge to flow. Meetings are just the tip of the iceberg of sharing. The connections can be made face to face or virtually. It is easier to create the relatedness and rapport face to face but virtual connections speed the exchange of knowledge and maintain more regular contact and communication. These connections may be via monthly meetings, regular telephone meetings, a discussion forum, or a shared social networking space such as Ning (www.ning.com).

An understanding of purpose

In BP all networks had some sort of governance document; a Terms of Reference or Charter. This document at a minimum included the raison d'être of the community, the objectives, principles or guidelines of how the members would conduct themselves and a brief description of the processes. Uppermost in the guidelines for conduct are responsiveness to requests and the creation of a culture of trust and reciprocity. When someone asks for help the community rallies round and finds a response.

A form of facilitating and/or leading

Usually this is a single person or small group of people, who are not experts but know enough about the topic. They are good at connecting people, and they would be good party hosts.

A regular rhythm

Using a combination of face-to-face and virtual connections it is important that the facilitator ensures there are frequent reasons to collaborate. For some it is not a natural habit so they must be prompted and learn a different way of working.

A process for packaging knowledge

The internet provides instant access to a multitude of information. The problem is that it is not distilled to give us a summary of what we need. Knowledge assets structured to give us the top ten things we need to know (FAQs) – with some generalized principles linked to real experiences and then to resources – makes it easier for those needing the knowledge to navigate to what they need.

Life cycle

Networking requires different processes and interventions depending on how long a network has existed. We can think of this as a life cycle of a network. Stages in the life cycle may include, but are not limited to: planning, launching, building momentum, sustaining and termination. The phase that a network finds itself in will determine the requirements and thus the choices for the various processes. The processes required to start a network, for instance, are very different from those needed when it has been functioning for a couple of years. Finally we need to know when to call it a day, when the community has served its usefulness, and when to close down the network.

Summary

Knowledge networking is a key approach to capacity development that seeks not only to help an individual build capacity but also to enable a large number of people to help develop each other's capacity at the same time. As we have seen from the examples on AIDS, SARS and organic rice farming, knowledge networking is demand driven and releases potential. It enables knowledge to be reused at scale and to create new knowledge (innovation). It is flexible, speedy, cost-effective and builds social capital.

To use the power of knowledge networking, practitioners need to tackle some of the barriers to sharing: a lack of time, being too proud to learn, hierarchy and formal conceptions of organization, perceptions of 'knowledge as power' and competition for resources. We can start by examining our own response.

What does it mean for capacity development practitioners? It requires a shift in our way of working and our way of thinking. We must lessen the distinctions of service provider and victim, donor and recipient, expert and uneducated person, rich and poor and think much more openly. We are all human! We all have something to share and we all have something to learn. Before offering our carefully packaged solutions we must learn to listen harder. It requires us to go beyond the standard roles of teachers, trainers or experts and participate actively in the change processes that our clients or partners are undertaking. What can they and *we* learn from what others have already done? As we have seen with the example on building the capacity to respond to AIDS, we can encourage the NGO participants to learn horizontally from peers and to shift from being 'providers of services' to people who facilitate communities to determine their own response. And we in turn can act in similar ways in supporting them to do so.

Knowledge networking will help us all access the knowledge that already exists and to build on that to innovate where there are no solutions. The practitioner will have to deal with three dimensions of knowledge networking:

- building a community of people who collaborate;
- having a focused topic of knowledge;
- facilitating organizational processes to ensure regular and meaningful dialogue.

Together these can enhance the flow of knowledge and support capacities to grow quickly, cost-effectively and at scale.

Recommended readings

This chapter links to several other chapters in this volume. Knowledge networking elements appear especially in Chapter 2 on multi-stakeholder engagement, Chapter 12 on public accountability and the use of information and media, Chapter 14 on an agricultural value chain and Chapter 16 on leadership development. Other linkages include the conclusions on the roles of advisors/facilitators in Chapter 4 and on balancing sectoral and change expertise in Chapter 5. The following is a short selection of useful resources as a starting point for further reading on the topic of knowledge networking.

Don Cohen and Larry Prusak (2001) *In Good Company – How Social Capital makes Organizations Work,* Harvard Business School Press, Boston, MA

This book discusses issues such as social capital, trust, and connections. Chapter 3 focuses on networks and communities, social talk and story-telling.

Chris Collison and Geoff Parcell (2004) *Learning to Fly – Practical Knowledge Management from Leading and Learning Organizations,* John Wiley, Chichester: second edition

This very practical book shares the experiences of a number of organizations applying such knowledge management techniques as self-assessment (Chapter 6) and peer assist (Chapter 7). Chapter 11 goes into detail on the life cycle of communities of practice.

Malcolm Gladwell (2001) *Tipping Point – How Little Things Can Make a Big Difference,* Abacus, London

Gladwell looks at a variety of examples to draw out three rules of the tipping point – the point at which the spread of a virus or product or knowledge becomes unstoppable: The Law of the Few (Connectors – the people who connect the right people, Mavens who are the educators – those with the knowledge, and Salesmen, the evangelists that spread the message), the Stickiness Factor (how to make the message irresistible) and the Power of Context (we are very sensitive to changes in the context the message is being received in).

Geoff Parcell and Chris Collison (2009) *No More Consultants,* Wiley, Chichester.

This book takes you on a journey of discovery along the river of insight, improvement and innovation. With inspiring stories and expert advice from their years of experience in helping organizations to value their own experience and reduce their dependency on consultants, the authors chart a course towards an engaged workforce and a successful business. The book describes in detail how to construct a self-assessment framework as a means of finding the knowledge in your organization.

James Surowiecki (2004) *The Wisdom of Crowds,* Abacus, London

This book is based on the thesis that under the right circumstances, groups of people are smarter than the smartest person in them. Characteristics of wise crowds are: diversity of opinion, independence, decentralization and aggregation (a process for turning private judgements into collective decision). He redefines diversity in terms of cognitive diversity which is a useful concept when getting a group of peers together to assist someone. So the wisdom of a network should be far greater than that of the company expert, providing the characteristics are adhered to.

Etienne Wenger, Richard McDermott and William Snyder (2002) *Cultivating Communities of Practice,* Harvard Business School Press, Boston, MA

If you want to go into Communities of Practice in detail then this is a good book to read. The authors argue that Communities need to be purposefully developed and integrated into the strategy of organizations. They come up with seven principles for cultivating a community: 1 Design for evolution, 2 Open a dialogue between inside and outside perspective, 3 Invite different levels of participation, 4 Develop both public and private community spaces, 5 Focus on value, 6 Combine familiarity and excitement and 7 Create a rhythm for the community.

Part IV

Improving on Results

Evidence that capacity has been developed should show in changes in performance of the actors concerned. With increased capacities these actors will be able
to address their own, as well as shared, goals and ambitions in addressing social,
economic or ecological issues. The four chapters in Part IV discuss how one can
operationalize a firm orientation on results in capacity development and learn at
the same time.

Chapter 18 reviews various ways in which monitoring and evaluation (M&E)
of capacity development and its results can be undertaken, based on elements
of two main 'schools of thought' in M&E. The subject of Chapter 19 is the challenge of maintaining a balance between short-, medium- and long-term ambitions.
Chapter 20 explores innovative and practical ways in which practitioners can
benefit from the information generated by M&E to foster self-reflection. Finally,
Chapter 21 shows that the often suggested dichotomy between 'accountability for
results' and 'learning while doing' is false, and discusses the principles for effectively combining these.

18

Measuring Capacity Development

Assessing progress and achievements in capacity development is a challenge. The drive for accountability is pushing monitoring and evaluation (M&E) of capacity development, and development in general, in two different directions that a practitioner needs to be aware of. One reflects a traditional results-based, log-frame approach to intentional change. The other relies on an open systems way of thinking, and the related interactive M&E methods.

In this chapter, David Watson acknowledges the merits of conventional results-based approaches but outlines their limitations when applied to more complex situations and to the multi-faceted nature of capacity itself. With extensive references to literature and cases available, he goes on to review examples of successful and innovative M&E methods and shows how these combine 'the best of two worlds'. The range of insights, clues and references provided can help the reader to think through their present or improved M&E logics and practices.

Combining the 'Best of Two Worlds' in Monitoring and Evaluation of Capacity Development

David Watson

Introduction

The term 'monitoring and evaluation' (M&E) tends to conjure up the immediate impression that it is 'something which donors want done'. This chapter attempts to demystify the term and argues that this function needs a broader interpretation and can be seen as an integral process in all effective organizations or systems.

The European Centre for Development Policy Management (ECDPM) conducted a Study of Capacity Change and Performance (Baser and Morgan,

2008) based on 18 detailed case studies as well as a comprehensive literature review. These cases illustrate different motives for undertaking M&E in general, and of M&E of capacity development in particular. On the one hand development cooperation agencies strive to demonstrate the effectiveness of their funding. On the other hand, some non-governmental organizations (NGOs) and other development practitioners emphasize participation in learning from experience as a means of self-improvement. The approaches to M&E of capacity development in the ECDPM sample also differed significantly. Donors tended to use logical frameworks or project frameworks for programme planning and monitoring. Those NGOs in the cases which had developed a degree of independence of donor funding tended to use approaches encouraging interaction between stakeholders, using 'stories' to illustrate important changes and to inform debate on the best way ahead.

These distinctions throw into sharp relief the various notions of, and ways of thinking about, 'capacity'. Donors tend to seek primarily 'performance improvement' and view it virtually as a proxy for 'capacity'. 'Performance' in this context is seen as the 'delivery' of predefined results (outputs). However, the insights from the ECDPM study identified other important features of 'capacity'. These are summarized in what the study calls five 'core capabilities'. In addition to the ability to produce development results, these are: the ability to create 'operating space' and sound relationships; the ability to self-organize and act; the ability to create coherence and direction, and the ability to learn and adapt to changing circumstances over time (see also Chapter 1).

This chapter starts with a brief discussion of planned or 'reductionist' thinking, compared to 'complex adaptive systems' notions of capacity and capacity development. Several case studies in appropriate application of each approach are presented, partly to illustrate how they complement each other. We then introduce some innovative approaches to M&E of capacity development.[1] The important notion of accountability is addressed by suggesting two distinct categories of accountability: 'exogenous' (accountability to donors), and 'endogenous' (accountability to domestic stakeholders and service users). Finally, Box 18.2 illustrates how at least some donors are beginning to change their practices of M&E of capacity development from 'planned' towards more flexible pragmatic approaches. It must be noted that the chapter's case studies are deliberately biased towards positive experiences, on the grounds that any reader who has dwelt upon the subject of M&E for long needs every encouragement possible.

Notions of capacity: 'Reductionism' to 'systems thinking'

Behind any discussion of 'M&E of capacity' is the challenge that 'capacity' is an ill-understood concept. It is not yet a well-defined area of practice. Nor is there a generally accepted definition of 'capacity' in the literature. Those in doubt are encouraged to refer to the accompanying volume of a recent discussion of capacity development (Taylor and Clarke, 2008) which lists definitions of 'capacity' and capacity development' used by various agencies.

The recent study by ECDPM referred to above has defined 'capacity' as 'that emergent combination of attributes, assets, capabilities and relationships that enables a human system to perform, survive and self-renew'. Based on 18 case studies of organizations and networks around the world, the study concludes that there are *multiple* dimensions of 'capacity': the five 'core capabilities'. The clear implication is that we need to recognize and acknowledge *all* of these dimensions in capacity development efforts, and to cater for them in approaches to the M&E of capacity.

However, the dominant capacity 'paradigm' adopted by donors to date posits a 'linear' connection between the various aspects of capacity development initiatives: from the provision of inputs (technical assistance and equipment, for example) to the delivery of outputs (e.g. more able, competent individuals or service units). Based on certain assumptions, these inputs and outputs are expected to lead to better 'performance' (for example 'improved health service delivery') and ultimately achievement of development goals (improved health in a population). The 'project framework or logical framework' enshrines this logic of 'cause and effect' relationships between inputs, outputs, performance and development goals, and and is often used to focus on 'delivery' of pre-defined outputs. This is also the basis of the 'results based management' approach. This methodological tool is often used to assess the need for, to design in detail, and to monitor progress of development programmes.

Achieving improvements in public sector organizational performance is often a major priority objective for donors. Indeed, 'performance' tends to be seen as a proxy for 'capacity' (if an organization is by some measure performing better, it is assumed to have improved its 'capacity'). These approaches have been termed 'technocratic' and 'reductionist' (i.e. they see organizations as 'machines', amenable to discrete 'fixes'; they 'reduce' complex problems and systems to their constituent components). The project framework's indicators of progress in relation to objectives become the yardsticks for the purposes of monitoring over time.

But the ECDPM study further concluded that, given the multi-dimensional nature of 'capacity', efforts to enhance organizational capacities were not amenable to 'linear' and neat 'if this, then that' thinking. The nature of the organizations studied was more akin to that of living organisms. This perspective has been conceptualized in a body of management literature known as 'complex adaptive systems (CAS) thinking'. This 'school' of thought sees capacity as being associated with multiple causes, solutions and effects, some of them unintended. Interaction between stakeholders over time matters a lot: yet these dynamics are often not necessarily controllable and potentially quite unpredictable. Detailed performance- (or capacity-) improvement plans are less easy to make, seen from this perspective. The study observed that capacity tends to 'emerge' over time, affected by many factors. Thus in the (plentiful!) jargon – it is an 'emergent' property. Critics of the planning- and control-oriented 'reductionist' approaches also argue that preoccupation with monitoring progress in relation to pre-determined 'indicators' detracts attention from less tangible and more relational/attitudinal dimensions of capacity and from broader learning from experience. In many cases unanticipated results or insights may prove more important to development effectiveness than what was 'planned'.[2]

Case study evidence of where different approaches to M&E have worked best

It is important to stress that evaluations of capacity development experience do not point unambiguously towards one or other of the above 'schools' of thought as being 'better' than the other. The cases reviewed in the ECDPM Capacity Study – and others mentioned below – indicate that both have their merits and uses, depending on circumstances, and the reason for embarking on some form of organizational development initiative. Indeed, there are several cases which illustrate complementarities between the different approaches. See, for example, the Ceja Andina programme case study in Ambrose's article in the September 2006 edition of *Capacity.org* referred to in the 'recommended readings' section.

Planned approaches to capacity development

Carefully planned 'reductionist' approaches to monitoring capacity tend to work best in circumstances where:

- an organization 'signs up' voluntarily to accept capacity development support;
- stakeholders themselves are willing and able to assess the capacities they need;
- the abilities required can be defined precisely and unambiguously (from the author's experience this is often 'easier said than done' in the public sector);
- there are incentives to improve performance; and
- leadership of the organization is firmly behind the capacity-improvement programme and thus there is unambiguous 'ownership'.

A number of cases discussed in the ECDPM study, such as those of the Rwanda Revenue Authority (see www.ecdpm.org/dp57d, accessed September 2009) and the Philippines–Canada Local Government Support Programme (www.ecdpm. org/dp57n, accessed September 2009), offer positive examples of where these factors prevailed, and contributed to successful capacity development outcomes using a project framework-based, results-based management logic. See Box 18.1 for another example that concerns municipal government capacity development in Pakistan.

Complex adaptive systems approaches

Other cases in the ECDPM study illustrate circumstances where a CAS approach to organizational development and monitoring proved effective. These include the Environmental Action Programme (ENACT) programme in Jamaica (www. ecdpm.org/dp57j, accessed September 2009) and the regional organization International Union for the Conservation of Nature (IUCN) in Asia (www.ecdpm. org/dp57m, accessed September 2009). They provide important and encouraging insights with regard to monitoring. They illustrate how positive impacts on capacity were achieved when the organizations were encouraged to learn lessons from their own experiences, and evolved approaches to developing their own

---

Box 18.1 Supporting capacity development in Faisalabad, Pakistan

Faisalabad City District Government (CDGF), serving nearly 7 million people, was supported for just four years by a largely national-staffed technical assistance team. Three factors allowed its project framework-based design and monitoring indicators to contribute to its success. First, flexibility of the donor, the UK Department for International Development (DFID) permitted a lengthy consensus-building process to define the mission of the CDGF and disseminate it throughout the organization. This took six months, led by the Strategic Policy Unit (staffed by key CDGF staff and consultants). The second factor was the close collaboration between staff and consultants in analysing the current situation, and defining together Strategic Operational Plans for all key departments. These became the basis for regular monitoring of progress and problems by the newly-constituted top management team. The case illustrates how regular internal reporting on, and close collective monitoring of, progress by top management sitting together (in meetings unprecedented before the start of the project) was crucial in changing the 'culture' of communication, co-operation and learning in the organization. The third major 'success' factor in the case was the early introduction of custom-designed management information systems to aid collection and analysis of basic data (for the first time, CDGF knew how many staff it employed, and the size of its financial deficit). Thus top management meetings knew the facts and 'how their departments, and CDGF, were doing'. The case illustrates how a 'hard' M&E tool was used in an organization with a clear, formally-agreed mandate to drive a process of change in management style and culture. How and why change happened in CDGF is accessibly documented in a series of 22 well-illustrated case studies at www.spu.com.pk/short_cs.htm, accessed November 2009.

---

capacity accordingly. These cases also note how donors can be supportive of the organizations in ways that responded to the uncertainties they faced, by demonstrating flexibility.

In the ENACT case, the donor, Canadian International Development Agency (CIDA) abandoned a project framework-based monitoring system in favour of a more process-oriented approach to monitoring progress and capacity development. In the IUCN case, its funders allowed it to experiment and maintain a spirit of innovation and creativity. Staff exchanges between some donor organizations and IUCN have taken place, providing insights for them into how each other's organizations work, and enhancing mutual trust. The Director of IUCN created an 'enabling environment' for creative team formation, based on shared values, and continuous re-thinking and re-fashioning. 'I do not have a road map, only a goal (which can change)' she acknowledged. While formal training has contributed to individuals' development, the predominant training modes are experiential, and include mentoring.

Common features across both approaches

Common themes relevant for monitoring represented in the ECDPM cases which illustrate CAS approaches yet are also features of the most successful 'results-based management' cases (such as the CDGF case cited above) include:

- identifying clear overall goals and organizational mission – and awareness of these throughout the organization – with an emphasis on commonly shared values that should be reflected in achieving these goals;
- leadership: especially empowerment by the leader of principal staff to encourage experimentation, changes in team structures and approaches, and defining what resources were needed and when;
- providing regular opportunities for learning from experience, self-assessment, and the identification of 'stories' involving positive examples or experiences, significant changes or errors;
- emphasizing on-the-job development of individuals' skills, though participative, face-to-face and 'hands-on' approaches;
- adopting functional M&E systems that were responsive to the needs of staff or clients, which enabled them to learn from their collective experience.

Recent innovations in M&E methodology and applications: The way forward?

In the last ten years, several innovative approaches to monitoring and evaluation in capacity development programmes have been developed and refined. These include 'Most Significant Change' developed by Jessica Dart and Rick Davies (see the recommended readings section); the Accountability, Learning and Planning System in ActionAid (Guijt, 2004), and Outcome Mapping (Earl et al, 2001).[3]

Common characteristics of these innovative approaches – tending to 'resonate' with CAS approaches – are that:

- they involve structured interactions among stakeholders based on day-to-day experiences using 'work stories' as a means of 'making sense' out of what changes are happening, and why;
- they are not exclusively concerned with quantitative measurement but with creating consensus on what constitutes qualitative improvements that will contribute to the broad goals of the systems involved;
- they tend to demystify 'M&E' and allow even the most vulnerable stakeholders or beneficiaries to have a voice in periodic reflection. The capacities of beneficiaries for critical analysis, debate and decision taking are thereby improved.

The accountability issue: Exogenous and endogenous

There is evidence that donors face accountability pressures from their domestic 'constituencies' (ministers, parliaments, audit bodies, press and indeed public opinion). They must accordingly demonstrate 'results' from development programmes they fund. The project framework (or close variants on it) is virtually universally adopted as a programme planning, design and monitoring tool, being deemed the most suitable basis for monitoring and (sometimes) evaluating progress. The majority of international NGOs (INGOs) – which tend to depend on donors for significant proportions of their funding – tend therefore to use this approach as well (see HLM Consult, 2008, for a recent account of M&E practices among Danish INGOs). In this context, the NGO cases featured in the ECDPM study are therefore unusual in moving away from, or never having used, such approaches.

However, if we reflect on the CAS cases cited above, in these accountability is also an important driver. Yet the stress appears different. In these cases the systems or organizations are accountable to their own clients, local politicians, members, or users of its services. This might be called 'endogenous' accountability. At this point, it may be helpful to draw a distinction between 'endogenous' and 'exogenous' accountability. 'Exogenous' accountability applies to 'recipients' – be they sovereign governments, consultant contractors or NGOs – having to account to donors for the use of funds.

The evidence from the ECDPM study appears to indicate that innovative (informal) monitoring mechanisms, based on CAS thinking, tend to be more supportive of 'endogenous' accountability. In turn, these mechanisms are often more effective in encouraging better performance and greater 'ownership' than the results-based management monitoring mechanisms that are applied by donors.

In cases where national governments' own resources are used to establish and manage development programmes, there may be the opportunities for 'endogenous' accountability to encourage innovation, and 'learning-by-doing'. Several of the successful service-delivery cases identified in a recent Asian Development Bank (ADB) study conducted in Pakistan (EAD/ADB, 2008) illustrate conspicuous improvements in service delivery, in the absence of detailed plans, *with* 'protection' of, and accountability to, a politically-influential patron (in what is a notoriously problematic public sector environment). See in particular the Sindh National Water Course Upgrading programme, and National Highways and Motorways Police as encouraging examples of where clear endogenous accountability in a permissive (but protected) environment produced extraordinary results.

How M&E can contribute to effective capacity development

A recent contribution to the debate illustrates how M&E might (better) contribute to capacity development processes. Alfredo Ortiz and Peter Taylor of the Institute of Development Studies (IDS), University of Sussex, ask the question 'what would we want from learning approaches to M&E of capacity development that donor 'accounting' approaches are unable to deliver?' (Ortiz and Taylor, 2008a, p19). They argue for more encouragement of 'stories' from key players about how they think change and development are happening. In this way, they envisage not just invoking energy and better interpretation of the meaning of what has changed on the part of key players, but a better application of 'strategic thinking': 'an intangible that is difficult to capture with indicators, but which is clearly important to long-term performance'. They argue that 'observation and study, learning, abstract framing, adaptive management and agility in changing plans and putting learning into practice are more important than rigorous tracking of outputs that ultimately do not reflect at all the reality of the situation they are describing' (Ortiz and Taylor, 2008a, pp20–21). Thus they appear to agree that the more informal approaches to M&E, where endogenous accountability is served, tend to encourage ownership of the capacity development process and strategic thinking. Both are essential factors for better performance. The Faisalabad case mentioned above illustrates how a formal approach to monitoring, serving endogenous accountability, also contributed strongly to capacity development and better organizational performance.

Conclusions for practitioners: Building capacities to deliver

So how can we boil the above account down to basics, for operational purposes? We can conclude that the evidence from the cases cited demonstrate that both approaches to M&E have their merits. The case studies of successful organizations illustrate how in fact they tend to combine elements of both. Given the multi-dimensional nature of 'capacity', CAS thinking is undoubtedly relevant in selecting M&E approaches. There are several innovative, yet tried-and-tested methods and approaches to M&E that have been proved to contribute to capacity development. It is no coincidence that they tend to strengthen 'endogenous' accountability, and ownership of the capacity development process. There is evidence that some bilateral donors are moving away from strict 'control'-oriented planning and monitoring, towards more nuanced approaches which reflect not only the complexity of partner organizations and service delivery systems, but also the challenges of sustainably developing their capacities.

Box 18.2 Examples of changes in donor practices in M&E of capacity development

In preparing this chapter, the author contacted several bilateral donors that had been involved in capacity development-related projects connected to the ECDPM study on Capacity Change and Performance to find out if and how recent M&E of capacity development practices had changed. Both the Australian Agency for International Development (AusAID) and the German Federal Ministry for Economic Development Cooperation (BMZ) reported that they had abandoned logical frameworks in planning programmes. BMZ now uses 'results chains' (sketching how change is envisaged); only outcome targets and indicators are pre-determined. AusAID also only sets objectives, and broad parameters. In both cases, details of implementation (inputs, activities and outputs) are to be worked out by the implementing teams and their partners. These can and should be adjusted over time according to conditions and changes in needs.

In AusAID an Independent Monitoring Group usually assesses progress up to twice a year, which includes a review of the detailed work-plans and progress against them. The approach to M&E in BMZ has reportedly not yet captured fully the implications of this more flexible approach to planning and programming. This challenge is recognized, and is currently being tackled.

Piloting of monitoring of progress in the 'five capabilities' inherent in the definition of capacity hypothesized in the ECDPM approach is ongoing in a major AusAID-supported law and justice reform programme in Papua New Guinea. 'Most Significant Change' methodology has been used on occasions by AusAID through its managing contractors. Most effort is devoted to assessing whether there is any improvement in development outcomes: capacity development per se is often implicitly a 'means to an end' in these cases. However, greater stress is being put on monitoring and evaluating capacity development and capacity development processes themselves. An example is in the Solomon Islands, where government expectations for more development of the capacities of counterparts to technical advisers have been instrumental in closer scrutiny of, and pressures for, more attention to individual and organizational capacity development. Nevertheless, AusAID is still coming to grips with the M&E of capacity development and capacity development processes, noting that this is still a relatively new field and that methodologies must not burden partner agencies and staff, and must be seen as relevant to them.

Notes

1   The basic sources for this chapter are:
    ECDPM Discussion Paper 58B, available from www.ecdpm.org/dp58b (accessed on 7 September 2009), which reviews some of the literature on the topic; distils the M&E-related features and issues raised in the ECDPM study cases; synthesizes contributions from champions of systems thinking; and summarizes some innovative approaches including those mentioned in this chapter.

The *Pelican Initiative (Platform for Evidence-Based Learning and Communications for Social Change)* is an internet-based discussion forum addressing the question 'How can we learn more from what we do while having the biggest impact on the social change processes in which we engage?' The group is moderated by Niels Keijzer in ECDPM (nk@ecdpm.org). Pelican archives are accessible via inserting pelican@dgroups.org in your browser. The forum regularly addresses M&E of capacity development.

2   Readers who wish to pursue this in more detail are advised first to read ECDPM Policy Management Brief No. 22 (www.ecdpm.org/Web_ECDPM/Web/Content/Download. nsf/0/5E619EA3431DE022C12575990029E824/$FILE/PMB22_e_CDapproaches-capacitystudy.pdf, accessed September 2009) on the results of the study, which provides a useful tabulation illustrating distinctions in terms and perspective between the two 'schools'.

3   Appendix 2 of the Theme Paper on M&E of capacity prepared for the ECDPM study describes these approaches in more detail.

References

EAD/ADB (2008) *Scoping Study on Capacity Building for Service Delivery & Aid Effectiveness in Pakistan*, Economic Affairs Division, Asian Development Bank, Manila, Philippines. Currently available as *Effective Technical Cooperation for Capacity Development – Pakistan Country Case Study*, JICA Joint Study on Effective TC for Capacity Development, www.jica.go.jp/cdstudy/about/output/pdf/Pakistan.pdf, accessed September 2009

Earl, S., Carden, F. and Smutylo, T. (2001) *Outcome Mapping: The Challenges of Assessing Development Impacts: Building Learning and Reflection into Development Programmes*, IDRC, Ottawa

Engel, P., Land, A. and Keijzer, N. (2006) 'A balanced approach to the M&E of capacity and performance', ECDPM Discussion Paper No. 58E, Maastricht

Guijt, I. (2004) *ALPS in Action: A Review of the Shifts in ActionAid towards a New Accountability, Learning and Planning System*, ActionAid International, London

HLM Consult (2008) *Mapping of Monitoring and Evaluation Practices of Danish NGOs*, Danida, Ministry of Foreign Affairs Evaluation Department, Copenhagen

Land, A., Hauck, V. and Baser, H. (2009) *Capacity Development: Between Planned Interventions and Emergent Processes: Implications for Development Co-operation*, ECDPM Policy Management Brief No. 22, March 2009. Maastricht

Ortiz, A. and Taylor, P. (2008a) 'Learning purposefully in capacity development:Why, when and what to measure?', Opinion Paper for IIEP, Institute of Development Studies (IDS), Brighton, Sussex. This can be accessed via www.mande.co.uk or www.impactalliance.org/ev_en.php?ID=47298_201&ID2=DO_TOPIC, accessed September 2009

Taylor, P. and Clarke, P. (2008) 'Capacity for a change', a document based on outcomes of a 'Capacity Collective' workshop, IDS, Brighton, Sussex

Recommended readings

This chapter links to and is complemented by several other chapters. ECDPM's 'five core capabilities' (5C's) model is more extensively introduced in Chapter 1, while Chapter 11 discusses how CD efforts take place within the setting of multi-actor relations, institutions and politics. Chapter 12 discusses ways in which public accountability can be used to stimulate performance. And finally, Chapter 21 further explores the perceived opposition between results-orientation and learning and, in line with this chapter, shows that they can actually be combined well.

For further reading it is suggested you also look at the list of references above, which does not purport to be exhaustive, but represents a distillation of some of the most accessible and (actually or potentially) influential literature relevant to the M&E of capacity development, from both 'schools' mentioned in the chapter, together with a small selection of donor-generated materials, including positive cases from Pakistan. For additional insights we suggest the following resources relating specifically to the application of M&E method-ologies, and Systems Thinking and Complexity approaches.

The Theme Paper Monitoring and Evaluation of Capacity Development, ECDPM Discussion Paper 58B, available from www.ecdpm.org/dp58b (accessed 7 September 2009). See especially Section 3 on 'Emerging Approaches to the M&E of Capacity Issues' in Chapter 8.

Ambrose, M. (2006) 'Enhancing learning in the M&E process; Outcome Mapping in Ecuador', *Capacity.org*, Issue 29, pp.12–13, illustrates how a range of stakeholders in community-based natural resource management were engaged in M&E which satisfied both imperatives: accountability and learning, using Outcome Mapping as a complement to Logical Framework approaches. The article is available online at www.capacity.org/en/journal/practice_reports/enhancing_learning_in_the_m_e_process, accessed September 2009.

Dart, J. and Davies, R. (2003) 'A dialogical story-based evaluation tool: The most significant change technique', *American Journal of Evaluation*, vol 24, no 2.

The article outlines the origins, philosophy and practicalities of this inno-vative technique for M&E of capacity development and change processes. It is available on a very useful website www.mande.co.uk under 'Rick's Methods' (accessed on 7 September 2009). Managed by Rick Davies, the site is dedicated to providing news of M&E methods relevant to development programmes with social development objectives.

Complexity Thinking and Social Development: Connecting the Dots, by Alan Fowler in (web-based) The Broker: Connecting Worlds of Knowledge, 7 April 2008, via www.thebrokeronline.eu/en, accessed September 2009, is one of the more accessible sources making the case for introducing more complexity-based frameworks into the capacity-related development field.

19

Time Matters

In capacity development, time is an ever present force. But how time influences and complicates a practitioner's work is not fully appreciated. This chapter highlights different ways in which time appears in capacity-development initiatives. It discusses the often competing demands of different actors' time frames, cycles and core processes that must somehow be brought together.

A case example introduces a model which shapes the primary process of a capacity-development support organization. It helps the practitioner to work consciously across short-, medium- and long-term objectives and time frames depending on the scale of ambition involved. The approach described shows how practitioners can apply adaptive planning and 'learning in action'.

Effective Capacity Development: The Importance of Connecting Time Frames

Heinz Greijn and Alan Fowler

Introduction

To say that time is important in capacity development is to state the obvious. Time permeates everything that we do so deeply that, like gravity, its force is exerted without a full appreciation of what it implies for capacity development in practice. But there are many ways of experiencing and being able to cope with the factor of time in capacity-development activity and relationships.

The first part of this chapter therefore sets out ways of appreciating time as it appears in a practitioner's work. This step is important because it is critical to understand various 'types' of time and to be aware of their influence on capacity and its development. Part two explores common problems involved when different features of time have to be connected to achieve development impact. Part three discusses a 'working model' developed by the SNV Netherlands Development

Organisation to support practitioners in consciously working with different time frames beyond the standard project cycle. It demonstrates one way in which – depending on the scale of ambition – a quality-focused and result-oriented approach to capacity development can ensure that short-term actions fit into and advance long-term strategies.

Unpacking time: Frames, cycles and core processes

The aid system functions on the basis of time 'units' with different durations. The Millennium Development Goals (MDGs), adopted by member states of the United Nations, span 15 years. National governments also have long- and medium-term goals, plans and measures, as have many non-governmental organizations (NGOs). Within long time lines, these and other stakeholders create multiple, shorter time units that should be internally aligned with each other as well as with time units used by others. In short, multiple demands for aligning or connecting different time spans need practical resolution. Seeing what this requirement looks like in reality means being familiar with the 'varieties' of time that practitioners have to deal with. There are three basic 'types' of time used in development: frames, cycles and core processes.

Time in frames: Linking intended effect and necessary duration

Progress in development is judged in terms of a time frame that makes sense in relation to the type and scale of result that people have in mind. With logical frameworks as a classic example, variation in time frames is recognized in differences between short-term (project) outputs, medium-term behavioural, skill or capability outcomes and long-term impact on improved performance and well-being. The time-bound relationship between these three degrees of change is built into the logic of the model.

For example improved capacity by increasing women's pre-natal knowledge about good nutrition is a short-term, personally enduring, change. This insight can give a capability leading to decrease in infant mortality in the medium term; with a child growing up to realize its full potential as an adult in the long term. In this example, a shorter-term gain for one child should lead to a long-term individual effect.

An alternative example is one that anticipates a collective impact in the long term. Here, citizens acting 'politically' on the basis of education about their civic rights and responsibilities is a short-term activity. Medium-term effects might be seen in greater voter engagement and the change of regimes because of insistence on free and fair electoral processes. Ultimately, such dynamics can produce a cumulative long-term, institutional effect of more accountable governance.

The general point is to be clear about what time frame(s) matter for what kind of intended results at any level or scale of ambition.

Time in cycles: The importance of nests and rhythms

Much of life moves in cycles. Seasonality is an obvious example that can affect almost every facet of development work. Seasonality is all-embracing and cannot be hurried. At best we cope with its uncertainties. Its impact on capacity-development efforts can be felt, for example, in the ebb and flow of labour demands and people's uneven availability to 'participate' in training and other events. This is especially so when seasonal variation in time demands exclude the poorest from capacity-development initiatives. Consequently, a practitioner's work frequently needs to be season-sensitive, illustrated in the case of increasing agricultural production in Ethiopia described later in this chapter.

Next to seasonal variations and forces, organizations rely on internal cycles to give coherence, direction, 'predictive' order and stability. In most cases combinations of time cycles add up to a rhythm or sense of regularity that is part and parcel of organizational life and culture. Typically, organizational cycles nest in each other where shorter repetitions, say, three-monthly accounting and reporting, sit inside annual budgeting and reporting, which sit within multi-year strategic objectives.

Yearly financial budgeting and accounting often dictate a basic cycle of planning, expenditure and reflection. In international development, complications can arise when 'annual' requirements have start and end dates that differ between countries providing and receiving aid. Practitioners' adherence to their organization's own standards and timings may be disrupted when there is dependency on other basic cycles that do not match.

Overall, the presence of 'nested' cycles in development work requires a practitioner to stand back and see where the timings of their intended intervention are located within the internal 'clock' of the organization as well as the 'rhythm' of the external system.

Time in relation to core processes and funding base

The way in which time is employed in capacity-development work depends also on the funding base of the service provider. A useful division is between funding provided as a subsidy and that gained through commercial competition and contracting.

Many development organizations rely on a direct (multi-year) subsidy or programme funding. Consequently, they are expected to be 'in control' of time by being accountable for self-determined measures of performance tied to the capacity-development and general programme results they have committed to. In such cases competitive charging rates and costs are not an *a priori* or sole measure for an adviser's performance or that of the organization overall. However, a subsidized organization is directly accountable for its development contribution alongside a selected client.

Many other providers of capacity-development services operate on commercial terms driven by competition for contracts and economic viability that often translate into 'selling' a necessary minimum of billable days for a consultant. Capacity-development providers may establish themselves in specialist niches, for example developing experience and reputations in 'technical sectors', such as water, agriculture or health or in processes such as network facilitation, human resource development or financial management. Such consultants usually operate on the basis of contracts and not subsidy. Correspondingly, time measures have a clear financial, profit and loss grounding. But there is less reliance on an overarching organizational accountability in terms of contributing towards development goals per se. This is the task of the client.

So logics of direct subsidy and of commerce bring with them different approaches to time, which also influence the ways external advisers engage with a client system. Subsidized providers can more easily opt for longer-term and flexible accompaniment. By the nature of their financing, commercial providers will often be more geared towards delivery of specific results in an agreed time frame. Activities from both kinds of actors can strongly overlap. Moreover, organizations can also combine subsidized and fee-for-services operations. It is not a question of one being better or worse than the other. But the key point here is that the funding base does indeed influence the 'value' of a practitioner's time and the ways in which it is dealt with.

Where direct subsidy for service provision is in play, quality assurance is one way of marrying the personal accountability of adviser with that of his or her organization's demonstrating results and that of the client selected for capacity-development support. Showing how this can be done is the subject of the case study below. But before getting there it is useful to apply the lens of time to challenges in the design of capacity-development interventions: the following topic for discussion.

Time and capacity-development interventions: Common challenges

Capacity development is all about increasing the performance of human systems over time. In a dynamic process, achieving certain purposes needs to connect to time frames, cycles and rhythms. The way that time is framed in cycles and processes will have implications for monitoring anticipated progress, evaluating results and learning from doing. There are, therefore, a number of frequent and tricky time-related issues that a practitioner has to take into account.

Downstream knock on effects

Aided capacity-building processes are probably more subject to the time behaviour of funders than that of other actors. Delays in budget approvals, erratic disbursements, and so on, all contribute to uncertainties – for example in moment of start up or continuation into a next phase – that can plague capacity-development design, planning and effectiveness. Assessing time-related vulnerability to resourcing channels is a prudent step to take.

Multiplicities of time frames

A practitioner working with multiple stakeholders, or even with parts of big organizations, will be confronted with (perhaps substantial) variations in the speed of the pace of change and the time horizons of different actors. When thinking about a capacity-development intervention it therefore makes sense to take a reading of differences in time frames and find out why they occur, particularly in relation to the inter-dependencies in play.

Span of client attention

A client organization's rhythms and cycles will usually generate an uneven and insufficient allocation of time for capacity-development efforts. This reality is often aggravated by the fact that the energy required for capacity development comes on top of daily work scheduling. Seldom is time freely available to draw on, even where management and/or staff are deeply committed to change. Time becomes a critical limiting quantity in intervention design that a practitioner probably needs to negotiate.

The year end rush

After budget approval comes scheduling for disbursement. Because the latter often gets out of step with what was planned, there can be a last minute rush to allocate and spend before the end of the financial year. Capacity development can get caught up in this reaction which gives incentives to cut corners in design and hence compromise on quality.

Results and learning

Monitoring, evaluating and learning from capacity-development initiatives have their own repetitions or cycles with implications for time-related design. Depending on context, substance and scale of intended change, a set up for assessing alterations in different elements of capacity or capabilities described in Chapter 1 may not readily match the core business or (funding) time frames a client relies on. A practitioner will need to clearly establish how assessment and learning in relation to various dimensions of capacity can best link to a client's monitoring and evaluation (M&E) rhythms, particularly in relation to external financing.[1]

An overall challenge for a practitioner is to work out with the client what the short-, medium- and long-term goals are, what time frames will go with these and what sort of frequency and pace are required to track and learn from results over time. In a commercial contract this is usually laid down in some form of Terms of Reference (ToR) document and possibly an underlying project plan. Subsidized providers also use some form of project or programme plan. Whatever the case, a critical issue is how to connect different types of time together in a logical, coherent practice. To explore one approach, the following section discusses a generic 'working model' that seeks to assist practitioners in working across different time frames and marrying their processes with the clients' view of aims and time. The illustrative model is used as a quality assurance tool within SNV Netherlands Development Organisation.

Managing for results over time

Practitioners have to be on their guard for myopia in terms of time and context. Being constantly in action mode often makes it hard to gauge whether you are still on track vis-à-vis medium- and long-term aims projected in the future that may have been formulated years ago. This is especially difficult because over time societal changes, perceptions and new insights occur that may place the initial aims in a different light.

This makes it important for practitioners to step back and look at the bigger picture from time to time. This involves reflecting on where you came from and where you are going so as to determine if the desired end state still makes sense or whether it is necessary to adjust the approach or even the intended outcome of the capacity-development effort. As noted earlier, such moments of reflection are rare amidst day-to-day project demands. In many situations what is urgent today takes priority over what is important for achieving results in the long run. But even at those rare moments when a reflective 'time-out' is taken, a systematic approach for how to go about this is often lacking. With this in mind, the following case presents a practical approach that stimulates the practitioner to maintain a reflective stance through different time frames, cycles and processes described above.

Background: SNV's advisory practice

As a result of internal reflection and learning, starting in 2000[2] SNV has undertaken a major shift in its development practice. It has done so by moving away from 'implementing projects' towards 'capacity development through providing advisory services'. A rationale behind this fundamental policy change was the need to de-emphasize the traditional focus on donor-driven financial accountability and to find innovative ways to engage better with, and contribute to, genuine capacity development of SNV's local clients and partners. To help implement this shift, SNV adopted a capacity-development approach with the following key characteristics.

- A focus on delivering advisory services to 'meso level' organizations (at provincial and district levels) that cannot afford to pay commercial rates for such advice.
- The recognition that clients are 'in the driver's seat', with SNV's role being to assist them in achieving their development ambitions. Services are thus 'demand-oriented and client centred' as opposed to 'donor and adviser-driven'.
- At the same time SNV, as a development organization, wants to contribute to development impact. Therefore SNV works in specific sectors or themes, where impact targets are formulated through dialogue with its clients and other stakeholders.

• SNV's ultimate goal is to ensure that its clients and partners achieve impact. Hence, SNV contributes to the improved performance of its clients to achieve such impacts.
• To a considerable extent, SNV can carry out its advisory work on the basis of a core subsidy and some programme funding. Consequently, the organization is able to work flexibly with existing clients, while simultaneously seeking to strategically engage with new clients as demand and need arise.

In many development contexts, advisory work is carried out as part of major projects and programmes that have been formulated between a government and a donor, or by a local NGO or network with international support. The associated agreements and documents usually establish the parameters of the work required. In other cases, advisory work can develop much more flexibly. For example, in responding to local demand, financial support may only become available later or may actually not be needed to a significant degree. Whatever the specific situation on the ground, SNV felt a strong need to create a working model or approach that would help practitioners continuously monitor the (changing) relation between their short-term activities and longer-term strategic objectives. A particular challenge was to develop a result-management logic that would help practitioners move away from the principles that governed the project-implementation era. In other words, not to focus so much on tallying physical implementation targets (such as schools, bridges or water points) but on finding ways to identify and measure the capacities developed and to link these to improvements in the lives of poor people.

Towards a new conceptual framework to manage results over time

Managing for other types of results, within and over different time frames, involved a lot more than target setting, or routine monitoring and evaluation. It had to encompass SNV's complete 'primary process', which starts with understanding a country's complex societal structures and dynamics, identifying existing home-grown development strategies and aligning SNV's strategy with them. The process also involves selecting clients with the leverage to change things, setting capacity-development targets with them, supporting their own efforts, assessing the results, as well as being able to relate a client's change in capacity to impact in terms of poverty indicators and improved governance.

Application of this new orientation to day-to-day advisory work, therefore, called for a matching conceptual framework to link the daily practice of providing capacity-development support to a specific client to achieving higher level and longer-term results. Such a framework was also needed in order to set long-term impact orientations, and make well-considered decisions with regard to the selection of clients and the type of support given to these clients.

Based on all these considerations, it was critical that the approach taken should encourage SNV staff to 'learn as they go' if they were to support the capacity development of clients in a complex and constantly changing environment. It was concluded that the new approach should be cyclical to ensure that lessons learned

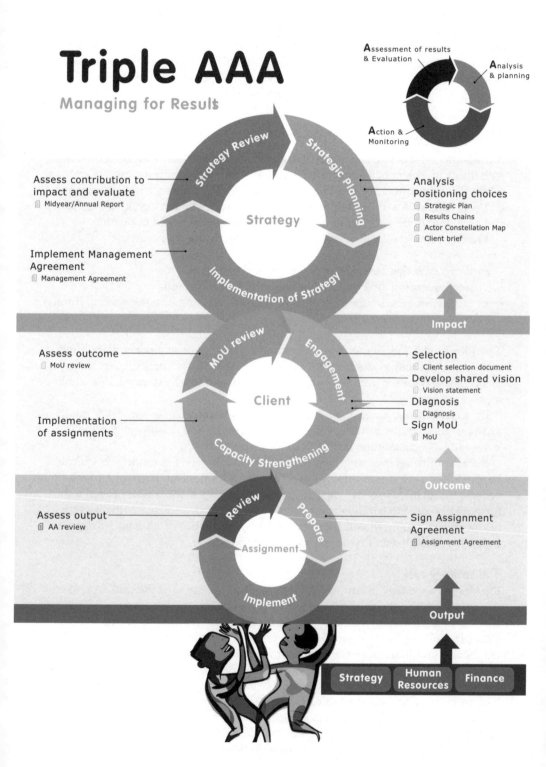

Figure 19.1 *SNV's primary process for capacity-development service provision*

would feed into the next cycle and contribute to a growing body of knowledge. And such cycles were needed at the level of country strategy, the duration of a memorandum of understanding of a client and at the level of a single assignment. The overarching idea was that every adviser should at all times be able to explain how his/her decision to work with a specific client – or even the result of a single assignment – contributes to long-term strategic goals.

The AAA model

A small internal task force was charged with facilitating a collective thinking process, with the involvement of a large number of field staff representing a wealth of experience. From this iterative process, a model for SNV's primary process emerged that was named 'AAA' or 'Triple A', signifying the continuous cycle of Analysis and planning, Action and monitoring, and Assessing results and evaluation.

The AAA model actually distinguishes three interconnected cycles:

- a *strategy cycle* that stretches over 3 years and longer;
- a *client engagement cycle* with a time frame of 1–3 years; and
- an *assignment cycle* for an individual activity or grouping of tasks ranging from a few weeks to a few months.

The idea is that individual practitioners and practitioner teams regularly apply analysis, action and assessment for each cycle. That is, for their specific assignments, but also for the overall relation with a client and for the strategy for a whole sector or country.

By treating these three time cycles as mutually interactive, the AAA model provides an adaptive working logic in which results and lessons at the various levels (and associated time frames) can influence each other.

Because of its relative simplicity and appeal to advisers, the model was quickly adopted within the organization. However, it also became clear that in order for it to become useful in day-to-day capacity-development work, the model needed to be further elaborated to specify the key steps to be followed, decision moments, types of documents required, and the roles and responsibilities of all actors involved. Below is a breakdown of basic steps and principles.

The strategy cycle

Developing a strategy in country A or sector B is done against the background of the overall SNV policies and history. For a particular country or sector it starts with strategic planning (Step 1). In Box 19.1 Rem Neefjes, Director SNV in Ethiopia, and Yohannes Agonafir, Senior Adviser, explain the steps in the strategic cycle and how these result in a firm impact orientation. The outcomes of the planning exercise provide the foundation for implementation (Step 2): the engagement with specific clients in that sector or country (see client cycle below). The strategy cycle is concluded with a strategy review (Step 3) which consists of an assessment of results with various clients and an evaluation of the outcome and impact results and perspectives. Questions raised here include: To what results have we contributed in this sector or country? Were the initial hypotheses correct?

Box 19.1 The strategy cycle

'Triple AAA helps us to get our primary process in good shape. Capacity development in a country starts with understanding the society you are working in. In Ethiopia we conducted a thorough context analysis as the foundation of our 3-year strategic programme. Subsequently we conducted an internal analysis to find out whether we have the resources to provide meaningful support in developing specific strategic capacities. For example with regards to the oilseed sector we concluded that we indeed have something valuable to add. After the planning phase we implement our strategic plan, which consists of supporting portfolios of carefully selected clients in each of the selected sectors. At the end of the strategy cycle we **assess the impact** we have achieved in each of these sectors. We also **evaluate** what went right and wrong and we try to understand why. These lessons learned we use while planning for our next cycle'.

Rem Neefjes and Yohannes Agonafir, SNV Ethiopia

Do we work with the right clients? Did the approaches adopted work? What are SNV's strengths and weaknesses? Such reviews are done in a light manner every year and more thoroughly at the end of a 3-year strategy cycle or formal evaluation moment. Lessons derived from these reviews will feed into the analysis and planning phase of the next annual and strategy cycle.

The client cycle
Within the strategy set, SNV establishes its client portfolio in a given sector or country. In order to maximize its contribution to impact, SNV has to be selective about which local actors it will support. For each client a cycle of SNV support, lasting between one to three years, has three steps again: engagement, capacity strengthening and MoU review. In Box 19.2 an SNV Ethiopia adviser explains how the client cycle works using the concrete example of the oilseed sector. He also indicates how lessons gained in client work feed the strategy cycle again.

The assignment cycle
An assignment is the smallest work cycle, covering a concrete piece of work of several weeks or months. Preparation of an assignment includes a demand/issue analysis and results in an assignment agreement on the intended output. This is usually related to a specific capability or set of capabilities to be strengthened. The implementation of the assignment is followed by an assignment review. This includes more than assessing the degree to which inputs lead to output. It is also a monitoring moment in the client cycle. The client and SNV reflect on whether the work is still moving in the right direction in view of broader outcomes and impact envisaged. Hypotheses and assumptions of the diagnosis are checked with new insights gained. This may lead to adjustments in the capacity-development approach. The quality of relationship between the parties is also examined.

Box 19.2 Client selection and accompanying

Clients usually come to us but we may also spot interesting opportunities. With limited resources, we need to select clients carefully and for that also use a checklist of criteria. When we think a real difference can be made, we make a commitment to support them in developing their capacity. Before starting together the first question we need to ask is 'Where are we going?' Therefore we ensure that together with the client we *develop a shared vision* about the outcome and impact we want to achieve, captured in a baseline. Having agreed on 'where we are going' the next question is: 'What do we need to get there?' We determine this through a *diagnosis* or capacity needs assessment. With the shared vision, targets and the diagnosis we have all the ingredients to draft a *Memorandum of Understanding* (MoU) which serves as a reference document for our collaboration. Implementation usually consists of several, sometimes many, assignments. At key moments during and at the end of a client cycle we check whether a client's performance is improving or has improved. We *review the MoU* which involves measuring outcomes. We also annually reflect on whether with this portfolio of clients and this approach we are likely to make a change in the lives of poor people. If this is not the case we reflect on whether we have overlooked some important actors or factors and review our value chain or result chain analysis. Maybe some unexpected events occurred. A MoU review and even individual assignments may thus lead to changes in our overall strategy.'

Eleni Abraham, Adviser, Economic Development, SNV Ethiopia

The three cycles described above form the Triple A working logic. It has been further elaborated in a set of standards against which adequate compliance can be judged and improvements introduced.

Using quality standards

While the above may sound fairly structured and even rigid, in fact the steps outlined above provide a flexible, negotiated way to connect a client's demands, perspectives and time horizon with that of SNV as a subsidized service provider, with its own strategy and accountability for results.

Assuring quality and maintaining focus on results over time is challenging. It requires advisers and teams to be curious about the results of their own day-to-day performance against the backdrop of a much bigger picture and time frame. Similarly to scientific work, it requires a certain amount of self discipline to document the evidence and observations from time to time, which can be challenging for some who experience this as time-consuming bureaucracy. One prerequisite to manage time and other relational challenges is to have a well thought-out set of standards firmly embedded in the business processes to ensure that at least the basic elements of the practice are adhered to by all. Triple A has been translated in SNV into a set of standards in which key decisions, progress and reviews are also documented. Evidence shows that SNV can achieve the following basics in capacity development with this model.

- Synergy between individual and team efforts over a longer period of time and within the framework of an SNV strategy at the national level. The collective effort is thus 'more than the sum of the individual efforts'.
- Quality towards clients in the sense that no services will be provided to clients: (a) without the practitioner engaging in a dialogue with the client about their vision for the future; (b) without establishing some kind of capacity baseline; (c) without explicitly being in agreement with the client about the tentative steps required to make the transition from the baseline towards the vision for the future; (d) without considering whether the resources required for this transition are proportionate in view of the expected results.
- A stimulus for strategic learning and results orientation in SNV and with clients in the sense that: (a) results at assignment, client and strategy level are made explicit regularly allowing for critical reflection on the hypotheses and assumptions that underlie the CD approach; (b) learning in different directions is stimulated: practical experiences inform broader strategies and adjusted strategies inform practical choices and approaches; and (c) short- and medium-term achievements with a client are verified to be in alignment with SNV's longer-term strategic orientations.

Conclusion

Time is an important dimension of capacity-development work. It is a constant companion as practitioners determine strategies, engage with clients and deal with inevitable variations between what should and what did happen. This chapter argues that time awareness is a vital factor when working with change processes and that, while uncertainties and lack of synchronization cannot be prevented, their effects can be proactively responded to by focusing on results in a systematic way that everyone can understand.

The Triple A model discussed has a results orientation that is flexible and open for learning on the way. It basically supports the practitioner in: (a) thinking across different time frames regularly; and (b) doing this in direct interaction with their clients. Its innovation lies in two mutually supportive features, differentiating it from a conventional log-frame approach. First is a 'nested logic', recognizing that cycles operating around assignment, client and strategy are interactive. By implication, second, the cyclical character makes it possible that adaptations of approach within one type of cycle can lead to adaptations in the other two. The cycles are not repetitions on the spot. They are structured processes that continually move forward over time in a reflective and adaptive way. Undoubtedly SNV will continue fine tuning and tinkering with it in order it to match it even more with the realities and needs of practioners and clients. From the experiments with AAA a number of general lessons and insights can be drawn.

- It is important to treat the strategy, client and assignment levels (or comparable distinctions) as mutually interactive. This is an important step forward from many conventional log-frame applications. It deliberately allows changes and experiences at each level (short-term assignment, medium-term client relation, long-term (sector) strategy) to mutually influence each other.

- When such levels or time frames are linked into an annual planning cycle, this can foster space for 'adaptive planning' and 'learning in action'.
- Such a generic and basic working model can also help to deal with 'holding' the variety of time frames and perspectives that may be at play in a development programme with several actors and funders.
- And finally such a model can help in dealing with the challenge to connect a client's time profile and accountabilities to those of the adviser or supporting agency without the latter dominating.

We can conclude that an essential challenge for individual practitioners and teams is, indeed, to consciously and continuously see their own efforts in different time frames and related ambition levels. Meeting this challenge through the learning-in-action described above can prevent different time frames from complicating and confusing capacity-development work. So that time is on our side.

Notes

1   Comments by Paul Engel on the DGroup: 'Pelican Initiative: Platform for Evidence-based Learning and Communications for Social Change', dgroups.org/groups/pelican, accessed 5 November 2009.
2   Contained in SNV's *Strategy Paper, October 2000.*

Recommended readings

The perspectives on time and the working model discussed in this chapter are connected to issues of scale discussed in Chapter 3 and the use of information about results generated by M&E cycles as a basis for a practitioner's self reflection described in Chapter 20. The learning and accountability features of AAA are related to the discussion on learning and accountability in Chapter 21. Some other relevant readings are given below.

Rondinelli, D. (1983) *Development Projects as Policy Experiments: An Adaptive Approach to Development Administration*, Methuen, London

As old as it may be, this book captures the essence of an adaptive approach to aided-development initiatives, translated by the AAA model into an organizational style and core business practice.

Capacity.org, Issue 33, April, 2008

This edition of *Capacity.org* contains a number of articles that have a bearing on the learning dimensions of this chapter. The following three are of particular interest.

Heinz Greijn, 'Learning for organizational development' (www.capacity.org/en/content/pdf/4167, accessed 20 June 2010)

This article analyses why despite the many new approaches to learning that have emerged in recent years, too many development agencies still underestimate the importance of learning and do not systematically practise learning.

Ben Ramalingam, 'Organisational learning for aid, and learning aid organisations' (www.capacity.org/en/content/pdf/4169,. accessed 20 June 2010)

Ben Ramalingam researched over a dozen aid organizations and found that they are rather poor learners. Formal learning is frequently seen as a non-essential support function – one, moreover, that is dominated by training and technology.

Although intrinsic factors in the aid sector explain why this is the case up to a point, there is no excuse for aid organizations not to try harder.

Charles G. Owusu 'Linking learning to decision making' (www.capacity.org/en/content/pdf/4174, accessed 20 June 2010)

In many aid agencies the rhetoric of learning is rarely matched in practice. Charles Owusu describes the efforts of ActionAid to make systems and structures part of the solution to becoming a learning organization, rather than part of the problem.

20

Self-Reflection

As they are intervening in complex human systems, capacity-development practitioners need to be flexible, adaptable and willing to learn from what they do. An important source of learning in real time is the processes and results of monitoring and evaluation (M&E).

Bruce Britton explains M&E activities as they are commonly pursued and explores creative ways in which practitioners can use them for personal learning and self-reflection. He also provides suggestions on how this can be done under non-conducive organizational conditions.

Monitoring and Evaluation for Personal Learning

Bruce Britton

By three methods we may learn wisdom: first, by reflection, which is noblest; second, by imitation, which is easiest; and third by experience, which is the bitterest.

(Confucius)

Introduction

Capacity development practitioners collaborate in efforts to improve the capabilities of complex human systems that operate and connect at different levels. First and foremost, capacity development is a process based on the assumption that better understanding and knowledge will bring about change. Also, the planning for capacity development interventions typically rely on variations of the Logical Framework Approach (LFA), which encourage careful thinking about expected outcomes and impacts. By its very nature LFA assumes that intended results of an initiative can be established in advance because the path that a capacity development process will take can be adequately assured, which requires a reasonably stable operating environment. The reality is usually very different.

Reflecting the perspective of other chapters in this volume, capacity development processes often evolve in ways we cannot anticipate. Their paths are rarely predictable and sometimes seem to defy the logic that was used to plan them. Consequently, by requiring progress to be assessed against pre-determined outcomes – which time and experience may demonstrate are unrealistic – organizations providing capacity development services can sabotage the very process they wish to support. In doing so they can undermine the self-confidence of the practitioners involved. The negative effects of this are experienced in different ways: at an organizational level in terms of frustration over unachieved goals and at an individual level as poor performance and de-skilling. However, there is another way of viewing deviation from plans, namely by using divergence as experience-based opportunities for reflection.

In other words, the unpredictability and fluid nature of capacity development can be viewed not as a failure of planning but as an indication of the need for adaptability and an opportunity for learning. As capacity development practitioners become more experienced, they develop a deepening understanding of the complexity of the issues with which they are working. Using the insights generated through reflection, advisers can become more adaptable and flexible in dealing with the unexpected challenges and problems that arise in day-to-day work with clients.

So, how can practitioners accelerate the pace at which they deepen their mastery of capacity development? One powerful way is through experience-based learning processes such as shadowing, coaching and action-learning. Unfortunately, not all practitioners have access to these structured experiential learning opportunities. However, practitioners can also develop their expertise using personal techniques for reflecting on and learning directly from their work. Using the formal feedback mechanisms of monitoring and evaluation is an important and often overlooked way to do so. This being said, using monitoring and evaluation in this way can be difficult because most of these systems are designed with other purposes in mind.

The conventional view of monitoring and particularly evaluation sees them as processes that are used primarily for assessing performance and ensuring accountability, not for reflection and learning. Reasons for this are explored in detail in Chapter 21. Consequently, if monitoring and evaluation rigidly focus on performance management it may be necessary for the practitioner to 'subvert' these systems – in the sense of challenging and expanding their intended purpose – in order to maximize the learning opportunities they offer.

This chapter examines how capacity development practitioners can use formal and informal monitoring and evaluation systems not only to assess progress towards intended outcomes but also, and just as importantly, for the purposes of self-improvement. In addition, by taking a creative approach to informal monitoring, practitioners can also create valuable opportunities for strengthening mutual support with colleagues.

The rest of the chapter is organized as follows. We begin with a brief introduction to the monitoring and evaluation of capacity development initiatives, also discussed in more detail in Chapter 18. The chapter then focuses on what can be characterized as the conventional purposes and uses of both monitoring and evaluation, which are contrasted with a more creative, learning-oriented approach. Thereafter, suggestions are made for how capacity development professionals can strengthen their own practice and influence the development of a more reflective approach to capacity development in their work. The chapter ends with suggestions about resources that can help capacity development practitioners make use of monitoring and evaluation for personal development through self-reflection.

Monitoring and evaluating capacity development

Monitoring and evaluation are usually spoken of together as in the abbreviation 'M&E'. The abbreviation gives the impression that the 'M' and the 'E' are inseparable or even interchangeable processes. The two terms are joined together because of their similarities. However, it is equally important to recognize the differences between monitoring and evaluation in order to identify how each can contribute to personal reflection and learning. A short examination of the usual understanding of monitoring and of evaluation can shine some light on the often untapped potential of each as a trigger for one's professional development as a practitioner.

What is monitoring?

Monitoring is commonly described as the systematic and continuous assessment of the progress of a piece of work over time. Monitoring activities check that things are 'going according to plan', enabling adjustments to be made in a methodical way. This conventional type of definition underplays the reflective, learning aspect of monitoring. A more comprehensive description of monitoring can be found in the Barefoot Collective's *Guide to Working with Organizations and Social Change*. This valuable publication explains that 'Monitoring should be seen as a reflective practice that assists learning to take place, enabling improvement in practice, including possible rethinking and re-planning. It can also be an important affirming practice of what is going well' (Barefoot Collective, 2009, p154).

Monitoring is an integral part of management systems. It is typically carried out by those who are involved in the work on a day-to-day basis. It usually involves gathering data in a number of ways including examining work records (often, but not exclusively, in the form of quantitative data), holding meetings, interviewing those involved, using participatory techniques, using secondary information (from documents) and observing activities. The most common tangible outputs of this data-gathering are client records and regular progress reports. Examples are: monthly contract reports; quarterly reports to clients and senior managers and annual reports to clients, board members and, if relevant, donor organizations that support the capacity development initiative.

It is still common to hear the complaint from practitioners that monitoring creates 'one-way traffic'. Information flows from the place where the work is being undertaken upwards or inwards through an organization. But analysis rarely flows back to those who gathered the data in the first place. The underlying and usually unspoken principle that guides many monitoring systems is 'no news is good news'. In other words, the only reason that those who generate the monitoring data may receive feedback from those who examine and analyse the data is when there is a discrepancy between what was supposed to happen in the 'plan' and what actually happened in practice. When feedback is given in these circumstances, it can take the form of criticism for a 'failure' to deliver agreed targets or to deliver them on time. Even if the intention is not to criticize, that is often how the feedback is perceived by the practitioners on the receiving end. It is hardly surprising that such monitoring systems create an (albeit unintended) disincentive to report truthfully and hence limit the formal opportunities for practitioners to honestly reflect on and learn from their experience. In contrast, 'good monitoring shows a genuine interest in what is being done and a constant and curious questioning of activities and their emerging effects... If monitoring is separated from learning it risks becoming a policing function' (Barefoot Collective, 2009, p154).

What is evaluation?

Evaluation is the most formal way in which work is examined and feedback generated. Evaluation involves the periodic assessment of the relevance, performance, efficiency or impact of activities with respect to their purpose and objectives. Evaluation is often carried out at some significant stage in a change-oriented process, for example towards the end of a planning period, as the work moves to a new phase, or in response to a particular critical issue (Bakewell et al, 2003). Usually, but not always, evaluation involves one or more people from outside the organization working as independent evaluators or, together with staff from the organization, forming part of an evaluation team.

When evaluations are conducted there is often a lot at stake. Future funding streams; staffing levels; accountability for the use of resources; career development decisions and professional reputations may all apparently depend on a 'positive' evaluation. On the face of it, this does not appear to be fertile ground for reflection and learning. Anxiety and stress levels can be high. There may be an understandable fear about exposing unintended outcomes and unachieved goals to wider scrutiny. Much depends, of course, on how the evaluation is conducted. A generally agreed basic principle is that the monitoring and evaluation of a capacity development initiative should itself contribute to developing capacity. Although it can be difficult to achieve this in practice, some external evaluators of capacity development initiatives do take this responsibility seriously. Horton et al (2003, pvi) describe this in the following way: 'When we take people through a process of evaluation – at least in any kind of stakeholder involvement or participatory process – they are, in fact, learning things about evaluation culture and often learning how to think in these ways. The learning that occurs as a result of these processes is twofold:

- the evaluation can yield specific insights and findings that can change practices and be used to build capacity, and
- those who participate in the inquiry learn to think more systematically about their capacity for further learning and improvement.'

What typically gets monitored and evaluated in a capacity development initiative?

What gets monitored and evaluated depends, of course, on the objectives and scope of the capacity development initiative. There is an understandable tendency for organizations to monitor what is measurable in a capacity development process, for example, the number of training workshops run, or the introduction of a new finance software system. However, the tendency to monitor the more easily measurable activities and outputs of capacity development interventions often means that the purpose and 'invisible' dimensions of this effort become lost. This may also mean that the monitoring system is blind to the unintended effects – both positive and negative – of the capacity development initiative because there are no indicators to measure them. Most significantly, for the development of the practitioner, there may be no focus at all on the unfolding process of the capacity development initiative. But this need not be the case.

Among the most well-developed tools for monitoring and evaluating capacity development are those that examine and assess changes in *organizational* capacity. Organizational assessment (OA) tools go beyond the output measures of counting, for example, the number of participants attending training courses. Such information tells us little about consequent changes in the workshop participants' competencies and even less about how they subsequently apply their new knowledge and skills in pursuit of their organization's goals. Whilst OA tools may have their faults (and some can be time-consuming, difficult to validate or based on culturally inappropriate concepts), they do focus on outcomes – acknowledged changes in organizational capacities – so they provide a gauge of the *effects* of an organizational capacity development intervention, not simply a record of activities undertaken.

However, even well-designed OA tools do not usually elicit explanations of why and how some organizational capacities have developed more than others and what the capacity development practitioner did to facilitate or hinder those changes. Answers to these questions are of considerable importance to the thoughtful practitioner who wishes to strengthen their practice. Because the answers are often of less immediate concern to a practitioner's own organization, the questions may not be asked as part of the formal monitoring process and hence important opportunities for feedback, learning and professional development are lost.

So, as we have seen, focusing only on the conventional uses of monitoring and evaluation can overlook their potential for helping capacity development practitioners to reflect on and learn from their experience. Practitioners, as outsiders or as staff, may view monitoring or evaluation as external, demand-driven processes designed by someone else to generate data for their managers to make judgements about their performance and achievement of targets. Monitoring is thus seen as a chore and evaluation treated as an unpleasant but necessary task that is demanded by others but remains disconnected from the day-to-day reality of developing the quality of work practice. However, this situation is not inevitable if creativity is applied.

Creative approaches to monitoring and evaluation in capacity development

There are proven ways to turn the processes and information generated by monitoring and evaluation into potentials for self-development. Three examples are explored below.

Living the principles of reflective practice

When a capacity development practitioner embraces the idea of learning from evaluation and particularly from monitoring they demonstrate a commitment to what is often referred to as 'reflective practice'. Reflective practitioners apply a powerful combination of self-awareness, critical thinking and analytic ability allied to a commitment to continuously apply on-the-job learning to their work.

Reflective practice involves the professional stepping back from an experience to make sense of it, understand what it means, learn from it and apply that learning to future situations. Applying critical thinking to experience develops and deepens insights. But what makes reflective practice different from other approaches to learning is the focus on action. Reflective practice is more than examining the past to identify 'what went well' or 'what could have been done better'. Reflective practice occurs when the practitioner initiates a cycle of action learning. The key to being a reflective practitioner is combining genuine inquisitiveness with a commitment to do things differently based on careful consideration of alternatives. The process of reflective practice can be summarized as a cycle comprising six steps.

1 Experience: Select a 'critical incident' to reflect on
2 Appraisal: Describe and unpack the experience
3 Analysis: Examine the experience
4 Discovery: Interpret and draw realizations from the experience
5 Integration: Explore the alternatives and re-think future action
6 Informed Action: Take action with new intent

By following these steps, the process of reflective practice brings together the skills of self-understanding, critical thinking, analysis and experience-based learning. These are skills that practitioners can readily learn and develop, given the right conditions.

Using monitoring as a springboard for learning – a practical example

Framework is a collective of consultants working with not-for-profit organizations worldwide. Currently the membership is six consultant practitioners. Each is self-employed and of equal status: there is no management hierarchy. A key organizing principle in Framework is mutual accountability for high quality.

Framework practitioners have developed tools for enabling reflective practice and experiential learning, the most important of which is peer supervision. This process involves a circular arrangement with each consultant supervising a colleague and, in turn, being supervised by another. The following example demonstrates peer supervision focusing on the on-going monitoring of contracts.

Box 20.1 The value of peer support

'I was in an awkward situation. I had been contracted by a client organization to help them develop a strategy for organizational learning. A week interviewing staff and other stakeholders led to an understanding of what was working well and some ideas for how learning could be organized more strategically. But at the same time I was increasingly aware that interviews had been used by staff as an opportunity to ventilate their feelings about the organization's leadership. It was uncomfortable to hear the criticism and I was finding it difficult to work out how to handle the situation. Although a small steering group had been set up within the organization to manage the strategy development process I was not sure how best to raise the concerns with them. I decided to talk through my concerns at my next peer supervision session. Before the session I reflected on the progress I had expected to achieve at this stage in the contract against the agreed timeline for the work. I also developed a list of what was going well with my work and where my anxieties lay. During the peer supervision session, I reviewed the progress I had made on the contract and reassured myself that I had enough good quality data to make a comprehensive assessment of the current situation. My colleague then helped talk through my feelings about the concerns that had been expressed about the organization's leadership. Through the sensitive use of questioning my colleague helped me realize that this 'critical incident', that is a willingness of staff to express their criticisms rather than keep them private, was a positive sign. This created an opportunity for change that was in the best interest of the organization. I began to recognize that my worries related mainly to a need to feel in control of the situation: I was worried that by passing on the critical feedback I might open up a 'can of worms' leading to internal conflict with negative consequences for the organization. Worse still, if relationships in the organization deteriorated it would be my fault! My colleague also helped me to see that my own discomfort in facing this potential conflict was a reflection of the discomfort that was held by many in the organization. I could see that I had a responsibility to share all the data that was relevant to the work. Leadership style was an important part of that data because it influenced the organization's learning culture. The key then was to design a process that would enable the organization to express and hear the different viewpoints, draw conclusions without those involved becoming defensive and then work out ways of improving the situation. With a peer review, I developed a strategy for discussing my concerns with the steering group and with the leadership. I then developed some new proposals for the design of a feedback and planning workshop. Reflecting on the progress of this contract with a valued colleague helped me to develop a much clearer understanding of the boundaries of my responsibilities and gave me the confidence to communicate this to my client. Those insights continue to shape my work'.

Reflective practice flourishes in a supportive environment and fails to thrive when circumstances are inhospitable. Organizations employing capacity development practitioners as staff or as external advisers have a crucial role to play in encouraging and supporting reflective practice by 'nurturing a culture of critical self-reflection and self-evaluation' (Dlamini, 2006, p13). A useful way for managers to think about this is to consider the motive, means and opportunity for reflective practice. 'Motive, means and opportunity' is a tool that detectives use to investigate crimes. It provides a useful metaphor for understanding what needs to be put in place to encourage learning and reflection (Britton, 2005). In the context of reflective practice, the 'motive' refers to understanding the nature of reflective practice and why it is important. The 'means' involves having the models, methods and sources of support necessary for reflective practice. And the 'opportunity' refers to creating the spaces for reflective practice. In criminal investigations, all three must be established to ensure a 'watertight case'. So if an organization providing capacity development wishes to encourage reflective practice, it needs to ensure that practitioners have the motive, the means *and* the opportunity.

Unfortunately, not all organizations are willing or able to create these conditions and capacity development practitioners may find themselves relatively unsupported in their attempts to reflect on and learn from their experience. In this case, the practitioner may need to demonstrate another important characteristic of reflective practice, namely self-reliance!

Developing a personal action learning system

If the monitoring system used by their organization does not encourage reflection and learning, practitioners may need to develop their skills of reflective practice by putting in place their own personal action learning system. This may sound time-consuming but many of the most useful tools and techniques for reflective practice are deceptively simple. Some practical ideas can be found in the following section.

Tools and techniques for reflective practice

Use critical incident technique. Critical incidents are short descriptions of experiences that have particular meaning to the practitioner. In this context, the word 'critical' means 'of crucial importance'. These experiences can be used as the basis of critical incident technique – a tool that can be used systematically to examine, reflect and learn from positive and negative incidents. See the 'Recommended readings' section for details of a manual by Hettlage and Steinlin (2006) that covers the practicalities of learning from critical incidents.

Ask interesting questions. When, as practitioners, we ask ourselves interesting or searching questions the process of answering often encourages a deep reflective approach to our practice. As Dlamini puts it, 'A questioning orientation should... lie at the heart of monitoring and evaluation and be integral to the orientation, culture and practice of the organizational whole and all those within it' (Dlamini, 2006, p5). Sometimes it is the simplest questions that generate the deepest insights. Asking: 'Why did I decide to do things that way?' can bring to the surface deeply held beliefs that may act as an obstacle to facilitating genuinely developmental processes. If, for example, the practitioner becomes aware of their need to be seen as an 'expert who can be relied on to come up with an answer to any challenge', they will find it difficult to work with clients who prefer to work more collaboratively or to deal with new challenges outside their normal realm of experience. This kind of insight based on a willingness to think deeply about our questions can be genuinely liberating, leading to greater humility and more authenticity in our work with clients and partners.

Draw a rich picture. Complex organizational issues always involve multiple inter-acting relationships. Pictures are a better medium than text for exploring complex relationships because they enable a more dynamic and holistic representation of the situation – in short they can provide a rich amount of information in an easily digestible form. The term 'rich picture' is borrowed from 'soft systems methodology' and simply means a visual (usually cartoon-type) drawing of an organizational problem, showing the main actors (including the practitioner) and the relationships between them. Figure 20.1 shows a number of dimensions of a breakdown in senior management: disconnection, facing in different direction, jumping ship. Can you see other issues?

Drawing a picture may feel uncomfortable at first but by helping us to make use of the right-hand side of the brain which is responsible for creativity, intuition and synthesis, drawing can facilitate deep intuitive understanding of complex issues.

Keep a journal. Keeping a personal journal or diary is a simple but powerful way for practitioners to develop and learn from their own self-directed monitoring

Figure 20.1 *A rich picture*

process. At different stages of a capacity development process, practitioners can write in their journal their thoughts, feelings, questions and learning points about their work – the things that do not usually find their way into the formal monitoring or recording system. By reading through the journal from time to time, reflecting on the questions posed and looking for critical incidents or patterns that shed light on work practices, the capacity development practitioner can readily create a platform for the six steps of reflective practice referred to earlier. Some practitioners take journalling a stage further in terms of openness by using an online blog to make their journal more widely available, although it is important to bear confidentiality issues in mind when reflecting on experiences that involve clients and colleagues!

Develop a timeline. A timeline is a simple technique for showing events over time in a graphic way. It can be used to examine a critical incident by looking at the circumstances, decisions and actions that led up to the incident and the consequences (both intended and unintended) that followed. Timelines lend themselves well to exploring the often enlightening question 'Why then?' In the illustration in Figure 20.2, what might the sequence of events have to do with a funding crisis? Timelines are also very useful ways of examining inter-relationships between apparently disconnected events, activities or decisions because they allow the practitioner to step back and see the context and patterns of decision-making more clearly.

Write a mini case study. The process of writing a short, one- or two-page mini 'case study' on a piece of work for discussion with colleagues can be extremely enlightening even before the discussion takes place. Using some specific headings and questions can make it easier and less time-consuming to write the case study and also encourages a more self-critical approach.

Hold an 'after action review'. An after action review (AAR) is a meeting of colleagues to reflect on an event or task they have just accomplished. The purpose of an AAR is to learn from the team's experience in order to take the lessons learned into the next phase of the work or to accomplish the team's task more effectively the next time it is done (Serrat, 2008).

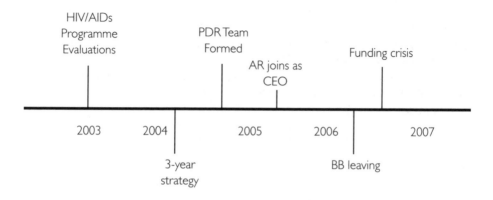

Figure 20.2 *Timeline example*

Develop monitoring and evaluation systems towards reflective learning

Practitioners often experience one or more of the following obstacles in learning from monitoring and evaluation systems: limited experience in analysing monitoring data; ineffective processes for discussing and identifying action points arising from monitoring data and evaluation recommendations; and structural barriers to making changes in capacity development initiatives that are under way because of organizational or contractual constraints.

Applying a utilization focus to monitoring as well as evaluation can be one way to overcome these obstacles. Carlsson and Wohlgemuth (undated) suggest some basic principles for improving the learning potential of evaluations and these principles can be applied equally well to systems for monitoring: the intended users must be identified at the beginning of an evaluation process; the evaluation should be planned and designed with utilization in mind; stakeholders should be involved in the whole evaluation process not just at the data-collection stage; and finally, recommendations should make clear who should act on them and results should be widely distributed.

When practitioners are expected to log their time use under different categories, there are some very practical improvements that can be made to time-recording and time-management systems. For example, reflection time is often overlooked as a category. As a result, practitioners understandably give priority to activities that are seen as more 'legitimate' and may believe that they have to use their personal 'non-work' time for reflection. Time-recording systems should include a category for agreed time spent on focused reflection.

A further strategy is to create opportunities for joint reflection in regular one-to-one meetings between practitioners and their colleagues or supervisors. Time to discuss a specific piece of work can be prioritized in managerial supervision and team meetings. Supervisors can encourage practitioners to discuss issues that arise from their individual reflection. Preparing critical incident studies or examining unanticipated outcomes gives focus and structure to these discussions. A simple form comprising a few key questions makes it easier for busy capacity development practitioners to prepare their critical incident studies. It is surprising just how many insights can emerge from as little as half an hour spent preparing a critical incident study.

Finally, peer review can be a powerful method for creating a more open and reflective working environment. When practitioners engage in discussions with their peers to interpret the data from monitoring, each learns in the process. Peers can also be involved in evaluating each other's capacity development initiatives.

Conclusions

What the individual capacity development practitioner can do to make more creative and personally developmental use of monitoring and evaluation to a large extent depends on how much influence they have on the design and implementation of the systems they use in their daily work practice.

As an individual, the practitioner can develop their personal action-learning system: expanding their 'toolbox' of techniques for reflective practice using, as a springboard, the techniques described in the section on tools and techniques. They may also consider 'subverting' their existing monitoring and evaluation systems to create new opportunities for reflection and learning. As a colleague or team member, the capacity development practitioner can work with other practitioners to develop peer review and feedback mechanisms which will help to create a working environment that provides the 'motive, means and opportunity' for reflective practice. Finally, as a member of a capacity development organization, the practitioner may have enough influence to initiate a re-examination of the systems used for monitoring and evaluation and, if necessary, help to redesign the systems to place greater emphasis on learning from experience.

References

Bakewell, O., Adams, J. and Pratt, B. (2003) *Sharpening the Development Process: A Practical Guide to Monitoring and Evaluation*, Praxis Guide No 1, INTRAC, Oxford

Barefoot Collective (2009), www.barefootguide.org/Book/Barefoot_Guide_to_ Organizations_Whole_Book.pdf>, p154, accessed May 2009

Britton, B. (2005) *Organizational Learning in NGOs: Creating the Motive, Means and Opportunity*, Praxis Paper No 3, INTRAC, Oxford, www.intrac.org/docs. php/241/PraxisPaper3%2008%20update.pdf, accessed April 2009

Carlsson, J. and Wohlgemuth, L. (eds.) (undated) 'Learning in development cooperation', SIDA, www.egdi.gov.se/pdf/carlsson-wohlgemuth.pdf, accessed April 2009

Dlamini, N. (2006) *Transparency of Process: Monitoring and Evaluation in the Learning Organization*, CDRA, Woodstock, South Africa, www.cdra.org. za/AnnualRep/2006%20-%20M%20and%20E%20in%20Learning%20 Organizations.doc, accessed April 2009

Horton, D., Alexaki, A., Bennett-Lartey, S., Brice, K.N., Campilan, D., Carden, F., de Souza Silva, J., Duong, L.T., Khadar, I., Maestrey Boza, A., Kayes Muniruzzaman, I., Perez, J., Somarriba Chang, M., Vernooy, R. and Watts, J. (2003) *Evaluating Capacity Development: Experiences from Research and Development Organizations around the World*, International Service for National Agricultural Research (ISNAR), The Netherlands; International Development Research Centre (IDRC), Canada; ACP-EU Technical Centre for Agricultural and Rural Cooperation (CTA), The Netherlands

Serrat, O. (2008) *Conducting After-Action Reviews and Retrospects*, Asian Development Bank, Manila, www.adb.org/Documents/Information/Knowledge-Solutions/Conducting-After-Action-Reviews.pdf, accessed April 2009

Recommended readings

The topics in this chapter have interesting connections to others in this volume. Readers may wish to look at Chapter 4 which describes advisers' roles as well as Chapter 5 which addresses combining technical and change expertise that would both be a source of reflection on M&E information. Chapters 18 and 21 cover the monitoring and evaluation of capacity development and its relation to learning and on accountability. The following is a short selection of useful resources as a starting point for further reading on this topic.

The Barefoot Guide to Working with Organisations and Social Change (2009), www.barefootguide.org

The Barefoot Collective is an international group of development practitioners who have written a practical and engaging do-it-yourself guide for leaders and facilitators wanting to help organizations to function and to develop in more healthy, human and effective ways as they strive to make their contributions to a more humane society. Their inspiring *Barefoot Guide*, together with a range of practical resources related to organizational development, change, monitoring and evaluation and learning are available from www.barefootguide.org, accessed November 2009.

Hettlage, R. and Steinlin, M. (2006) 'The Critical Incident Technique in Knowledge Management-Related Contexts: A tool for exploration/planning, evaluation and empowerment/animation', Zürich: IngeniousPeoplesKnowledge, www.i-p-k.ch/files/CriticalIncidentTechnique_in_KM.pdf, accessed April 2009

Although the illustrative examples focus on knowledge management, this is an excellent introduction to the use of critical incident technique for the purposes of planning, evaluation and empowerment.

International Fund for Agricultural Development (2002) A Guide for Project M&E, IFAD, www.ifad.org/evaluation/guide/m_e_guide.zip, accessed May 2009

More than most other guides to monitoring and evaluation, this comprehensive and well-written manual emphasizes the importance of critical reflection and learning. The focus is on projects but the lessons are equally applicable to capacity development. Section 8 is a particularly valuable source of practical ideas for reflective practice.

Serrat, O. (2009) *Knowledge Solutions: Tools, methods, approaches to drive development and enhance its effects*, www.adb.org/Documents/Information/Knowledge-Solutions/Knowledge-Solutions-1-38.pdf, accessed June 2009

The Asian Development Bank's knowledge management specialist has put together a wide-ranging compendium describing 38 tools almost all of which are directly relevant to developing reflective practice.

Watson, D. (2006) 'Monitoring and evaluation of capacity and capacity development', Discussion Paper No 58b, European Centre for Development Policy Management

This paper provides an excellent overview of how to overcome the particular challenges of monitoring and evaluating capacity development. The emphasis on systems thinking and learning together with a comprehensive bibliography make it an invaluable source of ideas.

21

Accountability and Learning

When accountability is understood as reporting on pre-defined deliverables, it is often considered to be irreconcilable with learning. This conventional wisdom inhibits an appreciation of their connection.

In this chapter, Irene Guijt exposes the flaws and traps in reasoning that keep accountability and learning apart. She provides practitioners with principles and basic good ideas that open up prospects for accountability and learning to complement each other.

Exploding the Myth of Incompatibility between Accountability and Learning

Irene Guijt

You cannot be accountable if you do not learn. And you need to know how well you live up to performance expectations in order to learn. The tug-of-war between learning and accountability is nonsensical. They need each other. Understanding effectiveness requires both.

However, that is the theory. The daily reality is that tensions between the two are alive and kicking. This results in major headaches for many organizations and individuals, straining relationships up and down the 'aid chain'. Official policies that profess the importance of learning are often contradicted by bureaucratic protocols and accounting systems which demand proof of results against pre-set targets. In the process, data are distorted (or obtained with much pain) and learning is aborted (or is too haphazard to make a difference).

Monitoring and evaluation (M&E) is a common site of a tug-of-war between the need for 'accountability' and the desire to ensure 'learning'. Often neither term is defined very clearly. Yet, people *do* seem convinced the two are methodologically and practically irreconcilable. This chapter first sets out reasons behind the perceptions and stubborn dilemmas that many working in aided-development processes face in satisfying demands to be both accountable and to learn. The issues involved are not unique to aid. They also hamper performance and innovation in business and government (Perrin, 2002). However, this chapter focuses on experiences in development initiatives that receive external funding.

The next section reviews underlying reasons for assuming incompatibility between accountability and learning. This setting the scene is followed by a section identifying two traps that appear to perpetuate the tensions, and then two ideas that offer scope for reconciliation. Section three moves us on by discussing what kinds of capacities may be needed for both functions. The chapter ends with principles, practices and simple good ideas that open up prospects for accountability and learning to complement each other.

Understanding the tug-of-war

So where does the purported tension lie? Development initiatives that receive external funding – be it from government, business or aid agencies – must sooner or later present their intentions following a certain format. This format requires statements about predefined goals and a specification of the activities and interim results that will lead to their achievement. These formats are known by many names: log-frame approach, goal-oriented project planning (ZOPP in German), results-based management (RBM), the list goes on. Informally, donors see the need for a more open-ended approach – without compromising the spirit of

Figure 21.1 *Reconciling incompatibility*

accountability – yet staff charged with monitoring progress refer rigidly to original plans (cf Guijt, 2008).[1]

Documents produced by planning processes are, of course, only theories about what people think might happen. But they often become reality – the 'map' becomes the 'world'. And in so doing, it often turns into a rigidly followed contract that requires proof of deliverables as the heart of development effectiveness. This perspective is motivated by a need for 'accountability' and driven by a logic that views development as 'projectable change' (Reeler, 2007). In this way planning processes lock down plans into watertight projections of change which dictate the spirit of development as a controllable process in mutually reinforcing cycles.

And yet, every day, the world surprises us with its unexpected twists of events, which arise out of multiple variables and strands of efforts. Conscious labours to make a difference are part of a maelstrom of societal change that is dynamic, unpredictable and non-linear. Twenty years of efforts may eventually culminate in one giant policy victory – or not. Hence, the need to keep an eye on the context and 'learn one's way towards a solution'. Viewing development as an adaptive management process is often agreed as important, at least informally, by those involved. And in some organizations and donor–grantee relationships, plans are allowed to evolve, indicators are allowed to (dis)appear, strategies allowed to shift.

Notwithstanding such examples, accountability is a recurrent winner. There is a fundamental disconnect between the rhetoric about the need for learning in development and the reality of procedures that funding agencies require. How can it be that such patent contradiction exists in the rhetoric and practice of aid policy and allocation? My own experiences suggest that the following factors may play a role.

Practical limitations

The most heard refrain from organizations seeking to be learning-oriented is 'we don't have time'. Reflection requires time to gather evidence, meet, analyse, agree and embed in new practices and policies. A culture of doing and delivering is common in development, and so reflection and learning have to be highly functional (Guijt, 2008a). This is compounded by overly ambitious goal-setting by development organizations themselves.

Capacity constraints

Clearly, different skills are needed to do statistical analysis than to facilitate transformational conversations in organizations – but often staff are not hired from a clear understanding of the capacities needed for accountability *and* learning. This issue is dealt with in more detail below.

Economic and political trends

The development sector is increasingly competitive in a world in economic crisis; there are more organizations and less money to go around. Profiling organizational uniqueness is increasingly important. Showing success using 'hard data' – of millions fed or schooled or housed or organized better – has an impact. Telling a more nuanced story about social change, involving contextual difficulties, messy partnerships and intangible but essential outcomes gets one nowhere.

Context constraints (and incentives)

Some contexts (organizational or societal) are too closed to allow even minimum debate. Rigid administrative and legal regulations can paralyse potential learning processes or flexibility with accountability requirements. Incentives focus on meeting pre-set performance agreements and rarely applaud fundamental question-asking that may argue for strategic changes. Rigid accountability systems hinder learning. Staff may be punished for not achieving original agreed objectives even though they have learned what *is* feasible and effective. The simple solution would be to allow plans that do not live up to initial expectations to be renegotiated. But many (many!) people have suffered from frankly stupid accountability systems. These systems reward those with timid goals and punish those with ambitious goals. They reward those who make precise specifications of what will happen, and therefore reward those whose guesses will inevitably be shown to be wrong as 'life happens'. In so doing, they reward those who do not learn and adapt what they are doing – and punish those who do.[2]

Organizational culture

Resources and responsibilities need to be allocated to accountability *and* learning. They *both* need to be embedded in specifications for project design or they won't happen. The nature of the senior managers is critical for the entire culture: the more curious, risk taking, feedback-asking, the more likely this will spawn similar behaviour elsewhere. In other cases, accountability may dominate.

Philosophical simplicity

According to Reeler, the frameworks that dictate accountability in funding relationships are part of that problem. 'Created to help control the flow of resources, these frameworks have, by default, come to help control almost every aspect of development practice across the globe. Social processes are subordinated to the logistics of resource control, infusing a default paradigm of practice closely aligned with conventional business thinking'. This one-size-fits-all approach means that many managers act based on the assumption that there is more predictability and order in the world than actually exists (Snowden and Boone, 2007). They look at accountability and learning from an oversimplified understanding of reality. I will return to this critical issue below.

There are undoubtedly other drivers. But even this short list suggests that the dualistic behaviour of aid is a systemic property – a phenomenon that arises from the wider aid system and not from any individual component. In particular, these drivers all point to power dynamics as a key to break the status quo that locks the system into non-learning forms of accountability. This helps understand the tenacity of the problem, and implies that resolving the tension requires a new ideas set, not just changes in organizational systems and practices. It needs ideas that include reconciling the anomalies between funders that stipulate funding conditionalities that encourage (dependent) grantees to report on results that may not have happened or do not result from their efforts. And so the system kids itself at deep levels. Tensions will continue to exist as long as these power inequalities are not challenged.[3] While the issue of power is significant for much that this chapter deals with, it is not the point of concentration.

Notwithstanding the aid sector's ongoing contradiction regarding power, a word of caution is needed here. There is a danger of creating and perpetuating a stereotype that pits the 'poor learning underdog' against the evils of 'accountability-obsessed funders.' While some organizations have only recently taken on the discipline of programme logic and have yet to experience its limitations, others are questioning the merits of this perspective and practice. The United Nations Development Programme (UNDP) recently produced a scathing evaluation of its own use of results-based management, opening the way for improvement (UNDP, 2007). Similarly, the German technical cooperation agency, Deutsche Gesellschaft für Technische Zusammenarbeit (GTZ), has acknowledged that its assumption that 'quality at entry' – involving a detailed situation analysis and goal-oriented planning – automatically led to quality and success has been contradicted by project practice. And some donors do give room to manoeuvre to grantees to shift plans or have flexible, responsive funding options, such as the UK Department for International Development (DFID) multi-year outcome based Challenge grants.

Is there a way to more systematically approach the supposed tug-of-war that enables greater synergy between these two needs? A new ideas set is part of the way forward.

Ideas that trap and ideas that liberate

The aid system is trapped by two ideas that keep accountability and learning apart. First, accountability is, somehow, *not* considered learning. Second, the world and its processes of change are viewed in overly idealized terms that set up unrealistic accountability expectations. An alternative idea is proposed for each trap.

Trap 1: Defining learning and accountability to see convergence

Is learning at odds with accountability? What *are* they about in essence? We begin with the nature of learning.

Understanding learning
Learning in development has countless interpretations. Keeping it simple here, I consider learning to be the process of continual reflection about visions, strategies, actions and contexts that enable continual readjustments. Below are two useful distinctions in relation to capacity for learning: purposes and levels.

Purposes (and loops) of learning Learning is needed for several purposes: (1) practical improvements, (2) strategic adjustments and changes, and (3) rethinking the core driving values. These differences give rise to what is commonly known as single, double and triple loop learning. Single loop learning and questioning focuses on 'are we doing things well' without questioning assumptions. Double loop questioning wonders 'are we doing the right things' which forces exploration of assumptions. Triple loop questioning bumps it up to another level by asking 'How do we know what it is "right' to do?"[4]

Learning entails not just pragmatic problem-solving but also reflection on the process by which this happens and the underlying perspective on knowledge. Seen like this, learning requires capacities for critical reflection, identifying assumptions, seeking evidence about what is going well or not, analysing multiple lines of evidence, relating evidence to expectations, and analysing and negotiating possible consequences. These processes all require connecting people and their perspectives. Therefore the capacity to deal with power dynamics becomes essential.

Levels of learning Similar to multiple levels of capacity explored in Chapter 3, learning processes differ greatly in form and focus depending on the type and level at which they are pitched: individual, group, partnership, sector or societal or hierarchical.

Enabling learning at the individual level, in adults as the core implementers, is often linked to experiential learning. This framework for understanding adult learning processes is also used to structure collective learning. But collective learning takes place at different levels, each requiring additional skills. In my work in Brazil, for example, collective learning at the simplest level involved small groups around thematic interests, such as farmers involved in agro-forestry or honey production. Another collective level is organizational learning which occurs within the farmer trade unions or NGOs that support farmers. A third level is that of the partnership, which involves the different organizations and groups, each with their constituencies, staff or members.

But two other levels of learning are relevant for the aid sector, in general: sector-wide learning and societal learning. Sector-wide learning requires convening a large diversity of actors to reflect on ways forward. Such forms of learning are rare to find. Examples that I know include smaller initiatives with a sectoral focus, such as the Sustainable Food Lab (www.sustainablefoodlab.org, accessed November 2009) or large events such as the biannual International Aids Conference. Finally, societal learning occurs when different groups, communities and multi-stakeholder constituencies in society engage actively in a communicative process of understanding problematic situations, conflicts and social dilemmas and paradoxes, creating strategies for improvement, and working through the implementation.

When considering learning in terms of levels, additional capacities needed include facilitation, convening relevant people, process design, creative thinking and conflict resolution. And finally, it requires the capacity to read the context in order to give direction to the desired learning process:

- *Who* is being expected to learn?
- What *purpose* is the learning supposed to serve?
- What *level* is the learning process aimed at?

Understanding accountability

If learning is understood in the way described above, the connection to and potential for synergy with *accountability* can become clearer. But this also calls for a rethinking of how accountability is currently portrayed. The common view is this. When promises are made or finances (in the form of taxes, voluntary donations or membership fees) are raised on behalf of a group of people or a cause, it is considered justified to expect some feedback on how the money was used and if promises were kept, that is, 'answerability'. If such feedback is found lacking, then sanctions may ensue: 'enforcement'. Hence accountability is essentially relational – as in answerable to others within a relationship of power (Goetz and Jenkins, 2005). 'To define accountability principles means to define who has the power to call for an account and who is obligated to give an explanation for their actions' (Newell and Bellour, 2002, p2).

However, there are variations modifying this term. There is *managerial accountability* which requires sending information 'upward', toward a Board or funding agencies. You can talk about *representative accountability*, when referring to the obligations of representatives to constituents. There is the option of *social accountability* with civil society exacting accountability, *principal–agent accountability* (motivating agents to achieve the goals of superiors), *mutual accountability*, in which values, aspirations and social relations form the glue. Increasingly, as used by Newell and Balfour and others, '*political* accountability' is extending beyond holding government and the judiciary to account, to including institutions that affect the poor, such as the World Trade Organization and the corporate sector. In this case, accountability is downward – citizens demanding of institutions that they be accountable to them. In all these variations, much effort is focused on compliance-checking and financial accountability – hence performing an external controlling function.

Critically important – and one of the places where accountability and learning converge – is that accountability can also be taken to mean taking responsibility for oneself. Understanding what you've done, being able to respond to questions about the basis of strategic decisions, the underlying theory of change and, of course, how money was spent. Such *strategic accountability* seeks to answer the question 'Did I/others/organizations/institutions act as effectively as possible?' In this sense, accountability is intrinsically about identity – feeling committed to one's ideas and strategies (Fry, 1995). Ebrahim (2005) echoes this by saying that: 'Organizational learning is more likely if internal accountability to mission, rather than upward accountability to donors, guides NGO reporting'. Being held accountable thus means having 'respond-ability'.

When considering accountability, the capacities needed include an ability to formulate clear performance expectations (of others and of self), gather and analyse evidence to understand effectiveness, draw conclusions about consequences, and engage in a dialogue with those holding to account. Importantly, it requires reading the context in order to understand which version of accountability is operating (see Box 21.1).

An initial glance at the capacities required for accountability shows a certain degree of convergence because the core tasks are similar. I return to this feature in section three.

Box 21.1 Clarifying what is meant by accountability in your context

Who is seeking accountability?
From whom (or what) is accountability sought?
Where (in which forums and over what extent of geographic coverage) is accountability being sought?
How (through which means) are the powerful being held to account?
For what (which actions, and against which norms) is accountability being sought?

Source: Goetz and Jenkins, 2005, p4

Idea 1: Clarifying learning purposes – including accountability

'Would you tell me, please, which way I ought to go from here?' Alice speaks to the Cheshire Cat. 'That depends a good deal on where you want to get to,' said the Cat.

Lewis Carroll, *Alice in Wonderland*

Perhaps the words from *Alice in Wonderland* are a bit tired and overused. But how valid they remain! 'Learning' is one term much bandied around with little care as to its direction (see 'Trap 1' above).

During work on participatory monitoring in Brazil in the late 1990s with farmers, trade unions and NGOs, time and again the question returned of 'who will use this data'. Each time we thought we had agreed on end users of the data, practice proved otherwise. A publicly stated intention by the NGO or the trade unions that they would use the data meant nothing. The penny dropped when we started asking 'but what purpose will this information serve?'

Akin to the fundamental question of 'capacity for what', clarifying purpose means focusing on what the learning is *for*, not only what one is learning *about*. And in this process, *accountability becomes one among various learning purposes* – seeking and sharing information to ensure financial management and stability. This is why this idea focuses on clarifying 'learning' – it automatically brings you to 'accountability'.

The Brazilian experience focused on learning for those engaged in concerted action for institutional transformation. Increasingly, partnerships or alliances are emerging as the mechanism for social change endeavours. Five of these pertain to management of the development intervention: financial accountability; operational improvement; strategic adjustment; contextual understanding; and capacity strengthening. Four learning purposes are also part of the development interventions themselves: research; self-auditing; advocacy; and sensitization (see Table 21.1).

Table 21.1 *Purposes served by 'learning'*

Type of learning	Core purpose
1 Financial accountability	Maintain financial viability or security
2 Operational improvement	Adjust implementation to be more efficient, effective
3 Strategic readjustment	Examine/question strategy (e.g. by identifying and testing underlying assumptions)
4 Capacity strengthening	Improve individual performance or that of the organization
5 Contextual understanding	Keep up-to-date on the context of implementation
6 Deepening understanding (research)	Understand key uncertainties better and to formulate new questions on which to focus
7 Self-auditing	Maintain transparency and therefore trust in (collective) use of resources
8 Advocacy	Push for political change/in public policies/with decision-makers
9 Sensitization	Sensitize others to build and sustain support for concerted action

Source: Guijt, 2008

Not all purposes will be equally important to each organization or partnership at any one time, and some might not be needed, for example 'self-auditing' or 'policy influencing'. My point here is that 'learning' requires direction. This helps make it operational in terms of time frame, required evidence-base, engagement of stakeholders, and importantly, required capacities. Each purpose, including financial and strategic accountability, can thus bring forth a custom-built learning process with purpose-specific capacities.

Trap 2: Predicting and controlling an idealized world

> Nasrudin found a weary falcon sitting one day on his window-sill. He had never seen a bird like this before. 'You poor thing', he said, 'how were you allowed to get into this state?' He clipped the falcon's talons and cut its beak straight, and trimmed its feathers. 'Now you look more like a bird', said Nasrudin.
>
> Source: Shah, 1979, p223

In many ways, this trap concerns a more pernicious and entrenched idea than the first trap. But it is also more straightforward. It concerns a relentless pursuit of change based on an idealized image of the world and of the change process itself. Yet, like Nasrudin, we want the world to be a certain way, to be able to mould it, shape it, know it and control it.

In responding to uncertainty, Kurtz and Snowden (2006) usefully make a distinction between *naturalized* and *idealized* thinking. Those with *idealistic* glasses on seek to close the gap between an ideal future state and their perception of the present. Those with a *naturalistic* take on life strive to understand enough of the present in order to be able to stimulate its evolution. They compare the two perspectives in terms of where expertise lies and the knowing–acting cycle as the core of an important aspect of capacity:

> Idealistic approaches tend to privilege *expert* knowledge, analysis and inter-pretation. Naturalistic approaches emphasise the inherent un-knowability of current and future complexities, and thus they de-privilege expert interpretation in favour of enabling emergent meaning at the *ground level*.

Shifting towards a more naturalized take on development means being willing and able to invest in resilience, act adaptively and accept rolling with the punches. This requires the ability to continually scan the context and have the creativity required to deal with what is perceived. Critical is figuring out what capacities make people and their efforts better able to cope with the certainty of change and the uncertainty this brings. Here context analysis is essential.

Idea 2: Adapting expectations of accountability and learning to contextual characteristics

Being clear about the nature of the context in which one is operating can help understand what is needed and what is feasible in connecting accountability and learning. Put another way, from a capacity development perspective the nature of the context can give pointers towards priorities in terms of the type of capabilities and links required.

Figure 21.2 shows one framework that helps to clarify diversity of context. The 'Cynefin framework' provides a basic understanding of how to act in situations with different degrees of complexity, that is where cause–effect linkages become more or less clear and reliable (Snowden and Boone, 2007). The power of the framework lies in forcing the question of what can realistically be expected of deci-sion-making responses, knowledge management processes, and general working procedures, given that one is dealing with situations that have inherently different characteristics.

Both the 'simple' and 'complicated' domains are ordered and are well suited to fact-based management and capacities that are repetitious or routine. In the *simple domain*, expectations are clear, cause and effect are directly related and the known can be predicted, repeated and perceived. Deviations and variance from what was anticipated signal problematic procedures and suggest concrete directions for remedial action. Accountability is relatively straightforward in being outcome-oriented. In this domain, learning and accountability can be better linked by addressing the five reasons for disconnection discussed above.

The *complicated domain* relates to situations with more variables and elements that shape causes that, over time, exert their effects. Importantly, these effects can be known with expert input (anyone with relevant knowledge and experience). Analysis is needed to make sense of the interaction of different variables. Rather than categorization, 'sensing' what is happening is the entry point into analysis

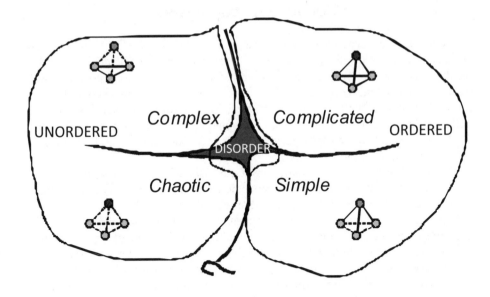

Figure 21.2 *Locating complexity: the Cynefin framework (Source: David Snowden, the Cognitive Edge)*

that enables a response or set of responses. Scenario planning and 'good practice' are at home in this domain. Accountability can remain outcome-oriented but, because more attention is paid to unpredictability and what can go awry, investing in learning becomes more critical. Expert consultation becomes a joint learning process and expected outcomes may shift as a result.

The domain that offers a 'liberating idea' is the *complex*. Here change follows an unpredictable trajectory. Cause and effect is only coherent retrospectively and cannot be repeated. It requires probing of actionable options through safe-fail experimentation. It is the domain where accountability and learning depend on each other. Accountability is demonstrated by showing how learning has led to adaptation or 'response-ability'. Capacity development is then about increasing abilities to gather the right information in order to make sense of what is going on in real time and adjust accordingly.

This leaves us with the *chaotic domain* in which no clear cause–effect linkage can be discerned and one is dealing with unknowables. Again, management best takes place through ongoing analysis of emerging patterns but requires action, then sensing what next step is needed and responding. Learning is embedded, while accountability becomes more akin to asking 'Did we act as well as we could, given the little we knew under quickly changing circumstances?' Crisis task forces are at home within this domain.

Determining in what context one is operating – simple, complicated, complex, chaotic or disordered – allied to the purposes of learning and type of accountability enables appropriate capacity development choices. In other words; different capacities are needed to manage under distinct conditions.

Converging capacities

In section two, capacities were identified as derived from the tasks that learning and accountability implied. If learning is to be a process of reflection that takes on the practical, the strategic and the transformational (and varied purposes), then diverse capacities are needed. The wide variety of different 'accountabilities' means that talking about capacity for accountability requires a choice. For accountability, I distinguish two core types – compliance-checking and strategic. Table 21.2 summarizes how these capacities relate to 'accountability' and 'learning', a list to which more could be added.

Two observations can be made about this table. First, there appears to be remarkable 'natural' convergence of capacities. This illustrates that there is greater overlap in terms of required capacities than perhaps seems obvious.

Second, hidden within generic 'capacities' are important differences. For example, evidence gathering and analysis include a wide range of methodological options that will further dictate capacities. The capacity to undertake randomized control trials in order to 'prove impact' will require vastly different skills than undertaking a participatory impact assessment related to less tangible shifts in people's self-image. Hence it is critical to be precise about what, for example, process design capacities or reporting capacities are needed in order to ensure compliance versus those that are needed to ensure strategic accountability, or learning.

Table 21.2 *Capacities needed for accountability and learning under more complex conditions*

| Capacities | Accountability | | Learning |
	Compliance	Strategic	
Process design (research and/or reflection)	×	×	×
Understand the context	×	×	×
Frame and revisit a theory of change	×	×	×
Formulate clear performance expectations	×	×	×
Identify assumptions	×	×	×
Make astute methodological choices	×	×	×
Gather evidence	×	×	×
Analyse multiple lines of evidence	×	×	×
Report findings and implications	×	×	×
Sense-making and critical reflection	×	×	×
Facilitation of reflection and dialogue		×	×
Creative thinking (consequences, alternatives)		×	×
Convene appropriate stakeholders		×	×
Negotiate differences and deal with power dynamics	×	×	×
Address cognitive biases and hazards	×	×	×

Arm-in-arm: Principles, practices and basic good ideas to resolve the tension

Resolving the tension between accountability and learning is not about 'making it productive', a platitude that one often hears in relation to stubborn problems. It is about seeing them as part and parcel of the same need – a need for 'respond-ability' – akin to the notion of 'responsiveness' described in Chapter 5. These principles may offer some guidance for proceeding arm-in-arm.

1 Be clear that being accountable requires active learning activities and that engaging in learning includes processes to discover whether one has delivered as promised. Therefore, there is *no inherent contradiction* between accountability and learning: 'The acid test of a good accountability system is that it encourages responsibility and promotes better performance' (Rogers, 2004). And this requires learning.
2 Establish capacity development *pre-conditions by ensuring clarity*. Agree what one means by accountability (see Box 21.1) and what one can be held accountable for. And agree what one means by 'learning'. Such clarity will make more apparent any big gap between expected processes, evidence, analysis, timing and capacities.
3 Merge the *rhythms* of accountability with the learning rhythm of the organization or partnership. Identify when particular accountability needs must be met. Schedule learning processes to facilitate meeting of accountability requirements. For example, evidence gathering can be timed to feed into annual participatory reviews that generate conclusions and insights, which are subsequently shared with funding agencies and constituents.
4 *Creatively merge needs*, for example, upward accountability requirements with strategic accountability and organizational learning needs. VECO Indonesia – a programme of Vredeseilanden Belgium – has opted to work with outcome mapping as it encourages more internal strategic reflection and accountability. At the same time, its main funder insists on a log-frame format. VECO has constructed a format based on outcome mapping that dovetails with the log-frame format, thus enabling donor financial accountability as a by-product.
5 Understand the *nature* of one's intended change process and accommodate these methodologically and in terms of capacity. Start taking non-linearity and non-predictability more seriously *where this is appropriate*. Not everything is complex, nor is everything completely unpredictable.
6 Processes of learning and accountability are essentially about bringing people and their perspective together to make sense of information and value performance in order to be able to respond. This means *engaging with the power dynamics* that exist between people, in hierarchies and in the aid sector in general. Having the skills to apply a power lens to these processes can help to strategize and create space for learning-oriented accountability – or accountability that feeds into learning.

Notes

1   See Schulpen and Ruben (2006) for a damning critique with respect to Netherlands official aid.
2   With thanks to Patricia Rogers for these ideas.
3   With thanks to Annelies Heijman.
4   Another version of triple loop learning considers 'are we learning as well as we can?' but this could be considered a special case of single and double loop learning.

References

Ebrahim, A. (2005) 'Accountability myopia can impede NGO learning and mission', *Nonprofit and Voluntary Sector Quarterly*, vol 34, no 1, pp56–87
Fry, R. E. (1995) 'Accountability in organizational life: Problem or opportunity for non-profits?' *Non-profit Management and Leadership*, 6, pp181–195
Goetz, A. and Jenkins, R. (2004) *Reinventing Accountability: Making Democracy Work for the Poor*, Palgrave, London
Guijt, I. (2008) 'Seeking Surprise: Rethinking monitoring for collective learning in rural resource management', PhD thesis, Wageningen University, Wageningen
Guijt, I. (2008a) 'Assessing and Learning for Social Change', Discussion paper, Institute of Development Studies, Brighton
Kurtz, C. and Snowden, D. (2006) 'Bramble bushes in a thicket' www.cognitive-edge.com/ceresources/articles/52_Bramble_Bushes_in_a_Thicket.pdf
Newell, P. and Bellour, S. (2002) 'Mapping accountability: origins, contexts and implications for development', IDS Working Paper 168, Institute of Development Studies, Brighton
Perrin, B. (2002) 'Towards a new view of accountability', paper presented to the European Evaluation Society annual conference, October 2002, Seville, Spain
Reeler, D. (2007) 'A theory of social change and implications for practice, planning, monitoring and evaluation', Community Development Resource Association, Cape Town
Rogers, P.J. (2004) 'Accountability' in Mathison, S. (ed) *Encyclopedia of Evaluation*, Sage Publications, Newbury Park, CA
Schulpen, L. and Ruben, R. (2006) *Een gevoelige selectie. Analyse van de beoor-delingssystematiek in het nieuwe Medefinancieringsstelsel* [A sensitive selection: Analysis of the assessment system in the new co-financing framework], CIDIN, Nijmegen
Shah, I. (1985) *The Exploits of the Incomparable Mulla Nasrudin*, Octagon Press
Snowden, D. and Boone, M. (2007) 'A leader's framework for decision making', *Harvard Business Review*, November 2007, pp69–76
UNDP (2007) *Evaluation of Results-based Management in UNDP*, UNDP, New York

Recommended readings

The topics in this chapter have interesting connections to others in this volume. Readers may wish to look at Chapter 12 which elaborates on public accountability which is tied to the area of monitoring and evaluation covered in Chapter 18. Chapters 19 and 20 provide a complement in terms of time frames for learning cycles and competencies and tools that support self-reflection. The following is a short selection of useful resources as a starting point for further reading on this topic.

Argyris, C. and Schön, D. (1978) *Organizational Learning: A Theory of Action Perspective*, Addison Wesley, Reading, MA. For an introduction to the core ideas, see: www.infed.org/thinkers/argyris.htm, accessed November 2009.

This classic text outlines key terms in organizational learning, both of which are central to surfacing and addressing assumptions and governing values. The first set of terms – theory-in-action and espoused theory – relates to the difference between the theories that are implicit in what we do (often tacit) and those that we use to explain to others or ourselves what we think we do. The second set of terms relates to whether learning occurs within the framework of given or chosen goals, plans, values, rules – so-called single loop learning. Another level of learning, that requires questioning of the assumed validity of these goals and plans, is double loop learning, which can reframe the basic premises on which an organization operates. The book details how the two sets of ideas are related.

Ebrahim, A. (2005) *NGOs and Organizational Change. Discourse, Reporting and Learning,* Cambridge University Press

This book explores change processes in NGOs, focusing on the relationships with international funders. This relationship impacts strongly on NGO change processes, leading to tensions in reporting requirements but also strategies used by NGOs to go their own way. It illustrates in sharp and insightful ways how the reporting requirements force conceptualizations of work that in turn shape long-term development.

Land, T., Hauck, V. and Baser, H. (2009) *Capacity Change and Performance. Capacity Development: Between Planned Interventions and Emergent Processes. Implications for Development Cooperation,* Policy Management Brief 22, European Centre for Development Policy Management, Maastricht

This brief provides a good introduction to how complexity thinking can help to reframe the expectations about capacity development as both process and product. It provides a useful comparison between planned interviews and emergent approaches by discussing key variables important in designing and implementing capacity development. It offers 12 implications for aid agencies that want to improve the capacity development they support.

Snowden, D. and Boone, M. (2007) 'A leader's framework for decision making', *Harvard Business Review*, November 2007, pp69–76

An excellent overview of the Cynefin framework that focuses on the implications for leadership. It offers several ideas for managing under complex conditions and provides ample illustrations of how the simple, complicated, complex and chaotic demand different managerial responses.

Part V

Looking Ahead

To look ahead, this closing section starts by looking back. Chapter 22 takes stock of what the preceding chapters have told us about capacity and its development, as seen through the eyes of practitioners. It draws on this evidence base to discuss recent steps in the understanding and evolution of capacity development as a professional domain. It also formulates an emerging practitioner profile and key challenges and orientations for the future.

With this picture in mind, Chapter 23 draws on a multi-country study to take a closer look at the emerging service sector for CD and specific demand, supply and finance dynamics. Important bottlenecks are identified in demand articulation, the quality of supply, the outreach towards sub-national levels and the characteristics of financing streams. What can be done to alter this situation is set out as a possible future strategic agenda, specifically in relation to increasing demand power, stimulating the quality and quantity of support services, and improving funding logics. Chapter 24 continues this forward-looking perspective in a complementary way by describing what steps could be undertaken to enhance the professionalism of this field of work.

As a package, these chapters provide for one view on the state-of-the-art of capacity development as a professional field and propose a number of essential perspectives and challenges for its further evolution.

22

Taking Stock

This chapter takes a step back and above by drawing on the richness of preceding contributions to consolidate what we can learn about capacity and its development. It first summarizes essential insights into the nature of capacity and its deliberate enhancement. It then distils an indicative practitioners' profile, integrating core elements of the wide variety of contributions to this volume. The explanation moves on to discuss the evolution of this area of work as a professional domain and identifies key challenges for the next stages of progress. Several ways forward are identified and explored. Two are elaborated in subsequent chapters on market dynamics and on perspectives for professionalization.

Learning about the Field of Capacity Development: Characteristics, Practitioner Challenges and Future Perspectives

Jan Ubels, Alan Fowler and Naa-Aku Acquaye-Baddoo

Introduction

This volume was conceived as and designed to be practice-based. Contributions by experienced practitioners explain and discuss the capacity development approaches they use as well as share their insights and lessons. This chapter will use this rich stock of information to look at the capacity development field overall and discuss answers to the questions 'How far have we come?' and 'Where do we go next?'

While the original topics for inclusion were selected from the editors' own experience, as the project developed the substance of contributions combined in such a way that the field of practice 'revealed' itself, so to speak. During this process, we found that several of our original ideas did not work well enough and needed revision. As draft chapters started to arrive, new authors and topics popped up that made more sense. In addition, authors often brought new perspectives to or seriously reoriented their assigned topics. In several instances they challenged our framing and concepts of capacity development. Towards the end, it became clear that our initial selection of topics was pretty appropriate, but the overall organizing structure required significant adjustment.

Thus the nature of 'the terrain' of capacity development is becoming much clearer. We started better to notice where the landscape was well-mapped as well as areas that remain ill-explored. As a way of taking stock, this chapter sketches the 'broader landscape' arising from the perspectives of the various texts and cases. We will first look at the nature of capacity and its development. Contours of a practitioner profile and the status of evolution of CD as a professional field are discussed next. Finally we move to the key challenges and perspectives that we see ahead of us.

The introduction to this book acknowledged the many definitions of capacity, not one of which is ideal or without its problems. We chose to work with the formulation 'capacity is the power of a human system to perform, sustain and self-renew'. Now, after some 20 substantive chapters, do we have a better idea of what capacity is and how it comes about?

The nature of capacity ...

On the basis of the contributions found in this volume, as well as many other sources cited in recommended readings, it is possible to describe five 'defining' character-istics of capacity and, from there, also discuss features of its development.

Capacity is about real-life issues and results

The rich and varied cases explored in this volume show that capacity is about practical issues and overcoming concrete challenges to people's well-being. It is about an ability to manage forests, to provide drinking water, to increase income for farmers and others, to provide good education to children, to build roads, or protect people in one's community against HIV/AIDS. It is not vague and far removed from real action. It is about achieving concrete results that make a differ-ence in the lives of (poor) people. The capacity described is impact-oriented and developmentally relevant.

Capacity is multi-faceted

Capacity is not a specific ability or competency nor a secret ingredient. It exists on the basis of multiple elements and factors and these can differ very much depending on the nature of the organization or situation in which it is embedded. The first three chapters of the book set out different dimensions of capacity (multiple elements, multiple actors and multiple levels). These perspectives are drawn from careful reflections on practical experience. They were not a precon-ceived framework. One could say that these three 'multis' invite a simple form of open systems thinking. They help a practitioner and a client to appreciate a situation from multiple angles and ask themselves what specific elements, what specific actors and what specific levels of functioning influence capacity here? How do these interrelate and how can one start to strengthen capacity here?

Capacity is relational

It is very clear from the above and all the cases discussed in this volume that, indeed, capacity is highly relational. Chapter 2 introduced an interesting concept here in distinguishing three forms of relating: (a) with oneself; (b) with others; and (c) with the wider world. Almost all other chapters discuss and reveal different dimensions of, and approaches to, working with relationships in order to enhance capacities.

Capacity is political

More than we expected, the fact that capacity is political came to the fore again and again. Capacity is about the power 'to' do certain things, but consequently also deals directly with power of some actors 'over' others and the way that power differences are used and mediated. This is reflected in, for example, issues of stakeholders' governance and accountability. It is about contending values and the degree to which these can be made productive. Many chapters discuss how engagement of multiple stakeholders was required to develop better mutual understanding and opportunities of joint gains or collective solutions. All these chapters either directly address power or touch on practical experiences of dealing with power in capacity development processes.

Capacity is tangible and intangible

Though we said that capacity is about real-life issues and results, this does not mean that it is necessarily concrete, instrumental and tangible. It is not just about observable skills or organizational procedures. These factors are embedded in something else, in attitudes, beliefs and cultural perceptions. Capacity also deals with the 'software' of how people see themselves, others and the world. Consequently understanding capacity and helping to develop it requires the ability to 'read' behind observable features and situations. It also calls for an ability to appreciate and deal with how actors see the world around them as well as themselves. It means recognizing and working positively with differences in values and the dynamic connections between actors, and with the ways these are rooted in deeper institutions and societal value systems.

... and capacity's (deliberate) development

Capacity is about real-life issues and results. It is multi-faceted, relational and political, tangible as well as intangible at the same time. What, then, have we learned and can we conclude about its development?

Capacity development is ongoing

It is important to acknowledge that capacity is always in a state of development. Any form of human organization is dynamic and 'living'. And thus there are internal and external forces that impinge on the existing capacity and make it change, evolve, stagnate, deepen, erode or stabilize. Consequently, even a period of relative stagnation is determined by an ever changing interplay of forces. And one can thus say that capacity development is going on continuously, in more intensive or gentle, positive or more negative ways. Consequently, any deliberate capacity development intervention steps into an ongoing, living process, will need to work with that reality and eventually move out.

Capacity development is an 'inside-out' process but can also have significant 'outside-in' dynamics

Ownership, responsibility and sustainability – and therefore capacity development as an 'inside-out' change process – are important themes across this volume. At the same time, Parts I and III show that while the practice of capacity development is anchored within a specific organizational entity, its growth is strongly influenced by external factors as well. The case of the multi-stakeholder processes in an agricultural value chain in Uganda in Chapter 14 showed that such growth can originate from the space between different actors. That is, it stems from improvements in their relationships rather than from within the specific actors. In addition, shifts in context and dissatisfactions about performance – and hence capacity – are often signalled through external relations that cannot be ignored indefinitely.

In sum, while capacity development must be carried from within, the triggers for doing so are often responses to external developments or pressures. By the same token, external forces may also be influential enabling factors in the eventual success (or failure) of a capacity development effort. Effective capacity development interventions deliberately work with, engage and use external dynamics.

Capacity development requires multi-actor engagement

An employee returning from a training event will have to deal with her team, manager or subordinates if she wants to use what she learned to change her day-to-day way of working. Likewise, capacity development efforts of a larger magnitude inevitably require the engagement of multiple actors. Capacity development approaches focused on single entities have, therefore, tended to be limited in their impact, because they do not sufficiently deal with the actors and relations implicated in creating effective results. A multi-actor perspective is therefore essential to inform any deliberate capacity development process, even if in itself it does not deal with the engagement of multiple actors directly.

The capacity development repertoire is expanding

Cases discussed in the chapters of Part III provide examples of how traditional capacity development tools and methods – typically focused on instilling certain skills or improving specific organizational procedures and functioning – have been successfully integrated with new approaches. Sources of innovation are found in accountability, value chains, micro–macro linkages or knowledge networking. These and other drivers challenge a practitioner to work more intensively with methods of dialogue, brokering, facilitation and mediation. Such innovations are opening up and expanding the relatively new and still developing area of multi-actor interventions. These more holistic and system-responsive approaches take in political, institutional and governance dimensions of capacity and start to deal with the value networks that exist between actors. We believe this is a very important development and step for the capacity development field, as it helps to embed seemingly discrete capacity development interventions and programmes in the real-life (inter)actions and 'business processes' of the actors and sectors concerned.

Capacity development occurs at varying scales and time frames

Does the importance of connections mean that one always has to go for big programmes covering many aspects and actions? Not necessarily. Small or 'single focus' interventions – such as training on a specific set of skills – are relevant. But, as many cases in this volume have shown, if one wants to achieve concrete results in the 'real' world – improving forestry management or the effectiveness of local government, for instance – connections, scale and time frame matter. In other words, small and single-focused interventions must be strategically understood and responsively located in bigger and longer-term processes. Therefore a prac-titioner needs to have short-, medium- and long-term ambitions and related time frames in mind. This requirement translates into an ability to consciously 'shift gear' between the short-term requirements of a specific assignment and longer-term perspectives and forces of change.

Capacity development is an iterative process of 'learning in action'

The multiple dimensions and relational nature of capacity lead to another main lesson. It is difficult to undertake the development of capacity as a linear, certain, pre-planned process. Sudden changes 'elsewhere' can impinge on a capacity development process. As a result, factors that were not thought to be very rele-vant often become apparently so. Effective capacity development thus has a char-acter of 'learning in action'. The chapters in Part IV all explore this challenge in different ways. They reveal that an often-perceived dichotomy between adopting a clear results-orientation to satisfy accountability and a learning-orientation is false. Both can be combined in very effective ways in concrete interventions and can be organized to reinforce each other.

Capacity development requires the practitioner to balance goal-driven engagement with some form of 'neutrality'

In international cooperation, capacity development seeks to realize societal change and pursues strategies towards this goal. Such change processes are inherently relational and political. But the capacity development practitioner is often called to have a more or less impartial role. Her role is usually not to lead the change, but rather to help people build the capacities to do so. This does not mean that she is a colourless or even a neutral player. The practitioner helps the process to achieve certain (collective) objectives. One could say that a practitioner has the role to be 'all-partisan' rather than just non-partisan. He or she can radiate values and principles that invigorate the process. And meaningful change processes usually require a high level of engagement, energy and dedication. Practitioners may also have a strong (social or ethical) connection to the substance or aims of the process. The case in Chapter 12, for example, illustrates an activist stance of a Tanzanian NGO that sought to improve education. But even here, an important principle of the NGO was not to rally or 'mobilize' citizens themselves but to offer them information and tools to self-organize. The essential principle to maintain is that the capacity development practitioner does not own or carry the process. But the practitioner is indeed a facilitator and is requested to serve the (common) goal of the stakeholders concerned (not necessarily all stakeholders).

An indicative professional profile

Previous sections in this chapter described five important characteristics of capacity and seven features of deliberate capacity development processes. The contributions to this volume show in many ways how practitioners work with these characteristics and features to develop and support effective capacity development activities. Based on this broad set of experiences and the two previous sections we believe it is possible to delineate some contours of the professional profile of a capacity development practitioner. Box 22.1 – and here we speak directly to a practitioner – summarizes what appear to be essential elements of effective and quality practice.

This characterization is not theoretical. It is extracted from the practical experiences brought together in this volume. We believe such a profile forms an interesting take on the set of competencies and abilities required of practitioners in order to be 'professional' in capacity development. With this substance in mind, Chapter 24 takes forward a concern of how 'professionalism' in capacity development can be promoted and developed with quality and scale.

Box 22.1 A practitioner profile

These are qualities of an effective CD practitioner or professional

1 **You articulate your own framework and ways of looking at capacity** (Chapters 1, 2, 3 and 8). You know key theories that underpin your analysis and choices and are conscious about what you are inclined to focus on and what you are not.

2 **You select between or combine different roles as appropriate** to the task and the client situation (Chapter 4). You know what roles you are good at and which less so. You can help to clarify roles and expectations and select appropriate role choices.

3 **You balance thematic understanding with change expertise.** You consciously hold and develop expertise on 'both sides of the coin' in order to be effective in the assignments and for the clients that you serve (Chapter 5).

4 **You are able to deal with multiple interests, politics, conflict, inequality and value differences and your own position in these** (Chapters 6, 7 and 11). You know and deepen your personal style in this respect and are clear about your boundaries, also to clients.

5 **You have the skill of 'reading situations'** (all chapters, especially Chapters 9 and 11) and see the uniqueness of each client or assignment. You develop a sense for discovering the pattern of existing energy and bottlenecks for change.

6 **You have developed your skills for interaction and listening** and a clear sense of your personal qualities and pitfalls in this respect. You have mastered your own selection of dialogue techniques and methods (Chapter 10).

7 **You are able to help clients develop connections between actors and levels.** You have a repertoire of specific approaches or methods for doing so (Chapters 11–17). If necessary and appropriate you also actively facilitate, mediate, catalyse or broker new connections.

8 **You have shaped your own concepts and methods about measuring capacity development and demonstrating its results.** You create clarity on this with clients and are able to hold different time frames (Chapters 18 and 19).

9 **You balance and link accountability and learning aims.** You are able to 'learn in action' and adjust the course of action on the basis of experiences, and exercise self-reflection (Chapters 18, 19, 20 and 21).

10 **You design, manage and review specific interventions.** You fine tune your interventions towards the needs, situation and dynamics of the client and other stakeholders. And you manage the relation with them in an accountable, transparent and ethical manner.

A major step in the evolution of the capacity development field

The emerging practitioner profile discussed above shows that important characteristics of (deliberate) capacity development processes are that they: (1) are ongoing with inside-out and outside-in dynamics; (2) require multi-actor engagement and an expanding intervention repertoire; (3) have strong elements of dialogue-facilitation, brokering and mediation; (4) can be applied at varying scales and time frames, through a 'learning in action' way of working; and (5) require the practitioner to balance an all-partisan attitude with goal-oriented 'engagement'.

Distilled from what the practitioner stories in this book have told us, these five key points represent something significant. This clearly is an understanding of capacity development that goes beyond the conventional notions of equipping individuals (training) or organizations (organizational development) to perform better. It brings capacity development into the realm of multi-actor processes. This does not negate ways of working oriented towards individuals or organizations. On the contrary. These are essential intervention focuses and practices that should be retained. But they are now placed within a broader perspective that also addresses multi-actor arrangements and interactions.

As already said, we believe this appreciation to be a major step in the evolution of capacity development as a professional endeavour. Why? Because most if not all development issues, whether they are social, economic or ecological, are not solved by a single actor but need the engagement of various players. Capacity development as an intervention discipline is now growing closer to this insight and more relevant to the multi-actor nature of the primary processes at stake, whether this concerns water provision, local governance, forest management or combating HIV/AIDS.

So, looking from the perspective of what capacity development was meant to do – as the opening sentences of this book states, to help better achieve development results – one could also say that capacity development as an intervention discipline has come of age in its really productive role.

Core bodies of knowledge

To date, capacity development has mainly been defined in relation to achieving broader development policy goals and surprisingly little effort has been expended on conceptualizing and deepening capacity development in terms of its professional sources of knowledge and quality. To some extent, this volume also reflects such a limitation, and deliberately so, because we wanted to talk from practice, building up our understanding based on real-life experience.

In taking stock in this chapter, however, some important characteristics of 'capacity' and its 'development' have been formulated, together with a conclusion that capacity development encompasses working with individuals, organizations and multi-actor systems. This and other insights allow us to look more clearly at the sources of professional knowledge it uses. The diverse cases and experiences discussed in this volume show that capacity development is an eclectic field of work that draws on many domains of knowledge and disciplines. However, there are some core bodies of knowledge that seem to have broader relevance. Most apparent are:

- organizational development and management science;
- multi-stakeholder processes and related insights from social and political science;
- pedagogy, behavioural psychology and group facilitation;
- change management and facilitation; and
- governance, public administration and institutional development.

The above listing provides one important and potentially significant way of defining the conceptual boundaries of, and content streams within, capacity development as a field of work. While this is an underdeveloped conversation, we feel confident to say, fed by practical evidence, that these five main types of knowledge are essential building blocks. And capacity development can be strengthened by using these sources more deliberately and more deeply. Doing so will add depth to answering an old question about if, and in what ways, capacity development is a distinct area of expertise.

An emerging professional domain?

The past 15 years have seen many people and organizations grappling with questions of how to understand capacity and what range of methods to work with for its development. The result of this search for answers has reached a level of maturity reflected in this volume and other sources. Perhaps now we can say with some cautious confidence that we understand what we are working with and what kinds of approaches and methods may be relevant. The various sections of this chapter have drawn the main lines of this understanding of capacity, its development, the practice of supporting it and the relevant bodies of knowledge.

One could compare the current situation to the early stages in the development of medical science. Or even, for that matter, the emergence of organizational development (OD) as a professional domain. We are at a stage where the medical (or OD) discipline began to have a fairly accurate understanding of the main parts and sub-systems of the body (the organization) and how these work and function in relation to the outside world. And thus we began to identify a basic repertoire for 'treating' medical (organizational) problems. In other words, with capacity development we are at a point in time similar to when it became possible to form and educate doctors or OD specialists more systematically. And where patients (or clients) started to become more vocal and making demands on what they expect and need; where they started to critically discuss the doctors (or OD consultants) available and select who they would like to consult.

As a recognized domain of practice – and in fact a sub-discipline within a wider science of social change and agency – in the field of capacity development we are probably at a point where purposeful approaches can and should now be used to expand and deepen professionalism. This moment suggests that we need to think of defining the field somewhat better. Areas to consider and of concern are: professional quality and its assurance; research and educational efforts; conditions under which it is practised; the nature of demand; the logic of financing; and position within society. Progress on these and many other fronts will, however, mean tackling some interesting challenges.

Two key challenges

So far in this chapter we have sketched a picture that suggests that the work terrain of capacity development is 'coming of age'. We have also suggested that reaching such a stage implies that there are new possibilities and needs to be dealt with. Here we would like to briefly suggest two new essential challenges for the capacity development field. These are 'demand–supply–financing dynamics' and issues of professionalization.

Demand–supply–financing dynamics and service models

The way that a profession is financed and how the demand–supply interface works strongly co-determine the ways in which professionals and organizations working in that field actually function. For example, in the medical field the differences between private and public arrangements may be big, for individual doctors, for the functioning of hospitals and for knowledge development. At the time of writing, President Obama of the Unites States is trying to develop a breakthrough in the US health system with stronger public roles to ensure that a significant part of the poor people in the US is served better. In some developing countries there are opposite moves away from dysfunctional public health systems to forms of private care that better respond to demands.

Similarly, for capacity development, the financing regime and the way that demand and supply meet each other (or the service models and nature of service organizations) are critical factors in shaping how capacity development is done, its quality as well as the drivers for its future development. It is clear that, in many countries of the South, practice is strongly oriented by the dynamics of the 'aid industry'. On the other hand there are plenty of examples – particularly in developing countries that are not that heavily dominated by aid – of more spontaneous, self-organized forms of capacity development. Capacity development is actually supported by a growing consultancy sector. Civil society organizations, networks and movements also play very important roles in developing a society's capabilities. And there are public entities that do such work. However, there has been little analysis of how this emerging 'service sector' or 'field of work' actually evolves. To help fill in this gap, Chapter 23 provides an interesting in-road into that conversation by analysing capacity development 'service environments' across a number of country settings. It will show that current financing patterns and delivery models used by aid agencies seriously limit the outreach, quality and effectiveness of capacity development investments. In response, perspectives for future improvement are proposed.

Professionalization

The second prominent challenge that appears on the agenda is the issue of professional quality. If there is so much investment in capacity development and the field starts to have some kind of recognizable contours and profile, then logically the question emerges whether one could better develop, stimulate and 'guarantee' the quality of work. This is even more necessary if a considerable amount of 'not-so-good' or mediocre work is seen. It will then become relevant to think about how one can promote professionalism.

Progress in this direction would ask how this field of work could establish an understanding of intervention quality. What could be done about professional standards, quality, innovation and research? What are the possibilities for practitioner development and learning? A brief exploration of these questions in Chapter 24 is intended to stimulate debate and invite new thinking in terms of future initiatives for fostering quality and professionalism.

Conclusions: Taking the next steps

In this chapter we have observed and argued that the work terrain of capacity development is 'coming of age'. We mean this in the sense that it presents a reasonably realistic and somewhat comprehensive picture of: (a) the nature of capacity; (b) important characteristics of its development; (c) its expansion to include individual, organizational and multi-actor focuses and related intervention repertoires; (d) an indicative professional profile; and (e) key bodies of knowledge it taps from. We have also suggested that reaching this stage brings new challenges now, especially to understand and influence demand–supply–financing dynamics and delivery models, and to start to promote professionalism in one way or the other.

However, as important as they may be, the context for these new steps may not necessarily be very conducive. As good change agents, the emerging professional community will do well in understanding the specific hurdles that one may meet. Four seem important.

First is a fixation on short-term projects, programmes and results as well as following development 'fashions'. The international development cooperation sector, broadly defined, is not known for its excellence in developing quality and maintaining focus over time. Second is a dominating logic of 'management for results'. An over-emphasis on this way of thinking about social change underplays the importance of understanding ways in which results have been achieved, or could have been achieved better. A third factor is that although the field of capacity development is young, there are large and strong institutions actively involved – multi-lateral and bilateral institutions, international NGOs and also recipient country actors – each pursuing their own concerns. Consequently, politics and institutional interests tend to get priority over quality and professionalism. Fourthly, development activities are overseen to a considerable extent by generalist foreign service professionals. While they may have excellent diplomatic qualities, they may not necessarily be conversant with, or able to stimulate, professional rigour and innovation. Singly and together, these factors do not necessarily create a strong development climate for improving capacity development as a professional practice.

Making the next steps in developing quality in this emerging professional domain will thus be challenging. But undoubtedly it is important. There are hundreds of thousands of practitioners in developing countries and elsewhere that apply the concepts and practices of capacity development. The state of understanding and practice of capacity development that has now been achieved – as portrayed in this volume – not only supports steps towards professionalization but also, in a sense, calls for them. There are significant and realistic opportunities. Funders can change financing strategies so they stimulate effective demand–supply dynamics and higher quality approaches. Individual practitioners can organize themselves better and engage in professional platforms and knowledge exchange. Development organizations and service providers that host or support capacity development work could collaborate better to enhance learning, research, quality initiatives and product development. Moreover, it provides an excellent opportunity for educational institutions and universities to develop new, relevant curricula.

And yes, the emphasis of all of such efforts does indeed need to be in the South. A growing community of all kinds of practitioners is taking shape there, but such endogenous processes are still ill-supported.

We believe that the individuals as well as the organizations active in this field will make the necessary next steps to enhance this professional field. If for no other reason than wanting to 'walk our talk'; out of a recognition that if the field of capacity development is to mature further, it needs to take a look at its own present performance and ask itself how its own capacities can further improve.

23

A Capacity Development Market?

Over the last 20 years, many countries receiving external support show a rapid growth in expertise for 'doing development'. For capacity development, this trend is reflected in the rise of home-grown specialized organizations and support structures. Unfortunately, there has been little analysis or discussion of how this 'service environment' for CD is evolving, or how it may be strategically supported.

This chapter shares the results of an initial effort to analyse the service environment for capacity development, including a sample of very different countries. It shows a pattern of strong centralization, patchy outreach to sub-national actors and little 'demand power'. In other words, capacity development outside national capitals and large urban locations is not well served by the present financing dynamics and provider community. A set of changes in financing logics and assistance strategies are proposed to better support the development of service environments for capacity development. In this way, Southern expertise can become more effective and better able to take the lead in developing the capacity of its own societies.

Stimulating the Provision of Local Capacity Development Support

Jan Ubels

Introduction

All societies need knowledge and expertise to solve their problems and achieve equitable and sustainable development. In so-called 'developed societies', private as well as public and social sector organizations also need and hire assistance in order to address emerging challenges, or simply to perform better. In most cases, they have at their disposal a wide selection of consultants, knowledge institutes and support structures that they can draw on for both their general as well as specialized capacity needs. Of course, in a globalizing economy, developing countries can also draw on international contacts and import necessary know-how and assist-ance. But for a society to steer and develop itself, it requires its own critical mass of capable human capital and organizations that understand their own context intimately and are able to bring about change and innovation to create unique solutions that draw on local knowledge.

Therefore, the critical site for increasing professional capabilities to support capacity development must be within developing countries themselves, reducing the dependency on external expertise. Drawing on a recent study, this chapter explores how this type of process could be accelerated.

In many developing countries a 'service sector' providing the necessary support to developing 'home-grown' capacity is emerging. Typically, this sector consists of (semi-) public entities such as training and research institutes, leading non-governmental organizations (NGOs), consultancy firms and independent consult-ants. This chapter refers to them as local capacity developers (LCDs).

However, little is known or documented about the quantity or quality of local capacity developers in the South. As a modest start to remedy this knowledge gap, supported by the UK Overseas Development Institute (ODI), SNV Netherlands Development Organisation undertook a general reconnaissance and country scoping studies to map this 'service environment'. The overall study sought answers to three broad questions: What is the current demand–supply dynamic? What is problematic in this equation? And how can this information inform strate-gies for funding and supporting capacity development in other ways? Although only an initial exploration, this chapter presents and discusses the preliminary findings of the study as a basis for thinking about ways to increase the number and competencies of local capacity developers.

Addressing the questions posed by the study requires starting with a consid-eration of what LCDs look like and how they are viewed. This is the focus of the first section of this chapter. An appreciation is also needed of the environments in which LCDs operate, the subject of section two. Against this background, section three presents major findings. And this leads, in section four, to a discussion of possible ways forward, particularly in terms of alternative financing arrangements and overall support strategies.

What are local capacity developers and what are their distinctive advantages?

A clear definition of what a local capacity developer is does not exist. In this text LCDs are taken to be 'organizations supporting capacity development that origi-nate from and belong financially and socio-culturally to the country or region in which they deliver their services'. Local capacity developers can operate at local, sub-national, national or even regional levels. They offer a variety of services and employ different working methods and techniques such as training, facilitation and coaching, organizational development advice, technical assistance and knowledge networking. Often, these techniques are combined with knowledge of, or expertise relating to, a particular sector such as infrastructure, health or agriculture. For some LCDs capacity development is their core business, for others it forms just a segment of their work. For example a university or research centre can provide paid or subsidized capacity development services next to its core research and educational programmes. There are consulting firms that have capacity development work as a core activity. Other firms may offer this type of service next to or as part of a main business in, for example, technical construction work in the water sector or accountancy. Similarly, within the NGO community there are specialists in capacity development and organizations that intertwine it very effectively with, for example, a core mandate for advocacy around a certain theme. Some LCDs are formally affiliated with an international consulting firm or an international NGO (INGO). And others are just individuals working on their own, who may pool their skills with those of colleagues or partners to create mutually supportive networks or associations.

The outcomes of several recent international policy processes, such as the Accra Agenda for Action in 2008, have merely reaffirmed what has been a longstanding discussion on the need to make better use of and stimulate development of Southern expertise for capacity development (see Box 23.1).

Box 23.1 How do donors and national government view local capacity developers?

The practice of employing local consultants goes back to an era when technical assistance was first provided to developing countries. Growing privatization in the 1980s and early 1990s stimulated major increases in national technical or 'hard' expertise. However, though uneven across the South, the 'soft' expertise – of institutional and organizational development, strategy work, policy advice, coaching, training, learning, and so on – typically lagged behind. For international development agencies, however, there were and are clear advantages of deploying local capacity developers, who:

- understand the local context and cultural sensitivities;
- speak the local languages;
- know the professional, formal and informal networks;
- enjoy legitimacy and recognition among peers;
- have institutional knowledge of national institutions;
- are familiar with the work environment and able to command lower costs;
- tend to have a better rapport with national decision-makers who prefer to see their compatriots employed in-country rather than losing people to better-paid jobs abroad.

However, there are also risks associated with increasing the involvement of local professional resources in capacity development initiatives. For example, care must be taken to ensure employing LCDs and similar technical service providers does not lead to an extraction of valuable resources, expertise and capacity from government organizations and other national institutions.

The Berg Report (UNDP, 1993), for instance, criticized technical assistance (TA) for being primarily donor-driven and based on interventions that were led by outside expertise. It noted that this contributed to limited sustainability because results were not sufficiently embedded in local capacities. At the time, the Berg Report received serious attention. But subsequently, progress has been quite modest. Much has been written about reforming TA, in which the rationale for capacity development in, by and for the South has been well explored. But there has been minimal debate on how local capabilities in capacity development can best be stimulated and developed.

The development of LCDs is also important in view of recent policy discussions on international development cooperation and capacity development, which include the Paris Declaration on aid effectiveness in 2005 and the follow-up Accra Agenda for Action in 2008. Signatories to the Third High Level Forum in Accra underlined the centrality of capacity development to sustainable development and committed themselves to 'the provision of technical cooperation by local and regional resources, including through South–South cooperation'.

Understanding CD 'service environments'

To increase understanding of the condition and status of local capacity developers, the SNV/ODI study examined their situation in five countries: Cameroon, Montenegro, Peru, Tanzania and Vietnam. A parallel analysis of a large number of existing support mechanisms for (local) capacity development was also undertaken (Tembo, 2008). Country reconnaissance basically involved a week of interviews and visits with a round-table meeting at the end. This was fed by specific inventories as well as broader intelligence on the basis of SNV's on-the-ground presence in the environments concerned. The teams involved looked at what gradually came to be referred to as the local capacity development 'service environment' and examined the nature and role of organizations providing capacity development support, the financing patterns, the working methods and types of support provided, and how the demand–supply–financing interactions steered the work. In line with SNV's focus on working with sub-national (meso-level) actors, special attention was given to the degree to which capacity development needs in provinces, districts and communities are served by the emerging support industry.

Combining 'market' and 'non-market' views

In general there is a separation between the ways that commercial (private sector) and non-commercial (NGO) actors talk about and operate in this service environment. In this study, however, a deliberate effort was made to combine these two perspectives.

Box 23.2 presents a rather 'stereotypical' view of both perspectives to help us appreciate that using both 'market development' and 'subsidized development' language offers a more comprehensive understanding of the service environment as a whole. In contexts where subsidized development language has been dominant, employing market terms and perspectives may provide new insights. A value

---

Box 23.2 Typical 'market' and 'non-market' terminology and perceptions of capacity development service environments

'Subsidized development' logics and language help to think in terms of:

- grants for CD projects;
- development objectives and results;
- less advantaged groups and their rights;
- collaboration between actors;
- participatory and empowering methods;
- governance, politics and institutions.

'Market development' terminology and logics helps to think in terms of:

- fees for CD services;
- consumers making choices;
- demand-orientation;
- competition;
- products and market dynamics;
- rate of return on investments.

---

chain analysis, for example, can reveal perspectives in demand, forces of competition, weak links in the chain, and so on. The converse is also true. Where market language is all-pervasive, using the development language and questions may help to discuss social and poverty dimensions that would otherwise not be touched.

Variations between countries

The broader context in each of the five countries surveyed differs significantly in terms of their mix of wealth and poverty and related scores on development indices; the nature of their economies; their political systems; the relations between civil society, the private sector and the government; the character and speed of decentralization processes; as well as their natural environments.

In Peru a relatively strong consultancy industry operates with several thousand professionals serving mainly the private sector and national (semi-)public agencies. A community of development-related NGOs also exists. In recent years both have crossed over into each other's terrain, with NGOs doing more 'fee-for-service' work and consultants bidding for development programmes.

There are indications that the number of LCDs operating as private businesses correlates with the size of the commercial sector in an economy. Thus the commercial capacity of the development sector is relatively strong in Cameroon, with its forestry and oil, and is developing quickly in the booming economy of Vietnam. The NGO sector is weak in Vietnam, however, due to its socialist history, but is relatively strong in Cameroon and Tanzania. Semi-public training and research institutes play a strong role in capacity development in Vietnam and have some prominence in Tanzania and Cameroon, but play only a minor role in liberalized Peru. With donor emphasis on 'national implementation' modalities over the last years, international consultancy firms have also started to focus on capacity development through their local offices and affiliates. But what do these various types of LCDs do?

Capacity development support – what methods are used?

From the country reconnaissance and general studies it became clear that the capacity development repertoire has clearly widened over recent years. A range of conventional and more advanced intervention approaches or methods are applied, as shown in Box 23.3.

In practice, at the sub-national level, training and workshops (often one-off) are the dominant support modalities. This preference is followed by, and sometimes combined with, technical advice and assistance in project-management. In the NGO realm, lobbying and advocacy support is also a conventional capacity development method and purpose. The other eight forms of assistance, generally focusing on supporting change in more comprehensive or deeper ways and possibly over longer periods of time, are quite rare.

One also has to recognize that the organizations providing capacity development support, whether commercial or not-for-profit, have very different roles and underlying motivations. Some do indeed operate as service providers, on a fee-for-

---

Box 23.3 Types of capacity development services

Conventional

- Training and related workshop forms
- Technical advice (often focused on specific systems and/or procedures)
- Support to project management
- Support to lobby and advocacy

More advanced

- Action research and action learning, including pilots and 'laboratories'
- Knowledge brokering and networking
- Various kinds of multi-stakeholder processes
- Stimulating mutual and public accountability mechanisms
- Coaching and mentoring
- Change and process facilitation
- Leadership development
- Value chain development

services basis, of one kind or the other. Others implement large programmes that allow and require them to actively support capacity development. Other LCDs may have a knowledge or advocacy role in a certain area that engages them in capacity development. Yet others are membership-based organizations that carry out capacity development support to their constituency (farmers' unions, women's organizations, chambers of commerce, etc). And there are units within government departments and research or education institutions that have formal capacity development mandates, or engage in fee-for-services work. These differences influence such organizations' assistance repertoire (see Box 23.3) and also the nature and quality of the relations that they have with clients, partners or beneficiaries. Nevertheless, the survey did not establish a strict correlation between the variety of methods distinguished above and the nature of the providers. The challenge of providing more advanced methods can be seen across the different types of actors.

Cross-cutting patterns emerging from the study

Despite the differences in the country settings of the study, some remarkably similar patterns emerged that were echoed by a wider inventory of capacity development support mechanisms.

Box 23.4 Systemic phenomena in CD service environments

- Most *funding* for capacity development is spent in the capital on national level programmes and activities (which may have an ambition for decentralized outreach).
- Most *services* are designed at the national level in interaction between the funder and the service provider, far away from local level clients' needs.
- Capacity development support *providers* tend to be concentrated in one or two major towns. At the sub-national level one often finds small(er) NGOs or temporarily-funded programmes.
- With regard to the type of *services,* training in standard modules is the norm combined with technical advice and project management. More advanced services are very rare.
- There is a large *knowledge* gap between national and local actors, both about professional capacity development and about the 'market' for capacity development-related services and funding.
- In terms of *prices* capacity development in its present form is an expensive product for clients at the sub-national level most of whom cannot afford 'national' consultancy fees, allowances, long-distance travel costs, and so on.
- For sub-national actors the capacity development *'market'* is largely inaccessible, not transparent, and the quality of services on offer is unpredictable.

Box 23.5 Some findings from the Tanzania reconnaissance

Tanzania is a good example of the divide between international and national capacity development dynamics on the one hand, and local realities on the other. While national and international attention on the need for capacity development is growing, local organizations find it difficult to access funds and assistance to strengthen their capacities. Here are some of the key conclusions from the country reconnaissance.

- Capacity development is a top-down process. Initiatives, programmes and funding streams are designed by national actors. It is assumed that receivers need capacities.
- Local initiatives are often ignored in capacity development programmes. Even where there are interesting examples of enhanced capacities, they remain isolated. Capacity development providers are not able to capture and nurture local initiatives for up-scaling, as they are driven by national agendas set by external actors.
- Many study participants recognized the 'micro–macro gap' in capacity development.

In terms of the dynamics of service provisioning, the following factors were in play.

- *Expression of demand:* local actors have insufficient capabilities and space to express demand and are thus simply recipients of capacity development interventions.
- *Quality of supply:* provision of capacity development support is skewed towards supply-driven products, subject to a central-urban bias and often based on standardized approaches.
- *Imperfect market:* while funding is becoming available at national levels for capacity development programmes and approaches, it often does not connect to local demand. Programmes are conceptualized at the centre and face a physical challenge (the urban–rural gap).

Although there are considerable variations between and within the countries, the patterns described above are clearly visible, to the extent that they may be regarded as systemic phenomena created and maintained by the way the aid system and developing societies work.

Two examples illustrate the scenario sketched in Boxes 23.4 and 23.5. In one, a senior Tanzanian official working with an international agency in the water sector explains how a new set of capacity development training modules has been developed and is now being rolled out in the sector. The modules were largely developed by international consultants, who were flown in from abroad. He concludes that, to his own frustration, local expertise and experiences have hardly been tapped in the process of compiling the modules. In another, an NGO in one of the regions of the country has a well established practice in budget expenditure tracking and helping district officials and citizens to jointly analyse, decide on, use and monitor funds. When asked whether such expertise is also available in, or is spreading to, other regions, the head of the NGO indicates this is hardly the case. He explains that he is limited to their funding agreement with a specific international NGO. There is a national platform that discusses these items with the government, but few actors or mechanisms that engage in the horizontal spreading of such effective practices.

Multiple types and tariffs

The service environments scanned by this study are clearly 'hybrid' in nature, populated with a mix of NGO, private sector and semi-public actors. These survive on funding from multiple sources: INGOs, the private sector, governments and donors. Over time, some 'providers' move from commercial to subsidized market segments or vice versa. NGOs, as well as commercial or semi-public entities, often use similar kinds of funding. It is not uncommon to combine different legal statuses in order to operate in this hybrid environment. Although there are clearly different segments, overall various forms of financing intertwine and form one larger market or service environment.

There are also enormous differences in prices charged. Despite variations between countries, however, one can still indicate a few broad lines. In the national arena consultancy rates of between US$100 to US$350 a day are normal for firms and NGOs, with higher fees charged for more specialized policy work. Some INGOs pay US$250–350 a day to preferred consultants. As a result their local partners at national and sub-national level face difficulties hiring these consultants because they cannot afford such rates. At a sub-national level, rates are often capped at around US$100 day but are typically a lot lower. Many local NGOs are totally dependent on one major donor or project and revert to employing just one or two staff until they find the next donor. This situation stems, in part, from a lack of choice.

Limited choice set against growing demand

There is growing demand for more and higher quality capacity development services. But the 'service delivery' concept may be part of the problem. Most capacity development assistance consists of relatively isolated training sessions or workshops, while there is little effective support to bring about longer-term change at the local level. Also, the number of lead actors in capacity development support for a sector or theme within a country is usually quite limited (often between three and eight). National and international agencies who are the principal funders often demand a standard repertoire from this limited set of providers. In round-table discussions held in the five countries as part of the study, participants regularly expressed a desire to work more innovatively to develop methods for better outreach and horizontal spreading of effective practices. But there is neither the time nor resources to do so.

In the meantime clients, even at the local level, have become more demanding. As a local mayor in southern Cameroon said: 'One-off training and technical design is not enough. If I want my water department to function better I need somebody to work with that team over a longer period, to look at the quality of working practices, their leadership, how they relate to citizens and user groups, their internal organization. But it is very difficult to get such support, for financial as well as technical reasons.'

This quote reflects an important development in quality of demand at the local level. It is not just technical advice or standard management practices that are lacking. What most actors seek and need is really support *to make things work*. As this volume shows, often this requires a responsive and flexible approach on the part of capacity development service providers, in which one can bring in different methods and elements as the client progresses to become more effective. This Cameroon example also confirms an observation that often, local advisors and facilitators need to have a combination of change and sector expertise. Of course many local actors still have difficulties in formulating their needs and demands well. But by now, many of them have had enough of the standard trainings and workshops that they are now and then invited (and paid) to participate in. A Tanzania NGO leader had a nice statement in that respect: 'Do you know what people start to think of when you use the word capacity development nowadays? Dull workshops and sitting allowances!'

With regard to the improvement of quality and relevance of capacity development support methods it is interesting to note that capacity development practices can be quite diverse across sectors, even within the same country. Models for 'business development services' used by LCDs within the agriculture or other private sector market chains, for example, may be transferrable to other fields. Similarly in the water sector, there is considerable experience with multi-actor platforms and processes that may be relevant elsewhere. In short, there is considerable potential for improvement through cross-fertilization of ideas and approaches between sectors. But this means more than just increasing numbers. It also means re-distributing capacity development provision outside of capital cities and major urban centres to where demand is multiplied.

Reaching below the 'glass floor'

At the sub-national level the local capacity development community consists predominantly of NGOs and individual consultants. This is because major funding is concentrated in the capital cities so that sub-national level clients can only afford the services of subsidized NGOs or individual consultants who charge affordable fees. Their outreach is likewise limited due to relatively low quantities of financing reaching this level. Therefore access to high quality services for localities and smaller municipalities is sorely limited. This is a serious limitation on the potential for providing capacity development services at scale in the areas where the demand may be highest.

As we have seen from the Tanzanian example of public expenditure tracking, in many sectors or themes there are 'pockets' of effective and successful capacity development practice. But these sources of effective practice consistently struggle to spread horizontally, often because they are dependent on a specific donor or programme. In addition, funding patterns in general do not stimulate horizontal expansion of local solutions. Funds come with their own sets of objectives and criteria, usually set from above. In general, funding is rarely responsive to ideas from below. Financing and accounting arrangements are often quite narrowly constructed, with little room for innovation or experimentation that could be spread. Beneficiaries are induced to apply for what a financier thinks is important. Funds are less inclined to follow local lessons, dynamics, innovations and opportunities.

A related finding was an enormous relational and knowledge barrier between actors that are part of the 'national arena' and those operating at sub-national levels. It was difficult to find examples of sub-national LCDs that had won government or donor contracts. This was the case even for work in 'their' region where significant advantages are likely in terms of local presence, knowledge, connections and networking, not to mention cost effectiveness. The above factors seem to conspire to create what one could call a 'glass floor' (rather than a glass ceiling) in the system.

We can thus conclude that capacity development support faces massive challenges if it is to reach beyond major cities to the need and (potentially huge) demand at the local level. This raises the question: which strategies or approaches can be adopted to enhance outreach?

Could solutions be found in measures to increase the number of local capacity developers operating at this level at affordable rates? Or should we focus on adopting more 'networked' approaches that operate through peer-to-peer learning and horizontal spreading and better pick-up of what really works locally? A solution can possibly be found in a combination of both. What is certain is that capacity development at sub-national levels and locations is not well served by the present financing dynamics and provider community. Changes in the funding–demand–supply pattern are needed. This will require innovative strategies as the next section suggests.

Ways forward

Outreach and a weak match between the quality of supply and what really works locally are key challenges, which current financing levels and support strategies cannot meet. So, are there cheaper, more effective, networked approaches to capacity development support? Would this help solve erratic, poor-quality outreach? In order to move forward and achieve a better service environment as is urgently needed, what issues need addressing? Our analysis so far leads us to suggest three important entries for improving support to local capacity development: better analysis and understanding of local service environments; changes in key elements of funding logics; and introducing some essential orientations in the broad strategic perspective used. We will discuss each of these below.

Improved analysis and understanding

We simply need to analyse better! There is remarkably little data or material on local service environments. For a deeper understanding, a 'value chain' perspective would help open up a range of relevant questions, for example: how does the capacity development support value chain actually work? How do demand, supply and financing meet and interface? What range of products and services is in use and how adequate is it? What 'delivery models' work most effectively and efficiently? How are prices determined and composed? What drives providers? How does innovation take place? At SNV we are presently experimenting with methodologies in this field, making use of a combination of 'market research' and 'network analysis' techniques.

When improved data and analysis become available these will not only help to inform intervention strategies; this information itself can also become an active stimulating factor. 'Markets' as well as networks thrive on good and reliable information. Understanding of approaches, products, prices and choices can empower demand and improve competition and innovation with providers. It is also the basis for peer-to-peer learning and horizontal spreading of effective practices.

Box 23.6 Five key shifts in funding logics

Localize decision-making: For local capacity development to work better it is important that decision-making is shifted more towards local actors. This will require some guidance and stimulation of 'demand expression', but local actors themselves should get the position and responsibility to determine what they think works best for their setting. This will require funders to be less focused on their criteria and more on the quality of engagement with local actors. Providers would need to be more responsive and do better exploration of actual demand.

Make market information available: There is insufficient market information for local actors (potential clients) to make conscious choices. What are the kinds of solutions and support available? Can one choose from different sources? What about price differences? What is the track record of certain methods or providers? If such information was made available, it would not only empower the demand but also foster competition and innovation among providers and inform funders to improve the strategic quality of their funding strategy.

Shared investment: Many CD interventions are supply-driven and relatively ineffective. Some form of contribution and/or co-investment by local actors would be a strong incentive to focus on sustainable solutions that have a sufficient benefit–cost ratio. It will also help to make the relation funder–beneficiary and beneficiary–provider more mature.

Reduce standardization: Contrary to the current situation, funding patterns should avoid prescribing standard (often supply-driven) solutions but foster the demand-driven development and evidence-based replication of approaches or services that effectively support local change and solutions. Providers will have to improve their adaptiveness and ability to tailor-make support to local requirements and dynamics.

Revise selection criteria: Financing entities should become selective in a different way than they are now. They should not be focused on qualifying against standard criteria, but behave more as an investor, and ask: do I believe I am really investing in a possible success here? If so, how can we help such a solution to become mature and gain scale in a responsive manner? This will stimulate local actors to take responsibility and providers to work on effectiveness as well as efficiency and scaling.

Changing funding logics

We have noted that the dominance of external funding has often made benefici-aries responsive to the priorities of financiers rather than the latter being respon-sive to what works and can be made successful locally. It must be acknowledged that local capacity development in many cases will remain a (partially) subsidized business. But to shift the inadequacies in the prevailing financing dynamics we like to suggest five (interconnected) elements which are summarized in Box 23.6.

Three broad strategic orientations

The above elements are tactical and technical changes to financing conventions and practices and are helpful, but they are not enough. Many present financing mechanisms are supply-driven, simply distributing funds under agreed criteria but not necessarily operating intelligently to strengthen the quality and dynamics of the capacity development service environment. Capacity development financing needs to be embedded within a strategic view of significant change in the capacity of the South (that is, local actors) to demand, develop and provide its (their) own capacity development expertise when and wherever it is required. The five concrete changes in financing logics and practices mentioned in the box above therefore need to be embedded in broader strategic orientations that offer a perspective of empowered, less dependent in-country support systems that are able to anticipate and solve their own societies' problems. We believe that three important changes in thinking and focus need to be adopted: from input to supporting local change and solutions; an improved understanding of achieving scale; and better support to spreading professionalism.

From inputs to supporting local change and solutions

Current capacity development inputs – especially standard training modules – are not necessarily helping achieve local change effectively. So a shift in thinking is needed on what capacity development itself is and how it works. A combination of better quality, proper demand orientation and the range of innovative meth-odologies described in this volume should help foster and facilitate local change and solutions. In general this means: (a) selection of proven approaches that are making a difference; (b) adopting forms of support that do not rigidly apply a single method but seek to combine different approaches as required for effective local change (for example combining training with coaching, some knowledge networking and support for multi-stakeholder engagement to realize a specific outcome); and (c) longer or periodic engagement to support concrete change and application in a responsive manner.

Achieving scale

Such capacity development approaches and solutions need to be scaleable. But the thinking on scale also needs to change. Currently, it is attempted by roll-out and replication of standard approaches from the centre. Instead, effective scale is often better achieved through 'horizontal learning' (Ellerman, 2001). Building peer-to-peer linkages, brokering knowledge, networking and using modern media and communication is one angle into this type of horizontal process. Such approaches link with the need for market information for local actors mentioned above and may also stimulate the development of more advanced services. In addition there seems to be a need for capacity development methods that influence groups of actors rather than individual clients, such as multi-actor processes, strengthening (public) accountability mechanisms and value chain improvement. The possibilities to use and combine both non-commercial and commercial, market and non-market drivers for change will need to become a specific point of attention and innovation.

Spreading professionalism

Professional development of CD practitioners and support organizations, especially those working at the sub-national level, needs to be enhanced. So far it seems this has not been a significant point of attention in most development programmes and strategies. Again we need a change in thinking. Much stronger support for local capacity development professionalism is crucial, alongside new approaches and key elements mentioned above. The specific, often non-commercial, characteristics of the sub-national capacity development support provision should orient the ways of working applied under such professional development strategies or programmes. Such programmes should themselves be guided by an understanding of value chain dynamics in the capacity development support environment and should adequately create conditions for innovation and horizontal spreading.

We have suggested three strategic orientations: from inputs to supporting local solutions, achieving scale and spreading professionalism. Overarching these three strategic orientations is a need to achieve a change in the dynamics of demand–supply–financing of 'service environments' over a longer period of time. Development programs, sector ministries and donors will have to learn to consider the development of the broader service context which, in a sense, requires applying 'systems thinking' rather than just pursuing short term delivery aims.

Conclusions: The need for strategic action

A 'capacity development service industry' is emerging in most countries. In general, however, existing policies, financing strategies and (sector) programmes only pay piecemeal attention to the structural improvement of the 'service environment' for capacity development. Capacity development can help transform poverty reduction ambitions into reality. Yet policies and national or macro-level programmes often face difficulties in stimulating local change. This 'macro–micro gap' stems, amongst other factors, from the lack and mal-distribution of capacity and abilities to increase this shortcoming from within. The findings discussed above show that this gap also applies to the capacity development service sector itself. In most environments we see centralization, a supply-driven approach, fragmentation and a lack of outreach. The limited outreach to, or access by, sub-national actors can be considered a significant factor in most countries' failure to achieve ambitions such as the Millennium Development Goals.

SNV Netherlands Development Organisation is already using insights gained through this study to engage better with local capacity developers as clients, sub-contractors and partners. The organization is also establishing 'Local Capacity Development Facilities' (LCDFs) in a number of countries. These facilities will basically combine two components: (a) brokering knowledge and market information to stimulate demand power and horizontal spreading and continuous innovation and (b) making available flexible and innovative funding to support 'scaling local solutions'. These facilities will be jointly funded, locally-governed and can be sector-focused or more generic. Essentially they will enable capacity development demand, and facilitate a more effective interface with services and finance. Updates on these initiatives will be found in SNV publications and reports in the years to come (www.snvworld.org).

In the meantime, the challenge for all of us is to move away from a focus on providing direct support to capacity development tied to our specific programme objectives. We need to start working in ways that consciously support the development of a broader service environment for capacity development. This chapter has articulated a preliminary understanding of these ideas and perspectives. We hope that much will happen in this direction in the next few years so that Southern expertise can indeed become more and more effective and take the lead in developing the capacity of its own societies.

References

Berg, E. (ed) (1993) *Rethinking Technical Cooperation: Reforms for Capacity Building in Africa*, UNDP, New York

Tembo, F. (2008) 'Study on capacity development support initiatives and patterns – LCDF research and development phase', Report for SNV Netherlands Development Organisation, ODI, London

Third High Level Forum on Aid Effectiveness (2008) *Accra Agenda for Action*, Ghana

Recommended readings

This chapter builds on the understanding of the multi-faceted nature of capacity in the Chapters 1, 2 and 3 in Part I of this volume. For the improvement of the quality of CD support it builds on approaches and examples of effective practice discussed in Chapters 4, 5 and 6 in Part II and working with multi-actor dynamics as discussed in Chapters 11, 12, 13, 14 and 17 in Part III.

There has been little analysis of and debate on local capacity development service environments. Consequently, recommending in-depth further readings is not possible. However, there are some writings which provide entry points into the topic worthy of mention.

'Local Capacity Developers', *Capacity.org*, issue 38, December 2009

This issue of the *Capacity.org* magazine is devoted to 'local capacity developers'. Amongst others, it contains an earlier and shorter version of the present chapter, a set of interviews with LCDs and an exploration of the knowledge architecture in the CD area.

Berg, E. (ed) (1993) *Rethinking Technical Cooperation: Reforms for Capacity Building in Africa*, UNDP, New York

In the early 1990s this report provoked a fundamental discussion on the use of foreign Technical Assistance in international cooperation and was a significant contribution to the broader capacity development discussion.

Bloom, E. et al, (2009) 'The Network Value Chain', Capacity Development Briefs, No 30, February, The World Bank Institute

This paper presents an interesting model for understanding capacity development in networks and the roles of networks in innovation and achieving scale.

Ellerman, D. (2001) 'Hirschmanian Themes of Social Learning and Change', Policy Research Working Paper No 2591, The World Bank, Washington; Ellerman, D. (2001) 'Helping People Help Themselves: Toward a Theory of Autonomy-Compatible Help', Policy Research Working Paper No 2693, The World Bank, Washington; and Ellerman, D. (2004) 'Autonomy-respecting assistance: toward an alternative theory of development assistance', *Review of Social Economy*, vol LXII, no 2

Former World Bank chief economist David Ellerman has consistently argued towards alternative forms of supporting development. One of his central concepts is that of 'decentralized social learning'. Backed by solid theory and evidence he shows how this concept helps to understand how innovations take place and how change in large systems really happens.

Third High Level Forum on Aid Effectiveness (2008)*Accra Agenda for Action*, Ghana

This high-level international agreement reflects the most recent policy understanding between donors and recipient countries. It has a strong emphasis on CD and lays out the international commitment to using more Southern expertise and strengthening it.

Tembo, F. (2008) 'Study on capacity development support initiatives and patterns – LCDF research and development phase', Report for SNV Netherlands Development Organisation, ODI, London

This is the report of a study of a considerable number of existing financing and support mechanisms for capacity development. It has interesting observations on funding logics and 'delivery models'.

SNV Netherlands Development Organisation (2008) 'Local Capacity Development Funding Mechanisms (LCDF), Research & Development Phase, Final Report', SNV Netherlands Development Organisation, The Hague.

This is the SNV internal consolidation of the five country reconnaissances and the ODI research (see above). It sets out the initial parameters of the LCDF initiative.

24

Becoming Professional

This last piece of the volume is intentionally 'impressionistic', forward looking and open ended. While grounded in reflections on practice, unlike many previous chapters it is not empirical or case-based because our purpose is to stimulate a conversation on the future of capacity development.

A comprehensive exploration of capacity development as a professional field in formation needs to be done, a task which is beyond the scope of this volume. Moreover, that conversation requires a process of interaction and engagement of a broader community of practitioners. Nevertheless, while our ideas and suggestions are limited, the substance of this volume offers ground and insights for advancing much-needed debate.

A Professional Field in Formation?

Naa-Aku Acquaye-Baddoo, Jan Ubels and Alan Fowler

Why is a discussion on professionalization relevant?

Based on the range of valuable contributions by the authors in this volume, we have looked (in Chapter 22) at capacity development and the progress made in advancing this as a distinct practice or field of work. This review included tracing the growing understanding of the 'theory' of what capacity is and how it comes about; distilling essential characteristics of the nature of capacity and of its development; and noting a meaningful and important growth in scope, beyond individuals and single organizations towards multi-actor arrangements. Here, we concluded that the field is becoming mature and beginning to deal with the interconnections relevant for addressing real-life issues and ambitions. As most development challenges are to be addressed by combinations of actors working together, they thus require capacities that live not only within them but also between them.

The previous chapter (Chapter 23) considers 'market dynamics' (demand, supply and financing) and on one hand notes the limitations of present financing regimes and challenges in extending outreach. On the other hand there is an observed expansion in range of services as well as opportunities for strengthening demand power, improving quality of support, 'scaling up local solutions' and reforming financing arrangements to support these. This assessment is undertaken with the knowledge that hundreds of thousands of people are involved in capacity development as their main activity or as a significant element of their work, and the recognition that there is a need to improve support to the quality and professionalism of these practitioners.

Gradually, the contributions in this volume started to mark out capacity development as a professional endeavour – a 'professional field in formation'. We feel there are good reasons to support this idea because of:

- the sheer number of people working in this domain, labelling all or significant parts of what they do as capacity development;
- the growing clarity among practitioners, of what capacity is and how its development can be effectively pursued or supported;
- the fact that capacity development is prominent and called for at global and national levels;
- the fact that one can delineate specific practices and interventions within capacity development and identify the different disciplines and bodies of knowledge which inform them;
- the progress made with the measuring and evaluation of capacity development.

Such perspective towards professionalization is possible because capacity development has established a distinct identity and is important because it helps stimulate quality. To help further discussion, the notion of a professional field can be approached from two perspectives. The first is that of the individual practitioner (to whom much of this volume is addressed) and the second is the field of capacity development overall.

The quality of the individual practitioner and the capacity development field as a whole

From the perspective of the individual, the table of practitioner competencies and abilities presented in Chapter 22 (p. 301) summarizes what we have distilled so far from the experiences brought forward in this collection. Described in this way, the combination of knowledge and abilities that practitioners need to demonstrate or master may be helpful in orienting their self-development, but it could also be further elaborated to inform the focus and design of practitioner learning trajectories.

When it comes to the field overall: capacity and its development is a complex, multifaceted and continually dynamic phenomenon and type of activity. But this does not mean that the question of a professional domain cannot be discussed rigorously. On the contrary a vigorous and meaningful conversation is necessary in order to address the issues of distinctiveness on one side and quality on the other. Dialogue is required to bring coherence (not homogeneity), structure (not control) and rigour (not prescription) into the way capacity development practitioners, their organizations and funding partners act and think together as co-shapers of this area of work.

Special professional challenges in capacity development

Discussing and stimulating professionalism in capacity development requires engagement with distinctive features of the functional terrain of international aid and cooperation that create unique challenges for the practitioner and which a journey towards professionalization will need to address.

One, almost defining, feature is the *separation between funders and clients.* The funders who pay for or subsidize capacity development interventions do not receive the service, but are clients nonetheless. Their interest and influence count. The duality of accountability (towards the paying party and the receiving party) can be problematic. Who is most directly able to determine priorities, orient a practitioner's assignment or question her professional quality? How do conflicting cultures, orientations and views of funder and recipient play out? Because demand is (partially) externally triggered, there are also issues around ownership and sustainability. The implications for professionalization need to be thought through. Another distinguishing feature is that shifts, crises, trends and dominant interests in *international geopolitics have direct implications* for the development sector. Direction and amount of funding for development processes are affected by wars, security concerns, financial constraints of major donor countries and power relations between rich and poor countries. It is difficult to sustain the necessary continuity and quality in capacity development support when shifting global priorities can affect the processes involved in such a direct manner. A discussion about an emerging professional field therefore needs to address the extent to which financing of capacity development may become self-sustaining.

The next feature to be confronted is that capacity development practice almost always happens in settings and contexts where *inequalities and social exclusion of different kinds abound.* These are persistent issues that may have deep, historical roots reflected and reinforced at multiple levels in a society. No single intervention will tackle the complex nests of factors which reinforce different forms of social injustice and under-development. How does a professional field respond to this reality in a realistic and at the same time engaged manner? How can such challenges inform intervention principles and approaches? What can capacity development practice contribute to a society's ability to start tackling these issues for itself?

Finally, although they may have great wealth of social and cultural capital, many capacity development contexts are unstable, fragile and resource-poor in terms of economic assets, adequate governance institutions and formal levels of education. A discussion about the quality of work in the field of capacity development has to include debate about engagement with and *gaining leverage from local or indigenous knowledge and socio-cultural capital* in the adaptation and innovation of interventions and practices.

Together, these and other features of international development cooperation set a particular operational context that professionalism must both reflect and qualitatively satisfy.

Three starting points for the discussion on professionalism

So, from the above, what does the development towards a professional field require? We look to propose three elements that are important in the first steps forward.

Taking a strong practitioner focus

The individuals doing the work and how they understand it is a necessary starting point for and a grounding to establishing professionalism. Practitioners must come together to critically reflect on their practice and distil insights and patterns from what they observe. This will provide a foundation for discussion about a 'profession' that is informed by actual experience of practice and what it demands. This 'enquiry' approach will also contribute new knowledge and stimulate innovation as practitioners come to a deeper understanding of what they do and why it works or not.

A more thorough examination of the variety of interventions

Intervening is what practitioners do even if it is in a facilitative or supporting role. Consequently, a 'complete' understanding and formation of capacity development as a profession will require more knowledge about the ins and outs of 'the art of intervening' than is currently available. For example, an intervention may be as light as connecting two people who need to talk to each or as complex as a multiple stakeholder process cutting across a whole sector and spanning many months or years. In the specific context of international development corporation, there needs to be more discussion about what informs the intervention choices that practitioners make. How can one arrive at a coherent grouping of the wide range of interventions, so that they are better understood in terms of what they aim to do and their limitations and potential depending on the context? How do we innovate in intervention design to respond to the unique features of the development terrain, and to trends such as the blurring of private, civil and public boundaries in development work?

A thorough conversation on 'intervening' may help practitioners to engage each other in deepening and bringing clarity to what is currently an eclectic area of work with different practices and approaches drawing from a wide range of knowledge domains and disciplines. The diverse nature of the work makes discussion about quality and standards difficult. At the same time, the wealth and variety of practices can also be seen as a rich basis for reaching a more coherent description of intervention dimensions or types with enough flexibility to accommodate different contexts, time and sectors in which capacity development is offered. Over many years, practitioners have built up a depth of understanding that can be better established and articulated in a systematic discussion about intervention.

Locate the debate and engagement around professionalization in the South

A large majority of practitioners operate in and originate from the South. It is also where 'capacity development' plays a special role in equipping the societies concerned with the expertise to solve their own problems and achieve equitable and sustainable development. This perspective equates to a call for Northern and Southern practitioners to engage each other in discussions about how the shaping of a capacity development professional field can contribute to a future where developing societies have access to high quality, context responsive and innovative capacity development expertise, services and support structures.

Professionalism as a work in progress

On a practical note, progress in these directions would be helped by new initiatives or the expansion and deepening of existing efforts. Here are some examples.

- Professionalism arises partly from trial and error, but also by *learning from conscious (comparative) testing of capacity development work* (using 'non-mechanical', complex approaches (on a small scale) alongside current mainstream 'mechanical' practice). Unlike dedicated research, this method of learning relies on critical reflection across assignments as they are commissioned, undertaken and completed.
- Mechanisms for peer *review and public debate* such as journals, conferences, associations or communities of practice, that provide spaces where practitioners and other stakeholders can take the various discussions forward.
- Initiatives that involve *peers coming together to form membership associations* with gradual progression towards a common set of standards or forms of accreditation that help to increase public confidence and respect.
- Greater access to *educational programmes and professional training* designed with a focus on practice improvement alongside technical or thematic knowledge.
- *Practitioner-led (action-) research* in collaboration with international and Southern-based knowledge and research institutions to deepen understanding of practice or provide insight into effectiveness of interventions.
- *Greater engagement with wider society, funders and governments* to promote understanding of the capacity development field and a better recognition of its practices.

Many of these activities exist already; offering scope for further development and wider involvement. But this will not be a straightforward path. Self-organization of practitioners will be important for a conversation about practice that must be led by them with an interest in the quality and effectiveness of what they do. This type of exchange will also need to deal with the dynamics and world views of civil, private sector and public organizations which are involved in development work and capacity development. Research and education institutes, especially those in the South, will also have an important role to play in supporting practitioners and their organizations and in challenging the field to question its ways of working in a more structured and rigorous manner. Funders will be required to show commitment to paying for quality and innovation initiatives. Development organizations and providers will need to demonstrate greater willingness to collaborate both in the development and innovation of interventions and learning – including learning from initiatives that do not work.

Energizing the debate

This is only the beginning of an international discussion on professionalization of capacity development that we hope will continue with many different parties and well beyond this volume. Amongst others, this type of dialogue needs to actively push forward on issues of effectiveness, quality, learning, standards and financing. To this end, we believe that the rich and varied practices portrayed in the texts of this volume illustrate the concrete nature of the work and, in so doing, reduce confusion and dispel vagueness. Such greater clarity will advance professionalism and prove invaluable to the thousands of practitioners who wish to be better at what they do.

Index